THE BOOK OF POWER

THE BOOK OF POWER

The Greatest Works of the Ages on Attaining Mastery, Magnetism, and Personal Power

EDITED AND INTRODUCED BY
MITCH HOROWITZ

Published 2022 by Gildan Media LLC
aka G&D Media
www.GandDmedia.com

THE BOOK OF POWER. Copyright © 2022 G&D Media. Introduction, *The Power of Sex Transmutation*, Abridgment of *The Prince*, and Appendix II © 2022 by Mitch Horowitz. See the Introduction for additional bibliographical information. All rights reserved.

No part of this book may be used, reproduced or transmitted in any manner whatsoever, by any means (electronic, photocopying, recording, or otherwise), without the prior written permission of the author, except in the case of brief quotations embodied in critical articles and reviews. No liability is assumed with respect to the use of the information contained within. Although every precaution has been taken, the author and publisher assume no liability for errors or omissions. Neither is any liability assumed for damages resulting from the use of the information contained herein.

Front cover design by David Rheinhardt of Pyrographx

Library of Congress Cataloging-in-Publication Data is available upon request

ISBN: 978-1-7225-0231-7

10 9 8 7 6 5 4 3 2 1

Contents

Introduction: *Power Without Apologies*
    by Mitch Horowitz 7

The Art of War
    by Sun Tzu 15

Crystallizing Public Opinion
    by Edward Bernays 85

The Science of Being Great
    by Wallace D. Wattles 219

The Power of Sex Transmutation
    by Mitch Horowitz 287

Your Invisible Power
    by Genevieve Behrend 315

At Your Command
    by Neville 373

The Magic Story
    by Frederick van Rensselaer Dey 401

The Prince
    by Niccolò Machiavelli 425

Introduction

Power Without Apologies

By Mitch Horowitz

I believe that the last thing the mature seeker needs in literature or talks today are chin-stroking ideas or "insights." The seeker requires power. Power—not force—to see through self-expressive wishes. Force dissipates and dies with its user. True power is generative: it creates and builds.

Ethical concerns necessarily accompany the exercise of power as they do all other exertions in life. Ethics are empathy. Although good ethics can be promoted in part through policies, they cannot be instilled in the individual who does not already possess a sensitive emotional nature. Hence, for the sensitive individual to defer the honesty and productiveness of power-seeking to some presumed higher stage of development is to cede the wielding of power itself to the insensitive.

I hope that the works collected in this volume provide you with actionable ideas, methods, and inroads to generative power. With that aim in mind, I comment here on each one.

The Art of War by Sun Tzu

The Art of War is at once among the most popular and yet misunderstood books in the catalogue of personal philosophy. The strategy classic was recorded around 500 BC by legendary general Sun Tzu. Little is known about Sun Tzu, who is estimated to have been born in 544 BC in the latter-era of China's Zhou dynasty and died in 496 BC. According to posthumous records, Sun Tzu—an honorific title meaning "Master Sun"—was a commander in the dynastic army. The work that bears his name is presented here in its gem-like 1910 translation by British sinologist Lionel Giles (1875–1958).* It is purposefully grouped with the Giles' significant 1905 translation of the *Tao Te Ching*. The two works are complementary. Although written from an unabashedly martial and even ruthless perspective, *The Art of War* is essentially a Taoist work. Its core principle is to blend with the natural order of things. That is the book's approach to conflict and friction as it is to restoration and maintenance of peace. I believe that Sun Tzu's outlook can be distilled to five basic points:

1. The greatest warrior prevails without fighting; rightness (or the Tao), preparation, and advantage make conflict unnecessary.
2. Beware the devastation of conflict; war should never be pursued lightly.
3. Be eminently watchful: know your enemy, know yourself, know your terrain. Fight only if victory is assured.
4. When you strike, concentrate fury and power at your enemy's weakest point.
5. When conflict ends, quickly restore peace. Protracted conflict destroys victor and vanquished alike.

Crystallizing Public Opinion by Edward Bernays

Although I do not personally admire PR maven Edward Bernays (1891–1995), who lent his skills as readily to productive causes as to corrupt ones—including promoting the CIA-backed coup against

---

* I explore the broader history of the work and its path into English in *The Art of War: Landmark Edition* (G&D Media, 2021).

Guatemala's democratically elected government in 1954—it must be granted that his 1923 book is an absolute must for anyone who wishes to influence others, which is nearly all of us. Bernays pointed out the efficacy of "discrediting the old authorities," using subtle props and visualizations to make your point, the need to understand the public's desire for spectacle and contest, and how to create the perception of newsworthy events. In my 2019 introduction to Bernays' book, I concluded: "If anger is required to sell something, I do not want a piece of it. But if I, as an author, can use Bernays' ideas to build an audience for a message that extols, let's say, the value of a broadly defined spiritual search, then I see such methods as fair game. I consider some variation of that true for every communicator."

The Science of Being Great by Wallace D. Wattles

This 1911 work is Wallace D. Wattles' (1860–1911) follow up to his 1910 mind-power classic, *The Science of Getting Rich,* a book with a stronger ethical core than is commonly understood. I include *The Science of Being Great* in this volume as a necessary counterbalance and corrective to some of the admittedly more amoral voices represented here. Self-refinement, Wattles wrote, is the key to transforming ourselves into vehicles for what he saw as the Higher Principle of life, which yearns for expression through you and can deliver you to greatness. You begin by doing small things in a great way. Everything that this good and thoughtful man believed necessary for a powerful life appears in this short and compelling book.

The Power of Sex Transmutation by Mitch Horowitz

This brief 2019 book explores what I consider one of the most effective and actionable ideas from the work of pioneering success writer Napoleon Hill (1883–1970), "sex transmutation." Since I believe that power requires workable methods, this short text explores and expands on a concrete and immediately usable technique. Hill viewed the urge toward sexuality as the principle of life itself seeking creative expression through the individual; but the urgency and energy behind sexuality need not be limited to physical release—these forces can also be applied to the critical tasks of life. This teaching appears in various forms in wide-ranging spiritual literature throughout history.

Your Invisible Power by Geneviève Behrend

This 1921 work by New Thought seeker Geneviève Behrend (1881–1960) is one of the most practical and no-nonsense books I know on maximizing the powers of your mind. Behrend's guidebook does not endorse the idea that your visualizing powers will "manifest" properties from the ether. Rather, the powers of causative thought can bring about extraordinary breakthroughs by *working through established and recognized channels of production and creativity*. We do not bend natural laws, Behrend notes; rather, we discover multitudinous possibilities within them. "We now fly through the air," she writes, "not because anyone has been able to change the laws of Nature, but because the inventor of the flying machine learned how to apply Nature's laws and, by making orderly use of them, produced the desired result."

At Your Command by Neville Goddard

I feel that I owe it to the reader to include certain texts of a more philosophically idealistic nature—and I know of few better than the premiere 1939 book by visionary spiritual thinker Neville Goddard (1905–1972). Neville's contention is simple as it is radical: your emotionalized thoughts and mental images out-picture into every facet of reality that you experience. Whether one takes a spiritual, by which I mean extra-physical, view of life, Neville's outlook of extreme philosophical idealism is worthy of personal experiment. If you knew beyond any doubt that the stakes are as high as Neville says, and that your mental pictures and emotions concretize your reality, how would that alter your life? I challenge you to try it and see.

The Magic Story by Frederick van Rensselaer Dey

Pulp writer Frederick van Rensselaer Dey's (1861–1922) two-part narrative, originally published in *Success Magazine* in December 1900 and January 1901, is one of the oddest and most compelling self-help works ever written. It tells the story within a story of a down-and-out seventeenth century craftsman who discovers a haunting presence hovering around his periphery. Dey's hero learns that his counter-self, or "plus-entity," is an actual part of him, one that is "calm, steadfast, and self-reliant." As soon as he comes to identify, literally, with this *plus-entity*—which some historical writers might call his daemon—his life is happily transformed. This eerie, metaphorical tale holds real-life lessons for every striver.

The Prince by Niccolò Machiavelli

I round out *The Book of Power* with a return to material pragmatism and realpolitik in a condensation of the posthumously published 1532 guidebook to statecraft by Italian diplomat and writer Niccolò Machiavelli (1469–1527). Although Machiavelli's name is synonymous with underhanded cunning (in the adjective Machiavellian), the author imbued his work with a greater sense of purpose and principle than is widely acknowledged. Machiavelli emphasized rewarding merit; leaving the public to its own devices and personal pursuits as much as possible (which is the essential ingredient to developing culture and commerce); surrounding oneself with wise counselors; avoiding and not exploiting civic divisions; and striving to ensure the public's general satisfaction. Machiavelli justifies resorting to deception or faithlessness only as a defense against the depravity of men, who shift alliances like the winds. This logic by no means approaches the morality of Christ's principle to be "wise as serpents and harmless as doves," but it belies the general notion that Machiavelli was a monochromatic schemer. Some contemporary critics suggest that *The Prince* is actually a satire of monarchy: that under the guise of a guide to ruthless conduct Machiavelli sends up the actions of absolute rulers and covertly calls for more republican forms of government. I think that assessment probably stretches matters. But it would be equally wrong, as noted, to conclude that Machiavelli was a narrow-eyed courtier bent on keeping others down. On balance, Machiavelli was a pragmatic tutor interested in promoting the unity, stability, and integrity of nations, chiefly his own Italy, in a Europe that lacked cohesive civics and reliable international treaties. My abridgment, which includes the author's full range of lessons but eliminates historical portraiture, is based on the 1910 Harvard Classics translation by Renaissance scholar N.H. Thomson.

Assembling this anthology has left unanswered for me one question: are the powerful born or made? I lean toward the former. Usually a deeply felt inner drive, one present from a person's earliest memories, a need to stretch or reach for something in order to feel a completed sense of self—and I believe we are too quick to judge or label such drives—place someone in the orbit of practices, disciplines, and methods that develop the psyche and body.

Such methods appear, in some significant measure, in the works assembled here. But to benefit from these writings, you must already possess an innate and even uncontainable urge toward self-growth and refinement. This further points to what I consider the "secret ingredient" in attainment of power or self-agency, by which I expressly mean the ability to see through some significant portion of your hallowed wishes and expressive urges in life. And that is *passion*. If you approach these pages with passion, I have little doubt of your discovering within them some greater measure of yourself.

Mitch Horowitz is a PEN Award-winning historian whose books include *Occult America, One Simple Idea, The Miracle Club, Daydream Believer,* and *Uncertain Places*. His work has been translated into Italian, Korean, Chinese, Spanish, French, and Portuguese. He is censored in China. Visit him @MitchHorowitz on Twitter, @MitchHorowitz23 on Instagram, and at MitchHorowitz.com.

THE ART OF WAR

by Sun Tzu

Translated by Lionel Giles
Annotated by Mitch Horowitz

Contents

- I. Laying Plans 17
- II. Waging War 19
- III. Attack By Stratagem 22
- IV. Tactical Dispositions 24
- V. Energy 26
- VI. Weak Points and Strong 29
- VII. Maneuvering 32
- VIII. Variation of Tactics 36
- IX. The Army On the March 37
- X. Terrain 41
- XI. The Nine Situations 45
- XII. The Attack By Fire 51
- XIII. The Use Of Spies 53

I.

Laying Plans

1. Sun Tzu said: The art of war is of vital importance to the State.
2. It is a matter of life and death, a road either to safety or to ruin. Hence it is a subject of inquiry which can on no account be neglected.
3. The art of war, then, is governed by five constant factors, to be taken into account in one's deliberations, when seeking to determine the conditions obtaining in the field.
4. These are:
    (1) The Moral Law;[1]
    (2) Heaven;
    (3) Earth;
    (4) The Commander;
    (5) Method and discipline.

5,6. *The Moral Law* causes the people to be in complete accord with their ruler, so that they will follow him regardless of their lives, undismayed by any danger.
7. *Heaven* signifies night and day, cold and heat, times and seasons.
8. *Earth* comprises distances, great and small; danger and security; open ground and narrow passes; the chances of life and death.
9. *The Commander* stands for the virtues of wisdom, sincerity, benevolence, courage and strictness.
10. By *Method and discipline* are to be understood the marshaling of the army in its proper subdivisions, the graduations of rank among the officers, the maintenance of roads by which supplies may reach the army, and the control of military expenditure.

---

1 This is sometimes translated as the Tao, or the Way, as explored in the introduction.

11. These five heads should be familiar to every general: he who knows them will be victorious; he who knows them not will fail.
12. Therefore, in your deliberations, when seeking to determine the military conditions, let them be made the basis of a comparison, in this wise:
13. (1) Which of the two sovereigns is imbued with the Moral law?
    (2) Which of the two generals has most ability?
    (3) With whom lie the advantages derived from Heaven and Earth?
    (4) On which side is discipline most rigorously enforced?
    (5) Which army is stronger?
    (6) On which side are officers and men more highly trained?
    (7) In which army is there the greater constancy both in reward and punishment?
14. By means of these seven considerations I can forecast victory or defeat.
15. The general that hearkens to my counsel and acts upon it, will conquer: let such a one be retained in command! The general that hearkens not to my counsel nor acts upon it, will suffer defeat: let such a one be dismissed!
16. While heading the profit of my counsel, avail yourself also of any helpful circumstances over and beyond the ordinary rules.
17. According as circumstances are favorable, one should modify one's plans.
18. All warfare is based on deception.[2]
19. Hence, when able to attack, we must seem unable; when using our forces, we must seem inactive; when we are near, we must make the enemy believe we are far away; when far away, we must make him believe we are near.
20. Hold out baits to entice the enemy. Feign disorder, and crush him.

---

2 This is Sun Tzu's key strategic point; most tactics in the book stem from this principle.

21. If he is secure at all points, be prepared for him. If he is in superior strength, evade him.
22. If your opponent is of choleric temper, seek to irritate him. Pretend to be weak, that he may grow arrogant.
23. If he is taking his ease, give him no rest. If his forces are united, separate them.
24. Attack him where he is unprepared, appear where you are not expected.
25. These military devices, leading to victory, must not be divulged beforehand.
26. Now the general who wins a battle makes many calculations in his temple ere the battle is fought. The general who loses a battle makes but few calculations beforehand. Thus do many calculations lead to victory, and few calculations to defeat: how much more no calculation at all! It is by attention to this point that I can foresee who is likely to win or lose.[3]

II.

Waging War

1. Sun Tzu said: In the operations of war, where there are in the field a thousand swift chariots, as many heavy chariots, and a hundred thousand mail-clad soldiers, with provisions enough to carry them a thousand *li*,[4] the expenditure at home and at the front, including entertainment of guests, small items such as glue and paint, and sums spent on chariots and armor, will reach the

---

[3] Sun Tzu had no respect for the commander who acted out of emotion or haste. Research, foreknowledge, deliberateness, and information-gathering are central to his system of warfare and are , he argued, the best guarantors of victory. See chapter IV of the *Tao Te Ching*: "The best soldiers are not warlike; the best fighters do not lose their temper."

[4] A traditional Chinese unit of measure, a "*li*" is about 500 meters.

total of a thousand ounces of silver per day. Such is the cost of raising an army of 100,000 men.
2. When you engage in actual fighting, if victory is long in coming, then men's weapons will grow dull and their ardor will be damped. If you lay siege to a town, you will exhaust your strength.
3. Again, if the campaign is protracted, the resources of the State will not be equal to the strain.[5]
4. Now, when your weapons are dulled, your ardor damped, your strength exhausted and your treasure spent, other chieftains will spring up to take advantage of your extremity. Then no man, however wise, will be able to avert the consequences that must ensue.
5. Thus, though we have heard of stupid haste in war, cleverness has never been seen associated with long delays.
6. There is no instance of a country having benefited from prolonged warfare.
7. It is only one who is thoroughly acquainted with the evils of war that can thoroughly understand the profitable way of carrying it on.
8. The skillful soldier does not raise a second levy, neither are his supply-wagons loaded more than twice.
9. Bring war material with you from home, but forage on the enemy. Thus the army will have food enough for its needs.[6]
10. Poverty of the State exchequer causes an army to be maintained by contributions from a distance. Contributing to maintain an army at a distance causes the people to be impoverished.
11. On the other hand, the proximity of an army causes prices to go up; and high prices cause the people's substance to be drained away.

---

[5] As seen in the ensuing lines, Sun Tzu warned against the drain of extended campaigns or drawn-out occupations. Compare to chapter VI in the *Tao Te Ching*: "The good man wins a victory and then stops; he will not go on to acts of violence." Also in that chapter: "Where troops have been quartered, brambles and thorns spring up. In the track of great armies there must follow lean years."
[6] Sun Tzu thought it vital to "live off the land"—no army or exploratory mission can possibly bring all of its supplies with it. Also, supply lines may get disrupted. Be prepared to supplement your supplies from the territory you enter.

12. When their substance is drained away, the peasantry will be afflicted by heavy exactions.
13,14. With this loss of substance and exhaustion of strength, the homes of the people will be stripped bare, and three-tenths of their income will be dissipated; while government expenses for broken chariots, worn-out horses, breast-plates and helmets, bows and arrows, spears and shields, protective mantles, draught-oxen and heavy wagons, will amount to four-tenths of its total revenue.
15. Hence a wise general makes a point of foraging on the enemy. One cartload of the enemy's provisions is equivalent to twenty of one's own, and likewise a single picul of his provender is equivalent to twenty from one's own store.
16. Now in order to kill the enemy, our men must be roused to anger; that there may be advantage from defeating the enemy, they must have their rewards.[7]
17. Therefore in chariot fighting, when ten or more chariots have been taken, those should be rewarded who took the first. Our own flags should be substituted for those of the enemy, and the chariots mingled and used in conjunction with ours. The captured soldiers should be kindly treated and kept.
18. This is called, using the conquered foe to augment one's own strength.
19. In war, then, let your great object be victory, not lengthy campaigns.
20. Thus it may be known that the leader of armies is the arbiter of the people's fate, the man on whom it depends whether the nation shall be in peace or in peril.

---

[7] Although Sun Tzu warns against anger as in a commander, he is not above using it as a tactical goad among troops or adversaries. Also, before looking for strict consistency in his statements it is worth noting from chapter VI in the *Tao Te Ching*: "The truest sayings are paradoxical."

III.

Attack By Stratagem

1. Sun Tzu said: In the practical art of war, the best thing of all is to take the enemy's country whole and intact; to shatter and destroy it is not so good. So, too, it is better to recapture an army entire than to destroy it, to capture a regiment, a detachment or a company entire than to destroy them.[8]
2. Hence to fight and conquer in all your battles is not supreme excellence; supreme excellence consists in breaking the enemy's resistance without fighting.[9]
3. Thus the highest form of generalship is to balk the enemy's plans; the next best is to prevent the junction of the enemy's forces; the next in order is to attack the enemy's army in the field; and the worst policy of all is to besiege walled cities.
4. The rule is, not to besiege walled cities if it can possibly be avoided. The preparation of mantlets,[10] movable shelters, and various implements of war, will take up three whole months; and the piling up of mounds over against the walls will take three months more.
5. The general, unable to control his irritation, will launch his men to the assault like swarming ants, with the result that one-third of his men are slain, while the town still remains untaken. Such are the disastrous effects of a siege.

---

8 As alluded earlier, Sun Tzu believed in repurposing the resources of the enemy for your own means.
9 This is another of Sun Tzu's key principles: to win without fighting. Strength and foreknowledge ideally make combat unnecessary; victory is won by outmaneuvering or outflanking the enemy and thus breaking his nerve or resolve. A display of overwhelming might will also deter your adversary. There is a subtler dimension to this point: dominant nature, composed of the Way, knowledge, and preparation create natural advantage. See chapter IV of the *Tao Te Ching*: "The greatest conquerors are those who overcome their enemies without strife."
10 These are screens or shields.

6. Therefore the skillful leader subdues the enemy's troops without any fighting; he captures their cities without laying siege to them; he overthrows their kingdom without lengthy operations in the field.
7. With his forces intact he will dispute the mastery of the Empire, and thus, without losing a man, his triumph will be complete. This is the method of attacking by stratagem.
8. It is the rule in war, if our forces are ten to the enemy's one, to surround him; if five to one, to attack him; if twice as numerous, to divide our army into two.
9. If equally matched, we can offer battle; if slightly inferior in numbers, we can avoid the enemy; if quite unequal in every way, we can flee from him.
10. Hence, though an obstinate fight may be made by a small force, in the end it must be captured by the larger force.
11. Now the general is the bulwark of the State; if the bulwark is complete at all points; the State will be strong; if the bulwark is defective, the State will be weak.
12. There are three ways in which a ruler can bring misfortune upon his army:
13. (1) By commanding the army to advance or to retreat, being ignorant of the fact that it cannot obey. This is called hobbling the army.
14. (2) By attempting to govern an army in the same way as he administers a kingdom, being ignorant of the conditions which obtain in an army. This causes restlessness in the soldier's minds.
15. (3) By employing the officers of his army without discrimination, through ignorance of the military principle of adaptation to circumstances. This shakes the confidence of the soldiers.
16. But when the army is restless and distrustful, trouble is sure to come from the other feudal princes. This is simply bringing anarchy into the army, and flinging victory away.

17. Thus we may know that there are five essentials for victory:
    (1) He will win who knows when to fight and when not to fight.
    (2) He will win who knows how to handle both superior and inferior forces.
    (3) He will win whose army is animated by the same spirit throughout all its ranks.
    (4) He will win who, prepared himself, waits to take the enemy unprepared.
    (5) He will win who has military capacity and is not interfered with by the sovereign.
18. Hence the saying: If you know the enemy and know yourself, you need not fear the result of a hundred battles. If you know yourself but not the enemy, for every victory gained you will also suffer a defeat. If you know neither the enemy nor yourself, you will succumb in every battle.

IV.

Tactical Dispositions

1. Sun Tzu said: The good fighters of old first put themselves beyond the possibility of defeat, and then waited for an opportunity of defeating the enemy.
2. To secure ourselves against defeat lies in our own hands, but the opportunity of defeating the enemy is provided by the enemy himself.
3. Thus the good fighter is able to secure himself against defeat, but cannot make certain of defeating the enemy.
4. Hence the saying: One may *know* how to conquer without being able to *do* it.[11]

---

11 This is natural law: where two parties are involved the outcome depends on the actions of both.

5. Security against defeat implies defensive tactics; ability to defeat the enemy means taking the offensive.
6. Standing on the defensive indicates insufficient strength; attacking, a superabundance of strength.
7. The general who is skilled in defense hides in the most secret recesses of the earth; he who is skilled in attack flashes forth from the topmost heights of heaven. Thus on the one hand we have ability to protect ourselves; on the other, a victory that is complete.
8. To see victory only when it is within the ken of the common herd is not the acme of excellence.
9. Neither is it the acme of excellence if you fight and conquer and the whole Empire says, "Well done!"[12]
10. To lift an autumn hair is no sign of great strength; to see the sun and moon is no sign of sharp sight; to hear the noise of thunder is no sign of a quick ear.[13]
11. What the ancients called a clever fighter is one who not only wins, but excels in winning with ease.
12. Hence his victories bring him neither reputation for wisdom nor credit for courage.[14]
13. He wins his battles by making no mistakes. Making no mistakes is what establishes the certainty of victory, for it means conquering an enemy that is already defeated.
14. Hence the skillful fighter puts himself into a position which makes defeat impossible, and does not miss the moment for defeating the enemy.

---

12 See also verse 12. The great warrior does his work without ever being apparent. His victory is so natural that it is not even noticed.
13 Do not credit yourself for ordinary means and methods; seek impeccable means. No one is rewarded for just doing his job.
14 This is one of Sun Tzu's subtlest and most overlooked points. The greatest commander prevails with such ease, possibly without fighting or casualties at all, that he is not the subject of "glory." His victories appear so natural that they go unnoticed. The commander who seeks glory is liable to risk, extended campaigns, and massive loss.

15. Thus it is that in war the victorious strategist only seeks battle after the victory has been won, whereas he who is destined to defeat first fights and afterwards looks for victory.
16. The consummate leader cultivates the moral law, and strictly adheres to method and discipline; thus it is in his power to control success.[15]
17. In respect of military method, we have, firstly, Measurement; secondly, Estimation of quantity; thirdly, Calculation; fourthly, Balancing of chances; fifthly, Victory.
18. Measurement owes its existence to Earth; Estimation of quantity to Measurement; Calculation to Estimation of quantity; Balancing of chances to Calculation; and Victory to Balancing of chances.
19. A victorious army opposed to a routed one, is as a pound's weight placed in the scale against a single grain.
20. The onrush of a conquering force is like the bursting of pent-up waters into a chasm a thousand fathoms deep.[16]

V.

Energy

1. Sun Tzu said: The control of a large force is the same principle as the control of a few men: it is merely a question of dividing up their numbers.
2. Fighting with a large army under your command is nowise different from fighting with a small one: it is merely a question of instituting signs and signals.

---

15 It is useful to note that Sun Tzu adheres not to inspiration, which can come and go, but to "method and discipline," where are permanent. Compare to chapter VI in the *Tao Te Ching*: "Winning, he boasteth not; he will not triumph; he shows no arrogance. He wins because he cannot choose [i.e., it is natural]; after his victory he will not be overbearing."
16 See chapter VI, verse 29, for an expansion on the qualities of water and warfare.

3. To ensure that your whole host may withstand the brunt of the enemy's attack and remain unshaken—this is affected by maneuvers direct and indirect.
4. That the impact of your army may be like a grindstone dashed against an egg—this is effected by the science of weak points and strong.
5. In all fighting, the direct method may be used for joining battle, but indirect methods will be needed in order to secure victory.
6. Indirect tactics, efficiently applied, are inexhaustible as Heaven and Earth, unending as the flow of rivers and streams; like the sun and moon, they end but to begin anew; like the four seasons, they pass away to return once more.[17]
7. There are not more than five musical notes, yet the combinations of these five give rise to more melodies than can ever be heard.
8. There are not more than five primary colors (blue, yellow, red, white, and black), yet in combination they produce more hues than can ever been seen.
9. There are not more than five cardinal tastes (sour, acrid, salt, sweet, bitter), yet combinations of them yield more flavors than can ever be tasted.
10. In battle, there are not more than two methods of attack—the direct and the indirect; yet these two in combination give rise to an endless series of maneuvers.
11. The direct and the indirect lead on to each other in turn. It is like moving in a circle—you never come to an end. Who can exhaust the possibilities of their combination?
12. The onset of troops is like the rush of a torrent which will even roll stones along in its course.[18]

---

[17] This precept should be read and considered carefully with the one immediately preceding it. In Sun Tzu's philosophy, principles of flexibility are vital. Combinations are limitless. A commander should never grow comfortable with any one tactic. Tactics may be repeated—but be cautious: losses often result from the reapplication of a tactic that formerly brought victory but is unsuited to a new challenge.

[18] Here and in the immediately following lines Sun Tzu is teaching that once an attack is decided on it must be carried out with absolute decisiveness, dedication, and ferocity. Otherwise it is better not to attack.

13. The quality of decision is like the well-timed swoop of a falcon which enables it to strike and destroy its victim.
14. Therefore the good fighter will be terrible in his onset, and prompt in his decision.
15. Energy may be likened to the bending of a crossbow; decision, to the releasing of a trigger.
16. Amid the turmoil and tumult of battle, there may be seeming disorder and yet no real disorder at all; amid confusion and chaos, your array may be without head or tail, yet it will be proof against defeat.
17. Simulated disorder postulates perfect discipline, simulated fear postulates courage; simulated weakness postulates strength.
18. Hiding order beneath the cloak of disorder is simply a question of subdivision; concealing courage under a show of timidity presupposes a fund of latent energy; masking strength with weakness is to be effected by tactical dispositions.
19. Thus one who is skillful at keeping the enemy on the move maintains deceitful appearances, according to which the enemy will act. He sacrifices something, that the enemy may snatch at it.
20. By holding out baits, he keeps him on the march; then with a body of picked men he lies in wait for him.
21. The clever combatant looks to the effect of combined energy, and does not require too much from individuals. Hence his ability to pick out the right men and utilize combined energy.[19]
22. When he utilizes combined energy, his fighting men become as it were like unto rolling logs or stones. For it is the nature of a log or stone to remain motionless on level ground, and to move when on a slope; if four-cornered, to come to a standstill, but if round-shaped, to go rolling down.

---

19 Sun Tzu is saying that you must not over-rely on any one person or factor.

23. Thus the energy developed by good fighting men is as the momentum of a round stone rolled down a mountain thousands of feet in height. So much on the subject of energy.

VI.

Weak Points and Strong

1. Sun Tzu said: Whoever is first in the field and awaits the coming of the enemy, will be fresh for the fight; whoever is second in the field and has to hasten to battle will arrive exhausted.[20]
2. Therefore the clever combatant imposes his will on the enemy, but does not allow the enemy's will to be imposed on him.
3. By holding out advantages to him, he can cause the enemy to approach of his own accord; or, by inflicting damage, he can make it impossible for the enemy to draw near.
4. If the enemy is taking his ease, he can harass him; if well supplied with food, he can starve him out; if quietly encamped, he can force him to move.
5. Appear at points which the enemy must hasten to defend; march swiftly to places where you are not expected.
6. An army may march great distances without distress, if it marches through country where the enemy is not.
7. You can be sure of succeeding in your attacks if you only attack places which are undefended. You can ensure the safety of your defense if you only hold positions that cannot be attacked.
8. Hence that general is skillful in attack whose opponent does not know what to defend; and he is skillful in defense whose opponent does not know what to attack.

---

20 This is one of Sun Tzu's most practical lessons: always arrive first.

9. O divine art of subtlety and secrecy! Through you we learn to be invisible, through you inaudible; and hence we can hold the enemy's fate in our hands.
10. You may advance and be absolutely irresistible, if you make for the enemy's weak points; you may retire and be safe from pursuit if your movements are more rapid than those of the enemy.
11. If we wish to fight, the enemy can be forced to an engagement even though he be sheltered behind a high rampart and a deep ditch. All we need do is attack some other place that he will be obliged to relieve.
12. If we do not wish to fight, we can prevent the enemy from engaging us even though the lines of our encampment be merely traced out on the ground. All we need do is to throw something odd and unaccountable in his way.
13. By discovering the enemy's dispositions and remaining invisible ourselves, we can keep our forces concentrated, while the enemy's must be divided.
14. We can form a single united body, while the enemy must split up into fractions. Hence there will be a whole pitted against separate parts of a whole, which means that we shall be many to the enemy's few.
15. And if we are able thus to attack an inferior force with a superior one, our opponents will be in dire straits.
16. The spot where we intend to fight must not be made known; for then the enemy will have to prepare against a possible attack at several different points; and his forces being thus distributed in many directions, the numbers we shall have to face at any given point will be proportionately few.
17. For should the enemy strengthen his van, he will weaken his rear; should he strengthen his rear, he will weaken his van; should he strengthen his left, he will weaken his right; should he strengthen

his right, he will weaken his left. If he sends reinforcements everywhere, he will everywhere be weak.
18. Numerical weakness comes from having to prepare against possible attacks; numerical strength, from compelling our adversary to make these preparations against us.
19. Knowing the place and the time of the coming battle, we may concentrate from the greatest distances in order to fight.
20. But if neither time nor place be known, then the left wing will be impotent to succor the right, the right equally impotent to succor the left, the van unable to relieve the rear, or the rear to support the van. How much more so if the furthest portions of the army are anything under a hundred *li* apart, and even the nearest are separated by several *li*!
21. Though according to my estimate the soldiers of Yueh exceed our own in number, that shall advantage them nothing in the matter of victory. I say then that victory can be achieved.
22. Though the enemy be stronger in numbers, we may prevent him from fighting. Scheme so as to discover his plans and the likelihood of their success.
23. Rouse him, and learn the principle of his activity or inactivity. Force him to reveal himself, so as to find out his vulnerable spots.
24. Carefully compare the opposing army with your own, so that you may know where strength is superabundant and where it is deficient.
25. In making tactical dispositions, the highest pitch you can attain is to conceal them; conceal your dispositions, and you will be safe from the prying of the subtlest spies, from the machinations of the wisest brains.
26. How victory may be produced for them out of the enemy's own tactics—that is what the multitude cannot comprehend.
27. All men can see the tactics whereby I conquer, but what none can see is the strategy out of which victory is evolved.

28. Do not repeat the tactics which have gained you one victory, but let your methods be regulated by the infinite variety of circumstances.
29. Military tactics are like unto water; for water in its natural course runs away from high places and hastens downwards.[21]
30. So in war, the way is to avoid what is strong and to strike at what is weak.
31. Water shapes its course according to the nature of the ground over which it flows; the soldier works out his victory in relation to the foe whom he is facing.[22]
32. Therefore, just as water retains no constant shape, so in warfare there are no constant conditions.
33. He who can modify his tactics in relation to his opponent and thereby succeed in winning, may be called a heaven-born captain.
34. The five elements (water, fire, wood, metal, earth) are not always equally predominant; the four seasons make way for each other in turn. There are short days and long; the moon has its periods of waning and waxing.

VII.

Maneuvering

1. Sun Tzu said: In war, the general receives his commands from the sovereign.

---

21 Take careful note of all of Sun Tzu's references to water. Water is humble and subtle. It dwells at low places. (On a related note, see chapter VIII in the *Tao Te Ching*: "He who raises himself on tiptoe cannot stand firm; he who stretches his legs wide apart cannot walk.") But when in a torrent or onrush, water proves irresistible. Like water, you must go unnoticed when observing your enemy. But when attacking you must strike overwhelmingly, crashing like a wave through his defenses at their weakest point. Also note line 20 in chapter IV: "The onrush of a conquering force is like the bursting of pent-up waters into a chasm a thousand fathoms deep." And in the *Tao Te Ching*, chapter II: "The highest goodness is like water, for water is excellent in benefiting all things, and it does not strive. It occupies the lowest place, which men abhor. And therefore it is near akin to Tao."
22 Sun Tzu is counseling flexibility, morphing, and ready response to changed circumstances. Do not be rigid.

2. Having collected an army and concentrated his forces, he must blend and harmonize the different elements thereof before pitching his camp.
3. After that, comes tactical maneuvering, than which there is nothing more difficult. The difficulty of tactical maneuvering consists in turning the devious into the direct, and misfortune into gain.
4. Thus, to take a long and circuitous route, after enticing the enemy out of the way, and though starting after him, to contrive to reach the goal before him, shows knowledge of the artifice of *deviation*.
5. Maneuvering with an army is advantageous; with an undisciplined multitude, most dangerous.
6. If you set a fully equipped army in march in order to snatch an advantage, the chances are that you will be too late. On the other hand, to detach a flying column for the purpose involves the sacrifice of its baggage and stores.
7. Thus, if you order your men to roll up their buff-coats, and make forced marches without halting day or night, covering double the usual distance at a stretch, doing a hundred *li* in order to wrest an advantage, the leaders of all your three divisions will fall into the hands of the enemy.
8. The stronger men will be in front, the jaded ones will fall behind, and on this plan only one-tenth of your army will reach its destination.
9. If you march fifty *li* in order to outmaneuver the enemy, you will lose the leader of your first division, and only half your force will reach the goal.
10. If you march thirty *li* with the same object, two-thirds of your army will arrive.
11. We may take it then that an army without its baggage-train is lost; without provisions it is lost; without bases of supply it is lost.
12. We cannot enter into alliances until we are acquainted with the designs of our neighbors.

13. We are not fit to lead an army on the march unless we are familiar with the face of the country—its mountains and forests, its pitfalls and precipices, its marshes and swamps.
14. We shall be unable to turn natural advantage to account unless we make use of local guides.
15. In war, practice dissimulation, and you will succeed.
16. Whether to concentrate or to divide your troops, must be decided by circumstances.
17. Let your rapidity be that of the wind, your compactness that of the forest.
18. In raiding and plundering be like fire, is immovability like a mountain.
19. Let your plans be dark and impenetrable as night, and when you move, fall like a thunderbolt.
20. When you plunder a countryside, let the spoil be divided amongst your men; when you capture new territory, cut it up into allotments for the benefit of the soldiery.
21. Ponder and deliberate before you make a move.
22. He will conquer who has learnt the artifice of deviation. Such is the art of maneuvering.
23. The Book of Army Management says: On the field of battle, the spoken word does not carry far enough: hence the institution of gongs and drums. Nor can ordinary objects be seen clearly enough: hence the institution of banners and flags.
24. Gongs and drums, banners and flags, are means whereby the ears and eyes of the host may be focused on one particular point.
25. The host thus forming a single united body, is it impossible either for the brave to advance alone, or for the cowardly to retreat alone. This is the art of handling large masses of men.
26. In night-fighting, then, make much use of signal-fires and drums, and in fighting by day, of flags and banners, as a means of influencing the ears and eyes of your army.

27. A whole army may be robbed of its spirit; a commander-in-chief may be robbed of his presence of mind.
28. Now a soldier's spirit is keenest in the morning; by noonday it has begun to flag; and in the evening, his mind is bent only on returning to camp.
29. A clever general, therefore, avoids an army when its spirit is keen, but attacks it when it is sluggish and inclined to return. This is the art of studying moods.
30. Disciplined and calm, to await the appearance of disorder and hubbub amongst the enemy: this is the art of retaining self-possession.
31. To be near the goal while the enemy is still far from it, to wait at ease while the enemy is toiling and struggling, to be well-fed while the enemy is famished: this is the art of husbanding one's strength.
32. To refrain from intercepting an enemy whose banners are in perfect order, to refrain from attacking an army drawn up in calm and confident array: this is the art of studying circumstances.
33. It is a military axiom not to advance uphill against the enemy, nor to oppose him when he comes downhill.
34. Do not pursue an enemy who simulates flight; do not attack soldiers whose temper is keen.
35. Do not swallow bait offered by the enemy. Do not interfere with an army that is returning home.
36. When you surround an army, leave an outlet free. Do not press a desperate foe too hard.[23]
37. Such is the art of warfare.

---

23 As noted in the introduction, Sun Tzu is teaching that by pressing a desperate foe and leaving him no way out, you ensure that he will fight to the death, with severe consequences on both sides. Giles observes that leaving an "outlet free" may also be a matter of strategic deception. He quotes Chinese poet Du Mu (803–852 A.D.) that the aim is "to make him believe that there is a road to safety and thus prevent his fighting with the courage of despair."

VIII.

Variation of Tactics

1. Sun Tzu said: In war, the general receives his commands from the sovereign, collects his army and concentrates his forces
2. When in difficult country, do not encamp. In country where high roads intersect, join hands with your allies. Do not linger in dangerously isolated positions. In hemmed-in situations, you must resort to stratagem. In desperate position, you must fight.
3. There are roads which must not be followed, armies which must be not attacked, towns which must be besieged, positions which must not be contested, commands of the sovereign which must not be obeyed.
4. The general who thoroughly understands the advantages that accompany variation of tactics knows how to handle his troops.
5. The general who does not understand these, may be well acquainted with the configuration of the country, yet he will not be able to turn his knowledge to practical account.
6. So, the student of war who is unversed in the art of war of varying his plans, even though he be acquainted with the Five Advantages, will fail to make the best use of his men.[24]
7. Hence in the wise leader's plans, considerations of advantage and of disadvantage will be blended together.
8. If our expectation of advantage be tempered in this way, we may succeed in accomplishing the essential part of our schemes.
9. If, on the other hand, in the midst of difficulties we are always ready to seize an advantage, we may extricate ourselves from misfortune.

---

24 For the "Five Advantages," see Sun Tzu's note on the "five essentials for victory" in chapter III.

10. Reduce the hostile chiefs by inflicting damage on them; and make trouble for them, and keep them constantly engaged; hold out specious allurements, and make them rush to any given point.
11. The art of war teaches us to rely not on the likelihood of the enemy's not coming, but on our own readiness to receive him; not on the chance of his not attacking, but rather on the fact that we have made our position unassailable.
12. There are five dangerous faults which may affect a general:
    (1) Recklessness, which leads to destruction;
    (2) cowardice, which leads to capture;
    (3) a hasty temper, which can be provoked by insults;
    (4) a delicacy of honor which is sensitive to shame;
    (5) over-solicitude for his men, which exposes him to worry and trouble.
13. These are the five besetting sins of a general, ruinous to the conduct of war.
14. When an army is overthrown and its leader slain, the cause will surely be found among these five dangerous faults. Let them be a subject of meditation.

IX.

The Army On the March

1. Sun Tzu said: We come now to the question of encamping the army, and observing signs of the enemy. Pass quickly over mountains, and keep in the neighborhood of valleys.
2. Camp in high places, facing the sun. Do not climb heights in order to fight. So much for mountain warfare.
3. After crossing a river, you should get far away from it.

4. When an invading force crosses a river in its onward march, do not advance to meet it in mid-stream. It will be best to let half the army get across, and then deliver your attack.
5. If you are anxious to fight, you should not go to meet the invader near a river which he has to cross.
6. Moor your craft higher up than the enemy, and facing the sun. Do not move up-stream to meet the enemy. So much for river warfare.
7. In crossing salt-marshes, your sole concern should be to get over them quickly, without any delay.
8. If forced to fight in a salt-marsh, you should have water and grass near you, and get your back to a clump of trees. So much for operations in salt-marshes.
9. In dry, level country, take up an easily accessible position with rising ground to your right and on your rear, so that the danger may be in front, and safety lie behind. So much for campaigning in flat country.
10. These are the four useful branches of military knowledge which enabled the Yellow Emperor to vanquish four several sovereigns.
11. All armies prefer high ground to low and sunny places to dark.
12. If you are careful of your men, and camp on hard ground, the army will be free from disease of every kind, and this will spell victory.
13. When you come to a hill or a bank, occupy the sunny side, with the slope on your right rear. Thus you will at once act for the benefit of your soldiers and utilize the natural advantages of the ground.
14. When, in consequence of heavy rains up-country, a river which you wish to ford is swollen and flecked with foam, you must wait until it subsides.
15. Country in which there are precipitous cliffs with torrents running between, deep natural hollows, confined places, tangled

thickets, quagmires and crevasses, should be left with all possible speed and not approached.

16. While we keep away from such places, we should get the enemy to approach them; while we face them, we should let the enemy have them on his rear.
17. If in the neighborhood of your camp there should be any hilly country, ponds surrounded by aquatic grass, hollow basins filled with reeds, or woods with thick undergrowth, they must be carefully routed out and searched; for these are places where men in ambush or insidious spies are likely to be lurking.
18. When the enemy is close at hand and remains quiet, he is relying on the natural strength of his position.
19. When he keeps aloof and tries to provoke a battle, he is anxious for the other side to advance.
20. If his place of encampment is easy of access, he is tendering a bait.
21. Movement amongst the trees of a forest shows that the enemy is advancing. The appearance of a number of screens in the midst of thick grass means that the enemy wants to make us suspicious.
22. The rising of birds in their flight is the sign of an ambuscade. Startled beasts indicate that a sudden attack is coming.
23. When there is dust rising in a high column, it is the sign of chariots advancing; when the dust is low, but spread over a wide area, it betokens the approach of infantry. When it branches out in different directions, it shows that parties have been sent to collect firewood. A few clouds of dust moving to and fro signify that the army is encamping.
24. Humble words and increased preparations are signs that the enemy is about to advance. Violent language and driving forward as if to the attack are signs that he will retreat.
25. When the light chariots come out first and take up a position on the wings, it is a sign that the enemy is forming for battle.

26. Peace proposals unaccompanied by a sworn covenant indicate a plot.
27. When there is much running about and the soldiers fall into rank, it means that the critical moment has come.
28. When some are seen advancing and some retreating, it is a lure.
29. When the soldiers stand leaning on their spears, they are faint from want of food.
30. If those who are sent to draw water begin by drinking themselves, the army is suffering from thirst.
31. If the enemy sees an advantage to be gained and makes no effort to secure it, the soldiers are exhausted.
32. If birds gather on any spot, it is unoccupied. Clamor by night betokens nervousness.
33. If there is disturbance in the camp, the general's authority is weak. If the banners and flags are shifted about, sedition is afoot. If the officers are angry, it means that the men are weary.
34. When an army feeds its horses with grain and kills its cattle for food, and when the men do not hang their cooking-pots over the camp-fires, showing that they will not return to their tents, you may know that they are determined to fight to the death.[25]
35. The sight of men whispering together in small knots or speaking in subdued tones points to disaffection amongst the rank and file.
36. Too frequent rewards signify that the enemy is at the end of his resources; too many punishments betray a condition of dire distress.
37. To begin by bluster, but afterwards to take fright at the enemy's numbers, shows a supreme lack of intelligence.
38. When envoys are sent with compliments in their mouths, it is a sign that the enemy wishes for a truce.
39. If the enemy's troops march up angrily and remain facing ours for a long time without either joining battle or taking themselves

---

25 Men eat grain; horses eat grass. Hence, the slaying of cattle means a preparation for the end.

off again, the situation is one that demands great vigilance and circumspection.
40. If our troops are no more in number than the enemy, that is amply sufficient; it only means that no direct attack can be made. What we can do is simply to concentrate all our available strength, keep a close watch on the enemy, and obtain reinforcements.
41. He who exercises no forethought but makes light of his opponents is sure to be captured by them.
42. If soldiers are punished before they have grown attached to you, they will not prove submissive; and, unless submissive, then will be practically useless. If, when the soldiers have become attached to you, punishments are not enforced, they will still be useless.
43. Therefore soldiers must be treated in the first instance with humanity, but kept under control by means of iron discipline. This is a certain road to victory.
44. If in training soldiers commands are habitually enforced, the army will be well-disciplined; if not, its discipline will be bad.
45. If a general shows confidence in his men but always insists on his orders being obeyed, the gain will be mutual.

X.

Terrain

1. Sun Tzu said: We may distinguish six kinds of terrain, to wit:
(1) Accessible ground;
(2) entangling ground;
(3) temporizing ground;
(4) narrow passes;
(5) precipitous heights;
(6) positions at a great distance from the enemy.

2. Ground which can be freely traversed by both sides is called accessible.
3. With regard to ground of this nature, be before the enemy in occupying the raised and sunny spots, and carefully guard your line of supplies. Then you will be able to fight with advantage.
4. Ground which can be abandoned but is hard to re-occupy is called entangling.
5. From a position of this sort, if the enemy is unprepared, you may sally forth and defeat him. But if the enemy is prepared for your coming, and you fail to defeat him, then, return being impossible, disaster will ensue.
6. When the position is such that neither side will gain by making the first move, it is called *temporizing* ground.
7. In a position of this sort, even though the enemy should offer us an attractive bait, it will be advisable not to stir forth, but rather to retreat, thus enticing the enemy in his turn; then, when part of his army has come out, we may deliver our attack with advantage.
8. With regard to *narrow passes*, if you can occupy them first, let them be strongly garrisoned and await the advent of the enemy.
9. Should the army forestall you in occupying a pass, do not go after him if the pass is fully garrisoned, but only if it is weakly garrisoned.
10. With regard to *precipitous heights*, if you are beforehand with your adversary, you should occupy the raised and sunny spots, and there wait for him to come up.
11. If the enemy has occupied them before you, do not follow him, but retreat and try to entice him away.
12. If you are situated at a great distance from the enemy, and the strength of the two armies is equal, it is not easy to provoke a battle, and fighting will be to your disadvantage.
13. These six are the principles connected with Earth. The general who has attained a responsible post must be careful to study them.

14. Now an army is exposed to six several calamities, not arising from natural causes, but from faults for which the general is responsible. These are:
(1) Flight;
(2) insubordination;
(3) collapse;
(4) ruin;
(5) disorganization;
(6) rout.
15. Other conditions being equal, if one force is hurled against another ten times its size, the result will be the *flight* of the former.
16. When the common soldiers are too strong and their officers too weak, the result is *insubordination*. When the officers are too strong and the common soldiers too weak, the result is *collapse*.
17. When the higher officers are angry and insubordinate, and on meeting the enemy give battle on their own account from a feeling of resentment, before the commander-in-chief can tell whether or not he is in a position to fight, the result is ruin.
18. When the general is weak and without authority; when his orders are not clear and distinct; when there are no fixes duties assigned to officers and men, and the ranks are formed in a slovenly haphazard manner, the result is utter *disorganization*.
19. When a general, unable to estimate the enemy's strength, allows an inferior force to engage a larger one, or hurls a weak detachment against a powerful one, and neglects to place picked soldiers in the front rank, the result must be *rout*.
20. These are six ways of courting defeat, which must be carefully noted by the general who has attained a responsible post.
21. The natural formation of the country is the soldier's best ally; but a power of estimating the adversary, of controlling the forces of victory, and of shrewdly calculating difficulties, dangers and distances, constitutes the test of a great general.

22. He who knows these things, and in fighting puts his knowledge into practice, will win his battles. He who knows them not, nor practices them, will surely be defeated.
23. If fighting is sure to result in victory, then you must fight, even though the ruler forbid it; if fighting will not result in victory, then you must not fight even at the ruler's bidding.
24. The general who advances without coveting fame and retreats without fearing disgrace, whose only thought is to protect his country and do good service for his sovereign, is the jewel of the kingdom.
25. Regard your soldiers as your children, and they will follow you into the deepest valleys; look upon them as your own beloved sons, and they will stand by you even unto death.
26. If, however, you are indulgent, but unable to make your authority felt; kind-hearted, but unable to enforce your commands; and incapable, moreover, of quelling disorder: then your soldiers must be likened to spoilt children; they are useless for any practical purpose.
27. If we know that our own men are in a condition to attack, but are unaware that the enemy is not open to attack, we have gone only halfway towards victory.
28. If we know that the enemy is open to attack, but are unaware that our own men are not in a condition to attack, we have gone only halfway towards victory.
29. If we know that the enemy is open to attack, and also know that our men are in a condition to attack, but are unaware that the nature of the ground makes fighting impracticable, we have still gone only halfway towards victory.
30. Hence the experienced soldier, once in motion, is never bewildered; once he has broken camp, he is never at a loss.
31. Hence the saying: If you know the enemy and know yourself, your victory will not stand in doubt; if you know Heaven and know Earth, you may make your victory complete.

XI.

The Nine Situations

1. Sun Tzu said: The art of war recognizes nine varieties of ground:
   (1) Dispersive ground;
   (2) facile ground;
   (3) contentious ground;
   (4) open ground;
   (5) ground of intersecting highways;
   (6) serious ground;
   (7) difficult ground;
   (8) hemmed-in ground;
   (9) desperate ground.
2. When a chieftain is fighting in his own territory, it is dispersive ground.
3. When he has penetrated into hostile territory, but to no great distance, it is facile ground.
4. Ground the possession of which imports great advantage to either side, is contentious ground.
5. Ground on which each side has liberty of movement is open ground.
6. Ground which forms the key to three contiguous states, so that he who occupies it first has most of the Empire at his command, is a ground of intersecting highways.
7. When an army has penetrated into the heart of a hostile country, leaving a number of fortified cities in its rear, it is serious ground.
8. Mountain forests, rugged steeps, marshes and fens—all country that is hard to traverse: this is difficult ground.
9. Ground which is reached through narrow gorges, and from which we can only retire by tortuous paths, so that a small number of

the enemy would suffice to crush a large body of our men: this is hemmed in ground.
10. Ground on which we can only be saved from destruction by fighting without delay, is desperate ground.
11. On dispersive ground, therefore, fight not. On facile ground, halt not. On contentious ground, attack not.
12. On open ground, do not try to block the enemy's way. On the ground of intersecting highways, join hands with your allies.
13. On serious ground, gather in plunder. In difficult ground, keep steadily on the march.
14. On hemmed-in ground, resort to stratagem. On desperate ground, fight.
15. Those who were called skillful leaders of old knew how to drive a wedge between the enemy's front and rear; to prevent co-operation between his large and small divisions; to hinder the good troops from rescuing the bad, the officers from rallying their men.
16. When the enemy's men were united, they managed to keep them in disorder.
17. When it was to their advantage, they made a forward move; when otherwise, they stopped still.
18. If asked how to cope with a great host of the enemy in orderly array and on the point of marching to the attack, I should say: "Begin by seizing something which your opponent holds dear; then he will be amenable to your will."
19. Rapidity is the essence of war: take advantage of the enemy's unreadiness, make your way by unexpected routes, and attack unguarded spots.
20. The following are the principles to be observed by an invading force: The further you penetrate into a country, the greater will be the solidarity of your troops, and thus the defenders will not prevail against you.

21. Make forays in fertile country in order to supply your army with food.
22. Carefully study the well-being of your men, and do not overtax them. Concentrate your energy and hoard your strength. Keep your army continually on the move, and devise unfathomable plans.
23. Throw your soldiers into positions whence there is no escape, and they will prefer death to flight. If they will face death, there is nothing they may not achieve. Officers and men alike will put forth their uttermost strength.
24. Soldiers when in desperate straits lose the sense of fear. If there is no place of refuge, they will stand firm. If they are in hostile country, they will show a stubborn front. If there is no help for it, they will fight hard.
25. Thus, without waiting to be marshaled, the soldiers will be constantly on the *qui vive*;[26] without waiting to be asked, they will do your will; without restrictions, they will be faithful; without giving orders, they can be trusted.
26. Prohibit the taking of omens, and do away with superstitious doubts. Then, until death itself comes, no calamity need be feared.
27. If our soldiers are not overburdened with money, it is not because they have a distaste for riches; if their lives are not unduly long, it is not because they are disinclined to longevity.
28. On the day they are ordered out to battle, your soldiers may weep, those sitting up bedewing their garments, and those lying down letting the tears run down their cheeks. But let them once be brought to bay, and they will display the courage of a Chu or a Kuei.[27]

---

26 I.e., on alert.
27 Sun Tzu refers here to the legendary Chinese warriors Chuan Chu (c. 6th century BC) and Ts'ao Kuei (c. 7th century BC). He is saying that if you leave your warriors with no way out they will fight with ferocity.

29. The skillful tactician may be likened to the *shuai-jan*.[28] Now the *shuai-jan* is a snake that is found in the Ch'ang mountains. Strike at its head, and you will be attacked by its tail; strike at its tail, and you will be attacked by its head; strike at its middle, and you will be attacked by head and tail both.
30. Asked if an army can be made to imitate the *shuai-jan*, I should answer, Yes. For the men of Wu and the men of Yueh are enemies; yet if they are crossing a river in the same boat and are caught by a storm, they will come to each other's assistance just as the left hand helps the right.
31. Hence it is not enough to put one's trust in the tethering of horses, and the burying of chariot wheels in the ground.[29]
32. The principle on which to manage an army is to set up one standard of courage which all must reach.
33. How to make the best of both strong and weak—that is a question involving the proper use of ground.
34. Thus the skillful general conducts his army just as though he were leading a single man, willy-nilly, by the hand.
35. It is the business of a general to be quiet and thus ensure secrecy; upright and just, and thus maintain order.
36. He must be able to mystify his officers and men by false reports and appearances, and thus keep them in total ignorance.
37. By altering his arrangements and changing his plans, he keeps the enemy without definite knowledge. By shifting his camp and taking circuitous routes, he prevents the enemy from anticipating his purpose.
38. At the critical moment, the leader of an army acts like one who has climbed up a height and then kicks away the ladder behind him. He carries his men deep into hostile territory before he shows his hand.

---

28 Sun Tzu refers here to a species of rapidly moving snake.
29 Here and in the preceding verse, Sun Tzu is counseling to fasten your army in one place, compel your forces to depend on each other for life, and they will fight fiercely and in concert.

39. He burns his boats and breaks his cooking-pots; like a shepherd driving a flock of sheep, he drives his men this way and that, and nothing knows whither he is going.[30]
40. To muster his host and bring it into danger: this may be termed the business of the general.
41. The different measures suited to the nine varieties of ground; the expediency of aggressive or defensive tactics; and the fundamental laws of human nature: these are things that must most certainly be studied.
42. When invading hostile territory, the general principle is, that penetrating deeply brings cohesion; penetrating but a short way means dispersion.
43. When you leave your own country behind, and take your army across neighborhood territory, you find yourself on critical ground. When there are means of communication on all four sides, the ground is one of intersecting highways.
44. When you penetrate deeply into a country, it is serious ground. When you penetrate but a little way, it is facile ground.
45. When you have the enemy's strongholds on your rear, and narrow passes in front, it is hemmed-in ground. When there is no place of refuge at all, it is desperate ground.
46. Therefore, on dispersive ground, I would inspire my men with unity of purpose. On facile ground, I would see that there is close connection between all parts of my army.
47. On contentious ground, I would hurry up my rear.
48. On open ground, I would keep a vigilant eye on my defenses. On ground of intersecting highways, I would consolidate my alliances.
49. On serious ground, I would try to ensure a continuous stream of supplies. On difficult ground, I would keep pushing on along the road.

---

30 The reference to burning boats and breaking cooking pots is akin to the Western expression to "burn the fleet"—in other words, to eliminate any way out and thus to guarantee victory or demise. This also makes a show of determination to troops and foes.

50. On hemmed-in ground, I would block any way of retreat. On desperate ground, I would proclaim to my soldiers the hopelessness of saving their lives.
51. For it is the soldier's disposition to offer an obstinate resistance when surrounded, to fight hard when he cannot help himself, and to obey promptly when he has fallen into danger.
52. We cannot enter into alliance with neighboring princes until we are acquainted with their designs. We are not fit to lead an army on the march unless we are familiar with the face of the country—its mountains and forests, its pitfalls and precipices, its marshes and swamps. We shall be unable to turn natural advantages to account unless we make use of local guides.
53. To be ignorant of any one of the following four or five principles does not befit a warlike prince.
54. When a warlike prince attacks a powerful state, his generalship shows itself in preventing the concentration of the enemy's forces. He overawes his opponents, and their allies are prevented from joining against him.
55. Hence he does not strive to ally himself with all and sundry, nor does he foster the power of other states. He carries out his own secret designs, keeping his antagonists in awe. Thus he is able to capture their cities and overthrow their kingdoms.
56. Bestow rewards without regard to rule, issue orders without regard to previous arrangements; and you will be able to handle a whole army as though you had to do with but a single man.
57. Confront your soldiers with the deed itself; never let them know your design. When the outlook is bright, bring it before their eyes; but tell them nothing when the situation is gloomy.[31]
58. Place your army in deadly peril, and it will survive; plunge it into desperate straits, and it will come off in safety.

---

31 In the first part of this principle, Sun Tzu is saying to focus troops on the goal not on the means to the goal.

59. For it is precisely when a force has fallen into harm's way that is capable of striking a blow for victory.
60. Success in warfare is gained by carefully accommodating ourselves to the enemy's purpose.
61. By persistently hanging on the enemy's flank, we shall succeed in the long run in killing the commander-in-chief.
62. This is called ability to accomplish a thing by sheer cunning.
63. On the day that you take up your command, block the frontier passes, destroy the official tallies, and stop the passage of all emissaries.
64. Be stern in the council-chamber, so that you may control the situation.
65. If the enemy leaves a door open, you must rush in.
66. Forestall your opponent by seizing what he holds dear, and subtly contrive to time his arrival on the ground.
67. Walk in the path defined by rule, and accommodate yourself to the enemy until you can fight a decisive battle.
68. At first, then, exhibit the coyness of a maiden, until the enemy gives you an opening; afterwards emulate the rapidity of a running hare, and it will be too late for the enemy to oppose you.

XII.

The Attack By Fire[32]

1. Sun Tzu said: There are five ways of attacking with fire. The first is to burn soldiers in their camp; the second is to burn stores; the third is to burn baggage trains; the fourth is to burn arsenals and magazines; the fifth is to hurl dropping fire amongst the enemy.

---

32 The tactics discussed in this chapter have one underlying theme: use the flow of nature, the essential Taoist principle.

2. In order to carry out an attack, we must have means available. The material for raising fire should always be kept in readiness.
3. There is a proper season for making attacks with fire, and special days for starting a conflagration.
4. The proper season is when the weather is very dry; the special days are those when the moon is in the constellations of the Sieve, the Wall, the Wing or the Cross-bar; for these four are all days of rising wind.
5. In attacking with fire, one should be prepared to meet five possible developments:
6. (1) When fire breaks out inside to enemy's camp, respond at once with an attack from without.
7. (2) If there is an outbreak of fire, but the enemy's soldiers remain quiet, bide your time and do not attack.
8. (3) When the force of the flames has reached its height, follow it up with an attack, if that is practicable; if not, stay where you are.
9. (4) If it is possible to make an assault with fire from without, do not wait for it to break out within, but deliver your attack at a favorable moment.
10. (5) When you start a fire, be to windward of it. Do not attack from the leeward.
11. A wind that rises in the daytime lasts long, but a night breeze soon falls.
12. In every army, the five developments connected with fire must be known, the movements of the stars calculated, and a watch kept for the proper days.
13. Hence those who use fire as an aid to the attack show intelligence; those who use water as an aid to the attack gain an accession of strength.
14. By means of water, an enemy may be intercepted, but not robbed of all his belongings.

15. Unhappy is the fate of one who tries to win his battles and succeed in his attacks without cultivating the spirit of enterprise; for the result is waste of time and general stagnation.
16. Hence the saying: The enlightened ruler lays his plans well ahead; the good general cultivates his resources.
17. Move not unless you see an advantage; use not your troops unless there is something to be gained; fight not unless the position is critical.
18. No ruler should put troops into the field merely to gratify his own spleen; no general should fight a battle simply out of pique.
19. If it is to your advantage, make a forward move; if not, stay where you are.
20. Anger may in time change to gladness; vexation may be succeeded by content.
21. But a kingdom that has once been destroyed can never come again into being; nor can the dead ever be brought back to life.[33]
22. Hence the enlightened ruler is heedful, and the good general full of caution. This is the way to keep a country at peace and an army intact.

XIII.

The Use Of Spies

1. Sun Tzu said: Raising a host of a hundred thousand men and marching them great distances entails heavy loss on the people and a drain on the resources of the State. The daily expenditure will amount to a thousand ounces of silver. There will be commo-

---

33 This point is at the heart of Sun Tzu's ethical philosophy and should be considered carefully by any would-be combatant. Note in chapter VI of the *Tao Te Ching*: "Weapons, however beautiful, are instruments of ill omen, hateful to all creatures. Therefore he who has Tao will have nothing to do with them." Also in chapter VIII of the *Tao Te Ching*: "The violent and stiff-necked die not by a natural death."

tion at home and abroad, and men will drop down exhausted on the highways. As many as seven hundred thousand families will be impeded in their labor.

2. Hostile armies may face each other for years, striving for the victory which is decided in a single day. This being so, to remain in ignorance of the enemy's condition simply because one grudges the outlay of a hundred ounces of silver in honors and emoluments, is the height of inhumanity.

3. One who acts thus is no leader of men, no present help to his sovereign, no master of victory.

4. Thus, what enables the wise sovereign and the good general to strike and conquer, and achieve things beyond the reach of ordinary men, is foreknowledge.

5. Now this foreknowledge cannot be elicited from spirits; it cannot be obtained inductively from experience, nor by any deductive calculation.

6. Knowledge of the enemy's dispositions can only be obtained from other men.

7. Hence the use of spies, of whom there are five classes:
   (1) Local spies;
   (2) inward spies;
   (3) converted spies;
   (4) doomed spies;
   (5) surviving spies.

8. When these five kinds of spy are all at work, none can discover the secret system. This is called "divine manipulation of the threads." It is the sovereign's most precious faculty.

9. Having *local spies* means employing the services of the inhabitants of a district.

10. Having *inward spies*, making use of officials of the enemy.

11. Having *converted spies*, getting hold of the enemy's spies and using them for our own purposes.

12. Having *doomed spies*, doing certain things openly for purposes of deception, and allowing our spies to know of them and report them to the enemy.
13. *Surviving spies*, finally, are those who bring back news from the enemy's camp.
14. Hence it is that which none in the whole army are more intimate relations to be maintained than with spies. None should be more liberally rewarded. In no other business should greater secrecy be preserved.
15. Spies cannot be usefully employed without a certain intuitive sagacity.
16. They cannot be properly managed without benevolence and straightforwardness.
17. Without subtle ingenuity of mind, one cannot make certain of the truth of their reports.
18. Be subtle! be subtle! and use your spies for every kind of business.
19. If a secret piece of news is divulged by a spy before the time is ripe, he must be put to death together with the man to whom the secret was told.
20. Whether the object be to crush an army, to storm a city, or to assassinate an individual, it is always necessary to begin by finding out the names of the attendants, the aides-de-camp, and door-keepers and sentries of the general in command. Our spies must be commissioned to ascertain these.
21. The enemy's spies who have come to spy on us must be sought out, tempted with bribes, led away and comfortably housed. Thus they will become converted spies and available for our service.
22. It is through the information brought by the converted spy that we are able to acquire and employ local and inward spies.
23. It is owing to his information, again, that we can cause the doomed spy to carry false tidings to the enemy.

24. Lastly, it is by his information that the surviving spy can be used on appointed occasions.
25. The end and aim of spying in all its five varieties is knowledge of the enemy; and this knowledge can only be derived, in the first instance, from the converted spy. Hence it is essential that the converted spy be treated with the utmost liberality.
26. Of old, the rise of the Yin dynasty was due to I Chih who had served under the Hsia. Likewise, the rise of the Chou dynasty was due to Lu Ya who had served under the Yin.[34]
27. Hence it is only the enlightened ruler and the wise general who will use the highest intelligence of the army for purposes of spying and thereby they achieve great results. Spies are a most important element in water, because on them depends an army's ability to move.

---

[34] Sun Tzu is observing that these dynasties arose due to shifting allegiances and changing of sides—hence, a former minister bringing vital information into another's camp.

TAO TE CHING

The Sayings of Lao Tzu

Contents

I. Tao in its Transcendental Aspect and in its Physical Manifestation 59

II. Tao as a Moral Principle, or "Virtue" 62

III. The Doctrine of Inaction 66

IV. Lowliness and Humility 68

V. Government 71

VI. War 74

VII. Paradoxes 75

VIII. Miscellaneous Sayings and Precepts 78

IX. Lao Tzu on Himself 82

I.

Tao in its Transcendental Aspect and in its Physical Manifestation

The Tao which can be expressed in words is not the eternal Tao; the name which can be uttered is not its eternal name. Without a name, it is the Beginning of Heaven and Earth; with a name, it is the Mother of all things. Only one who is eternally free from earthly passions can apprehend its spiritual essence; he who is ever clogged by passions can see no more than its outer form. These two things, the spiritual and the material, though we call them by different names, in their origin are one and the same. This sameness is a mystery,—the mystery of mysteries. It is the gate of all spirituality.

How unfathomable is Tao! It seems to be the ancestral progenitor of all things. How pure and clear is Tao! It would seem to be everlasting. I know not of whom it is the offspring. It appears to have been anterior to any Sovereign Power.

Tao eludes the sense of sight, and is therefore called colorless. It eludes the sense of hearing, and is therefore called soundless. It eludes the sense of touch, and is therefore called incorporeal. These three qualities cannot be apprehended, and hence they may be blended into unity.

Its upper part is not bright, and its lower part is not obscure. Ceaseless in action, it cannot be named, but returns again to nothingness. We may call it the form of the formless, the image of the imageless, the fleeting and the indeterminable. Would you go before it, you cannot see its face; would you go behind it, you cannot see its back.

The mightiest manifestations of active force flow solely from Tao.

Tao in itself is vague, impalpable,—how impalpable, how vague! Yet within it there is Form. How vague, how impalpable! Yet within it there is Substance. How profound, how obscure! Yet within it there is a Vital Principle. This principle is the Quintessence of Reality, and out of it comes Truth.

From of old until now, its name has never passed away. It watches over the beginning of all things. How do I know this about the beginning of things? Through Tao.

There is something, chaotic yet complete, which existed before Heaven and Earth. Oh, how still it is, and formless, standing alone without changing, reaching everywhere without suffering harm! It must be regarded as the Mother of the Universe. Its name I know not. To designate it, I call it Tao. Endeavoring to describe it, I call it Great. Being great, it passes on; passing on, it becomes remote; having become remote, it returns.

Therefore Tao is great; Heaven is great; Earth is great; and the Sovereign also is great. In the Universe there are four powers, of which the Sovereign is one. Man takes his law from the Earth; the Earth takes its law from Heaven; Heaven takes its law from Tao; but the law of Tao is its own spontaneity.

Tao in its unchanging aspect has no name. Small though it be in its primordial simplicity, mankind dare not claim its service. Could princes and kings hold and keep it, all creation would spontaneously pay homage. Heaven and Earth would unite in sending down sweet dew, and the people would be righteous unbidden and of their own accord.

As soon as Tao creates order, it becomes nameable. When it once has a name, men will know how to rest in it. Knowing how to rest in it, they will run no risk of harm.

Tao as it exists in the world is like the great rivers and seas which receive the streams from the valleys.

All-pervading is the Great Tao. It can be at once on the right hand and on the left. All things depend on it for life, and it rejects them not.

Its task accomplished, it takes no credit. It loves and nourishes all things, but does not act as master. It is ever free from desire. We may call it small. All things return to it, yet it does not act as master. We may call it great.

The whole world will flock to him who holds the mighty form of Tao. They will come and receive no hurt, but find rest, peace, and tranquility.

With music and dainties we may detain the passing guest. But if we open our mouths to speak of Tao, he finds it tasteless and insipid.

Not visible to the sight, not audible to the ear, in its use it is inexhaustible.

Retrogression is the movement of Tao. Weakness is the character of Tao.

All things under Heaven derive their being from Tao in the form of Existence; Tao in the form of Existence sprang from Tao in the form of Non-Existence.

Tao is a great square with no angles, a great vessel which takes long to complete, a great sound which cannot be heard, a great image with no form.

Tao lies hid and cannot be named, yet it has the power of transmuting and perfecting all things.

Tao produced Unity; Unity produced Duality; Duality produced Trinity; and Trinity produced all existing objects. These myriad objects leave darkness behind them and embrace the light, being harmonized by the breath of Vacancy.

Tao produces all things; its Virtue nourishes them; its Nature gives them form; its Force perfects them.

Hence there is not a single thing but pays homage to Tao and extols its Virtue. This homage paid to Tao, this extolling of its Virtue, is due to no command, but is always spontaneous.

Thus it is that Tao, engendering all things, nourishes them, develops them, and fosters them; perfects them, ripens them, tends them, and protects them.

Production without possession, action without self-assertion, development without domination this is its mysterious operation.

The World has a First Cause, which may be regarded as the Mother of the World. When one has the Mother, one can know the Child. He who knows the Child and still keeps the Mother, though his body perish, shall run no risk of harm.

It is the Way of Heaven not to strive, and yet it knows how to overcome; not to speak, and yet it knows how to obtain a response; it calls not, and things come of themselves; it is slow to move, but excellent in its designs.

Heaven's net is vast; though its meshes are wide, it lets nothing slip through.

The Way of Heaven is like the drawing of a bow: it brings down what is high and raises what is low. It is the Way of Heaven to take from those who have too much, and give to those who have too little. But the way of man is not so. He takes away from those who have too little, to add to his own superabundance. What man is there that can take of his own superabundance and give it to mankind? Only he who possesses Tao.

The Tao of Heaven has no favorites. It gives to all good men without distinction.

Things wax strong and then decay. This is the contrary of Tao. What is contrary to Tao soon perishes.

II.

Tao as a Moral Principle, or "Virtue"

The highest goodness is like water, for water is excellent in benefiting all things, and it does not strive. It occupies the lowest place, which men abhor. And therefore it is near akin to Tao.

When your work is done and fame has been achieved, then retire into the background; for this is the Way of Heaven.

Those who follow the Way desire not excess; and thus without excess they are forever exempt from change.

All things alike do their work, and then we see them subside. When they have reached their bloom, each returns to its origin. Returning to their origin means rest or fulfillment of destiny. This reversion is an eternal law. To know that law is to be enlightened. Not to know it, is misery and calamity. He who knows the eternal law is liberal-minded. Being liberal-minded, he is just. Being just, he is kingly. Being kingly, he is akin to Heaven. Being akin to Heaven, he possesses Tao. Possessed of Tao, he endures forever. Though his body perish, yet he suffers no harm.

He who acts in accordance with Tao, becomes one with Tao. He who treads the path of Virtue becomes one with Virtue. He who pursues a course of Vice becomes one with Vice. The man who is one with Tao, Tao is also glad to receive. The man who is one with Virtue, Virtue is also glad to receive. The man who is one with Vice, Vice is also glad to receive.

He who is self approving does not shine. He who boasts has no merit. He who exalts himself does not rise high. Judged according to Tao, he is like remnants of food or a tumor on the body—an object of universal disgust. Therefore one who has Tao will not consort with such.

Perfect Virtue acquires nothing; therefore it obtains everything. Perfect Virtue does nothing, yet there is nothing which it does not effect. Perfect Charity operates without the need of anything to evoke it. Perfect Duty to one's neighbor operates, but always needs to be evoked. Perfect Ceremony operates, and calls for no outward response; nevertheless it induces respect.

Ceremonies are the outward expression of inward feelings.

If Tao perishes, then Virtue will perish; if Virtue perishes, then Charity will perish; if Charity perishes, then Duty to one's neighbor will perish; if Duty to one's neighbor perishes, then Ceremonies will perish.

Ceremonies are but the veneer of loyalty and good faith, while ofttimes the source of disorder. Knowledge of externals is but a showy ornament of Tao, while oft-times the beginning of imbecility.

Therefore the truly great man takes his stand upon what is solid, and not upon what is superficial; upon what is real, and not upon what is ornamental. He rejects the latter in favor of the former.

When the superior scholar hears of Tao, he diligently practices it. When the average scholar hears of Tao, he sometimes retains it, sometimes loses it. When the inferior scholar hears of Tao, he loudly laughs at it. Were it not thus ridiculed, it would not be worthy of the name of Tao.

He who is enlightened by Tao seems wrapped in darkness. He who is advanced in Tao seems to be going back. He who walks smoothly in Tao seems to be on a rugged path.

The man of highest virtue appears lowly. He who is truly pure behaves as though he were sullied. He who has virtue in abundance behaves as though it were not enough. He who is firm in virtue seems like a skulking pretender. He who is simple and true appears unstable as water.

If Tao prevails on earth, horses will be used for purposes of agriculture. If Tao does not prevail, war-horses will be bred on the common.

If we had sufficient knowledge to walk in the Great Way, what we should most fear would be boastful display.

The Great Way is very smooth, but the people love the by-paths.

Where the palaces are very splendid, there the fields will be very waste, and the granaries very empty.

The wearing of gay embroidered robes, the carrying of sharp swords, fastidiousness in food and drink, superabundance of property and wealth: this I call flaunting robbery; most assuredly it is not Tao.

He who trusts to his abundance of natural virtue is like an infant newly born, whom venomous reptiles will not sting, wild beasts will not seize, birds of prey will not strike. The infant's bones are weak, its sinews are soft, yet its grasp is firm. All day long it will cry without its voice becoming hoarse. This is because the harmony of its bodily system is perfect.

Temper your sharpness, disentangle your ideas, moderate your brilliancy, live in harmony with your age. This is being in conformity with the principle of Tao. Such a man is impervious alike to favor and disgrace, to benefits and injuries, to honor and contempt. And therefore he is esteemed above all mankind.

In governing men and in serving Heaven, there is nothing like moderation. For only by moderation can there be an early return to man's normal state. This early return is the same as a great storage of Virtue. With a great storage of Virtue there is naught which may not be achieved. If there is naught which may not be achieved, then no one will know to what extent this power reaches. And if no one knows to what extent a man's power reaches, that man is fit to be the ruler of a State. Having the secret of rule, his rule shall endure. Setting the tap-root deep, and making the spreading roots firm: this is the way to ensure long life to the tree.

Tao is the sanctuary where all things find refuge, the good man's priceless treasure, the guardian and savior of him who is not good.

Hence at the enthronement of an Emperor and the appointment of his three ducal ministers, though there be some who bear presents of costly jade and drive chariots with teams of four horses, that is not so good as sitting still and offering the gift of this Tao.

Why was it that the men of old esteemed this Tao so highly? Is it not because it may be daily sought and found, and can remit the sins of the guilty? Hence it is the most precious thing under Heaven.

All the world says that my Tao is great, but unlike other teaching. It is just because it is great that it appears unlike other teaching. If it had this likeness, long ago would its smallness have been known.

The skillful philosophers of the olden time were subtle, spiritual, profound, and penetrating. They were so deep as to be incomprehensible. Because they are hard to comprehend, I will endeavor to describe them.

Shrinking were they, like one fording a stream in winter. Cautious were they, like one who fears an attack from any quarter. Circumspect were they, like a stranger guest; self-effacing, like ice about to melt; simple, like unpolished wood; vacant, like a valley; opaque, like muddy water.

When terms are made after a great quarrel, a certain ill-feeling is bound to be left behind. How can this be made good? Therefore, having entered into an agreement, the Sage adheres to his obligations, but does not exact fulfillment from others. The man who has Virtue attends to the spirit of the compact; the man without Virtue attends only to his claims.

He who tries to govern a kingdom by his sagacity is of that kingdom the despoiler; but he who does not govern by sagacity is the kingdom's blessing. He who understands these two sayings may be regarded as a pattern and a model. To keep this principle constantly before one's eyes is called Profound Virtue. Profound Virtue is unfathomable, far-reaching, paradoxical at first, but afterwards exhibiting thorough conformity with Nature.

III.

The Doctrine of Inaction

The Sage occupies himself with inaction, and conveys instruction without words. Is it not by neglecting self-interest that one will be able to achieve it?

Purge yourself of your profound intelligence, and you can still be free from blemish. Cherish the people and order the kingdom, and you can still do without meddlesome action.

Who is there that can make muddy water clear? But if allowed to remain still, it will gradually become clear of itself. Who is there that can secure a state of absolute repose? But let time go on, and the state of repose will gradually arise.

Be sparing of speech, and things will come right of themselves.

A violent wind does not outlast the morning; a squall of rain does not outlast the day. Such is the course of Nature. And if Nature herself cannot sustain her efforts long, how much less can man!

Attain complete vacuity, and sedulously preserve a state of repose.

Tao is eternally inactive, and yet it leaves nothing undone. If kings and princes could but hold fast to this principle, all things would work out their own reformation. If, having reformed, they still desired to act, I would have them restrained by the simplicity of the Nameless Tao. The simplicity of the Nameless Tao brings about an absence of desire. The absence of desire gives tranquility. And thus the Empire will rectify itself.

The softest things in the world override the hardest. That which has no substance enters where there is no crevice. Hence I know the advantage of inaction.

Conveying lessons without words, reaping profit without action,—there are few in the world who can attain to this!

Activity conquers cold, but stillness conquers heat. Purity and stillness are the correct principles for mankind.

Without going out of doors one may know the whole world; without looking out of the window, one may see the Way of Heaven. The further one travels, the less one may know. Thus it is that without moving you shall know; without looking you shall see; without doing you shall achieve.

The pursuit of book-learning brings about daily increase. The practice of Tao brings about daily loss. Repeat this loss again and again, and you arrive at inaction. Practice inaction, and there is nothing which cannot be done.

The Empire has ever been won by letting things take their course. He who must always be doing is unfit to obtain the Empire.

Keep the mouth shut, close the gateways of sense, and as long as you live you will have no trouble. Open your lips and push your affairs, and you will not be safe to the end of your days.

Practice inaction, occupy yourself with doing nothing.

Desire not to desire, and you will not value things difficult to obtain. Learn not to learn, and you will revert to a condition which mankind in general has lost.

Leave all things to take their natural course, and do not interfere.

IV.

Lowness and Humility

All things in Nature work silently. They come into being and possess nothing. They fulfill their functions and make no claim.

When merit has been achieved, do not take it to yourself; for if you do not take it to yourself, it shall never be taken from you.

Follow diligently the Way in your own heart, but make no display of it to the world.

Keep behind, and you shall be put in front; keep out, and you shall be kept in.

Goodness strives not, and therefore it is not rebuked.

He that humbles himself shall be preserved entire. He that bends shall be made straight. He that is empty shall be filled. He that is worn out shall be renewed. He who has little shall succeed. He who has much shall go astray.

Therefore the Sage embraces Unity, and is a model for all under Heaven. He is free from self-display, therefore he shines forth; from self-assertion, therefore he is distinguished; from self-glorification, therefore he has merit; from self-exaltation, therefore he rises superior to all. Inasmuch as he does not strive, there is no one in the world who can strive with him.

He who, conscious of being strong, is content to be weak, he shall be the paragon of mankind. Being the paragon of mankind, Virtue will never desert him. He returns to the state of a little child.

He who, conscious of his own light, is content to be obscure,—he shall be the whole world's model. Being the whole world's model, his Virtue will never fail. He reverts to the Absolute.

He who, conscious of desert, is content to suffer disgrace,—he shall be the cynosure of mankind. Being the cynosure of mankind, his Virtue then is full. He returns to perfect simplicity.

He who is great must make humility his base. He who is high must make lowliness his foundation. Thus, princes and kings in speaking of themselves use the terms "lonely," "friendless," "of small account." Is not this making humility their base?

Thus it is that "Some things are increased by being diminished, others are diminished by being increased." What others have taught, I also teach; verily, I will make it the root of my teaching.

What makes a kingdom great is its being like a down-flowing river,—the central point towards which all the smaller streams under Heaven converge; or like the female throughout the world, who by quiescence always overcomes the male. And quiescence is a form of humility.

Therefore, if a great kingdom humbles itself before a small kingdom, it shall make that small kingdom its prize. And if a small kingdom humbles itself before a great kingdom, it shall win over that great kingdom. Thus the one humbles itself in order to attain, the other attains because it is humble. If the great kingdom has no further desire than to bring men together and to nourish them, the small kingdom will have no further desire than to enter the service of the other. But in order that both may have their desire, the great one must learn humility.

The reason why rivers and seas are able to be lords over a hundred mountain streams, is that they know how to keep below them. That is why they are able to reign over all the mountain streams.

Therefore the Sage, wishing to be above the people, must by his words put himself below them; wishing to be before the people, he must put himself behind them. In this way, though he has his place above them, the people do not feel his weight; though he has his place before them, they do not feel it as an injury. Therefore all mankind delight to exalt him, and weary of him not.

The Sage expects no recognition for what he does; he achieves merit but does not take it to himself; he does not wish to display his worth.

I have three precious things, which I hold fast and prize. The first is gentleness; the second is frugality; the third is humility, which keeps me from putting myself before others. Be gentle, and you can be bold; be frugal, and you can be liberal; avoid putting yourself before others, and you can become a leader among men.

But in the present day men cast off gentleness, and are all for being bold; they spurn frugality, and retain only extravagance; they discard humility, and aim only at being first. Therefore they shall surely perish.

Gentleness brings victory to him who attacks, and safety to him who defends. Those whom Heaven would save, it fences round with gentleness.

The best soldiers are not warlike; the best fighters do not lose their temper. The greatest conquerors are those who overcome their enemies without strife. The greatest directors of men are those who yield place to others. This is called the Virtue of not striving, the capacity for directing mankind; this is being the compeer of Heaven. It was the highest goal of the ancients.

V.

Government

Not exalting worth keeps the people from rivalry. Not prizing what is hard to procure keeps the people from theft. Not to show them what they may covet is the way to keep their minds from disorder.

Therefore the Sage, when he governs, empties their minds and fills their bellies, weakens their inclinations and strengthens their bones. His constant object is to keep the people without knowledge and without desire, or to prevent those who have knowledge from daring to act. He practices inaction, and nothing remains ungoverned.

He who respects the State as his own person is fit to govern it. He who loves the State as his own body is fit to be entrusted with it.

In the highest antiquity, the people did not know that they had rulers. In the next age they loved and praised them. In the next, they feared them. In the next, they despised them.

How cautious is the Sage, how sparing of his words! When his task is accomplished and affairs are prosperous, the people all say: "We have come to be as we are, naturally and of ourselves."

If anyone desires to take the Empire in hand and govern it, I see that he will not succeed. The Empire is a divine utensil which may not be roughly handled. He who meddles, mars. He who holds it by force, loses it.

Fishes must not be taken from the water: the methods of government must not be exhibited to the people.

Use uprightness in ruling a State; employ stratagems in waging war; practice non-interference in order to win the Empire. Now this is how I know what I lay down:—

As restrictions and prohibitions are multiplied in the Empire, the people grow poorer and poorer. When the people are subjected to overmuch government, the land is thrown into confusion. When the people are skilled in many cunning arts, strange are the objects of luxury that appear.

The greater the number of laws and enactments, the more thieves and robbers there will be. Therefore the Sage says: "So long as I do nothing, the people will work out their own reformation. So long as I love calm, the people will right themselves. If only I keep from meddling, the people will grow rich. If only I am free from desire, the people will come naturally back to simplicity."

If the government is sluggish and tolerant, the people will be honest and free from guile. If the government is prying and meddling, there will be constant infraction of the law. Is the government corrupt? Then uprightness becomes rare, and goodness becomes strange. Verily, mankind have been under delusion for many a day!

Govern a great nation as you would cook a small fish.

If the Empire is governed according to Tao, disembodied spirits will not manifest supernatural powers. It is not that they lack supernatural power, but they will not use it to hurt mankind. Again, it is not that they are unable to hurt mankind, but they see that the Sage also does not hurt mankind. If then neither Sage nor spirits work harm, their virtue converges to one beneficent end.

In ancient times those who knew how to practice Tao did not use it to enlighten the people, but rather to keep them ignorant. The difficulty of governing the people arises from their having too much knowledge.

If the people do not fear the majesty of government, a reign of terror will ensue.

Do not confine them within too narrow bounds; do not make their lives too weary. For if you do not weary them of life, then they will not grow weary of you.

If the people do not fear death, what good is there in using death as a deterrent? But if the people are brought up in fear of death, and we can take and execute any man who has committed a monstrous crime, who will dare to follow his example?

Now, there is always one who presides over the infliction of death. He who would take the place of the magistrate and himself inflict death, is like one who should try to do the work of a master-carpenter. And of those who try the work of a master-carpenter there are few who do not cut their own hands.

The people starve because those in authority over them devour too many taxes; that is why they starve. The people are difficult to govern because those placed over them are meddlesome; that is why they are difficult to govern. The people despise death because of their excessive labor in seeking the means of life; that is why they despise death.

A Sage has said: "He who can take upon himself the nation's shame is fit to be lord of the land. He who can take upon himself the nation's calamities is fit to be ruler over the Empire."

Were I ruler of a little State with a small population, and only ten or a hundred men available as soldiers, I would not use them. I would have the people look on death as a grievous thing, and they should not travel to distant countries. Though they might possess boats and carriages, they should have no occasion to ride in them. Though they might own weapons and armor, they should have no need to use them. I would make the people return to the use of knotted cords. They should find their plain food sweet, their rough garments fine. They should be content with their homes, and happy in their simple ways. If a neighboring State was within sight of mine—nay, if we were close enough to hear the crowing of each other's cocks and the barking of each other's dogs—the two peoples should grow old and die without there ever having been any mutual intercourse.

VI.

War

He who serves a ruler of men in harmony with Tao will not subdue the Empire by force of arms. Such a course is wont to bring retribution in its train.

Where troops have been quartered, brambles and thorns spring up. In the track of great armies there must follow lean years.

The good man wins a victory and then stops; he will not go on to acts of violence. Winning, he boasteth not; he will not triumph; he shows no arrogance. He wins because he cannot choose; after his victory he will not be overbearing.

Weapons, however beautiful, are instruments of ill omen, hateful to all creatures. Therefore he who has Tao will have nothing to do with them.

Where the princely man abides, the weak left hand is in honor. But he who uses weapons honors the stronger right. Weapons are instruments of ill omen; they are not the instruments of the princely man, who uses them only when he needs must. Peace and tranquility are what he prizes. When he conquers, he is not elate. To be elate were to rejoice in the slaughter of human beings. And he who rejoices in the slaughter of human beings is not fit to work his will in the Empire.

On happy occasions, the left is favored; on sad occasions, the right. The second in command has his place on the left, the general in chief on the right. That is to say, they are placed in the order observed at funeral rites. And, indeed, he who has exterminated a great multitude of men should bewail them with tears and lamentation. It is well that those who are victorious in battle should be placed in the order of funeral rites.

A certain military commander used to say: "I dare not act the host; I prefer to play the guest. I dare not advance an inch; I prefer to retreat a foot."

There is no greater calamity than lightly engaging in war. Lightly to engage in war is to risk the loss of our treasure.

When opposing warriors join in battle, he who has pity conquers.

VII.

Paradoxes

Among mankind, the recognition of beauty as such implies the idea of ugliness, and the recognition of good implies the idea of evil. There is the same mutual relation between existence and non-existence in the matter of creation; between difficulty and ease in the matter of accomplishing; between long and short in the matter of form; between high and low in the matter of elevation; between treble and bass in the matter of musical pitch; between before and after in the matter of priority.

Nature is not benevolent; with ruthless indifference she makes all things serve their purposes, like the straw dogs we use at sacrifices. The Sage is not benevolent: he utilizes the people with the like inexorability.

The space between Heaven and Earth,—is it not like a bellows? It is empty, yet inexhaustible; when it is put in motion, more and more comes out.

Heaven and Earth are long-lasting. The reason why Heaven and Earth can last long is that they live not for themselves, and thus they are able to endure.

Thirty spokes unite in one nave; the utility of the cart depends on the hollow centre in which the axle turns. Clay is moulded into a vessel; the utility of the vessel depends on its hollow interior. Doors and windows are cut out in order to make a house; the utility of the house depends on the empty spaces.

Thus, while the existence of things may be good, it is the non-existent in them which makes them serviceable.

When the Great Tao falls into disuse, benevolence and righteousness come into vogue. When shrewdness and sagacity appear, great hypocrisy prevails. It is when the bonds of kinship are out of joint that filial piety and paternal affection begin. It is when the State is in a ferment of revolution that loyal patriots arise.

Cast off your holiness, rid yourself of sagacity, and the people will benefit an hundredfold. Discard benevolence and abolish righteousness, and the people will return to filial piety and paternal love. Renounce your scheming and abandon gain, and thieves and robbers will disappear. These three precepts mean that outward show is insufficient, and therefore they bid us be true to our proper nature;—to show simplicity, to embrace plain dealing, to reduce selfishness, to moderate desire.

A variety of colors makes man's eye blind; a diversity of sounds makes man's ear deaf; a mixture of flavors makes man's palate dull.

He who knows others is clever, but he who knows himself is enlightened. He who overcomes others is strong, but he who overcomes himself is mightier still. He is rich who knows when he has enough. He who acts with energy has strength of purpose. He who moves not from his proper place is long-lasting. He who dies, but perishes not, enjoys true longevity.

If you would contract, you must first expand. If you would weaken, you must first strengthen. If you would overthrow, you must first raise up. If you would take, you must first give. This is called the dawn of intelligence.

He who is most perfect seems to be lacking; yet his resources are never outworn. He who is most full seems vacant; yet his uses are inexhaustible.

Extreme straightness is as bad as crookedness. Extreme cleverness is as bad as folly. Extreme fluency is as bad as stammering.

Those who know do not speak; those who speak do not know.

Abandon learning, and you will be free from trouble and distress.

Failure is the foundation of success, and the means by which it is achieved. Success is the lurking-place of failure; but who can tell when the turning-point will come?

He who acts, destroys; he who grasps, loses. Therefore the Sage does not act, and so does not destroy; he does not grasp, and so he does not lose.

Only he who does nothing for his life's sake can truly be said to value his life.

Man at his birth is tender and weak; at his death he is rigid and strong. Plants and trees when they come forth are tender and crisp; when dead, they are dry and tough. Thus rigidity and strength are the concomitants of death; softness and weakness are the concomitants of life.

Hence the warrior that is strong does not conquer; the tree that is strong is cut down. Therefore the strong and the big take the lower place; the soft and the weak take the higher place.

There is nothing in the world more soft and weak than water, yet for attacking things that are hard and strong there is nothing that surpasses it, nothing that can take its place.

The soft overcomes the hard; the weak overcomes the strong. There is no one in the world but knows this truth, and no one who can put it into practice.

Those who are wise have no wide range of learning; those who range most widely are not wise.

The Sage does not care to hoard. The more he uses for the benefit of others, the more he possesses himself. The more he gives to his fellow-men, the more he has of his own.

The truest sayings are paradoxical.

VIII.

Miscellaneous Sayings and Precepts

By many words wit is exhausted; it is better to preserve a mean. The excellence of a dwelling is its site; the excellence of a mind is its profundity; the excellence of giving is charitableness; the excellence of speech is truthfulness; the excellence of government is order; the excellence of action is ability; the excellence of movement is timeliness.

He who grasps more than he can hold, would be better without any. If a house is crammed with treasures of gold and jade, it will be impossible to guard them all.

He who prides himself upon wealth and honor hastens his own downfall. He who strikes with a sharp point will not himself be safe for long.

He who embraces unity of soul by subordinating animal instincts to reason will be able to escape dissolution. He who strives his utmost after tenderness can become even as a little child.

If a man is clear-headed and intelligent, can he be without knowledge?

The Sage attends to the inner and not to the outer; he puts away the objective and holds to the subjective.

Between yes and yea, how small the difference!

Between good and evil, how great the difference!

What the world reverences may not be treated with disrespect.

He who has not faith in others shall find no faith in them.

To see oneself is to be clear of sight. Mighty is he who conquers himself.

He who raises himself on tiptoe cannot stand firm; he who stretches his legs wide apart cannot walk.

Racing and hunting excite man's heart to madness.

The struggle for rare possessions drives a man to actions injurious to himself.

The heavy is the foundation of the light; repose is the ruler of unrest.

The wise prince in his daily course never departs from gravity and repose. Though he possess a gorgeous palace, he will dwell therein with calm indifference. How should the lord of a myriad chariots conduct himself with levity in the Empire? Levity loses men's hearts; unrest loses the throne.

The skillful traveler leaves no tracks; the skillful speaker makes no blunders; the skillful reckoner uses no tallies. He who knows how to shut uses no bolts—yet you cannot open. He who knows how to bind uses no cords—yet you cannot undo.

Among men, reject none; among things, reject nothing. This is called comprehensive intelligence.

The good man is the bad man's teacher; the bad man is the material upon which the good man works. If the one does not value his teacher, if the other does not love his material, then despite their sagacity they must go far astray. This is a mystery of great import.

As unwrought material is divided up and made into serviceable vessels, so the Sage turns his simplicity to account, and thereby becomes the ruler of rulers.

The course of things is such that what was in front is now behind; what was hot is now cold; what was strong is now weak; what was complete is now in ruin. Therefore the Sage avoids excess, extravagance, and grandeur.

Which is nearer to you, fame or life? Which is more to you, life or wealth? Which is the greater malady, gain or loss?

Excessive ambitions necessarily entail great sacrifice. Much hoarding must be followed by heavy loss. He who knows when he has enough will not be put to shame. He who knows when to stop will not come to harm. Such a man can look forward to long life.

There is no sin greater than ambition; no calamity greater than discontent; no vice more sickening than covetousness. He who is content always has enough.

Do not wish to be rare like jade, or common like stone.

The Sage has no hard and fast ideas, but he shares the ideas of the people and makes them his own. Living in the world, he is apprehensive lest his heart be sullied by contact with the world. The people all fix their eyes and ears upon him. The Sage looks upon all as his children.

I have heard that he who possesses the secret of life, when traveling abroad, will not flee from rhinoceros or tiger; when entering a hostile camp, he will not equip himself with sword or buckler. The rhinoceros finds in him no place to insert its horn; the tiger has nowhere to fasten its claw; the soldier has nowhere to thrust his blade. And why? Because he has no spot where death can enter.

To see small beginnings is clearness of sight. To rest in weakness is strength.

He who knows how to plant, shall not have his plant uprooted; he who knows how to hold a thing, shall not have it taken away. Sons and grandsons will worship at his shrine, which shall endure from generation to generation.

Knowledge in harmony is called constant. Constant knowledge is called wisdom. Increase of life is called felicity. The mind directing the body is called strength.

Be square without being angular. Be honest without being mean. Be upright without being punctilious. Be brilliant without being showy.

Good words shall gain you honor in the marketplace, but good deeds shall gain you friends among men.

To the good I would be good; to the not-good I would also be good, in order to make them good.

With the faithful I would keep faith; with the unfaithful I would also keep faith, in order that they may become faithful.

Even if a man is bad, how can it be right to cast him off?

Requite injury with kindness.

The difficult things of this world must once have been easy; the great things of this world must once have been small. Set about difficult things while they are still easy; do great things while they are still small. The Sage never affects to do anything great, and therefore he is able to achieve his great results.

He who always thinks things easy is sure to find them difficult. Therefore the Sage ever anticipates difficulties, and thus it is he never encounters them.

While times are quiet, it is easy to take action; ere coming troubles have cast their shadows, it is easy to lay plans.

That which is brittle is easily broken; that which is minute is easily dissipated. Take precautions before the evil appears; regulate things before disorder has begun.

The tree which needs two arms to span its girth sprang from the tiniest shoot. Yon tower, nine storeys high, rose from a little mound of earth. A journey of a thousand miles began with a single step.

A great principle cannot be divided; therefore it is that many containers cannot contain it.

The Sage knows what is in him, but makes no display; he respects himself, but seeks not honor for himself.

To know, but to be as though not knowing, is the height of wisdom. Not to know, and yet to affect knowledge, is a vice. If we regard this vice as such, we shall escape it. The Sage has not this vice. It is because he regards it as a vice that he escapes it.

Use the light that is in you to revert to your natural clearness of sight. Then the loss of the body is unattended by calamity. This is called doubly enduring.

In the management of affairs, people constantly break down just when they are nearing a successful issue. If they took as much care at the end as at the beginning, they would not fail in their enterprises.

He who lightly promises is sure to keep but little faith.

He whose boldness leads him to venture, will be slain; he who is brave enough not to venture, will live. Of these two, one has the benefit, the other has the hurt. But who is it that knows the real cause of Heaven's hatred? This is why the Sage hesitates and finds it difficult to act.

The violent and stiff-necked die not by a natural death.

True words are not fine; fine words are not true.

The good are not contentious; the contentious are not good.

This is the Way of Heaven, which benefits, and injures not. This is the Way of the Sage, in whose actions there is no element of strife.

IX.

Lao Tzu on Himself

Alas! the barrenness of the age has not yet reached its limit. All men are radiant with happiness, as if enjoying a great feast, as if mounted on a tower in spring. I alone am still, and give as yet no sign of joy. I am like an infant which has not yet smiled, forlorn as one who has nowhere to lay his head. Other men have plenty, while I alone seem to have lost all. I am a man foolish in heart, dull and confused. Other men are full of light; I alone seem to be in darkness. Other men are alert; I alone am listless. I am unsettled as the ocean, drifting as though I had no stopping-place. All men have their usefulness; I alone am stupid and clownish. Lonely though I am and unlike other men, yet I revere the Foster-Mother, Tao.

My words are very easy to understand, very easy to put into practice; yet the world can neither understand nor practice them.

My words have a clue, my actions have an underlying principle. It is because men do not know the clue that they understand me not.

Those who know me are but few, and on that account my honor is the greater.

Thus the Sage wears coarse garments, but carries a jewel in his bosom.

CRYSTALLIZING PUBLIC OPINION

Edward Bernays

To My Wife

Doris E. Fleischman

Contents

Foreword 89

Part I
Scope and Functions

1 The Scope of the Public Relations Counsel 91

2 The Public Relations Counsel; the Increased and Increasing Importance of the Profession 105

3 The Function of a Special Pleader 115

Part II
The Group and Herd

1 What Constitutes Public Opinion? 1210

2 Is Public Opinion Stubborn or Malleable? 126

3 The Interaction of Public Opinion with the Forces That Help to Make It 131

4 The Power of Interacting Forces That Go to Make up Public Opinion 137

5 An Understanding of the Fundamentals of Public Motivation Is Necessary to the Work of the Public Relations Counsel 144

6 The Group and Herd Are the Basic Mechanisms of Public Change 152

7 The Application of These Principles 157

Part III
Technique and Method

1 The Public Can Be Reached Only Through Established Mediums of Communication 161

2 The Interlapping Group Formations of Society, the Continuous Shifting of Groups, Changing Conditions and the Flexibility of Human Nature Are All Aids to the Counsel on Public Relations 170

3 An Outline of Methods Practicable in Modifying the Point of View of a Group 186

Part IV
Ethical Relations

1 A Consideration of the Press and Other Mediums of Communication in Their Relation to the Public Relations Counsel 192

2 His Obligations to the Public as a Special Pleader 212

Foreword

In writing this book I have tried to set down the broad principles that govern the new profession of public relations counsel. These principles I have on the one hand substantiated by the findings of psychologists, sociologists, and newspapermen—Ray Stannard Baker, W. G. Bleyer, Richard Washburn Child, Elmer Davis, John L. Given, Will Irwin, Francis E. Leupp, Walter Lippmann, William MacDougall, Everett Dean Martin, H. L. Mencken, Rollo Ogden, Charles J. Rosebault, William Trotter, Oswald Garrison Villard, and others to whom I owe a debt of gratitude for their clear analyses of the public's mind and habits; and on the other hand, I have illustrated these principles by a number of specific examples which serve to bear them out. I have quoted from the men listed here, because the ground covered by them is part of the field of activity of the public relations counsel. The actual cases which I have cited were selected because they explain the application of the theories to practice. Most of the illustrative material is drawn from my personal experience; a few examples from my observation of events. I have preferred to cite facts known to the general public, in order that I might explain graphically a profession that has little precedent, and whose few formulated rules have necessarily a limitless number and variety of applications.

This profession in a few years has developed from the status of circus agent stunts to what is obviously an important position in the conduct of the world's affairs.

If I shall, by this survey of the field, stimulate a scientific attitude towards the study of public relations, I shall feel that this book has fulfilled my purpose in writing it.

E. L. B., December, 1923.

Part I
Scope and Functions

1

The Scope of the Public Relations Counsel

A new phrase has come into the language—counsel on public relations. What does it mean?

As a matter of fact, the actual phrase is completely understood by only a few, and those only the people intimately associated with the work itself. But despite this, the activities of the public relations counsel affect the daily life of the entire population in one form or another.

Because of the recent extraordinary growth of the profession of public relations counsel and the lack of available information concerning it, an air of mystery has surrounded its scope and functions. To the average person, this profession is still unexplained, both in its operation and actual accomplishment. Perhaps the most definite picture is that of a man who somehow or other produces that vaguely defined evil, "propaganda," which spreads an impression that colors the mind of the public concerning actresses, governments, railroads. And yet, as will be pointed out shortly, there is probably no single profession which within the last ten years has extended its field of usefulness more remarkably and touched upon intimate and important aspects of the everyday life of the world more significantly than the profession of public relations counsel.

There is not even any one name by which the new profession is characterized by others. To some the public relations counsel is known by the term "propagandist." Others still call him press agent or publicity man. Writing even within the last few years, John L. Given, the author of an excellent textbook on journalism, does not mention the public relations counsel. He limits his reference to the old-time press agent. Many organizations simply do not bother about an individual name and assign to an existing officer the duties of the public relations counsel. One bank's vice-president is its recognized public relations counsel. Some dismiss the subject or condemn the entire profession generally and all its members individually.

Slight examination into the grounds for this disapproval readily reveals that it is based on nothing more substantial than vague impressions.

Indeed, it is probably true that the very men who are themselves engaged in the profession are as little ready or able to define their work as is the general public itself. Undoubtedly this is due, in some measure, to the fact that the profession is a new one. Much more important than that, however, is the fact that most human activities are based on experience rather than analysis.

Judge Cardozo of the Court of Appeals of the State of New York finds the same absence of functional definition in the judicial mind. "The work of deciding cases," he says, "goes on every day in hundreds of courts throughout the land. Any judge, one might suppose, would find it easy to describe the process which he had followed a thousand times and more. Nothing could be farther from the truth. Let some intelligent layman ask him to explain. He will not go very far before taking refuge in the excuse that the language of craftsmen is unintelligible to those untutored in the craft. Such an excuse may cover with a semblance of respectability an otherwise ignominious retreat. It will hardly serve to still the prick of curiosity and conscience. In moments of introspection, when there is no longer a necessity of putting off with a show of wisdom the uninitiated interlocutor, the troublesome problem will recur and press for a solution: What is it that I do when I decide a case?"[1]

From my own records and from current history still fresh in the public mind, I have selected a few instances which only in a limited measure give some idea of the variety of the public relations counsel's work and of the type of problem which he attempts to solve.

These examples show him in his position as one who directs and supervises the activities of his clients wherever they impinge upon the daily life of the public. He interprets the client to the public, which he is enabled to do in part because he interprets the public to the client. His advice is given on all occasions on which his client appears before the public, whether it be in concrete form or as an idea. His advice is given not only on actions which take place, but also on the use of mediums which bring these actions to the public it is desired to reach, no matter whether these mediums be the printed, the spoken or the visualized word—that is, advertising, lectures, the stage, the pulpit, the newspaper, the photograph, the wireless, the mail or any other form of thought communication.

A nationally famous New York hotel found that its business was falling off at an alarming rate because of a rumor that it was shortly going to close and that the site upon which it was located would be occupied by a department store. Few things are more mysterious than the origins of rumors, or the credence which they manage to obtain. Reservations at this hotel for weeks and months ahead were being canceled by persons who had heard the rumor and accepted it implicitly.

The problem of meeting this rumor (which like many rumors had no foundation in fact) was not only a difficult but a serious one. Mere

---

1 Cardozo, "The Nature of the Judicial Process" (page 9).

denial, of course, no matter how vigorous or how widely disseminated, would accomplish little.

The mere statement of the problem made it clear to the public relations counsel who was retained by the hotel that the only way to overcome the rumor was to give the public some positive evidence of the intention of the hotel to remain in business. It happened that the *maitre d'hotel* was about as well known as the hotel itself. His contract was about to expire. The public relations counsel suggested a very simple device.

"Renew his engagement immediately for a term of years," he said. "Then make public announcement of the fact. Nobody who hears of the renewal or the amount of money involved will believe for a moment that you intend to go out of business." The *maitre d'hotel* was called in and offered a five-year engagement. His salary was one which many bank presidents might envy. Public announcement of his engagement was made. The *maitre d'hotel* was himself something of a national figure. The salary stipulated was not without popular interest from both points of view. The story was one which immediately interested the newspapers. A national press service took up the story and sent it out to all its subscribers. The cancellation of reservations stopped and the rumor disappeared.

A nationally known magazine was ambitious to increase its prestige among a more influential group of advertisers. It had never made any effort to reach this public except through its own direct circulation. The consultant who was retained by the magazine quickly discovered that much valuable editorial material appearing in the magazine was allowed to go to waste. Features of interest to thousands of potential readers were never called to their attention unless they happened accidentally to be readers of the magazine.

The public relations counsel showed how to extend the field of their appeal. He chose for his first work an extremely interesting article by a well-known physician, written about the interesting thesis that "the pace that kills" is the slow, deadly, dull routine pace and not the pace of life under high pressure, based on work which interests and excites. The consultant arranged to have the thesis of the article made the basis of an inquiry among business and professional men throughout the country by another physician associated with a medical journal. Hundreds of members of "the quality public," as they are known to advertisers, had their attention focused on the article, and the magazine which the consultant was engaged in counseling on its public relations.

The answers from these leading men of the country were collated, analyzed, and the resulting abstract furnished gratuitously to newspapers, magazines and class journals, which published them widely. Organizations of business and professional men reprinted the symposium by the thousands and distributed it free of charge, doing so because the material contained in the symposium was of great interest. A distinguished visitor from abroad. Lord Leverhulme, became interested in the question while in this country and made the magazine and the article the basis of an address before a large and influential conference in England. Nationally and internationally the magazine was called to the attention of a public which had, up to that time, considered it perhaps a publication of no serious social significance.

Still working with the same magazine, the publicity consultant advised it how to widen its influence with another public on quite a different issue. He took as his subject an article by Sir Philip Gibbs, "The Madonna of the Hungry Child," dealing with the famine situation in Europe and the necessity for its prompt alleviation. The article was brought to the attention of Herbert Hoover. Mr. Hoover was so impressed by the article that he sent the magazine a letter of commendation for publishing it. He also sent a copy of the article to members of his relief committees throughout the country. The latter, in turn, used the article to obtain support and contributions for relief work. Thus, while an important humanitarian project was being materially assisted, the magazine in question was adding to its own influence and standing.

Now, the interesting thing about this work is that whereas the public relations counsel added nothing to the contents of the magazine, which had for years been publishing material of this nature, he did make its importance felt and appreciated.

A large packing house was faced with the problem of increasing the sale of its particular brand of bacon. It already dominated the market in its field; the problem was therefore one of increasing the consumption of bacon generally, for its dominance of the market would naturally continue. The public relations counsel, realizing that hearty breakfasts were dietetically sound, suggested that a physician undertake a survey to make this medical truth articulate. He realized that the demand for bacon as a breakfast food would naturally be increased by the wide dissemination of this truth. This is exactly what happened.

A hair-net company had to solve the problem created by the increasing vogue of bobbed hair. Bobbed hair was eliminating the use of the hair-net. The public relations counsel, after investigation, advised that the opinions of club women as leaders of the women of the country should be made articulate on the question. Their expressed opinion, he believed, would definitely modify the bobbed hair vogue. A leading artist was interested in the subject and undertook a survey among the club women leaders of the country. The resultant responses confirmed the public relations counsel's judgment. The opinions of these women were given to the public and helped to arouse what had evidently been a latent opinion on the question. Long hair was made socially more acceptable than bobbed hair and the vogue for the latter was thereby partially checked.

A real estate corporation on Long Island was interested in selling cooperative apartments to a high-class clientele. In order to do this, it realized that it had to impress upon the public the fact that this community, within easy reach of Manhattan, was socially, economically, artistically and morally desirable. On the advice of its public relations counsel, instead of merely proclaiming itself as such a community, it proved its contentions dramatically by making itself an active center for all kinds of community manifestations.

When it opened its first post office, for instance, it made this local event nationally interesting. The opening was a formal one. National figures became interested in what might have been merely a local event.

The reverses which the Italians suffered on the Piave in 1918 were dangerous to Italian and Allied morale. One of the results was the awakening of a distrust among Italians as to the sincerity of American promises of military, financial and moral support for the Italian cause.

It became imperative vividly to dramatize for Italy the reality of American cooperation. As one of the means to this end the Committee on Public Information decided that the naming of a recently completed American ship should be made the occasion for a demonstration of friendship which could be reflected in every possible way to the Italians.

Prominent Italians in America were invited by the public relations counsel to participate in the launching of the *Piave*. Motion and still pictures were taken of the event. The news of the launching and of its significance to Americans was telegraphed to Italian newspapers. At the same time a message from Italian-Americans was transmitted to Italy expressing their confidence in America's assistance of the Italian cause. Enrico Caruso, Gatti-Casazza, director of the Metropolitan Opera, and others highly regarded by their countrymen in Italy, sent inspiriting telegrams which had a decided effect in raising Italian morale, so far as it depended upon assurance of American cooperation. Other means employed to disseminate information of this event had the same effect.

The next incident that I have selected is one which conforms more closely than some of the others to the popular conception of the work of the public relations counsel. In the spring and summer of 1919 the problem of fitting ex-service men into the ordinary life of America was serious and difficult. Thousands of men just back from abroad were having a trying time finding work. After their experience in the war it was not surprising that they should be extremely ready to feel bitter against the Government and against those Americans who for one reason or another had not been in any branch of the service during the war.

The War Department under Colonel Arthur Woods, assistant to the Secretary of War, instituted a nation-wide campaign to assist those men to obtain employment, and more than that, to manifest to them as concretely as it could that the Government continued its interest in their welfare. The incident to which I refer occurred during this campaign.

In July of 1919 there was such a shortage of labor in Kansas that it was feared a large proportion of the wheat crop could not possibly be harvested. The activities of the War Department in the reemployment of ex-service men had already received wide publicity, and the Chamber of Commerce of Kansas City appealed directly to the War Department at Washington, after its own efforts in many other directions had failed, for a supply of men who would assist in the harvesting of the wheat crop. The public relations counsel prepared a statement of this opportunity for employment in Kansas and distributed it to the public through the newspapers throughout the country. The Associated Press sent the statement over its wires as a news dispatch. Within four days the Kansas City Chamber of Commerce wired to the War Department that enough labor had been secured to harvest the wheat crop, and asked the War Department to announce that fact as publicly as it had first announced the need for labor.

By contrast with this last instance, and as an illustration of a type of work less well understood by the public, I cite another incident from the same campaign for the reestablishment of ex-service men to normal economic and social relations. The problem of reemployment was, of course, the crux of the difficulty. Various measures were adopted to obtain the cooperation of business men in extending employment opportunities to ex-members of the Army, Navy and Marines. One of these devices appealed to the personal and local pride of American business men, and stressed their obligation of honor to reemploy their former employees upon release from Government service.

A citation was prepared, signed by the Secretary of War, the Secretary of the Navy and the Assistant to the Secretary of War for display in the stores and factories of employers who assured the War and Navy Departments that they would re-employ their ex-service men. Simultaneous display of these citations was arranged for Bastile Day, July 14, 1919, by members of the Fifth Avenue Association.

The Fifth Avenue Association of New York City, an influential group of business men, was perhaps the first to cooperate as a body in this important campaign for the reemployment of ex-service men. Concerted action on a subject which was as much in the public mind as the reemployment of ex-service men was particularly interesting. The story of what these leaders in American business had undertaken to do went out to the country by mail, by word of mouth, by newspaper comment. Their example was potent in obtaining the cooperation of business men throughout the land. An appeal based on this action and capitalizing it was sent to thousands of individual business men and employers throughout the country. It was effective.

An illustration which embodies most of the technical and psychological points of interest in the preceding incidents may be found in Lithuania's campaign in this country in 1919, for popular sympathy and official recognition. Lithuania was of considerable political importance in the reorganization of Europe, but it was a country little known or understood by the American public. An added difficulty was the fact that the independence of Lithuania would interfere seriously with the plans which France had for the establishment of a strong Poland. There were excellent historical, ethnic and economic reasons why, if Lithuania broke off from Russia, it should be allowed to stand on its own feet. On the other hand there were powerful political influences which were against such a result. The American attitude on the question of Lithuanian independence, it was felt, would play an important part. The question was how to arouse popular and official interest in Lithuania's aspirations.

A Lithuanian National Council was organized, composed of prominent American-Lithuanians, and a Lithuanian Information Bureau established to act as a clearing house for news about Lithuania and for special pleading on behalf of Lithuania's ambitions. The public relations counsel who was retained to direct this work recognized that the first problem to be solved was America's indifference to and ignorance about Lithuania and its desires.

He had an exhaustive study made of every conceivable aspect of the problem of Lithuania from its remote and recent history and ethnic origins to its present-day marriage customs and its popular recreations. He divided his material into its various categories, based primarily on the public to which it would probably make its appeal. For the amateur ethnologist he provided interesting and accurate data of the racial origins of Lithuania. To the student of languages he appealed with authentic and well written studies of the development of the Lithuanian language from its origins in the Sanskrit. He told the "sporting fan" about Lithuanian sports and told American women about Lithuanian clothes. He told the jeweler about amber and provided the music lover with concerts of Lithuanian music.

To the senators, he gave facts about Lithuania which would give them basis for favorable action. To the members of the House of Representatives he did likewise. He reflected to those communities whose crystallized opinion would be helpful in guiding other opinions, facts which gave them basis for conclusions favorable to Lithuania.

A series of events which would carry with them the desired implications were planned and executed. Mass meetings were held in different cities; petitions were drawn, signed and presented; pilgrims made calls upon Senate and House of Representatives Committees. All the avenues of approach to the public were utilized to capitalize the public interest and bring public action. The mails carried statements of Lithuania's position to individuals who might be interested. The lecture platform resounded to Lithuania's appeal. Newspaper advertising was bought and paid for. The radio carried the message of speakers to the public. Motion pictures reached the patrons of moving picture houses.

Little by little and phase by phase, the public, the press and Government officials acquired a knowledge of the customs, the character and the problems of Lithuania, the small Baltic nation that was seeking freedom.

When the Lithuanian Information Bureau went before the press associations to correct inaccurate or misleading Polish news about the Lithuanian situation, it came there as representative of a group which had figured largely in the American news for a number of weeks, as a result of the advice and activities of its public relations counsel. In the same way, when delegations of Americans, interested in the Lithuanian problem, appeared before members of Congress or officials of the State Department, they came there as spokesmen for a country which was no longer unknown. They represented a group which could no longer be entirely ignored. Somebody described this campaign, once it had achieved recognition for the Baltic republic, as the campaign of "advertising a nation to freedom."

What happened with Roumania is another instance. Roumania wanted to plead its case before the American people. It wanted to tell Americans that it was an ancient and established country. The original technique was the issuance of treatises, historically correct and ethnologically accurate. Their facts were for the large part ignored. The public relations counsel, called in on the case of Roumania, advised them to make these studies into interesting stories of news value. The public read these stories with avidity and Roumania became part of

America's popular knowledge with consequent valuable results for Roumania.

The hotels of New York City discovered that there was a falling off of business and profits. Fewer visitors came to New York. Fewer travelers passed through New York on their way to Europe. The public relations counsel who was consulted and asked to remedy the situation, made an extensive analysis. He talked to visitors. He queried men and women who represented groups, sections and opinions of main cities and towns throughout the country. He examined American literature—books, magazines, newspapers, and classified attacks made on New York and New York citizens. He found that the chief cause for lack of interest in New York was the belief that New York was "cold and inhospitable."

He found animosity and bitterness against New York's apparent indifference to strangers was keeping away a growing number of travelers. To counteract this damaging wave of resentment, he called together the leading groups, industrial, social and civic, of New York, and formed the Welcome Stranger Committee. The friendly and hospitable aims of this committee, broadcasted to the nation, helped to reestablish New York's good repute. Congratulatory editorials were printed in the rural and city journals of the country.

Again, in analyzing the restaurant service of a prominent hotel, he discovers that its menu is built on the desires of the average eater and that a large group of people with children desire special foods for them. He may then advise his client to institute a children's diet service.

This was done specifically with the Waldorf-Astoria Hotel, which instituted special menus for children. This move, which excited wide comment, was economically and dietetically sound.

In its campaign to educate the public on the importance of early radium treatments for incipient cancer, the United States Radium Corporation founded the First National Radium Bank, in order to create and crystallize the impression that radium is and should be available to all physicians who treat cancer sufferers.

An inter-city radio company planned to open a wireless service between the three cities of New York, Detroit and Cleveland. This company might merely have opened its service and waited for the public to send its messages, but the president of the organization realized astutely that to succeed in any measure at all he must have immediate public support. He called in a public relations counsel, who advised an elaborate inauguration ceremony, in which the mayors of the three cities thus for the first time connected, would officiate. The mayor of each city officially received and sent the first messages issued on commercial inter-city radio waves. These openings excited wide interest, not only in the three cities directly concerned, but throughout the entire country.

Shortly after the World War, the King and Queen of the Belgians visited America. One of the many desired results of this visit was that it should be made apparent that America, with all the foreign elements represented in its body, was unified in its support of King Albert and his country. To present a graphic picture of the affection which the national elements here had for the Belgian monarch, a performance was staged at the Metropolitan Opera House in New York City, at which the many nationalist groups were represented and gave voice to their approval. The story of the Metropolitan Opera House performance was spread in the news columns and by photographs in the press throughout the world. It was evident to all who saw the pictures or read the story that this king had really stirred the affectionate interest of the national elements that make up America.

An interesting illustration of the broad field of work of the public relations counsel to-day is noted in the efforts which were exerted to secure wide commendation and support among Americans for the League of Nations. Obviously a small group of persons, banded together for the sole purpose of furthering the appeal of the League, would have no powerful effect. In order to secure a certain homogeneity among the members of groups who individually had widely varied interests and affiliations, it was decided to form a non-partisan committee for the League of Nations.

The public relations consultant, having assisted in the formation of this committee, called a meeting of women representing Democratic, Republican, radical, reactionary, club, society, professional and industrial groups, and suggested that they make a united appeal for national support of the League of Nations. This meeting accurately and dramatically reflected disinterested and unified support of the League. The public relations counsel made articulate what would otherwise have remained a strong passive sentiment. The still insistent demand for the League of Nations is undoubtedly due in part to efforts of this nature.

Cases as diverse as the following are the daily work of the public relations counsel. One client is advised to give up a Rolls-Royce car and to buy a Ford, because the public has definite concepts of what ownership of each represents—another man may be given the contrary advice. One client is advised to withdraw the hat-check privilege, because it causes unfavorable public comment. Another is advised to change the façade of his building to conform to a certain public taste.

One client is advised to announce changes of price policy to the public by telegraph, another by circular, another by advertising. One client is advised to publish a Bible, another a book of French Renaissance tales.

One department store is advised to use prices in its advertising, another store not to mention them.

A client is advised to make his labor policy, the hygienic aspect of his factory, his own personality, part of his sales campaign.

Another client is advised to exhibit his wares in a museum and school.

Still another is urged to found a scholarship in his subject at a leading university.

Further incidents could be given here, illustrating different aspects of the ordinary daily functions of the public relations counsel—how, for example, the production of "Damaged Goods" in America became the basis of the first notably successful move in this country for overcoming the prudish refusal to appreciate and face the place of sex in human life; or how, more recently, the desire of some great corporations to increase their business was, through the advice of Ivy Lee, their public relations counsel, made the basis of popular education on the importance of brass and copper to civilization. Enough has been cited, however, to show how little the average member of the public knows of the real work of the public relations counsel, and how that work impinges upon the daily life of the public in an almost infinite number of ways.

Popular misunderstanding of the work of the public relations counsel is easily comprehensible because of the short period of his development. Nevertheless, the fact remains that he has become in recent years too important a figure in American life for this ignorance to be safely or profitably continued.

2

The Public Relations Counsel; The Increased and Increasing Importance of the Profession

The rise of the modern public relations counsel is based on the need for and the value of his services. Perhaps the most significant social, political and industrial fact about the present century is the increased attention which is paid to public opinion, not only by individuals, groups or movements that are dependent on public support for their success, but also by men and organizations which until very recently stood aloof from the general public and were able to say, "The public be damned."

The public to-day demands information and expects also to be accepted as judge and jury in matters that have a wide public import. The public, whether it invests its money in subway or railroad tickets, in hotel rooms or restaurant fare, in silk or soap, is a highly sophisticated body. It asks questions, and if the answer in word or action is not forthcoming or satisfactory, it turns to other sources for information or relief.

The willingness to spend thousands of dollars in obtaining professional advice on how best to present one's views or products to a public is based on this fact.

On every side of American life, whether political, industrial, social, religious or scientific, the increasing pressure of public judgment has made itself felt. Generally speaking, the relationship and interaction of the public and any movement is rather obvious. The charitable society which depends upon voluntary contributions for its support has a clear and direct interest in being favorably represented before the public. In the same way, the great corporation which is in danger of having its profits taxed away or its sales fall off or its freedom impeded by legislative action must have recourse to the public to combat successfully these menaces. Behind these obvious phenomena, however, lie three recent tendencies of fundamental importance; first, the tendency of small organizations to aggregate into groups of such size and importance that the public tends to regard them as semi-public services; second, the increased readiness of the public, due to the spread of literacy and democratic forms of government, to feel that it is entitled to its voice in the conduct of these large aggregations, political, capitalist or labor, or whatever they may be; third, the keen competition for public favor due to modern methods of "selling."

An example of the first tendency—that is, the tendency toward an increased public interest in industrial activity, because of the increasing social importance of industrial aggregations—may be found in an article on "The Critic and the Law" by Richard Washburn Child, published in the *Atlantic Monthly* for May, 1906.

Mr. Child discusses in that article the right of the critic to say uncomplimentary things about matters of public interest. He points out the legal basis for the right to criticize plays and novels. Then he adds, "A vastly more important and interesting theory, and one which must arise from the present state and tendency of industrial conditions, is whether the acts of men in commercial activity may ever become so prominent and so far reaching in their effect that they compel a universal public interest and that public comment is impliedly invited by reason of their conspicuous and semi-public nature. It may be said that at no time have private industries become of such startling interest to the community at large as at present in the United States." How far present-day tendencies have borne out Mr. Child's expectation of a growing and accepted public interest in important industrial enterprises, the reader can judge for himself.

With regard to the second tendency—the increased readiness of the public to expect information about and to be heard on matters of political and social interest—Ray Stannard Baker's description of the American journalist at the Peace Conference of Versailles gives an excellent picture. Mr. Baker tells what a shock American newspaper men gave Old World diplomats because at the Paris conference they "had come, not begging, but demanding. They sat at every doorway," says Mr. Baker. "They looked over every shoulder. They wanted every resolution and report and wanted it immediately. I shall never forget the delegation of American newspaper men, led by John Nevin, I saw come striding through that Holy of Holies, the French Foreign Office, demanding that they be admitted to the first general session of the Peace Conference. They horrified the upholders of the old methods, they desperately offended the ancient conventions, they were as rough and direct as democracy itself."

And I shall never forget the same feeling brought home to me, when Herbert Bayard Swope of the *New York World*, in the press room at the Crillon Hotel in Paris, led the discussion of the newspaper representatives who forced the conference to regard public opinion and admit newspaper men, and give out communiques daily.

That the pressure of the public for admittance to the mysteries of foreign affairs is being felt by the nations of the world may be seen from the following dispatch published in the *New York Herald* under the date line of the *New York Herald* Bureau, Paris, January 17, 1922: "The success of Lord Riddell in getting publicity for British opinion during the Washington conference, while the French viewpoint was not stressed, may result in the appointment by the Poincare Government of a real propaganda agent to meet the foreign newspaper men. The *Eclair* to-day calls on the new premier to 'find his own Lord Riddell in the French diplomatic and parliamentary world, who can give the world the French interpretation.'" Walter Lippmann of the *New York World* in his volume "Public Opinion" declares that "the significant revolution of modern times is not industrial or economic or political, but the revolution which is taking place in the art of creating consent among the governed." He goes on: "Within the life of the new generation now in control of affairs, persuasion has become a self-conscious art and a regular organ of popular government. None of us begins to understand the consequences, but it is no daring prophecy to say that the knowledge of how to create consent will alter every political premise. Under the impact of propaganda, not necessarily in the sinister meaning of the word alone, the only constants of our thinking have become variables. It is no longer possible, for example, to believe in the cardinal dogma of democracy, that the knowledge needed for the management of human affairs comes up spontaneously from the human heart. Where we act on that theory we expose ourselves to self-deception and to forms of persuasion that we cannot verify. It has been demonstrated that we cannot rely upon intuition, conscience, or the accidents of casual opinion if we are to deal with the world beyond our reach."[2]

In domestic affairs the importance of public opinion not only in political decisions but in the daily industrial life of the nation may be seen from numerous incidents. In the *New York Times* of Friday, May 20, 1922, I find almost a column article with the heading "Hoover Prescribes Publicity for Coal." Among the improvements in the coal industry generally, which Mr. Hoover, according to the dispatch, anticipates from widespread, accurate and informative publicity about the industry itself, are the stimulation of industrial consumers to more regular demands, the ability to forecast more reliably the volume of demand, the ability of the consumer to "form some judgment as to the prices he should pay for coal," and the tendency to hold down over-expansion in the industry by publication of the ratio of production to capacity. Mr. Hoover concludes that really informative publicity "would protect the great majority of operators from the criticism that can only be properly leveled at the minority." Not so many years ago neither the majority nor the minority in the coal industry would have concerned itself about public criticism of the industry.

From coal to jewelry seems rather a long step, and yet in *The Jeweler's Circular*, a trade magazine, I find much comment upon the National Jewelers' Publicity Association. This association began with the simple commercial ambition of acquainting the public with "the value of jewelry merchandise for gift purposes"; now it finds itself engaged in eliminating from the public mind in general, and from the minds of legislators in particular, the impression that "the jewelry business is absolutely useless and that any money spent in a jewelry store is thrown away."

Not so long ago it would scarcely have occurred to any one in the jewelry industry that there was any importance to be attached to the

---

2 Walter Lippmann, "Public Opinion" (page 248).

opinion of the public on the essential or non-essential character of the jewelry industry. To-day, on the other hand, jewelers find it a profitable investment to bring before the people the fact that table silver is an essential in modern life, and that without watches "the business and industries of the nations would be a sad chaos." With all the other competing interests in the world to-day, the question as to whether the public considers the business of manufacturing and selling jewelry essential or non-essential is a matter of the first importance to the industry.

The best examples, of course, of the increasing importance of public opinion to industries which until recently scarcely concerned themselves with the existence or non-existence of a public opinion about them, are those industries which are charged with a public interest.

In a long article about the attitude of the public towards the railroads, the *Railway Age* reaches the conclusion that the most important problem which American railroads must solve is "the problem of selling themselves to the public." Some public utilities maintain public relations departments, whose function it is to interpret the organizations to the public, as much as to interpret the public to them. The significant thing, however, is not the accepted importance of public opinion in this or the other individual industry, but the fact that public opinion is becoming cumulatively more and more articulate and therefore more important to industrial life as a whole.

The New York Central Railroad, for example, maintains a Public Relations Department under Pitt Hand, whose function it is to make it clear to the public that the railroad is functioning efficiently to serve the public in every possible way. This department studies the public and tries to discover where the railroad's service can be mended or improved, or when wrong or harmful impressions upon the public mind may be corrected.

This Public Relations Department finds it profitable not only to bring to the attention of the public the salient facts about its trains, its time tables, and its actual traveling facilities, but also to build up a broadly cooperative spirit that is indirectly of great value to itself and benefit to the public. It cooperates, for example, with such movements as the Welcome Stranger Committee of New York City in distributing literature to travelers to assist them when they reach the city. It cooperates with conventions, to the extent of arranging special travel facilities. Such aids as it affords to the directors of children's camps at the Grand Central Station are especially conspicuous for their dramatic effect on the general public.

Even a service which is in a large measure non-competitive must continually "sell" itself to the public, as evidenced by the strenuous efforts of the New York subways and elevated lines to keep themselves constantly before the people in the most favorable possible aspect. The subways strive in this regard to create a feeling of submissiveness toward inconveniences which are more or less unavoidable, and they strive likewise to fulfill such constructive programs as that of extending traffic on less frequented lines.

Let us analyze, for example, the activities of the health departments of such large cities as New York. Of recent years, Health Commissioner Royal S. Copeland and his statements have formed a fairly regular part of the day's news. Publicity is, in fact, one of the major functions of the Health Department, inasmuch as its constructive work depends to a considerable extent upon the public education it provides in combating evils and in building up a spirit of individual and group cooperation in all health matters. When the Health Department recognizes that such diseases as cancer, tuberculosis and those following malnutrition are due generally to ignorance or neglect and that amelioration or prevention will be the result of knowledge, it is the next logical step for this department to devote strenuous efforts to its public relations campaign. The department accordingly does exactly this.

Even governments to-day act upon the principle that it is not sufficient to govern their own citizens well and to assure the people that they are acting whole-heartedly in their behalf. They understand that the public opinion of the entire world is important to their welfare. Thus Lithuania, already noted, while it had the unbounded love and support of its own people, was nevertheless in danger of extinction because it was unknown outside of the immediate boundaries of those nations which had a personal interest in it. Lithuania was wanted by Poland; it was wanted by Russia. It was ignored by other nations. Therefore, through the aid of a public relations expert, Lithuania issued pamphlets, it paraded, it figured in pictures and motion pictures and developed a favorable sentiment throughout the world that in the end gave Lithuania its freedom.

In industry and business, of course, there is another consideration of first-rate importance, besides the danger of interference by the public in the conduct of the industry—the increasing intensity of competition. Business and sales are no longer to be had, if ever they were to be had for the asking. It must be clear to any one who has looked through the mass of advertising in street cars, subways, newspapers and magazines, and the other avenues of approach to the public, that products and services press hard upon one another in the effort to focus public attention on their offerings and to induce favorable action.

The keen competition in the selling of products for public favor makes it imperative that the seller consider other things than merely his product in trying to build up a favorable public reaction. He must either himself appraise the public mind and his relation to it or he must engage the services of an expert who can aid him to do this. He may to-day consider, for instance, in his sales campaign, not only the quality of his soap but the working conditions, the hours of labor, even the living conditions of the men who make it.

The public relations counsel must advise him on these factors as well as on their presentation to the public most interested in them.

In this state of affairs it is not at all surprising that industrial leaders should give the closest attention to public relations in both the broadest and the most practical concept of the term.

Large industrial groups, in their associations, have assigned a definite place to public relations bureaus.

The Trade Association Executives in New York, an association of individual executives of state, territorial or national trade associations, such as the Allied Wall Paper Industry, the American Hardware Manufacturers' Association, the American Protective Tariff League, the Atlantic Coast Shipbuilders' Association, the National Association of Credit Men, the Silk Association of America and some seventy-four others, includes among its associations' functions such activities as the following: cooperative advertising; adjustments and collections; cost accounting; a credit bureau; distribution and new markets; educational, standardization and research work; exhibits; a foreign trade bureau; house organs; general publicity; an industrial bureau; legislative work; legal aid; market reports; statistics; a traffic department; Washington representation; arbitration. It is noteworthy that forty of these associations have incorporated public relations with general publicity as a definite part of their program in furthering the interests of their organizations.

The American Telephone and Telegraph Company devotes effort to studying its public relations problems, not only to increase its volume of business, but also to create a cooperative spirit between itself and the public. The work of the telephone company's operators, statistics, calls, lineage, installations are given to the public in various forms. During the war and for a period afterwards its main problem was that of satisfying the public that its service was necessarily below standard because of the peculiar national conditions. The public, in response to the efforts of the company, which were analogous to a gracious personal apology, accepted more or less irksome conditions as a matter of course. Had the company not cared about the public, the public would undoubtedly have been unpleasantly insistent upon a maintenance of the pre-war standards of service.

Americans were once wont to jest about the dependence of France and Switzerland upon the tourist trade. To-day we see American cities competing, as part of their public relations programs, for conventions, fairs and conferences. The *New York Times* printed some time ago an address by the governor of Nebraska, in which he told a group of advertising men that publicity had made Nebraska prosper.

The *New York Herald* carried an editorial recently, entitled, 'It pays a state to advertise," centering about the campaign of the state of Vermont to present itself favorably to public attention. According to the editorial, the state publishes a magazine. *The Vermonter*, an attractive publication filled with interesting illustrations and well-written text. It is devoted exclusively to revealing in detail the industrial and agricultural resources of the state and to presenting Vermont's strikingly beautiful scenic attractions for the summer visitor. Similar instances of elaborate efforts, taking the form of action or the printed word, either to obtain public attention or to obtain a favorable attitude from the public for individual industries and groups of industries, will come readily to the reader's mind.

Without attempting to take too seriously an amusing story printed in a recent issue of a New York newspaper, leaders in movements and industries of modern life will be inclined to agree with the protagonist of publicity spoken of. According to the story, a man set out to prove to another that it was not so much what a man did as the way it was heralded which insures his place in history. He cited Barbara Frietchie, Evangeline, John Smith and a half dozen others as instances to prove that they are remembered not for what they did, but because they had excellent counsel on their public relations.

"'Very good,' agreed the friend. 'But show me a case where a person who has really done a big thing has been overlooked.'

"'You know Paul Revere, of course,' he said. 'But tell me the names of the two other fellows who rode that night to rouse the countryside with the news that the British were coming.'

"'Never heard of them,' was the answer.

"'There were three waiting to see the signal hung in the tower of the Old North Church,' he said. 'Every one of them was mounted and spurred, just as Mr. Longfellow described Paul Revere. They all got the signal. They all rode and waked the farmers, spreading the warning. Afterward one of them was an officer in Washington's army, another became governor of one of the States. Not one in twenty thousand Americans ever heard the names of the other two, and there is hardly a person in America who does not know all about Revere.'

"'Did Revere make history or did Longfellow?'"

3

The Function of a Special Pleader

Public opinion has entered life at many points as a decisive factor. Men and movements whose interests will be affected by the attitude of the public are taking pains to have themselves represented in the court of public opinion by the most skillful counselors they can obtain. The business of the public relations counsel is somewhat like the business of the attorney—to advise his client and to litigate his causes for him.

While the special pleader in law, the lawyer for the defense, has always been accorded a formal hearing by judge and jury, this has not been the case before the court of public opinion. Here mob psychology, the intolerance of human society for a dissenting point of view, have made it difficult and often dangerous for a man to plead for a new or unpopular cause.

The Fourth Estate, a newspaper for the makers of newspapers, says: "'Counsel on public relations' and 'director of public relations' are two terms that are being encountered more often every day. There is a familiar tinge to them, in a way, but in justice to the men who bear these titles and to the concerns which employ them, it should be said that they are—or can be—dissociated from the old idea of 'publicity man,' The very fact that many of the largest corporations in the country are recognizing the need of maintaining right relationships with the public is alone important enough to assure a fair and even favorable hearing for their public relations departments.

"Whether a man is really entitled to the appellation 'counsel on public relations' or whether he should merely be called 'publicity man' rests entirely with the individual and the firm that employs him. As we see it, a man who is really counsel or director of public relations has one of the most important jobs on the roster of any concern; but a man who merely represents the old idea of getting something for nothing from publishers is about *passé*. . . .

"So there is made plain the difference between two terms, the old and the new, both of which have occasioned much natural curiosity among newspaper men. When Napoleon said, 'Circumstance? I make circumstance,' he expressed very nearly the spirit of the public relations counsel's work. So long as this new professional branch live up to the possibilities that their title suggests, they are bound to accomplish general constructive good. Maybe they, at last, will make us forget that ingratiating though insidious individual, the publicity man."

As indicative perhaps of the growing importance of the profession, an article by Mary Swain Routzahn, in charge of the Department of Surveys and Exhibits of the Russell Sage Foundation, on "Woman's Chance as Publicity Specialist" published in the *New York Globe* of August 2nd, 1921, discusses the profession as one of recent development, but of such importance as to deserve the serious consideration of women who are interested in making a professional career for themselves.

The public relations counsel is first of all a student. His field of study is the public mind. His text books for this study are the facts of life; the articles printed in newspapers and magazines, the advertisements that are inserted in publications, the billboards that line the streets, the railroads and the highways, the speeches that are delivered in legislative chambers, the sermons issuing from pulpits, anecdotes related in smoking rooms, the gossip of Wall Street, the patter of the theater and the conversation of other men who, like him, are interpreters and must listen for the clear or obscure enunciations of the public.

He brings the talent of his intuitive understanding to the aid of his practical and psychological tests and surveys. But he is not only a student. He is a practitioner with a wide range of instruments and a definite technique for their use.

First of all, there are the circumstances and events he helps to create. After that there are the instruments by which he broadcasts facts and ideas to the public; advertising, motion pictures, circular letters, booklets, handbills, speeches, meetings, parades, news articles, magazine articles and whatever other mediums there are through which public attention is reached and influenced.

Now sensitiveness to the state of mind of the public is a difficult thing to achieve or maintain. Any man can tell you with more or less accuracy and clearness his own reactions on any particular issue. But few men have the time or the interest or the training to develop a sense of what other persons think or feel about the same issue. In his own profession the skilled practitioner is sensitive and understanding. The lawyer can tell what argument will appeal to court or jury. The salesman can tell what points to stress to his prospective buyers. The politician can tell what to emphasize to his audience, but the ability to estimate group reactions on a large scale over a wide geographic and psychological area is a specialized ability which must be developed with the same painstaking self-criticism and with the same dependence on experience that are required for the development of the clinical sense in the doctor or surgeon.

Of course, the public relations counsel employs all those practical means of gauging the public mind which modern advertising has developed and uses. He employs the research campaign, the symposium, the survey of a particular group or of a particular state of mind as a further aid, and confirmation or modification of his own appraisals and judgments.

Charles J. Rosebault, the author of an article in the *New York Times* recently, headed "Men Who Wield the Spotlight," remarks that the competent public relations counsel has generally had some newspaper training and that the value of this training "is a keen sense of the likes and dislikes of what we call the public—that is, the average of men and women. The needle of the compass is no more sensitive to direction, nor the mercury in the thermometer to variations of heat and cold than is this expert to the influence of publicity upon the mind and emotions of the man in the street."

It is not surprising that the growing interest of the public in men and movements should have led to the spontaneous creation of the new profession.

We have presented here, in very broad outline, a picture of the fundamental work of the public relations counsel and of the fundamental conditions which have produced him. On the one hand, a complex environment of which only small, disconnected portions are available to different persons; on the other hand, the great and increasing importance either of making one's case accessible to the public mind or of determining whether that case will impinge favorably or unfavorably upon the public mind—these two conditions, taken together, have resulted inevitably in the public relations counsel. Mr. Lippmann finds in these facts the underlying reason for the existence of what he calls the "press agent." "The enormous discretion," he says, "as to what facts and what impressions shall be reported is steadily convincing every organized group of people that, whether it wishes to secure publicity or to avoid it, the exercise of discretion cannot be left to the reporter. It is safer to hire a press agent who stands between the group and the newspapers."[3]

It is clear that the popular impression of the scope and functions of the counsel on public relations must be radically revised if any accurate picture of the profession is to be looked for. The public relations counsel is the lineal descendant, to be sure, of the circus advance-man and of the semi-journalist promoter of small-part actresses. The economic conditions which have produced him, however, and made his profession the important one it is to-day, have in themselves materially changed the character of his work.

His primary function now is not to bring his clients by chance to the public's attention, nor to extricate them from difficulties into which they have already drifted, but to advise his clients how positive results can be accomplished in the field of public relations and to keep them from drifting inadvertently into unfortunate or harmful situations. The public relations counsel will find that the conditions under which his client operates, be it a government, a manufacturer of food products or a railroad system, are constantly changing and that he must advise modifications in policy in accordance with such changes in the public point of view. As such, the public relations counsel must be alive to the events of the day—not only the events that are printed but the events which are forming hour by hour, as reported in the words that are spoken on the street, in the smoking cars, in the school room, or expressed in any of the other forms of thought communication that make up public opinion.

So long as the press remains the greatest single medium for reaching the public mind, the work of the public relations counsel will necessarily have close contacts with the work of the journalist. He transmits his ideas, however, through all those mediums which help to build public opinion—the radio, the lecture platform, advertising, the

---

[3] "Public Opinion" (page 342). Mr. Lippmann goes on to say that "having hired him, the temptation to exploit his strategic position is very great." As to that aspect of the situation, see later chapters.

stage, the motion picture, the mails. On the other hand, he is becoming to-day as much of an adviser on actions as he is the communicator of these actions to the public.

The public relations consultant is ideally a constructive force in the community. The results of his work are often accelerated interest in matters of value and importance to the social, economic or political life of the community.

The public relations counsel is the pleader to the public of a point of view. He acts in this capacity as a consultant both in interpreting the public to his client and in helping to interpret his client to the public. He helps to mould the action of his client as well as to mould public opinion.

His profession is in a state of evolution. His future must depend as much upon the growing realization by the public of the responsibility to the public of individuals, institutions and organizations as upon the public relations counsel's own realization of the importance of his work.

Part II
The Group and Herd

1

What Constitutes Public Opinion?

The character and origins of public opinion, the factors that make up the individual mind and the group mind must be understood if the profession of public relations counsel is to be intelligently practiced and its functions and possibilities accurately estimated. Society must understand the fundamental character of the work he is doing, if for no other reason than its own welfare.

The public relations counsel works with that vague, little-understood, indefinite material called public opinion.

Public opinion is a term describing an ill-defined, mercurial and changeable group of individual judgments. Public opinion is the aggregate result of individual opinions—now uniform, now conflicting—of the men and women who make up society or any group of society. In order to understand public opinion, one must go back to the individual who makes up the group.

The mental equipment of the average individual consists of a mass of judgments on most of the subjects which touch his daily physical or mental life. These judgments are the tools of his daily being and yet they are his judgments, not on a basis of research and logical deduction, but for the most part dogmatic expressions accepted on the authority of his parents, his teachers, his church, and of his social, his economic and other leaders.

The public relations counsel must understand the social implications of an individual's thoughts and actions. Is it, for example, purely an accident that a man belongs to one church rather than another or to any church at all? Is it an accident that makes Boston women prefer brown eggs and New York women white eggs? What are the factors that work in favor of conversion of a man from one political party to another or from one type of food to another?

Why do certain communities resist the prohibition law—why do others abide by it? Why is it difficult to start a new party movement—or to fight cancer? Why is it difficult to fight for sex education? Why does the free trader denounce protectionism, and vice versa?

If we had to form our own judgments on every matter, we should all have to find out many things for ourselves which we now take for granted. We should not cook our food or live in houses—in fact, we should revert to primitive living.

The public relations counsel must deal with the fact that persons who have little knowledge of a subject almost invariably form definite and positive judgments upon that subject.

"If we examine the mental furniture of the average man," says William Trotter, the author of a comprehensive study of the social psychology of the individual,[4] "we shall find it made up of a vast number of judgments of a very precise kind upon subjects of very great variety, complexity, and difficulty. He will have fairly settled views upon the origin and nature of the universe, and upon what he will probably call its meaning; he will have conclusions as to what is to happen to him at death and after, as to what is and what should be the

---

4 William Trotter, "Instincts of the Herd in Peace and War" (page 36).

basis of conduct. He will know how the country should be governed, and why it is going to the dogs, why this piece of legislation is good and that bad. He will have strong views upon military and naval strategy, the principles of taxation, the use of alcohol and vaccination, the treatment of influenza, the prevention of hydrophobia, upon municipal trading, the teaching of Greek, upon what is permissible in art, satisfactory in literature, and hopeful in science.

"The bulk of such opinions must necessarily be without rational basis, since many of them are concerned with problems admitted by the expert to be still unsolved, while as to the rest it is clear that the training and experience of no average man can qualify him to have any opinion upon them at all. The rational method adequately used would have told him that on the great majority of these questions there could be for him but one attitude—that of suspended judgment."

The reader will recall from his own experience an almost infinite number of instances in which the amateur has been fully prepared to deliver expert advice and to give final judgment in matters upon which his ignorance is patent to every one except himself.

In the Middle Ages, society was convinced that there were witches. People were so positive that they burned people whom they suspected of witchcraft. To-day there is an equal number of people who believe just as firmly, one way or the other, about spiritualism and spirits. They do not burn mediums. But people who have made no research of the subject pass strong denunciatory judgments. Others, no better informed, consider mediums divinely inspired. Not so long ago every intelligent man knew that the world was flat. To-day the average man has a belief just as firm and unknowing in the mysterious force which he has heard called atomic energy.

It is axiomatic that men who know little are often intolerant of a point of view that is contrary to their own. The bitterness that has been brought about by arguments on public questions is proverbial. Lovers have been parted by bitter quarrels on theories of pacificism or militarism; and when an argument upon an abstract question engages opponents they often desert the main line of argument in order to abuse each other.

How often this is true can be seen from the congressional records of controversies in which the personal attack supersedes logic. In a recent fight against the proposed tariff measures, a protagonist of protection published long vindictive statements, in which he tried to confound the character and the disinterestedness of his opponents. Logically his discussion should have been based only upon the sound economic, social and political value of the bill as presented.

A hundred leading American bankers, business men, professional men and economists united in public disapproval of this plan. They stated their opinion that the "American" Valuation Plan, as it was called, would endanger the prosperity of the country, that it would be inimical to our foreign relations and that it would injure the welfare of every country with whom our commercial and industrial ties were at all close. This group was a broadly representative group of men and women, yet the chairman of the Ways and Means Committee accused all these people of acting upon motives of personal gain and lack of patriotism. Prejudice superseded logic.

Intolerance is almost inevitably accompanied by a natural and true inability to comprehend or make allowance for opposite points of view. The skilled scientist who may be receptive to any promising suggestion in his own field may outside of his own field be found quite unwilling to make any attempt at understanding a point of view contrary to his own. In politics, for example, his understanding of the problem may be fragmentary, yet he will enter excitedly into discussions on bonus and ship subsidy, of which he has made no study. We find here with significant uniformity what one psychologist has called "logic-proof compartments."

The logic-proof compartment has always been with us. Scientists have lost their lives through refusing to see flaws in their theories.

Intelligent mothers give food to their babies that they would manifestly forbid other mothers to give their children. Especially significant is the tendency of races to maintain religious beliefs and customs long after these have lost their meaning. Dietary laws, hygienic laws, even laws based upon geographical conditions that have been changed for more than a thousand years are still maintained in the logic-proof compartment of dogmatic adherence. There is a story that certain missionaries give money to heathen at the time of conversion and that the heathen, having got their money, bathe away their conversion in sacred streams.

The characteristic of the human mind to adhere to its beliefs is excellently summarized in the volume by Mr. Trotter to which reference has been made before. "It is clear," says Mr. Trotter,[5] "at the outset that these beliefs are invariably regarded as rational and defended as such, while the position of one who holds contrary views is held to be obviously unreasonable.

"The religious man accuses the atheist of being shallow and irrational, and is met by a similar reply. To the Conservative the amazing thing about the Liberal is his incapacity to see reason and accept the only possible solution of public problems. Examination reveals the fact that the differences are not due to the commission of the mere mechanical fallacies of logic, since these are easily avoided, even by the politician, and since there is no reason to believe that one party in such controversies is less logical than the other. The difference is due rather to the fundamental assumptions of the antagonists being hostile, and these assumptions are derived from herd-suggestions; to the Liberal certain basal conceptions have acquired the quality of instinctive truth, have become *a priori* syntheses, because of the accumulated suggestions to which he has been exposed; and a similar explanation applies to the atheist, the Christian, and the Conservative. Each, it

---

5 "Instincts of the Herd in Peace and War," William Trotter (pages 36–37).

is important to remember, finds in consequence the rationality of his position flawless and is quite incapable of detecting in it the fallacies which are obvious to his opponent, to whom that particular series of assumptions has not been rendered acceptable by herd suggestion."

Thus the public relations counsel has to consider the *a priori* judgment of any public he deals with before counseling any step that would modify those things in which the public has an established belief.

It is seldom effective to call names or to attempt to discredit the beliefs themselves. The counsel on public relations, after examination of the sources of established beliefs, must either discredit the old authorities or create new authorities by making articulate a mass opinion against the old belief or in favor of the new.

2

Is Public Opinion Stubborn Or Malleable?

There is a divergence of opinion as to whether the public mind is malleable or stubborn—whether it is a passive or an active element. On the one hand is the profound belief that "you can't change human nature." On the other hand is the equally firm assurance that certain well-defined institutions modify and alter public opinion.

There is a uniformity of opinion in this country upon many issues. When this uniformity accords with our own beliefs we call it an expression of the public conscience. When, however, it runs contrary to our beliefs we call it the regimentation of the public mind and are inclined to ascribe it to insidious propaganda.

Uniformity is, in fact, largely natural and only partly artificial. Public opinion may be as much the producer of "insidious propaganda" as its product. Naturally enough, where broad ideas are involved, criticisms of the state of the public's mind and of its origin come most frequently from groups that are out of sympathy with the accepted point of view. They find the public unreceptive to their point of view, and justly or unjustly they attribute this to the influence of antagonistic interests upon the public mind.

These groups see the press, the lecture platform, the schools, the advertisements, the churches, the radio, the motion picture screen, the magazines daily reaching millions. They see that the preponderant point of view in most, if not all, these institutions conforms to the preponderant state of mind of the public.

They argue from the one to the other and reach their conclusions without much difficulty. They do not stop to think that agreement in point of view between the public and these institutions may often be the result of the control exercised by the public mind over these institutions.

Many outside forces, however, do go to influence public opinion. The most obvious of these forces are parental influence, the school room, the press, motion pictures, advertising, magazines, lectures, the church, the radio.

To answer the question as to the stubbornness or malleability of the public, let us analyze the press in its relation to public opinion, since the press stands preeminent among the various institutions which are commonly designated ?is leaders or moulders of the public mind. By the press, in this instance, I mean the daily press. Americans are a newspaper-reading public. They have become accustomed to look to their morning and evening papers for the news of the world and for the opinions of their leaders. And while the individual newspaper reader does not give a very considerable portion of his day to this occupation, many persons find time to read more than one newspaper every day.

It is not surprising that the man who is outside the current of prevailing public opinion should regard the daily press as a coercive force.

Discussions of the public's reaction to the press are two-sided, just as are discussions of the influence of the pulpit or other forces. Some authorities hold that the public mind is stubborn in regard to the press and that the press has little influence upon it. There are graphic instances of the stubbornness of the public point of view. A most interesting example is the reelection of Mayor Hylan of New York by an overwhelming majority in the face of the opposition of all but two of the metropolitan dailies. It is also noteworthy that in 1909, Gaynor was elected Mayor of New York with every paper except one opposing his candidacy. Likewise, Mayor Mitchel of New York was defeated for reelection in 1917, although all the New York papers except two Hearst papers and the *New York Call* supported him. In Boston, in a recent election, a man was elected as mayor who had been convicted of a penal offense, and elected in the face of the practically united opposition of all the newspapers of that city. How would such authors as Everett Dean Martin, Walter Lippmann and Upton Sinclair explain these incidents? How, on the theory of the regimentation of the public mind by the daily press, can such thinkers explain the sharpness with which the public sometimes rejects the advocacies of a united press? These instances are not frequent; but they show that other influences beside the press enter into the making of a public opinion and that these forces must never be disregarded in the estimate of the quality and stability of a prevalent public opinion.

Francis E. Leupp, writing in the *Atlantic Monthly* for February, 1910, on "The Waning Power of the Press," remarks that Mayor Gaynor's comments shortly after his election in 1909 "led up to the conclusion that in our common sense generation nobody cares what the newspapers say." Mr. Leupp continues: "Unflattering as such a verdict may be, probably the majority of a community if polled as a jury would concur in it. The airy dismissal of some proposition as 'mere newspaper talk' is heard at every social gathering until one who is brought up to regard the press as a mighty factor in modern civilization is tempted to wonder whether it has actually lost the power it used to wield among us."

And H. L. Mencken, writing in the same magazine for March, 1914, declares that "one of the principal marks of an educated man, indeed, is the fact that he does *not* take his opinions from newspapers—not, at any rate, from the militant, crusading newspapers. On the contrary, his attitude toward them is almost always one of frank cynicism, with indifference as its mildest form and contempt as its commonest. He knows that they are constantly falling into false reasoning about the things within his personal knowledge,—that is, within the narrow circle of his special education,—and so he assumes that they make the same, or even worse, errors about other things, whether intellectual or moral. This assumption, it may be said at once, is quite justified by the facts."

The second point of view holds that the daily press and the other leading forces merely accept, reflect and intensify established public opinion and are, therefore, responsible for the uniformity of public reaction. A vivid statement of the point of view of the man who typifies this group is found in Everett Dean Martin's volume on "The Behavior of Crowds." He says;[6] "The modern man has in the printing press a wonderfully effective means for perpetuating crowd-movements and keeping great masses of people constantly under the sway of certain crowd-ideas. Every crowd-group has its magazines, press agents, and special 'literature' with which it continually harangues its members and possible converts. Many books, and especially certain works of fiction of the 'best seller' type, are clearly reading mob phenomena."

There is a third group which perhaps comes nearer the truth, which holds that the press, just as other mediums of education or dissemination, brings about a very definite change in public opinion. A most graphic illustration of what such mediums can do to change opinions upon fundamental and important matters is the woman suffrage question and its victory over established points of view. The press, the pul-

---

6 Page 45.

pit, the lecture platform, the motion pictures and the other mediums for reaching the public brought about a complete popular conversion. Other examples of the change that may be brought about in public opinion in this way, by such institutions of authority, is the present attitude towards birth control and towards health education.

Naturally the press, like other institutions which present facts or opinions, is restricted, often unconsciously, sometimes consciously, by various controlling conditions. Certain people talk of the censorship enacted by the prejudices and predispositions of the public itself. Some, such as Upton Sinclair, ascribe to the advertisers a conscious and powerful control of publications. Others, like Walter Lippmann, find that an effective barrier between the public and the event exists in the powerful influence which, he says, is exerted in certain cases on the press by the so-called quality public which the newspapers' advertisers wish to reach and among whom the newspapers must circulate if the advertising is to be successful. Mr. Lippmann observes that although such a restriction may exist, much of what may be attributed to censorship in the newspaper, often is actually inadequate presentation of the events it seeks to describe.

On this point he says:[7] "It follows that in the reporting of strikes, the easiest way is to let the news be uncovered by the overt act, and to describe the event as the story of interference with the reader's life. This is where his attention is first aroused and his interest most easily enlisted. A great deal, I think myself, of the crucial part of what looks to the worker and the reformer as deliberate misrepresentation on the part of newspapers, is the direct outcome of a practical difficulty in uncovering the news, and the emotional difficulty of making distinct facts interesting unless, as Emerson says, we can 'perceive' (them) and can 'set about translating (them) at once into parallel facts.'"

---

[7] "Public Opinion" (page 350).

In view then of the possibility of a malleable public opinion the counsel on public relations, desiring to obtain a hearing for any given cause, simply utilizes existent channels to obtain expression for the point of view he represents. How this is done will be considered later.

Because of the importance of channels of thought communication, it is vital for the public relations counsel to study carefully the relationship between public opinion and the organs that maintain it or that influence it to change. We shall look into this interaction and its effect in the next chapter.

3

The Interaction of Public Opinion with the Forces that Help to Make It

The public and the press, or for that matter, the public and any force that modifies public opinion, interact. Action and interaction are continually going on between the forces projected out to the public and the public itself. The public relations counsel must understand this fact in its broadest and most detailed implications. He must understand not only what these various forces are, but he must be able to evaluate their relative powers with fair accuracy. Let us consider again the case of a newspaper, as representative of other mediums of communication.

"We print," says the *New York Times*, "all the news that's fit to print." Immediately the question arises (as Elmer Davis, the historian of the *Times* tells us that it did when the motto was first adopted) what news *is* fit to print? By what standard is the editorial decision reached which includes one kind of news and excludes another kind? The *Times* itself has not been, in its long and conspicuously successful career, entirely free from difficulties on this point.

Thus in "The History of The *New York Times*," Mr. Davis feels the need for justifying the extent to which that paper featured Theodore Tilton's action against the Rev. Henry Ward Beecher for alienation of Mrs. Tilton's affections and his conduct with her. Mr. Davis says (pages 124–125): "No doubt a good many readers of the *Times* thought that the paper was giving an undue amount of space to this chronicle of sin and suffering. Those complaints come in often enough even in these days from readers who appreciate the paper's general reluctance to display news of this sort, and wonder why a good general rule should occasionally be violated. But there was a reason in the Beecher case, as there has usually been a reason in similar affairs since. Dr. Beecher was one of the most prominent clergymen in the country; there was a natural curiosity as to whether he was practicing what he preached. One of the counsel at the trial declared that 'all Christendom was hanging on its outcome.' Full reporting of its course was not a mere pandering to vulgar curiosity, but a recognition of the value of the case as news."

The simple fact that such a slogan can exist and be accepted is for our purpose an important point. Somewhere there must be a standard to which the editors of the *Times* can conform, as well as a large clientele of constant readers to whom that standard is satisfactory. "Fit" must be defined by the editors of the *Times* in a way which meets with the approval of enough persons to enable the paper to maintain its reading public. As soon, however, as the definition is attempted, difficulties arise.

Professor W. G. Bleyer, in an article in his book on journalism, first stresses the importance of completeness in the news columns of a paper, then goes on to say that "the only important limitations to completeness are those imposed by the commonly accepted ideas of decency embodied in the words, 'All the news that's fit to print' and by the rights of privacy. Carefully edited newspapers discriminate between what the public is entitled to know and what an individual has a right to keep private."

On the other hand, when Professor Bleyer attempts to define what news is fit to print and what the public is entitled to know, he discusses generalizations capable of wide and frequently inconsistent interpretation. "News," says he, "is anything timely which is significant to newspaper readers in their relations to the community, the state and the nation."

Who is to determine what is significant and what is not? Who is to decide which of the individual's relations to the community are safeguarded by his right of privacy and which are not? Such a definition tells us nothing more definite than does the slogan which it attempts to define. We must look further for a standard by which these definitions are applied. There must be a consensus of public opinion on which the newspaper falls back for its standards.

The truth is that while it appears to be forming the public opinion on fundamental matters, the press is often conforming to it.

It is the office of the public relations counsel to determine the interaction between the public, and the press and the other mediums affecting public opinion. It is as important to conform to the standards of the organ which projects ideas as it is to present to this organ such ideas as will conform to the fundamental understanding and appreciation of the public to which they are ultimately to appeal. There is as much truth in the proposition that the public leads institutions as in the contrary proposition that the institutions lead the public.

As an illustration of the manner in which newspapers are inclined to accept the judgments of their readers in presenting material to them, we have this anecdote which Rollo Ogden tells in the *Atlantic Monthly* for July, 1906, about a letter which Wendell Phillips wished to have published in a Boston paper.

"The editor read it over, and said, 'Mr. Phillips, that is a very good and interesting letter, and I shall be glad to publish it; but I wish you would consent to strike out the last paragraph.'

"'Why,' said Phillips, 'that paragraph is the precise thing for which I wrote the whole letter. Without that it would be pointless.'

"'Oh, I see that,' replied the editor; 'and what you say is perfectly true! I fully agree with it all myself. Yet it is one of those things which it will not do to say publicly. However, if you insist upon it, I will publish it as it stands.'

"It was published the next morning, and along with it a short editorial reference to it, saying that a letter from Mr. Phillips would be found in another column, and that it was extraordinary that so keen a mind as his should have fallen into the palpable absurdity contained in the last paragraph."

Recognition of this fact comes from a number of different sources. H. L. Mencken recognizes that the public runs the press as much as the press runs the public.

"The primary aim of all of them," says Mr. Mencken,[8] "not less when they play the secular Iokanaan than when they play the mere newsmonger, was to please the crowd, and to give a good show; and the way they set about giving that good show was by first selecting a deserving victim, and then putting him magnificently to the torture.

"This was their method when they were performing for their own profit only, when their one motive was to make the public read their paper; but it was still their motive when they were battling bravely and unselfishly for the public good, and so discharging the highest duty of their profession."

There are interesting, if somewhat obscure, examples of the complementary working of various forces. In the field of the motion pictures, for example, the producers, the actors and the press, in their support, have continually waged a battle against censorship. Undoubtedly censorship of the motion pictures is in its practical workings an economic and artistic handicap. Censorship, however, will continue

---

8 *Atlantic Monthly*, March, 1914.

in spite of the producers as long as there is a willingness on the part of the public to accept this censorship. The public, on the whole, has refused to join the fight against censorship, because there is a more or less articulate belief that children, if not women, should be protected from seeing shocking sights, such as murders visibly enacted, the taking of drugs, immoralities and other acts which might offend or suggest harmful imitation.

"Damaged Goods," before its presentation to America in 1913, was analyzed by the public relations counsel, who helped to produce the play. He recognized that unless that part of the public sentiment which believed in education and truth could be lifted from that part of public opinion which condemned the mentioning of sex matters, "Damaged Goods" would fail. The producers, therefore, did not try to educate the public by presenting this play as such, but allowed group leaders and groups interested in education to come to the support of Brieux's drama and, in a sense, to sponsor the production.

Proof that the public and the institutions that make public opinion interact is shown in instances in which books were stifled because of popular disapproval at one time and then brought forward by popular demand at a later time when public opinion had altered. Religious and very early scientific works are among such books.

A more recent instance is the announcement made by *Judge*, a weekly magazine, that it would support the fight for light wine and beer. *Judge* took this stand because it believed in the principle of personal freedom and also because it deemed that public sentiment was in favor of light wine and beer as a substitute for absolute prohibition. *Judge* believed its stand would please its readers.

Presumably writing of newspaper morality, Mr. Mencken, in his article just quoted, finds at the end of it that he has "written of popular morality very copiously, and of newspaper morality very little.

"But," says Mr. Mencken, "as I have said before, the one is the other. The newspaper must adapt its pleading to its clients' moral limitation just as the trial lawyer also must adapt *his* pleading to the jury's limitations. Neither may like the job, but both must face it to gain the larger end."

Writing on the other hand from the point of view of the man who feels that the public taste requires no justification, Ralph Pulitzer nevertheless agrees with Mr. Mencken that the opinion of the press is set by the public; and he justifies "muckraking"[9] by finding it neither "extraordinary nor culpable that people and press should be more interested in the polemical than in the platitudinous; in blame than in painting the lily; in attack than in sending laudatory coals to Newcastle."

Even Mr. Leupp[10] concludes that "whatever we may say of the modern press on its less commendable side, we are bound to admit that newspapers, like governments, fairly reflect the people they serve. Charles Dudley Warner once went so far as to say that no matter how objectionable the character of a paper may be, it is always a trifle better than the patrons on whom it relies for its support."

Similarly, from an unusually wide experience on a paper as highly considered, perhaps, as any in America, Rollo Ogden claims this give and take between the public and the press is vital to a just conception of American journalism.

"The editor does not nonchalantly project his thoughts into the void. He listens for the echo of his words. His relation to his supporters is not unlike Gladstone's definition of the intimate connection between the orator and his audience. As the speaker gets from his hearers in mist what he gives back in shower, so the newspaper receives from the public as well as gives to it. Too often it gets as dust what it gives back as mud; but that does not alter the relation. Action and reaction are all the while going on between the press and its patrons. Hence it follows that the responsibility for the more crying evils of journalism must be divided."[11]

---

9 *Atlantic Monthly*, June, 1914.
10 Francis E. Leupp, "The Waning Power of the Press," *Atlantic Monthly*, July, 1910.
11 Rollo Ogden, "Some Aspects of Journalism," *Atlantic Monthly*, July, 1906.

The same interaction goes on in connection with all the other forces that mould public opinion. The preacher upholds the ideals of society. He leads his flock whither they indicate a willingness to be led. Ibsen creates a revolution when society is ripe for it. The public responds to finer music and better motion pictures and demands improvements. "Give the people what they want" is only half sound. What they want and what they get are fused by some mysterious alchemy. The press, the lecturer, the screen and the public lead and are led by each other.

4

The Power of Interacting Forces that Go to Make Up Public Opinion

The influence of any force which attempts to modify public opinion depends upon the success with which it is able to enlist established points of view. A middle ground exists between the hypothesis that the public is stubborn and the hypothesis that it is malleable. To a large degree the press, the schools, the churches, motion pictures, advertising, the lecture platform and radio all conform to the demands of the public. But to an equally large degree the public responds to the influence of these very same mediums of communication.

Some analysts believe that the public has no opinions except those which various institutions provide ready made for it. From Mr. Mencken and others it would almost seem to follow that newspapers and other mediums have no standards except those which the public provides, and that therefore they are substantially without influence upon the public mind. The truth of the matter, as I have pointed out, lies somewhere between these two extreme positions.

In other words, the public relations counsel who thinks clearly on the problem of public opinion and public relations will credit the two factors of public opinion respectively with their influence and effectiveness in mutual interaction.

Ray Stannard Baker says[12] that "while there was a gesture of unconcern, of don't care what they say, on the part of the leaders (of the Versailles conference), no aspect of the conference in reality worried them more than the news, opinions, guesses that went out by scores of thousands of words every night, and the reactions which came back so promptly from them. The problem of publicity consumed an astonishing amount of time, anxiety and discussion among the leaders of the conference. It influenced the entire procedure, it was partly instrumental in driving the four heads of States finally into small secret conferences. The full achievement of publicity on one occasion— Wilson's Italian note—nearly broke up the conference and overturned a government. The bare threat of it, upon other occasions, changed the course of the discussion. Nothing concerned the conference more than what democracy was going to do with diplomacy."

For like causes we find great industries—motion pictures being one and organized baseball another—appointing as directors of their activities men prominent in public life, doing this to assure the public of the honest and social-minded conduct of their members. The Franklin Roosevelts are in this class, the Will Hayses and the Landises.

A striking example of this interaction is illustrated in what occurred at the Hague Conference a few years ago. The effect of the Hague Conference's conduct upon the public was such that officials were forced to open the Conference doors to the representatives of newspapers. On June 16th, 1922, a note came from The Hague by the Associated Press that Foreign Minister Van Karnebeek of Holland capitulated to the world's desire to be informed of what was going on by admitting correspondents. Early announcement that "the press cannot be admitted" was, according to the report, followed by anxious

---

12 "Publicity at Paris," *New York Times*, April 2, 1922.

emissaries begging the journalists to have patience. Editorials printed in Holland pointed out that the best way to insure public cooperation was to take the public into its confidence. Minister van Karnebeek, who had been at Washington, was thoroughly awake to the invaluable service the press of the world rendered there. One editorial here pointed out that public statements "were used by the diplomats themselves as a happy means of testing popular opinion upon the various projects offered in council. How many 'trial balloons' were sent up in this fashion, nobody can recall. Nevertheless each delegation maintained clipping bureaus, which were brought up to date every morning and which gave the delegates accurate information as to the state of mind at home. Thus it came about that world opinion was ready and anxious to receive the finished work of the conference and that it was prompt to bring individual recalcitrant groups into line."

Let me quote from the *New York Evening Post* of July, 1922, as to the important interaction of these forces: "The importance of the press in guiding public opinion and the cooperation between the members of the press and the men who express public opinion in action, which has grown up since the Peace Conference at Paris, were stressed by Lionel Curtis, who arrived on the *Adriatic* yesterday to attend the Institute of Politics, which opens on July 27 at Williamstown. 'Perhaps for the first time in history,' he said, 'the men whose business it is to make public opinion were collected for some months under the same roof with the officials whose task in life is the actual conduct of foreign affairs. In the long run, foreign policy is determined by public opinion. It was impossible in Paris not to be impressed by the immense advantage of bringing into close contact the writers who, through the press, are making public opinion and the men who have to express their opinion in actual policy.'"

Harvard University, likewise, appreciating the power of public opinion over its own activities, has recently appointed a counsel on public relations to make its aims clear to the public.

The institutions which make public opinion conform to the demands of the public. The public responds to an equally large degree to these institutions. Such fights as that made by *Collier's Weekly* for pure food control show this.

The Safety First movement, by its use of every form of appeal, from poster to circular, from lecture to law enforcement, from motion pictures to "safety weeks," is bringing about a gradual change in the attitude of a safety-deserving public towards the taking of unnecessary risks.

The Rockefeller Foundation, confronted with the serious problem of the hookworm in the South and in other localities, has brought about a change in the habits of large sections of rural populations by analysis, investigation, applied medical principles, and public education.

The moulder of public opinion must enlist the established point of view. This is true of the press as well as of other forces. Mr. Mencken mixes cynicism and truth when he declares that the chief difficulty confronting a newspaper which tries to carry out independent and thoughtful policies "does not lie in the direction of the board of directors, but in the direction of the public which buys the paper."[13]

The *New York Tribune*, as an example of editorial bravery, points out in an advertisement published May 23, 1922, that though "news knows no order in the making" and though "a newspaper must carry the news, both pleasant and unpleasant," nevertheless, it is the duty of any newspaper to realize that there is a possibility of selective action, and that "in times of stress and bleak despair a newspaper has a hard and fast duty to perform in keeping up the morale of the community."

Indeed, the instances are frequent and accessible to the recollection of any reader in which newspapers have consciously maintained a point of view toward which the public is either hostile or cold.

---

13 H. L. Mencken on Journalism, *The Nation*, April 26, 1922.

Occasionally, of course, even the established point of view is alterable. The two Baltimore *Suns* do brave their public and have been braving their public for some time, not entirely without success. As severe a critic as Oswald Garrison Villard points out that though modern Baltimore is a difficult city to serve, yet the two *Suns* have courageously and consistently stood for the policies of their editors and have refused to yield to pressure from any source. To the public relations counsel this is a striking illustration of the give and take between the public and the institutions which attempt to mould public opinion. The two interact upon each other, so that it is sometimes difficult to tell which is one and which is the other.

The *World* and the *Evening World* of New York, pride themselves upon the following campaigns which are listed in *The World Almanac* of 1922. They illustrate this interaction.

*"Conference on Limitation of Armament
Grew from 'World's' Plea*

"Bearing in mind in 1921 the injunction of its founder, Joseph Pulitzer, to fight always for progress and reform, and having led the campaign for disarmament in advance of any other demand therefor, the *World* covered the Washington Conference on Limitation of Armament in a comprehensive way. . . .

"Measures Advocated by 'World' Made Law

"During the 1921 session of the New York Legislature many measures advocated by the *World* were enacted. One of this paper's chief achievements was the passage of a resolution broadening the power of the Lockwood Housing Committee, enabling it to inquire into high finance as related to the building trades situation.

"The *World* was instrumental in obtaining the Anti-Theater Ticket Speculator Law. It also brought about a change in bills to abolish the Daylight-Saving Law so that municipalities might enact their own daylight-saving ordinances. It was successful in its campaign against the search-and-seizure and other drastic features of the State Prohibition Enforcement Law.

"The 'World' Told Facts About Ku Klux Klan

"The *World* on September 6 commenced the publication of a series of articles telling the truth about the Ku Klux Klan. Twenty-six newspapers, in widely separated sections of the United States, joined the *World* in the publication; some had been invited to participate, others requested the *World* to let them use the articles. All these newspapers realized that the only motive back of the *World*'s publication was public service. It was their desire to share in this service, and the *World* is proud that they asked only assurance of its traditional accuracy and fairness before they saw their way clear to cooperation.

"The *World* is proud that the completed record shows no evidence either that it was terrified by threats or was goaded by abuse into departures from its object of presenting the facts honestly and without exaggeration.

"Changes in Motor Vehicle Laws

"As a result of a crusade to lessen automobile fatalities in New York City and State, the *World* won a victory when changes in the motor vehicle laws were made. The paper printed exclusive stories giving the motor and license numbers of cars stolen daily in this city, and started a campaign against outlaw taxicabs and financially irresponsible drivers and owners.

"Evening World's' Achievements

"The *Evening World* continued its campaign against the coal monopoly and the high coal prices charged in New York City—a state of affairs that has been constantly and vigorously exposed in *Evening World* columns. After consultation with leading Senators at Washington, several bills were introduced in Congress to alleviate the conditions."

I am letting the *World* speak for itself merely as an example of what many splendid newspapers have accomplished as leaders in public movements. The *New York Evening Post* is another example, it having long led popular demand for vocational guidance and control.

The public relations counsel cannot base his work merely upon the acceptance of the principle that the public and its authorities interact. He must go deeper than that and discover why it is that a public opinion exists independently of church, school, press, lecture platform and motion picture screen—how far this public opinion affects these institutions and how far these institutions affect public opinion. He must discover what the stimuli are to which public opinion responds most readily.

Study of the mirrors of the public mind—the press, the motion pictures, the lecture platform and the others—reveal to him what their standards are and those of the groups they reach. This is not enough, however. To his understanding of what he actually can measure he must add a thorough knowledge of the principles which govern individual and group action. A fundamental study of group and individual psychology is required before the public relations counsel can determine how readily individuals or groups will accept modifications of viewpoints or policies, which they have already imposed upon their respective mediums.

No idea or opinion is an isolated factor. It is surrounded and influenced by precedent, authority, habit and all the other human motivations.

For a lucid conception of the functions, power and social utility of the public relations counsel it is vitally important to have a clear grasp of the fundamentals with which he must work.

5

An Understanding of the Fundamentals of Public Motivation Is Necessary to the Work of the Public Relations Counsel

Before defining the fundamental motivations of society, let me mention those outward signs on which psychologists base their study of conditions.

Psychological habits, or as Mr. Lippmann calls them, "stereotypes," are shorthand by which human effort is minimized. They are so clearly and commonly understood that every one will immediately respond to the mention of a stereotype within his personal experience. The words "capitalist" or "boy scout" bring out definite images to the hearer. These images are more comprehensible than detailed descriptions. Chorus girl, woman lawyer, politician, detective, financier are clean-cut concepts and capable of definition. We all have stereotypes which minimize not only our thinking habits but also the ordinary routine of life.

Mr. Lippmann finds that the stereotypes at the center of the code by which various sections of the public live "largely determine what group of facts we shall see and in what light we shall see them." That is why, he says, "with the best will in the world, the news policy of a journal tends to support its editorial policy, why a capitalist sees one set of facts and certain aspects of human nature—literally sees them; his socialist opponent another set and other aspects, and why each regards the other as unreasonable or perverse, when the real difference between them is a difference of perception. That difference is imposed by the difference between the capitalist and socialist pattern of stereotypes. 'There are no classes in America,' writes an American editor. 'The history of all hitherto existing society is the history of class struggles,' says the Communist Manifesto. If you have the editor's pattern in your mind, you will see vividly the facts that confirm it, vaguely and ineffectively those that contradict. If you have the communist pattern, you will not only look for different things, but you will see with a totally different emphasis what you and the editor happen to see in common."

The stereotype is the basis of a large part of the work of the public relations counsel. Let us try to inquire where the stereotype originates—why it is so influential and why from a practical standpoint it is so tremendously difficult to affect or change stereotypes or to attempt to substitute one set of stereotypes for another.

Mr. Martin attempts to answer questions such as these in his volume on "The Behavior of Crowds." By "crowds" Mr. Martin does not mean merely a physical aggregation of a number of persons. To Mr. Martin the crowd is rather a state of mind, "the peculiar mental condition which sometimes occurs when people think and act together, either immediately where the members of the group are present and in close contact, or remotely, as when they affect one another in a certain way through the medium of an organization, a party or sect, the press, etc."

Motives of social behavior are based on individual instincts. Individual instincts, on the other hand, must yield to group needs. Mr. Martin pictures society as an aggregation of people who have sacrificed individual freedom in order to remain within the group. This sacrifice of freedom on the part of individuals in the groups leads its members to resist all efforts at fundamental changes in the group code. Because all have made certain sacrifices, reasons are developed why such sacrifices must be insisted upon at all times. The "logic-proof" compartment is the result of this unwillingness to accept changes.

"What has been so painstakingly built up is not to be lightly destroyed. Each group, therefore, within itself, considers its own standards ultimate and indisputable, and tends to dismiss all contrary or different standards as indefensible.

"Even an honest, critical understanding of the demands of the opposing crowd is discouraged, possibly because it is rightly felt that the critical habit of mind is as destructive of one crowd-complex as the other, and the old crowd prefers to remain intact and die in the last ditch rather than risk dissolution, even with the promise of averting a revolution. Hence the Romans were willing to believe that the Christians worshiped the head of an ass. The medieval Catholics, even at Leo's court, failed to grasp the meaning of the outbreak in North Germany. Thousands saw in the reformation only the alleged fact that the monk Luther wanted to marry a wife . . ."[14]

The main satisfaction, Mr. Martin thinks, which the individual derives from his group association is the satisfaction of his vanity through the creation of an enlarged self-importance.

The Freudian theories upon which Mr. Martin relies very largely for his argument lead to the conclusion that what Mr. Henry Watterson has said of the suppression of news applies equally to the suppression of individual desire. Neither v/ill suppress. With the normal person, the result of this social suppression is to produce an individual who conforms with sufficient closeness to the standards of his group to enable him to remain comfortably within it.

The tendency, however, of the instincts and desires which are thus ruled out of conduct is somehow or other, when the conditions are favorable, to seek some avenue of release and satisfaction. To the individual most of these avenues of release are closed. He cannot, for example, indulge his instinct of pugnacity without running foul of the law. The only release which the individual can have is one which

---

14 "The Behavior of Crowds" (page 193).

commands, however briefly, the approval of his fellows. That is why Mr. Martin calls crowd psychology and crowd activity "the result of forces hidden in a personal and unconscious psyche of the members of the crowd, forces which are merely released by social gatherings of a certain sort." The crowd enables the individual to express himself according to his desire and without restraint.

He says further, "Every crowd 'boosts for' itself, gives itself airs, speaks with oracular finality, regards itself as morally superior, and will, so far as it has the power, lord it over every one. Notice how each group and section in society, so far as it permits itself to think as crowd, claims to be 'the people.'"

As an illustration of the boosting principle Mr. Martin points out the readiness of most groups to enter upon conflict of one kind or another with opposing groups. "Nothing so easily catches general attention and grips a crowd as a contest of any kind," he says. "The crowd unconsciously identifies its members with one or the other competitor. Success enables the winning crowd to 'crow over' the losers. Such an action becomes symbolical, and is utilized by the ego to enhance its feeling of importance. In society this egoism tends to take the form of the desire for dominance." According to Mr. Martin, that is why ". . . whenever any attempt is being made to secure recruits for a movement or a point of view the leaders intuitively assume and reiterate the certainty of ultimate victory."

Two points which Mr. Martin makes seem to me most important. In the first place, Mr. Martin points out with absolute justice that the crowd-mind is by no means limited to the ignorant. "Any class," he says, "may behave and think as a crowd—in fact, it usually does so in so far as its class interests are concerned." Neither is the crowd mind to be found only when there is a physical agglomeration of people. This fact is important to an understanding of the problems of the public relations counsel, because he must bear in mind always that the readers of advertisements, the recipients of letters, the solitary listener at a radio speech, the reader of the morning newspapers are mysteriously part of the crowd-mind. When Bergson came to America about a decade ago, men and women flocked to his classes, both the French and the English sessions. It was obvious to the observer that numbers of disciples who conscientiously attended the full course of lectures understood almost nothing of what was being said. Their behavior was an instance of the crowd-mind.

Everybody read "Main Street." Each reader in his own study tried to react as a crowd-mind. They felt as they thought they ought to.

Initiation scandals, where the crowd-mind has created a brutality not possible to individuals, take place not only in brotherhoods among what Mr. Martin calls "the lower classes," but also among well-bred college youths and the fraternal orders of successful business and professional men. A more specific instance is the football game, with its manifestations of the crowd-mind among a selected group of individuals. The Ku Klux Klan has numbered among its violent supporters some of the "best" families of the affected localities.

The crowd is a state of mind which permeates society and its individuals at almost all times. What becomes articulate in times of stress under great excitement is present in the mind of the individual at most times and explains in part why popular opinion is so positive and so intolerant of contrary points of view. The college professor in his study on a peaceful summer day is just as likely to be reacting as a unit of a crowd-mind, as any member of a lynching party in Texas or Georgia.

Mr. Trotter in his book, "Instincts of the Herd in Peace and War,"[15] gives us further material for study. He discusses the underlying causes and results of "herd" tendencies, stressing the herd's cohesiveness.

The tendency the group has to standardize the habits of individuals and to assign logical reasons for them is an important factor in the

---

15 W. Trotter, "Instincts of the Herd in Peace and War."

work of the public relations counsel. The predominant point of view, according to Mr. Trotter, which translates a rationalized point of view into an axiomatic truth, arises and derives its strength from the fact that it enlists herd support for the point of view of the individual. This explains why it is so easy to popularize many ideas.

"The cardinal quality of the herd is homogeneity."[16] The biological significance of homogeneity lies in its survival value. The wolf pack is many times as strong as the combined strength of each of its individual members. These results of homogeneity have created the "herd" point of view.

One of the psychological results of homogeneity is the fact that physical loneliness is a real terror to the gregarious animal, and that association with the herd causes a feeling of security. In man this fear of loneliness creates a desire for identification with the herd in matters of opinion. It is here, says Mr. Trotter,[17] that we find "the ineradicable impulse mankind has always displayed towards segregation into classes. Each one of us in his opinions and his conduct, in matters of amusement, religion, and politics, is compelled to obtain the support of a class, of a herd within the herd."

Says Mr. Trotter:[18] "The effect of it will clearly be to make acceptable those suggestions which come from the herd, and those only. It is of especial importance to note that this suggestibility is not general, and it is only herd suggestions which are rendered acceptable by the action of instinct, and man is, for example, notoriously insensitive to the suggestions of experience. The history of what is rather grandiosely called human progress everywhere illustrates this. If we look back upon the developments of some such thing as the steam engine, we cannot fail to be struck by the extreme obviousness of each advance,

---

16 It should be explained at the very outset that Mr. Trotter does not use the term "herd" in any derogatory sense. He approaches the entire subject from the point of view of the biologist and compares the gregarious instinct in man to the same instinct in lower forms of life.
17 "Instincts of the Herd in Peace and War" (page 33).
18 *Ibid.*

and how obstinately it was refused assimilation until the machine almost invented itself."

The workings of the gregarious instinct in man result frequently in conduct of the most remarkable complexity, but it is characterized by all of the qualities of instinctive action. Such conduct is usually rationalized, but this does not conceal its real character.

We may sincerely think that we vote the Republican ticket because we have thought out the issues of the political campaign and reached our decision in the cold-blooded exercise of judgment. The fact remains that it is just as likely that we voted the Republican ticket because we did so the year before or because the Republican platform contains a declaration of principle, no matter how vague, which awakens profound emotional response in us, or because our neighbor whom we do not like happens to be a Democrat.

Mr. Lippmann remarks:[19] "For the most part we do not first see and then define, we define first and then see. In the great booming, buzzing confusion of the outer world we pick out of the clutter what is already defined for us, and we tend to perceive that which we have picked out in the form stereotyped for us by our culture."

Mr. Trotter cites as a few of the examples of rationalization the mechanism which "enables the European lady who wears rings in her ears to smile at the barbarism of the colored lady who wears her rings in her nose"[20] and the process which enables the Englishman "who is amused by the African chieftain's regard for the top hat as an essential piece of the furniture of state to ignore the identity of his own behavior when he goes to church beneath the same tremendous ensign."

The gregarious tendency in man, according to Mr. Trotter, results in five characteristics which he displays in common with all gregarious animals.

---

19 "Public Opinion" (page 81).
20 "Instincts of the Herd in Peace and War" (page 38).

1. *"He is intolerant and fearful of solitude, physical or mental."*[21] The same urge which drives the buffalo into the herd and man into the city requires on the part of the latter a sense of spiritual identification with the herd. Man is never so much at home as when on the band wagon.

2. *"He is more sensitive to the voice of the herd than to any other influence."* Mr. Trotter illustrates this characteristic in a paragraph which is worth quoting in its entirety. He says: "It (the voice of the herd) can inhibit or stimulate his thought and conduct. It is the source of his moral codes, of the sanctions of his ethics and philosophy. It can endow him with energy, courage, and endurance, and can as easily take these away. It can make him acquiesce in his own punishment and embrace his executioner, submit to poverty, bow to tyranny, and sink without complaint under starvation. Not merely can it make him accept hardship and suffering unresistingly, but it can make him accept as truth the explanation that his perfectly preventable afflictions are sublimely just and gentle. It is this acme of the power of herd suggestion that is perhaps the most absolutely incontestable proof of the profoundly gregarious nature of man."

3. *"He is subject to the passions of the pack in his mob violence and the passions of the herd in his panics."*

4. *"He is remarkably susceptible to leadership."* Mr. Trotter points out that the need for leadership is often satisfied by leadership of a quality which cannot stand analysis, and which must therefore satisfy some impulse rather than the demands of reason.

5. *"His relations with his fellows are dependent upon the recognition of him as a member of the herd."*

The gregarious tendency, Mr. Trotter believes, is biologically fundamental. He finds therefore that the herd reaction is not confined to outbreaks such as panics and mob violence, but that it is a constant

---

21 *Ibid* (page 112 *et seq.*). Italics mine.

factor in all human thinking and feeling. Discussing the results of the sensitiveness of the individual to the herd point of view, Mr. Trotter says in part, "To believe must be an ineradicable natural bias of man, or in other words, an affirmation, positive or negative, is more readily accepted than rejected, unless its source is definitely disassociated from the herd. *Man is not, therefore, suggestible by fits and starts, not merely in panics and mobs, under hypnosis, and so forth, but always, everywhere, and under any circumstances.*"

The suggestibility of people to ideas which are part of the standards of their groups could not be more succinctly expressed than in the old command, "When in Rome do as the Romans."

Psychologists have defined for the public relations counsel the fundamental equipment of the individual mind and its relation to group reactions. We have seen the motivations of the individual mind—the motivations of the group mind. We have seen the characteristics in thought and action of the individual and the group. All these things we have touched on, though briefly, since they form the ground-work of knowledge for the public relations counsel Their application will be discussed later.

6

The Group and Herd Are the Basic Mechanisms of Public Change

The institutions that make public opinion carry on against a background which is in itself a controlling factor. The real character of this controlling background we shall take up later. Let us first consider some examples that prove its existence—then we can look into its origin and its standards.

Powerful standards control the very institutions which are supposed to help form public opinion. It is necessary to understand the origin, the working and the strength of these institutions in order to understand the institutions themselves and their effect upon the public.

In tracing the interaction of institution upon public and public upon institution, one finds a circle of obedience and leadership. The press, the school and other leaders of thought are themselves working in a background which they cannot entirely control.

Let us turn to the press again for a text.

That the press is so frequently unable to achieve a result on which its combined members are unanimously set makes it evident that the press itself is working in a medium which it cannot entirely control. The *New York Times* motto, "All the news that's fit to print," drives this point home. The standards of fitness created in the minds of the publishers express the point of view of a mass of readers, and this enables the newspapers to achieve and maintain circulation and financial success.

The very fact that newspapers must sell to the public is an evidence that they must please the public and in a measure obey it. In the press there is a very human tendency to compromise between giving the public what it wants and giving the public what it *should* want. This is equally true in music, where artists like McCormack or Rachmaninoff popularize their programs. It is true in the drama, where managers, producers and authors combine to adjust plots, situations and endings to what the public will be willing to pay to see. It is true in art, in architecture, in motion pictures. It is true of the lecture platform and of the pulpit.

So-called radical preachers, for example, usually succeed in broadcasting their radical ideas only when their following is prepared to accept their views. The Rev. Percy Stickney Grant was a great problem to the upholders of the accepted order, only because there was so large a body of parishioners eager to hear and accept his *dicta*. The Rev. Billy Sunday, evangelist, derived his following from among people who were awaiting a faith-stirring appeal.

Another evidence of the fact that a powerful outside influence helps make the forces that mould public opinion is shown by the newspapers in the actual selection of news. The public actually demands that certain types of facts be omitted. The standing problem of every newspaper office—the winnowing of the day's news from the mass of material that reaches the editorial desks—illustrates pointedly the need there is to examine the reasons which prompt the editors in selection.

In an exceedingly interesting advertisement published by the *New York Tribune*, on April 19, 1922, the *Tribune*'s editors state the problem most graphically. The advertisement is headed, "What Else Happened That Day?" and it reads as follows:

"Madame Caillaux was on trial in Paris for killing Gaston Calmette.

"In Long Island a woman was mysteriously shot in a doctor's office while on a night visit.

"Forty-five stage coaches were held up in Yellowstone Park by two masked bandits who took all the cash of 165 tourists.

"Romantic crime, mystery crime, adventurous crime, a public eagerly interested—and they suddenly dropped from the newspapers. The public forgot them. As news, these events became as if they had never happened. Something else had happened.

"The day of Madame Caillaux's acquittal Austria declared war on Serbia. Russia mobilized fourteen army corps on the German border and the price of wheat in this country soared.

"All the news that a newspaper prints is affected by what else happened that day. If an earthquake occurs the day you announce your daughter's engagement her picture may be left out of the newspaper.

"The man who made a golf hole in one the day of the Dempsey-Carpentier fight was out of luck so far as an item on the sporting page was concerned.

"When real news breaks, semi-news must go. When real news is scarce, semi-news returns to the front page. A very great man picked out Sunday night to dine at a Bowery mission. Monday is usually a dull day for news, although some big events, notably the sinking of the Titanic, came over the wires Sunday night.

"All papers feature big news. When there is no big news, real editing is needed to select the real news from the semi-news.

"What you read on dull news days is what fixes your opinions of your country and of your compatriots. It is from the non-sensational news that you see the world and assess, rightly or wrongly, the true value of persons and events.

"The relative importance your newspaper gives to an occurrence affects your thought, your character, and your children's thought and character. For few daily habits are as firmly established as the habit of reading the newspaper."

Now each of the items mentioned in the *Tribune*'s advertisement was news. Comparison of the newspapers of that day will undoubtedly show a wide divergence in the manner in which these items were treated and in the relative importance assigned to each. The basis of the selection was clearly the general standard of the clientele of each individual paper.

And this selection of ideas for presentation goes on in every medium of thought communication.

This basis of selection has long been recognized. Thus in an article in the *Atlantic Monthly* for February, 1911, Professor Hargar, formerly head of the Department of Journalism at the University of Kansas, draws attention to it in regard to newspapers, and points out that "the province of the city paper is one of news selection.[22] Out of the vast skein of the day's happenings what shall it select? More 'copy' is thrown away than is used. The *New York Sun* is written as definitely for a given constituency as is a technical journal. Out of the day's news it gives prominence to that which fits into its scheme of treatment, and there is so much news that it can fill its columns with interesting materials, yet leave untouched a myriad of events. The *New York Evening Post* appeals to another constituency, and is made accordingly. The *World* and the *Journal* have a far different plan, and 'play up' stories that are mentioned briefly, or ignored, by some of their contemporaries. So the writer on the metropolitan paper is trained to sift news, to choose from his wealth of material that which the paper's traditions demand shall receive attention; and so abundant is the supply that he can easily set a feast without exhausting the market's offering. Unconsciously he becomes an epicure, and knows no day will dawn without bringing him his opportunity."

Mr. Lippmann makes the same observation. He says:[23] "Every newspaper when it reaches the reader is the result of a whole series of selections as to what items shall be printed, in what position they shall be printed, how much space each shall occupy, what emphasis each shall have. There are no objective standards here. There are conventions. Take two newspapers published in the same city on the same morning.

The headline of one reads: 'Britain pledges aid to Berlin against French Aggression. France Openly Backs Poles.' The headline of the second is: 'Mrs. Stillman's Other Love.' Which you prefer is a matter of taste, but *not entirely a matter of the editor's taste. It is a matter of his judgment as to what will absorb the half hour's attention a certain set of readers will give to his newspaper.*"

---

22 Bleyer, "The Profession of Journalism" (page 269).
23 "Public Opinion" (page 354).

The American stage continually bows to public demand and consciously ascribes to the public the changes it undergoes. The character of advertising has definitely yielded to public demand and fake advertising has been to a great extent eliminated. Motion pictures have responded, too, to public taste and public pressure, both as to the kind of picture presented and, in isolated instances, to the type of action permitted to appear.

It is therefore apparent that these and the other institutions which modify public opinion carry on against a background which is also in itself a controlling factor. What the real character of this controlling background is we shall now consider.

7

The Application of These Principles

Both Trotter, Martin and the other writers we have quoted confirm what the actual experience of the public relations counsel shows—that the cause he represents must have some group reaction and tradition in common with the public he is trying to reach. This must exist before they can react sympathetically upon one another. Given these common fundamentals, much can be done to capitalize or destroy them. It is as untrue to contend that public opinion is manufactured as it is to contend that public opinion governs the agencies which mould it.

The public relations counsel must continually realize that there are always these limitations to his effectiveness.

The very "leaders," men who have been selected from the mass to "lead the nation," live with their ears to the ground for every slight rumbling of public sentiment. Preachers, acknowledged to be the ethical leaders of their flocks, express obedience to public opinion.

The critics who hold these extreme points of view about public opinion have too easily confused cause and effect. The sympathy between the orator and his audience is not one which the orator can create. He can intensify it, or by tactless speaking he can dissipate it, but he cannot manufacture it from thin air.

Margaret Sanger, a leader in the fight for education on birth control, will evoke enthusiasm when she addresses an audience that approves of her sentiments. When, however, she injects her point of view into groups that have a preconceived aversion to them, she is in danger of abuse, if not of actual physical violence. Likewise, a man who would talk of prison reform at a time when the public is aroused by an unwonted crime wave will find little response. On the other hand, when Madam Curie, co-discoverer of radium, came to America, she found a country that was prepared to meet her because of intensive effort on the part of a large radium corporation and a committee of women formed by Marie B. Meloney, to apprise the public of the importance of her visit. Had she come two years sooner, she might have been ignored save by a few scientists.

A historic incident illustrative of the interaction between a leader and a public is that of the sudden turn in the affairs of Rear Admiral Dewey. The idol of the Spanish American War, he nevertheless alienated popular affection by giving to his wife a house which had been presented to him by an admiring public. For some reason the public failed to sympathize with Admiral Dewey's own undoubtedly sound and worthy reasons.

To say, therefore, as some persons have said at great length and with considerable vehemence, that the public relations counsel is responsible for public opinion, is not true. The public relations counsel is not needed to persuade people to standardize their points of view or to persist in their established beliefs. The established point of view becomes established by satisfying some real or assumed human need.

In common with the scenario writer, the preacher, the statesman, the dramatist, the public relations counsel, has his share in making up the mind of the public. The public quite as truly makes up the mind of the journalist, the pamphleteer, the scenario writer, the preacher and the statesman. The main direction of the public mind is often irrevocably set for its leaders.

Hendrik Van Loon, in his "Story of Mankind," paints a picture of the action and interaction between Napoleon the Great and his public in a way that might well have been made to illustrate our point. When Napoleon led the public truly in the direction towards which it was headed, that is, towards democracy and equality, he was its successful leader and its idol, says Van Loon. When in the latter part of his career he turned back to a goal which the public had discarded and was eager to forget, that is, Bourbonism, Napoleon met with irresistible defeat.

"Damaged Goods" was able to make the American public accept the word "syphilis" because the counsel on public relations projected the doctrine of sex hygiene through those groups and sections of the public which were prepared to work with him.

Public opinion is the resultant of the interaction between two forces.

This may help us to see with greater clarity the position the public relations counsel holds in relation to the world at large, and what the factors are with which he is concerned and by which he accomplishes his work.

We have gone somewhat elaborately into the fundamental equipment of the individual mind and its relation to the group mind because the public relations counsel in his work in these fields must constantly call upon his knowledge of individual and group psychology. The public relations counsel can come forward, first, as the representative of established things when their security is shaken, or when they desire greater power; and second, as the representative of the group which is struggling to establish itself.

Mr. Lippmann says propaganda is dependent upon censorship. From my point of view the precise reverse is more nearly true. Propaganda is a purposeful, directed effort to overcome censorship—the censorship of the group mind and the herd reaction.

The average citizen is the world's most efficient censor. His own mind is the greatest barrier between him and the facts. His own "logic-proof compartments," his own absolutism are the obstacles which prevent him from seeing in terms of experience and thought rather than in terms of group reaction.

The training of the public relations counsel permits him to step out of his own group to look at a particular problem with the eyes of an impartial observer and to utilize his knowledge of the individual and the group mind to project his clients' point of view.

Part III
Technique and Method

1

The Public Can Be Reached Only Through Established Mediums Of Communication

When the United States was made up of small social units with common traditions and a small geographic and social area, it was comparatively simple for the proponent of a point of view to address his public directly. If he represented a social or a political idea, he could, at no very great expense and with no very great difficulty in the early Eighteenth Century, cover New England with his pamphlets. He could arouse the thirteen colonies with his journals and brochures. That was because the heritage of these groups made them sensitive to the same stimuli. One man, remarks Mr. Lippmann, then was able single-handed to crystallize the common will of his country in his day and generation. To-day the greatest superman as yet developed by humanity could not accomplish the same result with the United States.

Populations have increased. In this country geographical areas have increased. Heterogeneity has also increased. A group living in any given area is now extremely likely to have no common ancestry, no common tradition, as such, and no cohesive intelligence. All these elements make it necessary to-day for the proponent of a point of view to engage an expert to represent him before society, an expert who must know how to reach groups totally dissimilar as to ideals, customs and even language. It is this necessity which has resulted in the development of the counsel on public relations.

Now it must be understood that the proponent of a point of view, whether acting alone or under the guidance of a public relations counsel, must utilize existing avenues of approach. Modern conditions are such that it is not feasible to build up independent organs. Innovators and innovations cannot create their own channels of communication. They must for a great part work through the existing daily press, the existing magazine, the existing lecture circuit, existing advertising mediums, the existing motion picture channels and other means for the communication of ideas. The public relations counsel, on behalf of the groups he represents, must reach majorities and minorities through their respective approaches.

If the public relations counsel can succeed in presenting ideas and facts to the public in spite of the heterogeneity of society, in spite of the vast psychological and geographic problems, in spite of the difficulties, monetary and otherwise, of reaching and influencing populations numbering millions—if he can succeed in overcoming these difficulties by a skillful understanding of the situation, his profession is socially valuable.

Absolute homogeneity, resulting in a dead level of uniformity in public and individual reaction, is undesirable. On the other hand, agreement on broad social purposes is essential to progress. Agreement on broad industrial purposes may be equally desirable. Without such agreement, without unified purposes, there can be no progress and the unit must fall. The men who were most effective in stimulating national morale during the war never lost sight of these underlying needs, whether they stimulated a whole nation to ration itself voluntarily and give up the eating of sugar, or whether they stimulated knitting and Red Cross activities and voluntary contributions to funds.

Three ways are cited by Mr. Lippmann to obtain cohesive force among the special and local interests which make up national and social units. The public relations counsel avails himself only of the third. The first method which is described is that of "patronage and pork." This is very largely the method relied upon by certain legislative bodies to-day to maintain cohesive force. As an instance of this, the investigations of the methods used in connection with the bills to secure the building of local post offices or the dredging of harbors or rivers seem to point out that a representative from one community will promise reciprocal support to the member from another community, if he in turn will act favorably on another item. This method intensifies the feeling that all are working together, even though they may not be working for the highest interests of the country. Similarly the chief executive of a city may institute certain measures to placate school teachers. He will expect the school teachers to support him on some other project at some other period.

The second method named by Mr. Lippmann[24] is "government by terror and obedience."

The third method is "government based on such a highly developed system of information, analysis and self-consciousness that 'the knowledge of national circumstances and reasons of state' is evident to all men. The autocratic system is in decay. The voluntary system is in its very earliest development and so, in calculating the prospects of associations among large groups of people, a league of nations, industrial government, or a federal union of states, the degree to which the material for a common consciousness exists determines how far cooperation will depend upon force, or upon the milder alternative

---

24 "Public Opinion" (page 292).

to force, which is patronage and privilege. The secret of great state builders, like Alexander Hamilton, is that they know how to calculate these principles."

The method of education by information, which was to a great extent relied upon by the United States, for example, was evidenced in the formation during the war of such agencies as the Committee on Public Information. The public relations counsel, through the mediums chosen by him, presented to the public the information necessary to aid in understanding America's war aims and ideals. George Creel and his organization reached vast groups, representing every phase of our national elements, in every modern method of thought communication. But even in the United States the other two methods were used to obtain cohesive force.

In fact the method least relied upon in any of the belligerent countries was that of "government based on such a highly developed system of information, analysis and self-consciousness that 'the knowledge of national circumstances and reasons of state' is evident to all men."

This breakdown did not occur among small, inefficiently organised groups. It occurred among the representatives of the highest development in social organization.

If this was the fate of the most highly organized social groups, consider then the problem which confronts the social, economic, educational or political groups in peace time, when they attempt to obtain a public hearing for new ideas. Innumerable instances have shown the difficulty that any group faces in gaining an acceptance for its ideas.

The development of the United States to its present size and diversification has intensified the difficulty of creating a common will on any subject because it has heightened the natural tendency of men to separate into crowds opposed to one another in point of view. This difficulty is further emphasized by the fact that often these crowds live in different traditional, moral and spiritual worlds. The physical difficulties of communication make group separation greater.

Mr. Trotter's conclusions from a study of the gregarious instinct are singularly apt on this point. He says that[25] "the enormous power of varied reaction possessed by man must render necessary for his attainment of the full advantages of the gregarious habit a power of inter-communication of absolutely unprecedented fineness. It is clear that scarcely a hint of such power has yet appeared, and it is equally obvious that it is this defect which gives to society the characteristics which are the contempt of the man of science and the disgust of the humanitarian."

When the worker was of the same ancestry as his employer, labor difficulties, for example, could be discussed in terms which were comprehensible to both parties. To-day the United States Steel Corporation must exert tremendous effort to present its view to its thousands of employees who are South Europeans, North Europeans, Americans.

Czechoslovakia, during the Peace Conference, wanted to appeal to its countrymen in America, but this group was vague and scattered in a population that lived in many cities throughout the country. The public relations counsel who was engaged to reach this scattered population had, therefore, to translate his appeals so that they might be understood logically and emotionally by the educated and the uneducated, the urban, the rural, the laboring and the professional man.

The same problem in a quite different guise presented itself to the public relations counsel who wanted to insure a public response to the appeal of the Diaghileff Russian Ballet, of which the public knew nothing. He had, therefore, to surmount the difficulties of dissimilar geographic and artistic heritage and taste, of unwillingness to accept novelty and of interests already firmly attached to other forms of amusement.

Dominant groups to-day are more secure in their position than was the most successful autocrat of several hundred years ago, because

---

25 "Instincts of the Herd in Peace and War" (page 62).

to-day the inertia which must be overcome in order to displace these groups is so much greater. So many persons with so many different points of view must be reached and unified before anything effective can be done. Unity can be secured only by finding the greatest common factor or divisor of all the groups; and it is difficult to find one common factor which will appeal to a large and unhomogeneous group.

A very simple and broadly appealing campaign for reaching the public was undertaken recently by the railroads in combination. They utilized the poster in graphic, fundamental appeal to awaken an instinct of carefulness in regard to crossing railroad tracks. When the government sought to reestablish ex-service men, the public relations counsel had to appeal vividly and quickly to employers and returned soldiers out of the vast complexity of their interests. He selected the most fundamental appeals of loyalty, fairness and patriotism in order to be understood actively.

Domination to-day is not a product of armies or navies or wealth or policies. It is a domination based on the one hand upon accomplished unity, and on the other hand upon the fact that opposition is generally characterized by a high degree of disunity. The institution of electing representatives to Congress is so firmly established that no existent force to-day can overthrow it. More specifically, why is it that the two parties, Republican and Democrat, have maintained themselves as the dominant force for so many years? Only the leadership of Theodore Roosevelt seemed for a time to supersede them; and events since then have shown that it was Roosevelt and not his party who succeeded. The Farmer-Labor Party, the Socialist Party despite years of campaigning have failed to become even strongly recognizable opponents to the established groups. The disunity of forces which seek to overthrow dominant groups is illustrated every day in every phase of our lives—political, moral and economic. A new point of view, although faced by the difficulty of unifying a group to concerted will or action, can seldom establish new mediums by which to approach those people to whom it wishes to appeal.

It is possible for advertising and pamphletizing to blanket the country at a cost. To establish a new lecture service in order to reach the public would be expensive, and effective only to a limited extent. To establish an independent radio station to broadcast an idea would be difficult and probably disproportionately expensive. To create a new motion picture and a distributing agency would be slow, and very difficult and costly, if possible at all.

The difficulty of establishing and building new channels of approach to the public is shown best by an examination of the principal mediums which are available to the public relations counsel who desires to direct public thought to the problems of the group he represents.

It is only necessary to picture the newspaper and magazine situation in the United States to-day to realize the difficulty of establishing a new medium for the representation of a point of view. Americans are accustomed to first-rate service from their press. They demand a high standard not only in the physical appearance of their newspapers but in the news service as well. Their daily paper must provide them with items of local, state and international interest and importance. In the complex activities of modern life, the newspaper must find and select the subjects which interest its readers. It must also give to its readers the news fresh from the making. Whatever vagueness there may be about the definition of news itself, one admitted constant is that it must be fresh.

The cost of establishing a paper with a wide appeal, which will have the facilities of gathering news, of printing and distributing it, is such that groups can no longer depend upon their own organs of expression. The Christian Science church does not depend upon its admirable publication, the *Christian Science Monitor* in order to reach its own and new publics. Even where the issue demands a partisan or class origin of a newspaper, as in the case of a political party, the results achieved by so expensive and laborious a step seldom justify it.

Mr. Given in his book "Making a Newspaper," points out the great expense that is attached to the publication of a large metropolitan daily. In proportion to their field of appeal and potential income, the smaller dailies undoubtedly face the same economic problems. Mr. Given says:[26] "Few persons not having intimate knowledge of a newspaper have any idea of the great amount of money required to start one, or to keep one running which is already established. The mechanical equipment and delivery service alone may demand an investment of several hundred thousand dollars—there is one New York paper whose mechanical equipment cost $1,000,000—supplies are in constant demand, and the salary list is a long and heavy one. For a new paper the salary list of the editorial department is especially formidable, as editors and reporters who have employment with well-established publications are always reluctant to change to a venture that at best is in for a rough voyage, and can be attracted only by high pay.

"A good many of the newspapers that are started soon become memories, and fewer than are generally supposed are paying their own way. The sum of $3,000,000 would hardly suffice at the present time to equip a first-class newspaper establishment in New York City, issue a morning and an evening edition paper, build up a circulation of 75,000 for each, and place the establishment on a money-making basis. Run on the lines of those already established and possessing no extraordinary features to recommend them to the public, the two papers might continue to lose money for twenty years. When one learns that there are in New York business managers who are compelled to reckon with an average weekly expense account of nearly $50,000, he can understand the possibility of heavy losses. And it might be added,

---

26 Given, "Making a Newspaper" (pages 306–307).

in contrast, that there are in New York newspapers which could not be bought for $10,000,000."

Discussing substantially the same point, Mr. Oswald Garrison Villard observes the narrowing down of the number of newspapers in our large cities and points out the imminent danger of a news monopoly in the United States. He says:[27] "It is the danger that newspaper conditions, because of the enormously increased costs and this tendency to monopoly, may prevent people who are actuated by passion and sentiment from founding newspapers, which is causing many students of the situation much concern. What is to be the hope for the advocates of newborn and unpopular reforms if they cannot have a press of their own, as the Abolitionists and the founders of the Republican party set up theirs in a remarkably short time, usually with poverty-stricken bank accounts?"

The public relations counsel must always subdivide the appeal of his subject and present it through the widest possible variety of avenues to the public. That these avenues must be existing avenues is both a limitation and an opportunity.

People accept the facts which come to them through existing channels. They like to hear new things in accustomed ways. They have neither the time nor the inclination to search for facts that are not readily available to them. The expert, therefore, must advise first upon the form of action desirable for his client and secondly must utilize the established mediums of communication, in order to present to the public a point of view. This is true whether it is that of a majority or minority, old or new personality, institution or group which desires to change by modification or intensification the store of knowledge and the opinion of the public.

---

27 "Press Tendencies and Dangers," *Atlantic Monthly*, January, 1918.

2

The Interlapping Group Formations Of Society, The Continuous Shifting Of Groups, Changing Conditions And The Flexibility Of Human Nature Are All Aids To The Counsel On Public Relations

The public relations counsel works with public opinion. Public opinion is the product of individual minds. Individual minds make up the group mind. And the established order of things is maintained by the inertia of the group. Three factors make it possible for the public relations counsel to overcome even this inertia. These are, first, the interlapping group formation of society; second, the continuous shifting of groups; third, the changed physical conditions to which groups respond. All of these are brought about by the natural inherent flexibility of individual human nature.

Society is not divided into two groups, although it seems so to many. Some see modern society divided into capital and labor. The feminist sees the world divided into men and women. The hungry man sees the rich and the poor. The missionary sees the heathen and the faithful. If society were divided into two groups, and no more, then change could come about only through violent upheaval.

Let us assume, for example, a society divided into capital and labor. It is apparent on slight inspection that capital is not a homogeneous group. There is a difference in point of view and in interests between Elbert H. Gary or John D. Rockefeller, Jr., on the one hand, and the small shopkeeper on the other.

Occasions arise, too, upon which even in one group sharp differences and competitive alignments take place.

In the capital group, on the tariff question, for example, the retailer with a net income of ten thousand dollars a year is apt to take a radically different position from the manufacturer with a similar income. In some respects the capitalist is a consumer. In other respects he is a worker. Many persons are at the same time workers and capitalists. The highly paid worker who also draws income from Liberty Bonds or from shares of stock in industrial corporations is an example of this.

On the other hand, the so-called workers do not consist of a homogeneous group with complete identity of interests. There may be no difference in economic situation between manual labor and mental labor; yet there is a traditional difference in point of view which keeps these two groups far apart. Again, the narrower field of manual labor, the group represented by the American Federation of Labor, is frequently opposed in sympathies and interests to the group of Industrial Workers of the World. Even in the American Federation of Labor there are component units. The locomotive engineer, who belongs to one of the great brotherhoods, has different interests from the miner, who belongs to the United Mine Workers of America.

The farmer is in a class by himself. Yet he in turn may be a tenant farmer or the owner of an estate or of a small patch of tillable soil.

That group so vaguely called "the public" consists of all sorts and conditions of men, the particular kind or condition depending upon the point of view of the individual who is making the observation or classification. This is true likewise of great and small subdivisions of the public.

The public relations counsel must take into account that many groups exist, and that there is a very definite interlapping of groups. Because of this he is enabled to utilize many types of appeal in reaching any one group, which he subdivides for his purposes.

The Federation for the Support of Jewish Charities recently instituted a campaign to raise millions of dollars for what it called its United

Building Fund. The directors of that campaign might have subdivided society for their purpose into two groups, the Jewish and the non-Jewish group, or they might have decided that there were rich people who could give and poor people who could not give. But they realized the interlapping nature of the groups they wanted to reach. They analyzed these component groups closely and divided them into groups which had common business interests. For instance, they organized a group of dentists, a group of bankers, a group of real estate operators, a group of cloak-and-suit-house operators, a group of motion picture and theatrical owners and others.

Through an approach to each group on the strongest appeal to which the members of the group as a group would respond, the charity received the support of the individuals who made it up. The social aspirations of the group, the ambitions for leadership of the group, the competitive desires and philanthropic tendencies of the individuals who made up these groups were capitalized.

The interlapping nature of these groups made it possible, too, for the public relations counsel to reach all the individuals by appeals that were directed not merely to the individual as a member of the business group with which he was aligned, but also as a member of a different group. For instance, as a humanitarian, as a public-spirited citizen, or as a devoted Jew. Because of this interlapping characteristic of groups, the organization was able to accomplish its purpose more successfully.

Society is made up of an almost infinite number of groups, whose various interests and desires overlap and interweave inextricably. The same man may be at the same time the member of a minority religious sect, supporter of the dominant political party, a worker in the sense that he earns his living primarily by his labor, and a capitalist in the sense that he has rents from real estate investments or interest from financial investments. In an issue which involves his religious sect he will align himself with one group. In an issue which involves the choice of a President of the United States he aligns himself with another group. In an industrial issue between capital and labor it might be very nearly impossible to estimate in advance how he would align himself. It is from the constant interplay of these groups and of their conflicting interests upon each other that progress results, and it is this fact that the public relations counsel takes into account in pleading his cause. A movement called "The Go-Getters," instituted by a magazine, as much to keep itself before the public eye as to stimulate commercial activity, found rapid acceptance throughout the country because it appealed to trades of every description, because each group had among its members men who belonged also to a large group, the group of salesmen.

Let us examine for a moment the personnel of the Horseshoe at the Metropolitan Opera House. It is composed of people who are rich, but this economic classification is only one, for the men and women who assemble there are presumably music lovers. But we may again break up this classification of music lovers and discover that this group contains art lovers as well. It contains sportsmen. It contains merchants and bankers. There are philosophers in it. There are motorists and amateur farmers. When the Russian Ballet came to America the essential parts of this group attended the performances, but in going after his public, the public relations counsel based his actions upon the interlapping of groups, and appealed to his entire possible audience through their various interlapping group interests. The art lover had been stimulated by hearing of the Ballet through his art group or the art publications and by seeing pictures of the costumes and the settings. The music lover who might have had his interest stimulated through seeing a photograph, also had his interest stimulated by reading about the music.

Every individual heard of the Russian Ballet in terms of one or more different appeals and responded to the Ballet because of these appeals. It is naturally difficult to say which one of them had its strongest effect upon the individual's mind. There was no doubt, however, that the interlapping group formation of society made it possible for more to be reached and to be moved than would have been the case if the Ballet had been projected on the world at large only as a well-balanced artistic performance.

The utilization of this characteristic of society was shown recently in the activities of a silk firm which desired to intensify the interest of the public in silks. It realized that fundamentally women were its potential buying public, but it understood, too, that the women who made up this public were members of other groups as well. Thus, to the members of women's clubs, silk was projected as the embodiment of fashion. To those women who visited museums, silk was displayed there as art. To the schools in the same town, perhaps, silk became a lesson in the natural history of the silkworm. To art clubs, silk became color and design. To newspapers, the events that transpired in the silk mills became news matters of importance.

Each group of women was appealed to on the basis of its greatest interest. The school teacher was appealed to in the schoolroom as an educator, and after school hours as a member of a women's club. She read the advertisements about silk as a woman reader of the newspapers, and as a member of the women's group which visited the museums, saw the silk there. The woman who stayed at home was brought into contact with the silk through her child. All these groups made up the potential market for silk, reached in this way in terms of many appeals to each individual. These are the implications present for the public relations counsel, who must take into account the interchange and interplay of groups in pleading his cause.

For society, the interesting outcome of this situation is that progress seldom occurs through the abrupt expulsion by a group of its old ideas in favor of new ideas, but rather through the re-arrangement of the thought of the individuals in these groups with respect to each other and with respect to the entire membership of society.

It is precisely this interlapping of groups—the variety, the inconsistency of the average man's mental, social and psychological commitments which makes possible the gradual change from one state of affairs or from one state of mind to another. Few people are life members of one group and of one group only. The ordinary person is a very temporary member of a great number of groups. This is one of the most powerful forces making for progress in society because it makes for receptivity and open-mindedness. The modification which results from the inconstancy of individual commitments may be accelerated and directed by conscious effort. These changes which come about so stealthily that they remain unobserved in society until long after they have taken place, can be made to yield results in chosen directions.

Changed external conditions must be taken into account by the public relations counsel in his work.

Such changes carry with them modifications in the interests and points of view of those they affect. They make it possible to modify group and individual reaction. The public relations counsel, too, can modify the results of the changed external condition by calling attention to it or interpreting it in terms of the interest of those affected.

The radio might be taken as an example. In considering the radio from the standpoint of his work, the public relations counsel has a new medium which can readily reach huge sections of the public with his message. The public relations counsel must be ready to estimate, too, what difference in viewpoint the radio will produce or has produced in any given section of the public it reaches. He will have to consider, for instance, that due to it the average farmer is much more closely in contact with the world's events than formerly.

In the case of the radio, too, if his clients be for instance, large manufacturers of radio supplies and demand acceleration of this changed external condition in order to increase their business, he may enlarge the radio's field, activity and effectiveness. Or, he may stress to the public the importance of this new instrument and strengthen its prestige, so that it may better fulfill its mission as a modifier of conditions.

Changed conditions can make possible modifications in the public point of view, as can be instanced by a campaign carried on by savings banks to encourage thrift. This campaign was successful at that time because inflation made it easy for the public to see the wisdom of the doctrines preached and to act upon them.

Another example of this modification in the public point of view due to a changed condition was the demand made by the Executive Committee of the Central Trades and Labor Council of New York for the government to take over the railways of the country. Public ownership had been a pet subject for school debate for more than two decades, but it had seldom passed into the field of serious consideration by the general public. Yet the conditions of hardship created by the last strike of the railroad shopmen caused a much greater receptivity in the public mind to this idea.

The airplane slowly emerges as an important factor in the daily life of the people. What it will mean in the psychology of the nation when commuters can settle within a radius of a hundred or more miles of cities is only to be guessed at. Cities may cease to exist except as industrial centers. There will be greater groups and broader interests. There will be fewer geographic divisions.

When the automobile was first used motoring was a dangerous and thrilling sport. To-day it is found that the automobile has altered the fundamental conception of daily life held by thousands of people, both in the urban and the rural population. The automobile has removed much of the isolation of country districts. It has increased the possibility of education in them. It has caused millions of miles of excellent roads to be laid.

Changed conditions can be national or local in their import and significance. They can be as national in scope as the revolutionary introduction over night of a national prohibition law or as local as a police captain's edict in Coney Island against stockingless feminine bathers. But they must be taken into consideration by the public relations counsel in his work if they concern in the slightest degree his particular public.

The basic elements of human nature are fixed as to desires and instincts and innate tendencies. The directions, however, in which these basic elements may be turned by skillful handling are infinite. Human nature is readily subject to modification. Many psychologists have attempted to define the component parts of human nature, and while their terminology is not the same, they do follow more or less the same general outlines.

Among the universal instincts are—self-preservation, which includes the desire for shelter, sex hunger and food hunger. It is only necessary to look through the pages of any magazine to see the way in which modern business avails itself of these three fundamentals to exert a coercive force upon the public it is trying to reach. The American Radiator advertisement with its cozy home, the family gathered around the radiator, the storm raging outside, definitely makes its appeal to the universal desire for shelter.

The Gulden Mustard advertisements with their graphic delineation of cold cuts and an inviting glass of what is presumably near-beer definitely appeal to our gustatory sense.

As for the sex appeal, the soap advertisements run a veritable race with these ends in view. Woodbury's "the skin you love to touch" is a graphic illustration.

The instinct of self-preservation, one of the most basic of human instincts, is most flexible. The dispensers of raisins, upon the advice of an expert on public opinion, adopted a slogan to appeal to this instinct: "Have you had your iron to-day?"—iron presumably strengthening a man and increasing his powers of resistance. The same man appealed to here will respond to the sales talk which persuades him that insurance may save him at a time of need.

An important hair-net manufacturer wanted to increase the sales of his product. The public relations counsel, therefore, appealed to the instinct of self-preservation of large groups of the public. He talked of self-preservation with respect to hygiene for food dispensers. He talked of self-preservation with respect to safety for women who work near exposed machinery.

The same instinct of preservation which may cause a worker to give up necessary food so that he may save a little money will cause him to contribute money to a common fund if he can be shown that this too is a safety measure.

The public relations counsel extracts from his clients' causes ideas which will capitalize certain fundamental instincts in the people he is trying to reach, and then sets about to project these ideas to his public.

William MacDougall, the psychologist, classifies seven primary instincts with their attendant emotions. They are flight-fear, repulsion-disgust, curiosity-wonder, pugnacity-anger, self-display-elation, self-abasement-subjection, parental-love-tenderness. These instincts are utilized by the public relations counsel in developing ideas and emotions which will modify the opinions and actions of his public.

The action of public health officials in stressing the possibility of a plague or epidemic is effective because it appeals to the emotion of fear, and presents the possibility of preventing the spread of the epidemic or plague. Of course, the element of flight in this particular situation is not one of movement, but of a desire to get away from the danger.

The instinct of repulsion with its attendant emotion of disgust is not often called upon by the public relations counsel in his work.

On the other hand, curiosity and wonder are continually employed. In Governmental work, particularly, the statesman who has an announcement to make is continually exhausting every effort to arouse public interest in advance of the actual announcement. Feelers are often sent out to the public to help create curiosity.

It is interesting to note, too, that even book publishers rely upon the element of wonder, termed suspense in drama, to increase their public and their sales. Our now famous "What is wrong with this picture?" advertisements, and those used for the O. Henry books illustrate this point.

Pugnacity with its attendant emotion of anger is a human constant. The public relations counsel uses this continually in constructing all kinds of events that will call it into play. Because of it, too, he is often forced to enact combats and create issues. He stages battles against evils in which the antagonist is personified for the public. New York City, when it wants to reduce the death rate from tuberculosis, aligns its citizens yearly in a fight against the disease and continues the idea of combat by announcing the number of victims from year to year. It uses the terminology of warfare in these bulletins. Such phrases in this or other health campaigns as "kill the germs," "swat the fly," illustrate this point. The public responds to a battle in a way that it might not respond to a plea to take care of itself or to do its civic duty.

Under pugnacity would come that technique of the public relations counsel which is continually devising tests and contests. Mr. Martin, in his experience as director of the Cooper Union Forum, noticed that the sort of interest which will most easily bring an assemblage of people together is most commonly an issue of some kind.

On the one hand, says Mr. Martin:[28] "I have seen efforts made in New York to hold mass meetings to discuss affairs of the very greatest importance, and I have noted the fact that such efforts usually fail to get out more than a handful of specially interested persons, no matter how well advertised, if the subject to be considered happens not to be of a controversial nature. On the other hand, if the matter to be considered is one about which there is keen partisan feeling and popular resentment—if it lends itself to the spectacular personal achievement of one whose name is known, especially in the face of opposition or difficulties—or if the occasion permits of resolutions of protest, of the

---

28 "The Behavior of Crowds" (pages 23–24).

airing of wrongs, of denouncing a business of some kind, or of casting statements of external principles in the teeth of 'enemies of humanity,' then, however trivial the occasion, we may count on it that our meeting will be well attended.

"It is this element of conflict, directly or indirectly, which plays an overwhelming part in the psychology of every crowd. It is the element of contest which makes baseball so popular. A debate will draw a larger crowd than a lecture. One of the secrets of the large attendance of the forum is the fact that discussion—'talking back'—is permitted and encouraged. The Evangelist Sunday undoubtedly owes the great attendance at his meetings in no small degree to the fact that he is regularly expected to abuse some one.

"Nothing so easily catches general attention and creates a crowd as a contest of any kind. The crowd unconsciously identifies its members with one or the other competitor. Success enables the winning crowd to 'crow' over the losers. Such an occasion becomes symbolic and is utilized by the ego to enhance its feeling of importance."

The public relations counsel finds in the instinct of pugnacity a powerful weapon for enlisting public support for or public opposition to a point of view in which he is interested. On this principle, he will, whenever possible, state his case in the form of an issue and enlist, in support of his side, such forces as are available.

The dangers of the method must be recognized and borne in mind. Pugnacity can be enlisted on the side of decency and progress. He who looks at it from that point of view will agree with Mr. Pulitzer, the great publisher, that it seems neither extraordinary nor culpable that "people and press should be more interested in the polemical than in the platitudinous; in blame than in painting the lily; in attack than in sending laudatory coals to Newcastle." On the other hand, the instinct of pugnacity can be utilized to suppress and to oppress. From the point of view of the public relations counsel, who is interested from day to day in accomplishing definite results on specific issues, the dangers of the method are only the ordinary dangers of every weapon, physical or psychological, which has been devised.

It is interesting in this connection to note that a newspaper uses the same methods to encourage interest in itself as do others. The *New York Times* promoted public interest in heavier-than-air-machines by creating sporting issues of contests between aviators on altitude records, continuous stays in the air, distance flying and so forth.

Mr. Lippmann comments on this same characteristic:

"But where pugnacity is not enlisted, those of us who are not directly involved find it hard to keep up our interest. For those who are involved the absorption may be real enough to hold them even when no issue is involved. They may be exercised by sheer joy in activity or by subtle rivalry or invention. But for those to whom the whole problem is external and distant, these other faculties do not easily come into play. In order that the faint image of the affair shall mean something to them, they must be allowed to exercise the love of struggle, suspense, and victory."[29]

We have to take sides. We have to be able to take sides. In the recesses of our being we must step out of the audience onto the stage and wrestle as the hero for the victory of good over evil. We must breathe into the allegory the breath of our life.

Recently a philanthropic group was advised to hold a prize fight for charity. This recognition of the importance of the principle of pugnacity was correct. It is a question whether the application was not somewhat ill advised and in bad taste. The Consumer's Committee of Women opposed to American Valuation was avowedly aligned to fight against a section of the tariff presented by Chairman Fordney. The Lucy Stone League, a group who wish to make it easy for married women to maintain their maiden names, dramatized the fight that they are making against tradition by staging a debate at their annual banquet.

---

29 Walter Lippmann, "Public Opinion."

Very often the public relations counsel utilizes the self-display-elation motive and draws public attention to particular people in groups, in order to give them a greater interest in the work they are espousing. It is often found to be true that when a man's adherence or allegiance to a movement is lukewarm and he is publicly praised for his adherence to it, he will become a forceful factor in it. That is why the intelligent hospital boards name rooms or beds after their donors. It is one of the reasons for the elaborate letterheads so many of our philanthropic organizations have.

Self-abasement and subjection, its attendant emotion, are seldom called upon. On the other hand, parental love and tenderness are continually employed, viz., the effort of the baby-kissing candidate for public office or the attempt to popularize a brand of silk by having a child present a silk flag to a war veteran at a public ceremony. The whole flood of post-war charity-drives was keyed to this pitch. The starving Belgian orphan personified in every picture, the starving Armenian, and then the hungry Austrian and German orphans appeared, and the campaigns all succeeded on this issue. Even issues where the child was not the predominant factor used this appeal.

Four other instincts are listed in this classification—gregariousness, individualism, acquisition and construction. We have already dealt with the first at length.

The gregarious instinct in man gives the public relations counsel the opportunity for his most potent work. The group and herd show everywhere the leader, who because of certain qualifications, certain points that are judged by the herd to be important to its life, stands out and is followed more or less implicitly by it.

A group leader gains such power with his group or herd that even on matters which have had nothing to do with the establishment or gaining of that leadership he is considered a leader and is followed by his group.

It is this attribute of men and women that again gives the public relations counsel free play.

A group leader of any given cause will bring to a new cause all those who have looked to his leadership. For instance, if the adherence of a prominent Republican is secured for the League of Nations, his adherence will probably bring to the League of Nations many other prominent Republicans.

The group leadership with which the public relations counsel may work is limited only by the character of the groups he desires to reach. After an analysis of his problem the subdivisions must be made. His action depends upon his selective capacity, and the possibility of approach to the leaders. These leaders may represent therefore a wide variety of interests—society leaders or leaders of political groups, leaders of women or leaders of sportsmen, leaders of divisions by geography, or divisions by age, divisions by language or by education. These subdivisions are so numerous that there are large companies in the United States whose business it is to supply lists of groups and group leaders in different fields.

This same mechanism is carried out in many other cases. In looking for group leaders, the public relations counsel must realize that some leaders have more varied and more intensified authority than others. One leader may represent the ideals and ideas of several or numerous groups. His cooperation on one basis may bring into alignment and may carry with it the other groups who are interested in him primarily for other reasons.

The public relations counsel, let us say, enlists the support of a man, president of two associations; (a) an economic association, (b) a welfare association. The issue is an economic one, purely. But because of his leadership, the membership of association (b), that is, the welfare group, joins him in the movement as interestedly as association (a) does, which has the more logical, direct reason for entering the field.

I have given this in general terms rather than as a specific instance. The principle which governs the interlapping and continually shifting group formation of society also governs the gregariousness.

Individualism, another instinct, is a concomitant of gregariousness, and naturally follows it. The desire for individual expression is always a trait of the individuals who go to make up the group. The appeal to individualism goes closely in hand with other instincts, such as self-display.

The instincts of acquisition and construction are minor instincts as far as the ordinary work of the public relations counsel is concerned. Examples of this type of appeal come readily to mind in the "Own your own home" and "Build your own home" campaigns.

The innate tendencies are susceptibility to suggestion, imitation, habit and play. Susceptibility to suggestion and imitation might well be classified under gregariousness, which we have already discussed.

Under habit would come one very important human trait of which the public relations counsel avails himself continually. The mechanism which habit produces and which makes it possible for the public relations counsel to use habit is the stereotype we have already touched upon.

Mental habits create stereotypes just as physical habits create certain definite reflex actions. These stereotypes or reflex images are a great aid to the public relations counsel in his work.

These short-cuts to reactions make it possible for the average mind to possess a much larger number of impressions than would be possible without them. At the same time these stereotypes or *clichés* are not necessarily truthful pictures of what they are supposed to portray. They are determined by the outward stimuli to which the individual has been subject as well as by the content of his mind.

To most of us, for example, the stereotype of the general is a stern, upright gentleman in uniform and with gold braid, preferably on a horse. The stereotype of a farmer is a slouching, overall-clad man with straw sticking out of his mouth and a straw hat on his head. He is supposed to be very shrewd when it comes to matters of his own farm and very ignorant when it comes to matters of culture. He despises "city fellers." All this is the connotation brought up by the one word "farmer."

The public relations counsel sometimes uses the current stereotypes, sometimes combats them and sometimes creates new ones. In using them he very often brings to the public he is reaching a stereotype they already know, to which he adds his new ideas, thus he fortifies his own and gives a greater carrying power. For instance, the public relations counsel might well advise Austria, which in the public mind might still represent a belligerent country, to bring forward other Austrian stereotypes, namely the Danube waltz stereotype and the Danube blue stereotype. An appeal for help would then come from the country of the well-liked Danube waltz and Danube blue—the country of gayety and charm. The new idea would be carried to those who accepted the stereotypes they were familiar with.

The combating of the stereotype is seen in the battle waged against the American Valuation Plan by the public relations counsel. The formulators of the plan dubbed it "American Valuation" in order to capitalize on the stereotype of "American." In fighting the plan, its opponents put the word "American" in quotation marks whenever reference was made to the subject in order to question the authenticity of the use of this stereotype. Thus patriotism was definitely removed from what was evidently an economical and political issue.

The public relations counsel creates new stereotypes. Roosevelt, his own best adviser, was an apt creator of such stereotypes—"square deal, delighted, molly-coddle, big stick," created new concepts for general acceptance.

Stereotypes sometimes become shop-worn and lose their power with the public that has previously accepted them. "Hundred per cent American" died from over use.

Visible objects as stereotypes are often used by the public relations counsel with great effectiveness to produce the desired impression. A national flag on the orator's platform is a most common device, A scientist must of necessity be in juxtaposition with his instruments. A chemist is not a chemist to the public unless test tubes and retorts are near him, A doctor must have his kit, or, formerly, a Van Dyke beard. In photographs of food factory buildings white is a good stereotype for cleanliness and purity. In fact, all emblems and trade-marks are stereotypes.

There is one danger in the use of stereotypes by the public relations counsel. That is, by the substitution of words for acts, demagogues in every field of social relationship can take advantage of the public.

Play as an innate tendency is utilized by the public relations counsel whenever conditions merit such an appeal. When a charity committee is advised to institute a street fair to gather money, the committee is recognizing this tendency. When a city government arranges fireworks for its citizens, when a metropolitan news-daily stages marble contests or horseshoe pitching events, the play tendency of human society finds an outlet and the initiators of the event find friends.

3

An Outline Of Methods Practicable In Modifying The Point Of View Of A Group

On the question of specific devices upon which the public relations counsel relies to accomplish his ends, volumes could probably be written without exhausting the subject. The detailed presentation is potentially endless. Pages could be filled with instances of the stimuli to which men and women respond, the circumstances under which they will respond favorably or unfavorably, and the particular application of each of these stimuli to concrete conditions. Such an outline, however, would have less value than an outline of fundamentals, since circumstances are never the same.

These principles, by and large, consist of fundamentals already defined, to which the public relations counsel has recourse in common with the statesman, the journalist, the preacher, the lecturer and all others engaged in attempting to modify public opinion or public conduct.

How does the public relations counsel approach any particular problem? First he must analyze his client's problem and his client's objective. Then he must analyze the public he is trying to reach. He must devise a plan of action for the client to follow and determine the methods and the organs of distribution available for reaching his public. Finally he must try to estimate the interaction between the public he seeks to reach and his client. How will his client's case strike the public mind? And by public mind here is meant that section or those sections of the public which must be reached.

Let us take the example of a public relations counsel who is confronted with the specific problem of modifying or influencing the attitude of the public toward a given tariff bill. A tariff bill, of course, is primarily the application of theoretical economics to a concrete industrial situation. The public relations counsel in analyzing must see himself simultaneously as a member of a large number of publics. He must visualize himself as a manufacturer, a retailer, an importer, an employer, a worker, a financier, a politician.

Within these groups he must see himself again as a member of the various subdivisions of each of these groups. He must see himself, for example, as a member of a group of manufacturers who obtain the bulk of their raw material within the United States, and at the same time as a member of a group of manufacturers who obtain large portions of their raw material from abroad and whose importations of raw material may be adversely affected by the pending tariff bill. He must see himself not only as a farm laborer but also as a mechanic in a large industrial center. He must see himself as the owner of the department store and as a member of the buying public. He must be able to generalize, as far as possible, from these points of view in order to strike upon the appeal or group of appeals which will be influential with as many sections of society as possible.[30]

Let us assume that our problem is the intensification in the public mind of the prestige of a hotel. The problem for the public relations counsel is to create in the public mind the close relationship between the hotel and a number of ideas that represent the things the hotel desires to stand for in the public mind.

The counsel therefore advises the hotel to make a celebration of its thirtieth anniversary which happens to fall at this particular time and suggests to the president the organization of an anniversary committee of a body of business men who represent the cream of the city's merchants. This committee is to include men who represent a number of stereotypes that will help to produce the inevitable result in the public mind. There are to be also a leading banker, a society woman, a prominent lawyer, an influential preacher, and so forth until a cross section of the city's most telling activities is mirrored in the committee. The stereotype has its effect, and what may have been an indefinite impression beforehand has been reenforced and concretized. The hotel remains preeminent in the public mind. The stereotypes have proved its preeminence. The cause has been strongly presented to the public by identification with different group stereotypes.

---

30 Mr. Given's definition of the qualifications of a good reporter applies very largely to the qualifications of a good public relations counsel. "There is undoubtedly a good deal of truth," says Mr. Given, "in the saying that good reporters are born and not made. A man may learn how to gather some kinds of news, and he may learn how to write it correctly, but if he cannot see the picturesque or vital point of an incident and express what he sees so that others will see as through his eyes, his productions, even if no particular fault can be found with them, will not bear the mark of true excellence; and there is, if one stops to think, a great difference between something that is devoid of faults and something that is full of good points. The quality which makes a good newspaper man must, in the opinion of many editors, exist in the beginning. But when it does exist, it can usually be developed, no matter how many obstacles are in the way."

Here is another example. A packing company desires to establish in the public mind the fact that the name of its product is synonymous with bacon. Its public relations counsel advises a contest on "Bring home the Beech-Nut," the contest to be open to salesmen and to be based on the best sale made by salesmen throughout the country during the month of August. But here again it is necessary to use a stereotype to help the possible contestant identify the cause. A committee of nationally known sales-managers is chosen to act as judges for the contest and immediately success is assured. Thousands of salesmen compete for the prize. The stereotype has bespoken the value of the contest.

The public relations counsel can try to bring about this identification by utilizing the appeals to desires and instincts discussed in the preceding chapter, and by making use of the characteristics of the group formation of society. His utilization of these basic principles will be a continual and efficient aid to him.

He must make it easy for the public to pick his issue out of the great mass of material. He must be able to overcome what has been called "the tendency on the part of public attention to 'flicker' and 'relax.'" He must do for the public mind what the newspaper, with its headlines, accomplishes for its readers.

Abstract discussions and heavy facts are the groundwork of his involved theory, or analysis, but they cannot be given to the public until they are simplified and dramatized. The refinements of reason and the shadings of emotion cannot reach a considerable public.

When an appeal to the instincts can be made so powerful as to secure acceptance in the medium of dissemination in spite of competitive interests, it can be aptly termed news.

The public relations counsel, therefore, is a creator of news for whatever medium he chooses to transmit his ideas. It is his duty to create news no matter what the medium which broadcasts this news. It is news interest which gives him an opportunity to make his idea travel and get the favorable reaction from the instincts to which he happens to appeal. News in itself we shall define later on when we discuss "relations with the press." But the word news is sufficiently understood for me to talk of it here.

In order to appeal to the instincts and fundamental emotions of the public, discussed in previous chapters, the public relations counsel must create news around his ideas. News will, by its superior inherent interest, receive attention in the competitive markets for news, which are themselves continually trying to claim the public attention. The public relations counsel must lift startling facts from his whole subject and present them as news. He must isolate ideas and develop them into events so that they can be more readily understood and so that they may claim attention as news.

The headline and the cartoon bear the same relation to the newspaper that the public relations counsel's analysis of a problem bears to the problem itself.

The headline is a compact, vivid simplification of complicated issues. The cartoon provides a visual image which takes the place of abstract thought. So, too, the analyses the public relations counsel makes, lift out the important, the interesting, and the easily understandable points in order to create interest.

"Yet human qualities are themselves," says Mr. Lippmann,[31] "vague and fluctuating. They are best remembered by a physical sign. And therefore the human qualities we tend to ascribe to the names of our impressions, themselves tend to be visualized in physical metaphors. The people of England, the history of England, condense into England, and England becomes John Bull, who is jovial and fat, not too clever, but well able to take care of himself. The migration of a people may appear to some as a meandering of a river, and to others like a devastating flood. The courage people display may be objectified

---

31 "Public Opinion" (page 160).

as a rock, their purpose as a road, their doubts as forks of the road, their difficulties as ruts and rocks, their progress as a fertile valley. If they mobilize their dreadnaughts they unsheath a sword. If their army surrenders they are thrown to earth. If they are oppressed they are on the rack or under the harrow."

Perhaps the chief contribution of the public relations counsel to the public and to his client is his ability to understand and analyze obscure tendencies of the public mind. It is true that he first analyzes his client's problem—he then analyzes the public mind; he utilizes the mediums of communication between the two, but before he does this he must use his personal experience and knowledge to bring two factors into alignment. It is his capacity for crystallizing the obscure tendencies of the public mind before they have reached definite expression, which makes him so valuable.

His ability to create those symbols to which the public is ready to respond; his ability to know and to analyze those reactions which the public is ready to give; his ability to find those stereotypes, individual and community, which will bring favorable responses; his ability to speak in the language of his audience and to receive from it a favorable reception are his contributions.

The appeal to the instincts and the universal desires is the basic method through which he produces his results.

Part IV
Ethical Relations

1

A Consideration Of The Press And Other Mediums Of Communication In Their Relation To The Public Relations Counsel

When the question of preparing and publishing this volume was first considered, the publishers wrote letters to several hundred prominent men asking their opinions, individually, as to the probable public interest in a work dealing with public relations. Newspaper editors and publishers, heads of large industries and public service corporations, philanthropists, university presidents and heads of schools of journalism, as well as other prominent men made up the number. Their replies are exceedingly interesting in as much as they show, almost uniformly, the increasing emphasis placed upon public relations by leaders in every important phase of American life. These replies show also a growing understanding of the need for specialized service in this field of specialized problems.

Particularly interesting were the comments of newspaper publishers and editors in response to Mr. Liveright's inquiry, for nothing could better indicate the light in which the public relations counsel is held by those very individuals who are supposed popularly to disparage his value in the social and economic scheme of things.

What are the relations of the public relations counsel to the various mediums he can employ to carry his message to the public? There is, of course, first and perhaps most important, the press. There is the moving picture; the lecture platform; there is advertising; there is the direct-by-mail effort; there is the stage—drama and music; there is word of mouth; there is the pulpit, the schoolroom, the legislative chamber—to all of these the public relations counsel has distinct relationship.

The journalist of to-day, while still watching the machinations of the so-called "press agent" with one half-amused eye, appreciates the value of the service the public relations counsel is able to give him.

To the newspaper the public relations counsel serves as a purveyor of news.

As disseminator of news the newspaper holds an important position in American life. This has not always been the case, for the emphasis upon the news side is a development of recent years. Originally, the name newspaper was scarcely an accurate or appropriate designation for the units of the American press. So-called newspapers were, in fact, vehicles for the expression of opinion of their editors. They contained little or no news, as that word is understood to-day—largely because difficulties of communication made it impossible to obtain any but the most local items of interest. The public was accustomed to look to its press for the opinion of its favorite editor upon subjects of current interest rather than for the recital of mere facts.

To-day, on the other hand, the expression of editorial opinion is only secondarily the function of a newspaper; and thousands of persons read newspapers with whose editorial policy they do not in the slightest agree. Such a situation would have been nearly impossible in the days of Horace Greeley.

The need which the American press is to-day engaged in satisfying is the need for news. "A paper," says Mr. Given,[32] "may succeed without printing editorials worth reading and without having any aim other than the making of money, but it cannot possibly thrive unless it gets the news and prints it in a pleasing and attractive form."

Writing from a long experience with the profession of journalism. Will Irwin reaches the conclusion that[33] "news is the main thing, the vital consideration of the American newspaper; it is both an intellectual craving and a commercial need to the modern world. In popular psychology it has come to be a crying primal want of the mind, like hunger of the body. Tramp wind-jammers, taking on the pilot after a long cruise, ask for the papers before they ask, as formerly, for fresh fruit and vegetables. Whenever, in our later Western advance, we Americans set up a new mining camp, an editor, his type slung on burro-back, comes in with the missionaries, evangel himself of civilization. Most dramatically the San Francisco disaster illuminated this point. On the morning of April 20, 1906, the city's population huddled in parks and squares, their houses gone, death of famine or thirst a rumor and a possibility. The editors of the three morning newspapers, expressing the true soldier spirit which inspires this most devoted profession, had moved their staffs to the suburb of Oakland, and there, on the presses of the *Tribune*, they had issued a combined *Call-Chronicle-Examiner*. When, at dawn, the paper was printed, an editor and a reporter loaded the edition into an automobile and drove it through the parks of the disordered city, giving copies away. They were fairly mobbed, they had to drive at top speed, casting out the sheets as they went, to make any progress at all. No bread wagon, no supply of blankets, caused half so much stir as did the arrival of the news.

"We need it, we crave it; this nerve of the modern world transmits thought and impulse from the brain of humanity to its mus-

---

32 Given, "Making a Newspaper."
33 "What Is News?" by Will Irwin, *Collier's*, March 18, 1911 (page 16).

cles; the complex organism of modern society could no more move without it than a man could move without filaments and ganglia. On the commercial and practical side, the man of even small affairs must read news in the newspapers every day to keep informed on the thousand and one activities in the social structure which affect his business. On the intellectual and spiritual side, it is—save for the Church alone—our principal outlook on the higher intelligence. The thought of legislature, university, study, and pulpit comes to the common man first—and usually last—in the form of news. The tedious business of teaching reading in public schools has become chiefly a training to consume newspapers. We must go far up in the scale of culture before we find an intellectual equipment more a debtor to the formal education of school and college than to the haphazard education of news."

The extent to which the editorial aspect of the newspaper has given way to an increased importance of the news columns is vividly illustrated in the anecdote about the *Philadelphia North American*, which Mr. Irwin relates. "The *North American*," says Mr. Irwin, "had declared for local option. A committee of brewers waited on the editor; they represented one of the biggest groups in their business. 'This is an ultimatum,' they said. 'You must change your policy or lose our advertising. We'll be easy on you. We don't ask you to alter your editorial policy, *but you must stop printing news of local-option victories,*'[34] So the deepest and shrewdest enemies of the body politic give practical testimony to the 'power of the press' in its modern form."

In the case of the brewers of Philadelphia it is my own opinion that if they had been well advised, instead of attempting to interfere with the policy of the *North American*, they would have made it a point to bring to the attention of the *North American* every instance of the defeat of local option. The newspaper would undoubtedly have published both sides of the story, as far as both sides consisted of news.

---

34 Italics mine.

It is because he acts as the purveyor of truthful, accurate and verifiable news to the press that the conscientious and successful counsel on public relations is looked upon with favor by the journalist. And in the Code of Ethics recently adopted in Washington by a national editors' conference, his function is given acknowledgment. Just as in the case of the other mediums for the dissemination of information, mediums which range from the lecture platform to the radio, the press, too, looks to the public relations counsel for information about the causes he represents.

Since news is the newspaper's backbone, it is obvious that an understanding of what news actually is must be an integral part of the equipment of the public relations counsel. For the public relations counsel must not only supply news—he must create news. This function as the creator of news is even more important than his others.

It has always been interesting to me that a concise, comprehensive definition of news has never been written. What news is, every newspaper man instinctively knows, particularly as it concerns the needs of his own paper. But it is almost as difficult to define news as it is to describe a circular staircase without making corkscrew gestures with one's hand, or as to define some of the abstruse concepts of the metaphysician, like space or time or reality.

What is news for one newspaper may have no interest whatever, or very little interest, for another newspaper. There are almost as many definitions of news as there are journalists who take the trouble to define it. Certain of the characteristics of news, of course, can be readily seized upon; and definitions of news generally consist of particular emphasis upon one or another of these characteristics. Mr. Given remarks that[35] "news was once defined as 'Fresh information of something that has lately taken place'...." The author of this definition puts the chief emphasis upon the element of timeliness. Undoubtedly

---

35 "Making a Newspaper" (page 168).

in most news that element must be present. It would not be true, however, to say that it must always be present, nor would it be true to say that everything which is timely is news. Obviously, the well-nigh infinite number of occurrences which take place in daily life throughout the world are timely enough, so far as each of them in its respective environment is concerned; but few of them ever become news.

Mr. Irwin defines news as "a departure from the established order." Thus, according to Mr. Irwin, a criminal act is news because it is a departure from the established order, and at the same time, an exceptional display of fidelity, courage or honesty is also news for the same reason.

"With our education in established order, we get the knowledge," he says,[36] "that mankind in bulk obeys its ideals of that order only imperfectly. When something brings to our attention an exceptional adhesion to religion, virtue, and truth, that becomes in itself a departure from regularity, and therefore news. The knowledge that most servants do their work conscientiously and many stay long in the same employ is not news. But when a committee of housewives presents a medal to a servant who has worked faithfully in one employ for fifty years, that becomes news, because it calls our attention to a case of exceptional fidelity to the ideals of established order. The fact that mankind will consume an undue amount of news about crime and disorder is only a proof that the average human being is optimistic, that he believes the world to be true, sound and working upward. Crimes and scandals interest him most because they most disturb his picture of the established order.

"That, then, is the basis of news. The mysterious news sense which is necessary to all good reporters rests on no other foundation than acquired or instinctive perception of this principle, together with a feeling for what the greatest number of people will regard as a depar-

---

36 "What is News?" Will Irwin, *Collier's*, March 18, 1911 (page 16).

ture from the established order. In Jesse Lynch William's newspaper play, 'The Stolen Story,' occurs this passage:

> "(*Enter Very Young Reporter; comes down to city desk with air of excitement.*)
>
> "Very Young Reporter (*considerably impressed*): 'Big story. Three dagoes killed by that boiler explosion!'
>
> "The City Editor (*reading copy. Doesn't look up*): 'Ten lines.' (*Continues reading copy.*)
>
> "Very Young Reporter (*looks surprised and hurt. Crosses over to reporters table. Then turns back to city desk. Casual conversational tone*): 'By the way. Funny thing. There was a baby carriage within fifty feet of the explosion, but it wasn't upset.'
>
> "The City Editor (*looks up with professional interest*): 'That's worth a dozen dead dagoes. Write a half column.'
>
> "(*Very Young Reporter looks still more surprised, perplexed. Suddenly the idea dawns upon him. He crosses over to table, sits down, writes.*)

"Both saw news; but the editor went further than the reporter. For cases of Italians killed by a boiler explosion are so common as to approach the commonplace; but a freak of explosive chemistry which annihilates a strong man and does not disturb a baby departs from it widely."

Here again it is dear that Mr. Irwin merely emphasized one of the features generally to be found in what we call news, without, however, offering us a complete or exclusive definition of news.

Analyzing further within his general rule that news is a departure from the established order, Mr. Irwin goes on to point out certain outstanding factors which enhance or create news value. I cite them here because all of them are unquestionably sound. On the other hand, analysis shows that some of them are directly contradictory to his main principle that only the departure from the established order is news. In Mr. Irwin's opinion, the four outstanding factors making for the creation or enhancement of news value are the following:[37]

1. *"We prefer to read about the things we like."* The result, he says, has been the rule: "Power for the men, affections for the women."
2. *"Our interest in news increases in direct ratio to our familiarity with its subject, its setting, and its dramatis personae."*
3. *"Our interest in news is in direct ratio to its effect on our personal concerns."*
4. *"Our interest in news increases in direct ratio to the general importance of the persons or activities which it affects."* This is so obvious that it scarcely needs comment.

Some notion of the diversity of news arising in a city may be obtained if one studies the points which are watched as news sources, either continuously or closely by metropolitan dailies. Mr. Given[38] lists the places in New York which are watched constantly:

"Police Headquarters.
Police Courts.
Coroner's Office.
Supreme Courts, New York County.
New York Stock Exchange.
City Hall, including the Mayor's Office, Aldermanic Chamber, City Clerk's Office, and Office of the President of Manhattan Borough.
County Clerk's office."

---
37 "What is News?" by Will Irwin, *Collier's*, March 18, 1911 (pages 17–18). Italics mine.
38 "Making a Newspaper." by Given (pages 59–62).

Those places, says Mr. Given, which the newspapers watch carefully, but not continually, are:

"City Courts (Minor civil cases).
Court of General Sessions (Criminal cases).
Court of Special Sessions (Minor criminal cases.)
District Attorney's Office.
Doors of Grand Jury rooms when the Grand Jury is in session (For indictments and presentments).
Federal Courts.
Post Office.
United States Commissioner's Offices, and Offices of the United States Secret Service officers.
United States Marshal's Office.
United States District Attorney's Office.
Ship News, where incoming and outgoing vessels are reported.
Barge Office, where immigrants land.
Surrogate's Office, where wills are filed and testimony concerning wills in litigation is heard.
Political Headquarters during campaigns."

Finally, "the following are visited by the reporters several times, or only once a day:

"Police Stations.
Municipal Courts.
Board of Health Headquarters.
Fire Department Headquarters.
Park Department Headquarters.
Building Department Headquarters.
Tombs Prison.
County Jail.

United States Sub-treasury.
Office of Collector of the Port.
United States Appraiser's Office.
Public Hospitals.
Leading Hotels.
The Morgue.
County Sheriff's Office.
City Comptroller's Office.
City Treasurer's Office.
Offices of the Tax Collector and Tax Assessors."

Mr. Given's example of the broker, John Smith, illustrates aptly the point I am making. "For ten years," said Mr. Given,[39] "he pursues the even tenor of his way and except for his customers and his friends no one gives him a thought. To the newspapers he is as if he were not. But in the eleventh year he suffers heavy losses and, at last, his resources all gone, summons his lawyer and arranges for the making of an assignment. The lawyer posts off to the County Clerk's office, and a clerk there makes the necessary entries in the office docket. Here in step the newspapers. While the clerk is writing Smith's business obituary, a reporter glances over his shoulder, and a few minutes later the newspapers know Smith's troubles and are as well informed concerning his business status as they would be had they kept a reporter at his door every day for over ten years. Had Smith dropped dead instead of merely making an assignment his name would have reached the newspapers by way of the Coroner's office instead of the County Clerk's office, and in fact, while Smith did not know it, the newspapers were prepared and ready for him no matter what he did. They even had representatives waiting for him at the Morgue. He was safe only when he walked the straight and narrow path and kept quiet."

---

39 Given, "Making a Newspaper" (page 57).

An overt act is often necessary before an event can be regarded as news.

Commenting on this aspect of the situation, Mr. Lippmann discusses this very example of the broker, John Smith, and his hypothetical bankruptcy. "That overt act," says Mr. Lippmann,[40] "'uncovers' the news about Smith. Whether the news will be followed up or not is another matter. The point is that before a series of events become news they have usually to make themselves noticeable in some more or less overt act. Generally, too, in a crudely overt act. Smith's friends may have known for years that he was taking risks, rumors may even have reached the financial editor if Smith's friends were talkative. But apart from the fact that none of this could be published because it would be libel, there is in these rumors nothing definite on which to peg a story. Something definite must occur that has unmistakable form. It may be the act of going into bankruptcy, it may be a fire, a collision, an assault, a riot, an arrest, a denunciation, the introduction of a bill, a speech, a vote, a meeting, the expressed opinion of a well-known citizen, an editorial in a newspaper, a sale, a wage-schedule, a price change, the proposal to build a bridge.... There must be a manifestation. The course of events must assume a certain definable shape, and until it is in a phase where some aspect is an accomplished fact, news does not separate itself from the ocean of possible truth."

From the point of view of the practical journalist, Mr. Irwin has applied this observation to the making of the news of the day. He says:[41] "I state a platitude when I say that government by the people is the essence of democracy. In theory, the people watch and know; when, in the process of social and industrial evolution, they see a new evil becoming important, they found institutions to regulate it or laws to repress it. They cannot watch without light, know without teachers. The newspaper, or some force like it, must daily inform them of things

---

40 "Public Opinion" (pages 339–340).
41 "All the News That's Fit to Print," Comer's, May 6, 1911 (page 18).

which are shocking and unpleasant in order that democracy, in its slow, wobbling motion upward, may perceive and correct. It is good for us to know that John Smith, made crazy by drink, came home and killed his wife. Startled and shocked, but interested, we may follow the case of John Smith, see that justice in his case is not delayed by his pull with Tammany. Perhaps, when there are enough cases of John Smith, we shall look into the first causes and restrain the groggeries that made him momentarily mad or the industrial oppression that made him permanently an undernourished, overnerved defective. It is good to know that John Jones, a clerk, forged a check and went to jail. For not only shall we watch justice in his case, but some day we shall watch also the fraudulent race-track gambling that tempted him to theft. If every day we read of those crimes which grow from the misery of New York's East Side and Chicago's Levee, some day democracy may get at the ultimate causes for overwork, underfeeding, tenement crowding.

"No other method is so forcible with the public as driving home the instance which points the moral. General description of bad conditions fails, somehow, to impress the average mind. One might have shouted to Shreveport day after day that low dives make dangerous negroes, and created no sentiment against saloons. But when a negro, drunk on bad gin which he got at such a dive, assaulted and killed Margaret Lear, a schoolgirl, Shreveport voted out the saloon."

For the great mass of activities there is no machinery of record whatever. How these are to be recorded when they are important is the real problem for the press.

In this field the public relations counsel plays a considerable part. His is the business of calling to the public attention, through the press and through every other available medium, the point of view, the movement or the issue which he represents. Mr. Lippmann has observed that it is for this reason that what he calls the "press agent" has become an important factor in modern life.

Mr. Lippmann's observation on this point deserves comment. He says:[42] "This is the underlying reason for the existence of the press agent. The enormous discretion as to what facts and what impressions shall be reported is steadily convincing every organized group of people that whether it wishes to secure publicity or to avoid it, the exercise of discretion cannot be left to the reporter. It is safer to hire a press-agent who stands between the group and the newspapers."

The really important function of the public relations counsel, in relation to the press as well as to his client, lies even beyond these considerations. He is not merely the purveyor of news; he is more logically the *creator* of news.

An amateur can bring a good story to the average newspaper office and receive consideration, although the amateur is only too likely to miss precisely those features of his story which give it news value, and to overlook precisely that element of the story which will make it interesting to the particular newspaper he is approaching.

The New York hotel proprietors were enforcing the prohibition law in relation to their own establishments, but saw that certain restaurants were violating the law with impunity. Realizing the injustice to them of this situation, they built a definite news event by going over the heads of the local law enforcement offices and wired an appeal direct to President Harding, asking for enforcement. This naturally became news of the first order.

The opening of a shop by prominent women in which were shown graphic examples of the effect of the tariff on women's wear was an event created to intensify interest in this subject.

The launching of battleships with ceremony; the laying of corner stones; the presentation of memorials; demonstration meetings, parties and banquets are all events created with a view to their carrying capacity in the various mediums that reach the public.

---

42 "Public Opinion" (page 344).

The departments of a modern newspaper will show the great variety of possible approaches on any subject from the standpoint of the press. When this is correlated to the possible approaches on any subject from the standpoint of human psychology, we see the diversification of methods to which the public relations counsel can have recourse to construct events.

In the metropolitan press, for instance, there are the news departments, the editorial departments, the letter-to-the-editor department, the women's department, the society department, the current events department, the sport department, the real estate department, the business department, the financial department, the shipping department, the investment department, the educational department, the photographic department and the other special feature writers and sections, different in different journals.

In a valuable study on the "Newspaper Reading Habits of Business Executives and Professional Men in New York" compiled by Professor George Burton Hotchkiss, Head of the Department of Advertising and Marketing, and Richard B. Franken, Lecturer in Advertising at New York University, there are several tables setting forth the features of morning and evening newspapers preferred as a whole by the group to whom the questionnaires were sent, and by various smaller groups within the main group.

The counsel on public relations not only knows what news value is, but knowing it, he is in a position to *make news happen*. He is a creator of events.

An organization held a banquet for a building fund to which the invitations were despatched on large bricks. The news element in this story was the fact that bricks were despatched.

In this capacity, as purveyor and creator of news for the press as well as for all other mediums of idea dissemination, it must be clear immediately that the public relations counsel could not possibly succeed unless he complied with the highest moral and technical requirements of those with whom he is working.

Writing on the profession of the public relations counsel, the author of an article in the *New York Times*[43] says "newspaper editors are the most suspicious and cynical of mortals, but they are as quick to discern the truth as to detect the falsehood." He goes on to discuss the particular public relations counsel whom he has in mind and whom he designates by the fictitious name Swift, and remarks that: "Irrespective of their position on ethics, Swift & Co. won't deal in spurious goods. They know that one such error would be fatal. The public might forget, but the editor never. Besides, they don't have to."

Truthful and accurate must be the material which the public relations counsel furnishes to the press and other mediums. In addition, it must have the elements of timeliness and interest which are required of all news—and it must not only have these elements in general, but it must suit the particular needs of each particular newspaper and, even more than that, it must suit the needs of the particular editor in whose department it is hoped that it will be published.

Finally, the literary quality of the material must be up to the best standards of the profession of journalism. The writing must be good, in the particular sense in which each newspaper considers a story well written.

In brief, the material must come to the editorial desk as carefully prepared and as accurately verified as if the editor himself had assigned a special reporter to secure and write the facts. Only by presenting his news in such form and in such a manner can the counsel on public relations hope to retain, in the case of the newspaper, the most valuable thing he possesses—the editor's faith and trust. But it must be clearly borne in mind that only in certain cases is the public relations counsel the intermediary between the news and the press. The event he has counseled upon, the action he has created finds its own level of expression in mediums which reach the public.

---

43 *Times Book Review and Magazine,* January 1, 1922. "Men Who Wield the Spotlight," by Charles J. Rosebault.

The radio stations offer an avenue of approach to the public. They are controlled by private organizations, large electrical supply companies, department stores, newspapers, telegraph companies and in some cases by the government. Their programs broadcast information and entertainment to those within their radius. These programs vary in different localities.

To the public relations counsel there is a wide opportunity to utilize the means of distribution the radio program affords. In partisan matters, the controllers of the radio insist upon the presentation of all points of view in order to have the onus of propaganda removed from their shoulders. The public relations counsel is therefore in a position to suggest to the broadcasting managers a symposium treatment of the subject in which he happens to be interested. Or in the case of information, which has not this partisan character, he is in a position to assure treatment of his subject by embodying his thesis in the form of a speech delivered by some individual of standing and reputation.

In the case of events which the public relations counsel may be instrumental in creating, such as large public meetings, the radio today becomes a natural form of distribution, just as news treatment in a newspaper does, and the broadcasting to thousands and thousands of people of the speeches becomes a corollary of the event itself. The broadcasting of Lord Robert Cecil's speech on the League of Nations, delivered at a banquet in New York, is a case in point.

Many magazines, for instance, are availing themselves of the radio stations to supply speeches on the particular topics they are most interested in. So the housekeeping magazines supply the radio stations with information about that phase of women's activities. The fashion magazines do likewise in their fields. And they thereby heighten their own prestige and authority in the minds of their hearers.

The use of the wireless telegraph in war time was an important factor in broadcasting information of war aims and war accomplishments to enemy countries. It was used successfully by both Allied and

Central powers. It was utilized even by the Soviet Government in the announcement of its communications. This form of propagation differs slightly from the radio, referred to previously, since it depends for its efficacy not upon reaching great numbers of hearers, but upon reaching newspapers and other mediums that give currency to the material broadcasted. The wireless telegraph of course was and is a valuable asset to the public relations counsel.

The lecture platform is another well-established means of idea communication.

The spoken word has to a certain extent lost its efficacy when the lecture platform alone is considered.

The appeal of the lecture platform is limited by the actual number of those who hear the message. It is possible to reach vaster numbers through the printed word or the motion picture or even the radioed word. Both the weakness of the human voice and the physical characteristics of the place of assemblage bring about this limitation.

The lecture platform, however, still retains its importance for the public relations counsel because it affords him the opportunity to speak before group audiences which in themselves have a news value, or because it presents the opportunity to stage dramatic events that bring intensification of interest and action on the part of larger audiences than those actually addressed.

The lecture field open to the public relations counsel for the propagation of information or ideas may be divided into several classifications. First there are the lecture managers and bureaus, which act as agents in booking lecturers to different kinds of group audiences throughout the country. The public relations counsel can, for instance, suggest to his client to secure a prominent person, who because of interest in a cause will be glad to undertake a lecture tour. Then a bureau may manage the tour. The tours of important proponents on such issues as the League of Nations fall in this class as well as the tours of prominent authors, arranged by publishers in their behalf.

Then there is the lecture tour managed by the client himself and arranged through the booking of engagements with such local groups as might be interested in assuming sponsorship for what is said. A soap company might engage a lecturer on cleanliness to speak in the schools of leading communities. Or a woolen firm arrange for a home economics authority to lecture to women's clubs on dress. These speeches of course, locally, gain a wider audience than the speaker would who addressed a single meeting because they give opportunity for treatment in newspapers, advertising, circularizing, and other mediums.

The lecture field offers another means of communication in as much as it gives the public relations counsel a range of group leaders to whom he can furnish the facts and ideas he is trying to propagate. The lecturers of Boards of Education in cities throughout the country, the lecturers before schools and other institutions of learning, the lecturers of one sort or another who address varied audiences can be reached directly and can become the carriers of the information the public relations counsel desires to give forth.

The meeting or public demonstration, at which prominent speakers voice their views upon the particular problem or problems at issue, would fall quite naturally under this same classification. Its main purpose, of course, is not so much to reach the audience being addressed as to make a focal point of interest for those thousands and millions who do not attend, but who get the reverberations of the speaker's voice through other mediums than their own auditory sensation.

Advertising is a medium open to the public relations counsel. In the sense in which the word is used here, the term applies to every form of paid space available for the carrying of a message. From the newspaper advertisement to the billboard, its forms are so varied that it has developed its own literature and its own principles and practice. In considering his objectives and the mediums through which his potential public can be reached the public relations counsel always considers advertising space as among his most important adjuncts. The wise public relations counsel calls into conference on the particular kinds of advertising to be used in a given problem the advertising agent who has made this study his lifework. The public relations counsel and the advertising agent then work out the problem in their respective fields.

Advertising up to the present time has laid its greatest stress upon the creation of demands and markets for specific goods. It is also applied with effectiveness to the propagation of ideas as well. It is peculiarly effective when used in combination with other methods of appeal.

Advertising controls the amount of physical space it occupies before the public eye. Advertising's dimensional qualities give it a facile flexibility that can be extended or limited at will. In a sense, too, this quality gives the special leader the opportunity to select his audience and to give them his message directly.

The field of cooperative advertising by combinations of advertisers in the same business or profession, by governments or their subdivisions, for one reason or another, is open to future possibilities.

The stage offers an avenue of approach to the public which must be regarded both from the standpoint of the numbers of individuals it reaches as well as from the circles of influence it creates by word of mouth and otherwise. To the public relations counsel therefore it offers a wide field.

Through cooperation with playwrights or managers, ideas can be given currency on the stage. When they can be translated to the action that takes place upon a stage, they are given emphasis by the visual and auditory presentation.

The motion picture falls into two fields for the purposes of the public relations counsel. There is the field of the feature film. Here any direct utilization of the public relations counsel's ideas must come indirectly and be taken by the producer of the film from some of the other organs of thought communication. The producer may adopt for the subject of a film some idea which the public relations counsel has agitated. The film, for instance, dealing with the drug traffic came very definitely as a result of the work carried on to help relieve the drug evil.

The second field is one the public relations counsel can employ more directly. Educational films are made to order to-day to illustrate specific points for public consumption, from showing how a product is made to showing the necessity for subway relief in a big city. These films are usually shown before a special group audience arranged for by the public relations counsel or before some other group interested in the idea the particular film stands for. Thus a Chamber of Commerce can further a film having to do with the need for better port facilities.

One phase of this kind of film is the news reel which, controlled by a private organization, films events and occasions which may have been created by the public relations counsel, but which carries because of its value in the competitive market of events.

Word of mouth is an important medium to be considered. Ideas and facts can be given currency by word of mouth. Here group leaders are strong factors in giving currency to ideas. The public relations counsel often communicates the ideas he wishes to promulgate to group leaders whose espousal of the idea he wishes to obtain.

The direct-by-mail campaign and the printed word afford the public relations counsel channels of approach to such individuals as he may desire to reach. Large companies have available for such purposes lists of individuals arranged according to innumerable criteria. There are geographical divisions, professional divisions, business divisions, and divisions of religion. There are classifications by economic position, classifications by all manner of preferences. This classification of his public into the right groups for the proper appeals is one of the most important functions of the public relations counsel, as we have pointed out. The direct-by-mail method of approach offers wide opportunities for capitalizing his training and experience along these lines. Telegraphic and wireless communications would of course come under this heading.

2

His Obligations To The Public As A Special Pleader

It has been the history of new professions—and every profession has been at some time a new profession—that they are accepted by the public and become firmly established only after two significant handicaps are overcome. The first of these, oddly enough, lies in public opinion itself; it consists of the public's reluctance to acknowledge a dependence, however slight, upon the ministrations of any one group of persons. Medicine, even to-day, is still fighting this reluctance. The law is fighting it. Yet these are established professions.

The second handicap is that any new profession must become established, not through the efforts and activities of others, who might be considered impartial, but through its own energy.

These handicaps are particularly potent in a profession of advocacy, because it is engaged in the partisan representation of one point of view. The legal profession is perhaps the most familiar example of this fact, and in this light at least a trenchant comparison may be drawn between the bar and the new profession of the public relations counsel.

Both these professions offer to the public substantially the same services—expert training, a highly sensitized understanding of the background from which results must be obtained, a keenly developed capacity for the analysis of problems into their constituent elements. Both professions are in constant danger of arousing crowd antagonism, because they often stand in frank and open opposition to the fixed point of view of one or another of the many groups which compose society. Indeed it is this aspect of the work of the public relations counsel which is undoubtedly the foundation of a good deal of popular disapproval of his profession.

Even Mr. Martin, who on several occasions in his volume talks with severe condemnation of what he calls propaganda, sees and admits the fundamental psychological factors which make the adherents to one point of view impute degraded or immoral motives to believers in other points of view. He says:[44]

"The crowd-man can, when his fiction is challenged, save himself from spiritual bankruptcy, preserve his defenses, keep his crowd from going to pieces, only by a demur. Any one who challenges the crowd's fictions must be ruled out of court. He must not be permitted to speak. As a witness to contrary values, his testimony must be discounted. The worth of his evidence must be discredited by belittling the disturbing witness. 'He is a bad man; the crowd must not listen to him.' His motives must be evil; he is 'bought up'; he is an immoral character; he tells lies; he is insincere or he 'has not the courage to take a stand' or 'there is nothing new in what he says.'

"Ibsen's 'Enemy of the People,' illustrates this point very well. The crowd votes that Doctor Stockman may not speak about the baths, the real point at issue. Indeed, the mayor takes the floor and officially announces that the doctor's statement that the water is bad is 'unreliable and exaggerated.' Then the president of the Householders' Association makes an address accusing the doctor of secretly 'aiming at revolution.' When finally Doctor Stockman speaks and tells his fellow citizens the real meaning of their conduct, and utters a few plain truths about 'the compact majority,' the crowd saves its face, not by proving the doctor false, but by howling him down, voting him an 'enemy of the people,' and throwing stones through the window."

---

44 "The Behavior of Crowds" (pages 128–129).

If we analyze a specific example of the public relations counsel's work, we see the workings of the crowd mind, which have made it so difficult for his profession to gain popular approval. Let us take, for example, the tariff situation again. It is manifestly impossible for either side in the dispute to obtain a totally unbiased point of view as to the other side. The importer calls the manufacturer unreasonable; he imputes selfish motives to him. For his own part he identifies the establishment of the conditions upon which he insists with such things as social welfare, national safety, Americanism, lower prices to the consumer, and whatever other fundamentals he can seize upon. Every newspaper report carrying the flavor of adverse suggestion, whether on account of its facts or on account of the manner of its writing, is immediately branded as untrue, unfortunate, ill-advised. It must, the importer concludes, it must have been inspired by insidious machinations from the manufacturers' interests.

But is the manufacturer any more reasonable? If the newspapers publish stories unfavorable to his interests, then the newspapers have been "bought up," "influenced"; they are "partisan" and many other unreasonable things. The manufacturer, just like the importer, identifies his side of the struggle with such fundamental standards as he can seize upon—a living wage, reduced prices to the consumer, the American standard of employment, fair play, justice. To each the contentions of the other are untenable.

Now, carry this situation one step further to the point at which the public relations counsel is retained, on behalf of one side or the other. Observe how sincerely each side and its adherents call even the verifiable facts and figures of the other by that dread name "propaganda." Should the importers submit figures showing that wages could be raised and the price to the consumer reduced, their adherents would be gratified that such important educational work should be done among the public and that the newspapers should be so fair-minded as to publish it. The manufacturers, on the other hand, will call such material "propaganda" and blame either the news-paper which publishes those figures or the economist who compiled them, or the public relations counsel who advised collating the material.

The only difference between "propaganda" and "education," really, is in the point of view. The advocacy of what we believe in is education. The advocacy of what we don't believe in is propaganda. Each of these nouns carries with it social and moral implications. Education is valuable, commendable, enlightening, instructive. Propaganda is insidious, dishonest, underhand, misleading. It is only to-day that the viewpoint on this question is undergoing a slight change, as the following editorial would indicate:

"The relativity of truth,"[45] says Mr. Elmer Davis, "is a commonplace to any newspaper man, even to one who has never studied epistemology; and, if the phrase is permissible, truth is rather more relative in Washington than anywhere else. Now and then it is possible to make a downright statement; such and such a bill has passed in one of the houses of Congress, or failed to pass; the administration has issued this or that statement; the President has approved, or vetoed, a certain bill. But most of the news that comes out of Washington is necessarily rather vague, for it depends on the assertions of statesmen who are reluctant to be quoted by name, or even by description. This more than anything else is responsible for the sort of fog, the haze of miasmatic exhalations, which hangs over news with a Washington date line. News coming out of Washington is apt to represent not what is so but what might be so under certain contingencies, what may turn out to be so, what some eminent personage says is so, or even what he wants the public to believe is so when it is not."

Most subjects on which there is a so-called definite public opinion are much more vague and indefinite, much more complex in their facts and in their ramifications than the news from Washington which the

---

45 "History of the *New York Times*" (pages 379–380).

historian of the *New York Times* describes. Consider, for example, what complicated issues are casually disposed of by the average citizen. An uninformed lay public may condemn a new medical theory on slight consideration. Its judgment is hit or miss, as medical history proves.

Political, economic and moral judgments, as we have seen, are more often expressions of crowd psychology and herd reaction than the result of the calm exercise of judgment. It is difficult to believe that this is not inevitable. Public opinion in a society consisting of millions of persons, all of whom must somehow or other reach a working basis with most of the others, is bound to find a level of uniformity founded on the intelligence of the average member of society as a whole or of the particular group to which one may belong. There is a different set of facts on every subject for each man. Society cannot wait to find absolute truth. It cannot weigh every issue carefully before making a judgment. The result is that the so-called truths by which society lives are born of compromise among conflicting desires and of interpretation by many minds. They are accepted and intolerantly maintained once they have been determined. In the struggle among ideas, the only test is the one which Justice Holmes of the Supreme Court pointed out—the power of thought to get itself accepted in the open competition of the market.

The only way for new ideas to gain currency is through the acceptance of them by groups. Merely individual advocacy will leave the truth outside the general fund of knowledge and beliefs. The urge toward suppression of minority or dissentient points of view is counteracted in part by the work of the public relations counsel.

The standards of the public relations counsel are his own standards and he will not accept a client whose standards do not come up to them. While he is not called upon to judge the merits of his case any more than a lawyer is called upon to judge his client's case, nevertheless he must judge the results which his work would accomplish from an ethical point of view.

In law, the judge and jury hold the deciding balance of power. In public opinion, the public relations counsel is judge and jury because through his pleading of a case the public is likely to accede to his opinion and judgment. Therefore, the public relations counsel must maintain an intense scrutiny of his actions, avoiding the propagation of unsocial or otherwise harmful movements or ideas.

Every public relations counsel has been confronted with the necessity of refusing to accept clients whose cases in a law court would be valid, but whose cases in the higher court of public opinion are questionable.

The social value of the public relations counsel lies in the fact that he brings to the public facts and ideas of social utility which would not so readily gain acceptance otherwise. While he, of course, may represent men and individuals who have already gained great acceptance in the public mind, he may represent new ideas of value which have not yet reached their point of largest acceptance or greatest saturation. That in itself renders him important.

As for the relations between the public relations counsel and his client, little can be said which would not be merely a repetition of that code of decency by which men and women make moral judgments and live reputable lives. The public relations counsel owes his client conscientious, effective service, of course. He owes to his client all the duties which the professions assume in relation to those they serve. Much more important than any positive duty, however, which the public relations counsel owes to his client is the negative duty—that he must never accept a retainer or assume a position which puts his duty to the groups he represents above his duty to his own standards of integrity—to the larger society within which he lives and works.

Europe has given us the most recent important study of public opinion and its social and historical effects. It is interesting because it indicates the sweep of the development of an international realization of what a momentous factor in the world's life public opinion is becoming. I feel that this paragraph from a recent work of Professor Von Ferdinand Tonnies is of particular significance to all who would feel that the conscious moulding of public opinion is a task embodying high ideals.

"The future of public opinion," says Professor Tonnies, "is the future of civilization. It is certain that the power of public opinion is constantly increasing and will keep on increasing. It is equally certain that it is more and more being influenced, changed, stirred by impulses from below. The danger which this development contains for a progressive ennobling of human society and a progressive heightening of human culture is apparent. The duty of the higher strata of society—the cultivated, the learned, the expert, the intellectual—is therefore clear. They must inject moral and spiritual motives into public opinion. Public opinion must become public conscience."

It is in the creation of a public conscience that the counsel on public relations is destined, I believe, to fulfill his highest usefulness to the society in which he lives.

THE SCIENCE OF BEING GREAT

Wallace D. Wattles

Contents

Chapter I   Any Person May Become Great 221
Chapter II   Heredity And Opportunity 224
Chapter III   The Source Of Power 226
Chapter IV   The Mind Of God 229
Chapter V   Preparation 232
Chapter VI   The Social Point Of View 234
Chapter VII   The Individual Point Of View 238
Chapter VIII   Consecration 240
Chapter IX   Identification 242
Chapter X   Idealization 244
Chapter XI   Realization 247
Chapter XII   Hurry And Habit 249
Chapter XIII   Thought 252
Chapter XIV   Action At Home 255
Chapter XV   Action Abroad 258
Chapter XVI   Some Further Explanations 261
Chapter XVII   More About Thought 263
Chapter XVIII   Jesus' Idea Of Greatness 267
Chapter XIX   A View Of Evolution 270
Chapter XX   Serving God 273
Chapter XXI   A Mental Exercise 276
Chapter XXII   A Summary Of The Science Of Being Great 279

Chapter I

Any Person May Become Great

There is a Principle of Power in every person. By the intelligent use and direction of this principle, man can develop his own mental faculties. Man has an inherent power by which he may grow in whatsoever direction he pleases, and there does not appear to be any limit to the possibilities of his growth. No man has yet become so great in any faculty but that it is possible for someone else to become greater. The possibility is in the Original Substance from which man is made. Genius is Omniscience flowing into man. Genius is more than talent. Talent may merely be one faculty developed out of proportion to other faculties, but genius is the union of man and God in the acts of the soul. Great men are always greater than their deeds. They are in connection with a reserve of power that is without limit. We do not know where the boundary of the mental powers of man is; we do not even know that there is a boundary.

The power of conscious growth is not given to the lower animals; it is mans alone and may be developed and increased by him. The lower animals can, to a great extent, be trained and developed by man; but man can train and develop himself. He alone has this power, and he has it to an apparently unlimited extent.

The purpose of life for man is growth, just as the purpose of life for trees and plants is growth. Trees and plants grow automatically and along fixed lines; man can grow, as he will. Trees and plants can only develop certain possibilities and characteristics; man can develop any power, which is or has been shown by any person, anywhere. Nothing that is possible in spirit is impossible in flesh and blood. Nothing that man can think is impossible-in action. Nothing that man can imagine is impossible of realization.

Man is formed for growth, and he is under the necessity of growing.

It is essential to his happiness that he should continuously advance.

Life without progress becomes unendurable, and the person who ceases from growth must either become imbecile or insane. The greater and more harmonious and well rounded his growth, the happier man will be.

There is no possibility in any man that is not in every man; but if they proceed naturally, no two men will grow into the same thing, or be alike. Every man comes into the world with a predisposition to grow along certain lines, and growth is easier for him along those lines than in any other way. This is a wise provision, for it gives endless variety. It is as if a gardener should throw all his bulbs into one basket; to the superficial observer they would look alike, but growth reveals a tremendous difference. So of men and women, they are like a basket of bulbs. One may be a rose and add brightness and color to some dark corner of the world; one may be a lily and teach a lesson of love and purity to every eye that sees; one may be a climbing vine and hide the rugged outlines of some dark rock; one may be a great oak among whose boughs the birds shall nest and sing, and beneath whose shade the flocks shall rest at noon, but everyone will be something worthwhile, something rare, something perfect.

There are undreamed of possibilities in the common lives all around us in a large sense, there are no "common" people. In times of national stress and peril the cracker-box loafer of the corner store and the village drunkard become heroes and statesmen through the quickening of the Principle of Power within them. There is a genius in every man and woman, waiting to be brought forth. Every village has its great man or woman; someone to whom all go for advice in time of trouble; someone who is instinctively recognized as being great in wisdom and insight. To such a one the minds of the whole community turn in times of local crisis; he is tacitly recognized as being great. He does small things in a great way. He could do great things as well if he did but undertake them; so can any man; so can you. The Principle of Power gives us just what we ask of it; if we only undertake little things, it only gives us power for little things; but if we try to do great things in a great way it gives us all the power there is.

But beware of undertaking great things in a small way: of that we shall speak farther on.

There are two mental attitudes a man may take. One makes him like a football. It has resilience and reacts strongly when force is applied to it, but it originates nothing; it never acts of itself. There is no power within it. Men of this type are controlled by circumstances and environment; their destinies are decided by things external to themselves. The Principle of Power within them is never really active at all. They never speak or act from within. The other attitude makes man like a flowing spring. Power comes out from the center of him. He has within him a well of water springing up into everlasting life, he radiates force; heist felt by his environment. The Principle of Power in him is in constant action. He is self-active. "He hath life in himself."

No greater good can come to any man or woman than to become self-active. All the experiences of life are designed by Providence to force men and women into self-activity; to compel them to cease being creatures of circumstances and master their environment. In his lowest stage, man is the child of chance and circumstance and the slave of fear. His acts are all reactions resulting from the impingement upon him of forces in his environment. He acts only as he is acted upon; he originates nothing. But the lowest savage has within him a Principle of Power sufficient to master all that he fears; and if he learns this and becomes self-active, he becomes as one of the gods.

The awakening of the Principle of Power in man is the real conversion; the passing from death to life. It is when the dead hear the voice of the Son of Man and come forth and live. It is the resurrection and the life. When it is awakened, man becomes a son of the Highest and all power is given to him in heaven and on earth.

Nothing was ever in any man that is not in you; no man ever had more spiritual or mental power than you can attain, or did greater things than you can accomplish. You can become what you want to be.

Chapter II

Heredity And Opportunity

You are not barred from attaining greatness by heredity. No matter who or what your ancestors may have been or how unlearned or lowly their station, the upward way is open for you. There is no such thing as inheriting a fixed mental position; no matter how small the mental capital we receive from our parents, it may be increased; no man is born incapable of growth.

Heredity counts for something. We are born with subconscious mental tendencies; as, for instance, a tendency to melancholy, or cowardice, or to ill temper; but all these subconscious tendencies may be overcome. When the real man awakens and comes forth he can throw them off very easily. Nothing of this kind need keep you down; if you have inherited undesirable mental tendencies, you can eliminate them and put desirable tendencies in their places. An inherited mental trait is a habit of thought of your father or mother impressed upon your subconscious mind; you can substitute the opposite impression by forming the opposite habit of thought. You can substitute a habit of cheerfulness for a tendency to despondency; you can overcome cowardice or ill temper.

Heredity may count for something, too, in an inherited conformation of the skull. There is something in phrenology, if not as much as its exponents claim; it is true that the different faculties are localized in the brain, and that the power of a faculty depends upon the number of active brain cells in its area. A faculty whose brain area is large is likely to act with more power than one whose cranial section is small; hence persons with certain conformations of the skull show talent as musicians, orators, mechanics, and so on. It has been argued from this that a man's cranial formation must, to a great extent, decide his station in life, but this is an error. It has been found that a small brain section, with many fine and active cells, gives as powerful expression to faculty as a larger brain with coarser cells; and it has been found that by turning the Principle of Power into any section of the brain, with the will and purpose to develop a particular talent, the brain cells may be multiplied indefinitely. Any faculty, power, or talent you possess, no matter how small or rudimentary, may be increased; you can multiply the brain cells in this particular area until it acts as powerfully as you wish. It is true that you can act most easily through those faculties that are now most largely developed; you can do, with the least effort, the things which "come naturally"; but it is also true that if you will make the necessary effort you can develop any talent. You can do what you desire to do and become what you want to be. When you fix upon some ideal and proceed as hereinafter directed, all the power of your being is turned into the faculties required in the realization of that ideal; more blood and nerve force go to the corresponding sections of the brain, and the cells are quickened, increased, and multiplied in number. The proper use of the mind of man will build a brain capable of doing what the mind wants to do.

The brain does not make the man; the man makes the brain.

Your place in life is not fixed by heredity.

Nor are you condemned to the lower levels by circumstances or lack of opportunity. The Principle of Power in man is sufficient for all the requirements of his soul. No possible combination of circumstances can keep him down, if he makes his personal attitude right and determines to rise. The power, which formed man and purposed him for growth, also controls the circumstances of society, industry, and government; and this power is never divided against itself. The power which is in you is in the things around you, and when you begin to move forward, the things will arrange themselves for your advantage, as described in later chapters of this book. Man was formed for growth, and all things external were designed to promote his growth. No sooner does a man awaken his soul and enter on the advancing way than he finds that not only is God for him, but nature, society, and his fellow men are for him also; and all things work together for his good if he obeys the law. Poverty is no bar to greatness, for poverty can always be removed. Martin Luther, as a child, sang in the streets for bread. Linnaeus the naturalist had only forty dollars with which to educate himself; he mended his own shoes and often had to beg meals from his friends. Hugh Miller, apprenticed to a stonemason, began to study geology in a quarry. George Stephenson, inventor of the locomotive engine, and one of the greatest of civil engineers, was a coal miner, working in a mine, when he awakened and began to think. James Watt was a sickly child, and was not strong enough to be sent to school. Abraham Lincoln was a poor boy. In each of these cases we see a Principle of Power in the man that lifts him above all opposition and adversity.

There is a Principle of Power in you; if you use it and apply it in a certain way you can overcome all heredity, and master all circumstances and conditions and become a great and powerful personality.

Chapter III

The Source Of Power

Man's brain, body, mind, faculties, and talents are the mere instruments he uses in demonstrating greatness; in themselves they do not make him great. A man may have a large brain and a good mind, strong faculties, and brilliant talents, and yet he is not a great man unless he uses all these in a great way. That quality which enables man to use his abilities in a great way makes him great; and to that quality we give the name of wisdom. Wisdom is the essential basis of greatness.

Wisdom is the power to perceive the best ends to aim at and the best means for reaching those ends. It is the power to perceive the right thing to do. The man who is wise enough to know the right thing to do, who is good enough to wish to do only the right thing, and who is able and strong enough to do the right thing is a truly great man. He will instantly become marked as a personality of power in any community and men will delight to do him honor.

Wisdom is dependent upon knowledge. Where there is complete ignorance there can be no wisdom, no knowledge of the right thing to do. Man's knowledge is comparatively limited and so his wisdom must be small, unless he can connect his mind with knowledge greater than his own and draw from it, by inspiration, the wisdom that his own limitations deny him. This he can do; this is what the really great men and women have done. Man's knowledge is limited and uncertain; therefore he cannot have wisdom in himself.

Only God knows all truth; therefore only God can have real wisdom or the right thing to do at all times, and man can receive wisdom from God. I proceed to give an illustration: Abraham Lincoln had limited education; but he had the power to perceive truth. In Lincoln we see pre-eminently apparent the fact that real wisdom consists in knowing the right thing to do at all times and under all circumstances; in having the will to do the right thing, and in having talent and ability enough to be competent and able to do the right thing. Back in the days of the abolition agitation, and during the compromise period, when all other men were more or less confused as to what was right or as to what ought to be done, Lincoln was never uncertain. He saw through the superficial arguments of the pro-slavery men;

he saw, also, the impracticability and fanaticism of the abolitionists; he saw the right ends to aim at and he saw the best means to attain those ends. It was because men recognized that he perceived truth and knew the right thing to do that they made him president. Any man who develops the power to perceive truth, and who can show that he always knows the right thing to do and that he can be trusted to do the right thing, will be honored and advanced; the whole world is looking eagerly for such men.

When Lincoln became president he was surrounded by a multitude of so-called able advisers, hardly any two of whom were agreed. At times they were all opposed to his policies; at times almost the whole North was opposed to what he proposed to do. But he saw the truth when others were misled by appearances; his judgment was seldom or never wrong. He was at once the ablest statesman and the best soldier of the period. Where did he, a comparatively unlearned man, get this wisdom? It was not due to some peculiar formation of his skull or to some fineness of texture of his brain. It was not due to some physical characteristic. It was not even a quality of mind due to superior reasoning power. Processes of reason do not often reach knowledge of truth. It was due to a spiritual insight. He perceived truth, but where did he perceive it and whence did the perception come? We see something similar in Washington, whose faith and courage, due to his perception of truth, held the colonies together during the long and often apparently hopeless struggle of the Revolution. We see something of the same thing in the phenomenal genius of Napoleon, who always knew, in military matters, the best means to adopt. We see that the greatness of Napoleon was in nature rather than in Napoleon, and we discover back of Washington and Lincoln something greater than either Washington or Lincoln. We see the same thing in all great men and women. They perceive truth; but truth cannot be perceived until it exists; and there can be no truth until there is a mind to perceive it. Truth does not exist apart from mind. Washington and Lincoln were in touch and communication with a mind that knew all knowledge and contained all truth. The same is true of all who manifest wisdom.

Wisdom is obtained by reading the mind of God.

Chapter IV

The Mind Of God

There is a Cosmic Intelligence that is in all things and through all things. This is the one real substance. From it all things proceed. It is Intelligent Substance or Mind Stuff. It is God. Where there is no substance there can be no intelligence; for where there is no substance there is nothing. Where there is thought there must be a substance which thinks. Thought cannot be a function; for function is motion, and it is inconceivable that mere motion should think. Thought cannot be vibration, for vibration is motion, and that motion should be intelligent is not thinkable. Motion is nothing but the moving of substance; if there be intelligence shown it must be in the substance and not in the motion. Thought cannot be the result of motions in the brain; if thought is in the brain it must be in the brain's substance and not in the motions which brain substance makes.

But thought is not in the brain substance, for brain substance, without life, is quite unintelligent and dead. Thought is in the life-principle that animates the brain, in the spirit substance, which is the real man. The brain does not think, the man thinks and expresses his thought through the brain.

There is a spirit substance that thinks. Just as the spirit substance of man permeates his body, and thinks and knows in the body, so the Original Spirit Substance, God, permeates all nature and thinks and knows in nature. Nature is as intelligent as man, and knows more than man; nature knows all things. The All-Mind has been in touch with all things from the beginning; and it contains all knowledge. Man's experience covers a few things, and these things man knows; but God's experience covers all the things that have happened since the creation, from the wreck of a planet or the passing of a comet to the fall of a sparrow. All that is and all that has been are present in the Intelligence that is wrapped about us and enfolds us and presses upon us from every side.

All the encyclopedias men have written are but trivial affairs compared to the vast knowledge held by the mind in which men live, move, and have their being.

The truths men perceive by inspiration are thoughts held in this mind. If they were not thoughts men could not perceive them, for they would have no existence; and they could not exist as thoughts unless there is a mind for them to exist in; and a mind can be nothing else than a substance which thinks.

Man is thinking substance, a portion of the Cosmic Substance; but man is limited, while the Cosmic Intelligence from which he sprang, which Jesus calls the Father, is unlimited. All intelligence, power, and force come from the Father. Jesus recognized this and stated it very plainly. Over and over again he ascribed all his wisdom and power to his unity with the Father, and to his perceiving the thoughts of God. "My Father and I are one." This was the foundation of his knowledge and power. He showed the people the necessity of becoming spiritually awakened; of hearing his voice and becoming like him. He compared the unthinking man who is the prey and sport of circumstances to the dead man in a tomb, and besought him to hear and come forth. "God is spirit," he said; "be born again, become spiritually awake, and you may see his kingdom. Hear my voice; see what I am and what I do, and come forth and live. The words I speak are spirit and life; accept them and they will cause a well of water to spring up within you. Then you will have life within yourself."

"I do what I see the Father do," he said, meaning that he read the thoughts of God. "The Father shows all things to the son." "If any man has the will to do the will of God, he shall know truth." "My teaching is not my own, but his that sent me." "You shall know the truth and the truth shall make you free." "The spirit shall guide you into all truth."

We are immersed in mind and that mind contains all knowledge and all truth. It is seeking to give us this knowledge, for our Father delights to give good gifts to his children. The prophets and seers and great men and women, past and present, were made great by what they received from God, not by what they were taught by men. This limitless reservoir of wisdom and power is open to you; you can draw upon it, as you will, according to your needs. You can make yourself what you desire to be; you can do what you wish to do; you can have what you want. To accomplish this you must learn to become one with the Father so that you may perceive truth; so that you may have wisdom and know the right ends to seek and the right means to use to attain those ends, and so that you may secure power and ability to use the means. In closing this chapter resolve that you will now lay aside all else and concentrate upon the attainment of conscious unity with God.

Oh, when I am safe in my sylvan home,
I tread on the pride of Greece and Rome;
And when I am stretched beneath the pines,
Where the evenings tar so holy shines,
I laugh at the lore and pride of man,
At the Sophist schools and the learned clan;
For what are they all in their high conceit,
When man in the bush with God may meet?

Chapter V

Preparation

"Draw nigh to God and He will draw nigh to you."

If you become like God you can read his thoughts; and if you do not you will find the inspirational perception of truth impossible. You can never become a great man or woman until you have overcome anxiety, worry, and fear. It is impossible for an anxious person, a worried one, or a fearful one to perceive truth; all things are distorted and thrown out of their proper relations by such mental states, and those who are in them cannot read the thoughts of God.

If you are poor, or if you are anxious about business or financial matters, you are recommended to study carefully the first volume of this series, *The Science of Getting Rich*. That will present to you a solution for your problems of this nature, no matter how large or how complicated they may seem to be. There is not the least cause for worry about financial affairs; every person who wills to do so may rise above want, have all he needs, and become rich. The same source upon which you propose to draw for mental unfolding and spiritual power is at your service for the supply of all your material wants. Study this truth until it is fixed in your thoughts and until anxiety is banished from your mind; enter the Certain Way, which leads to material riches.

Again, if you are anxious or worried about your health, realize it is possible for you to attain perfect health so that you may have strength sufficient for all that you wish to do and more. That Intelligence which stands ready to give you wealth and mental and spiritual power will rejoice to give you health also. Perfect health is yours for the asking, if you will only obey the simple laws of life and live aright. Conquer ill-health and cast out fear.

But it is not enough to rise above financial and physical anxiety and worry; you must rise above moral evil-doing as well. Sound your inner consciousness now for the motives that actuate you and make sure they are right. You must cast out lust, and cease to be ruled by appetite, and you must begin to govern appetite. You must eat only to satisfy hunger, never for gluttonous pleasure, and in all things you must make the flesh obey the spirit.

You must lay aside greed; have no unworthy motive in your desire to become rich and powerful. It is legitimate and right to desire riches, if you want them for the sake of the soul, but not if you desire them for the lusts of the flesh.

Cast out pride and vanity; have no thought of trying to rule over others or of outdoing them. This is a vital point; there is no temptation so insidious as the selfish desire to rule over others. Nothing so appeals to the average man or woman as to sit in the uppermost places at feasts, to be respectfully saluted in the market place, and to be called Rabbi, Master. To exercise some sort of control over others is the secret motive of every selfish person. The struggle for power over others is the battle of the competitive world, and you must rise above that world and its motives and aspirations and seek only for life. Cast out envy; you can have all that you want, and you need not envy any man what he has. Above all things see to it that you do not hold malice or enmity toward any one; to do so cuts you off from the mind whose treasures you seek to make your own. "He that loves not his brother, loves not God." Lay aside all narrow personal ambition and determine to seek the highest good and to be swayed by no unworthy selfishness.

Go over all the foregoing and set these moral temptations out of your heart one by one; determine to keep them out. Then resolve that you will not only abandon all evil thought but that you will forsake all deeds, habits, and courses of action which do not commend themselves to your noblest ideals. This is supremely important, make this resolution with all the power of your soul, and you are ready for the next step toward greatness, which is explained in the following chapter.

Chapter VI

The Social Point Of View

"*Without faith it is impossible to please God*," and without faith it is impossible for you to become great. The distinguishing characteristic of all really great men and women is an unwavering faith. We see this in Lincoln during the dark days of the war; we see it in Washington at Valley Forge; we see it in Livingstone, the crippled missionary, threading the mazes of the dark continent, his soul aflame with the determination to let in the light upon the accursed slave trade, which his soul abhorred; we see it in Luther, and in Frances Willard, in every man and woman who has attained a place on the muster roll of the great ones of the world.

Faith—not a faith in one's self or in one s own powers but faith in principle; in the Something Great which upholds right, and which may be relied upon to give us the victory in due time. Without this faith it is not possible for anyone to rise to real greatness. The man who has no faith in principle will always be a small man. Whether you have this faith or not depends upon your point of view. You must learn to see the world as being produced by evolution, as a something that is evolving and becoming, not as a finished work. Millions of years ago God worked with very low and crude forms of life, low and crude, yet each perfect after its kind. Higher and more complex organisms, animal and vegetable, appeared through the successive ages; the earth passed through stage after stage in its unfolding, each stage perfect in itself, and to be succeeded by a higher one. What I wish you to note is that the so-called "lower organisms" are as perfect after their kind as the higher ones; that the world in the Eocene period was perfect for that period; it was perfect, but God's work was not finished. This is true of the world today. Physically, socially, and industrially it is all good, and it is all perfect. It is not complete anywhere or in any part, but so far as the handiwork of God has gone it is perfect.

THIS MUST BE YOUR POINT OF VIEW: THAT THE WORLD AND ALL IT CONTAINS IS PERFECT, THOUGH NOT COMPLETED.

"All's right with the world." That is the great fact. There is nothing wrong with anything; there is nothing wrong with anybody. All the facts of life you must contemplate from this standpoint. There is nothing wrong with nature. Nature is a great advancing presence working beneficently for the happiness of all. All things in Nature are good; she has no evil. She is not completed; for creation is still unfinished, but she is going on to give to man even more bountifully than she has given to him in the past. Nature is a partial expression of God, and God is love. She is perfect but not complete.

So it is of human society and government. What though there are trusts and combinations of capital and strikes and lockouts and so on. All these things are part of the forward movement; they are incidental to the evolutionary process of completing society. When it is complete there will be harmony; but it cannot be completed without them. J. P. Morgan is as necessary to the coming social order as the strange animals of the age of reptiles were to the life of the succeeding period, and just as these animals were perfect after their kind, so Morgan is perfect after his kind. Behold it is all very good. See government, and industry as being perfect now, and as advancing rapidly toward being complete; then you will understand that there is nothing to fear, no cause for anxiety, nothing to worry about. Never complain of any of these things. They are perfect; this is the very best possible world for the stage of development man has reached.

This will sound like rank folly to many, perhaps to most people. "What!" they will say, "are not child labor and the exploitation of men and women in filthy and unsanitary factories evil things? Aren't saloons evil? Do you mean to say that we shall accept all these and call them good?"

Child labor and similar things are no more evil than the way of living and the habits and practices of the cave dweller were evil. His ways were those of the savage stage of man's growth, and for that stage they were perfect. Our Industrial practices are those of the savage stage of industrial development, and they are also perfect. Nothing better is possible until we cease to be mental savages in industry and business, and become men and women. This can only come about by the rise of the whole race to a higher viewpoint. And this can only come about by the rise of such individuals here and there as are ready for the higher viewpoint. The cure for all this inharmoniousness lies not with the masters or employers but with the workers themselves. Whenever they reach a higher viewpoint, whenever they shall desire to do so, they can establish complete brotherhood and harmony in Industry; they have the numbers and the power. They are getting now what they desire. Whenever they desire more in the way of a higher, purer, more harmonious life, they will receive more. True, they want more now, but they only want more of the things that make for animal enjoyment, and so industry remains in the savage, brutal, animal stage; when the workers begin to rise to the mental plane of living and ask for more of the things that make for the life of the mind and soul, industry will at once be raised above the plane of savagery and brutality. But it is perfect now upon its plane, behold, in fact it is all very good.

So it is true of saloons and dens of vice. If the majority of the people desire these things, it is right and necessary that they should have them. When the majority desires a world without such discords, they will create such a world. So long as men and women are on the plane of bestial thought, so long the social order will be in part disorder, and will show bestial manifestations. The people make society what it is, and as the people rise above the bestial thought, society will rise above the beastly in its manifestations. But a society which thinks in a bestial way must have saloons and dives; it is perfect after its kind, as the world was in the Eocene period, and very good.

All this does not prevent you from working for better things. You can work to complete an unfinished society, instead of to renovate a decaying one; and you can work with a better heart and a more hopeful spirit. It will make an immense difference with your faith and spirit whether you look upon civilization as a good thing that is becoming better or as a bad and evil thing that is decaying. One viewpoint gives you an advancing and expanding mind and the other gives you a descending and decreasing mind. One viewpoint will make you grow greater and the other will inevitably cause you to grow smaller. One will enable you to work for the eternal things; to do large works in a great way toward the completing of all that is incomplete and inharmonious; and the other will make you a mere patchwork reformer, working almost without hope to save a few lost souls from what you will grow to consider a lost and doomed world. So you see it makes a vast difference to you, this matter of the social viewpoint. "All's right with the world. Nothing can possibly be wrong but my personal attitude, and I will make that right. I will see the facts of nature and all the events, circumstances, and conditions of society, politics, government, and industry from the highest viewpoint. It is all perfect, though incomplete. It is all the handiwork of God; behold, it is all very good."

Chapter VII

The Individual Point Of View

Important as the matter of your point of view for the facts of social life is, it is of less moment than your viewpoint for your fellow men, for your acquaintances, friends, relatives, your immediate family, and, most of all, yourself. You must learn not to look upon the world as a lost and decaying thing but as a something perfect and glorious which is going on to a most beautiful completeness; and you must learn to see men and women not as lost and accursed things, but as perfect beings advancing to become complete. There are no "bad" or "evil" people. An engine, which is on the rails pulling a heavy train, is perfect after its kind, and it is good. The power of steam, which drives it, is good. Let a broken rail throw the engine into the ditch, and it does not become bad or evil by being so displaced; it is a perfectly good engine, but off the track. The power of steam that drives it into the ditch and wrecks it is not evil, but a perfectly good power. So that which is misplaced or applied in an incomplete or partial way is not evil. There are no evil people; there are perfectly good people who are off the track, but they do not need condemnation or punishment; they only need to get upon the rails again.

That which is undeveloped or incomplete often appears to us as evil because of the way we have trained ourselves to think. The root of a bulb that shall produce a white lily is an unsightly thing; one might look upon it with disgust. But how foolish we should be to condemn the bulb for its appearance when we know the lily is within it. The root is perfect after its kind; it is a perfect but incomplete lily, and so we must learn to look upon every man and woman, no matter how unlovely in outward manifestation; they are perfect in their stage of being and they are becoming complete. Behold, it is all very good.

Once we come into a comprehension of this fact and arrive at this point of view, we lose all desire to find fault with people, to judge them, criticize them, or condemn them. We no longer work as those who are saving lost souls, but as those who are among the angels, working out the completion of a glorious heaven. We are born of the spirit and we see the kingdom of God. We no longer see men as trees walking, but our vision is complete. We have nothing but good words to say. It is all good; a great and glorious humanity coming to completeness. And in our association with men this puts us into an expansive and enlarging attitude of mind; we see them as great beings and we begin to deal with them and their affairs in a great way. But if we fall to the other point of view and see a lost and degenerate race we shrink into the contracting mind; and our dealings with men and their affairs will be in a small and contracted way. Remember to hold steadily to this point of view; if you do you cannot fail to begin at once to deal with your acquaintances and neighbors and with your own family as a great personality deals with men. This same viewpoint must be the one from which you regard yourself. You must always see yourself as a great advancing soul. Learn to say: "There is THAT in me of which I am made, which knows no imperfection, weakness, or sickness. The world is incomplete, *but God in my own consciousness is both perfect and complete*. Nothing can be wrong but my own personal attitude, and my own personal attitude can be wrong only when I disobey THAT which is within. I am a perfect manifestation of God so far as I have gone, and I will press on to be complete. I will trust and not be afraid." When you are able to say this understandingly you will have lost all fear and you will be far advanced upon the road to the development of a great and powerful personality.

Chapter VIII

Consecration

Having attained to the viewpoint that puts you into the right relations with the world and with your fellow men, the next step is consecration; and consecration in its true sense simply means obedience to the soul. You have that within you that which is always impelling you toward the upward and advancing way; and that impelling something is the divine Principle of Power; you must obey it without question. No one will deny the statement that if you are to be great, the greatness must be a manifestation of something within; nor can you question that this something must be the very greatest and highest that is within. It is not the mind, or the intellect, or the reason. You cannot be great if you go no farther back for principle than to your reasoning power. Reason knows neither principle nor morality. Your reason is like a lawyer in that it will argue for either side. The intellect of a thief will plan robbery and murder as readily as the intellect of a saint will plan a great philanthropy. Intellect helps us to see the best means and manner of doing the right thing, but intellect never shows us the right thing. Intellect and reason serve the selfish man for his selfish ends as readily as they serve the unselfish man for his unselfish ends. Use intellect and reason without regard to principle, and you may become known as a very able person, but you will never become known as a person whose life shows the power of real greatness. There is too much training of the intellect and reasoning powers and too little training in obedience to the soul. This is the only thing that can be wrong with your personal attitude—when it fails to be one of obedience to the Principle of Power.

By going back to your own center you can always find the pure idea of right for every relationship. To be great and to have power it is only necessary to conform your life to the pure idea as you find it in the GREAT WITHIN. Every compromise on this point is made at the expense of a loss of power. This you *must* remember.

There are many ideas in your mind that you have outgrown, and which, from force of habit you still permit to dictate the actions of your life. Cease all this; abandon everything you have outgrown. There are many ignoble customs, social and other, which you still follow, although you know they tend to dwarf and belittle you and keep you acting in a small way. Rise above all this. I do not say that you should absolutely disregard conventionalities, or the commonly accepted standards of right and wrong. You cannot do this; but you can deliver your soul from most of the narrow restrictions that bind the majority of your fellow men. Do not give your time and strength to the support of obsolete institutions, religious or otherwise; do not be bound by creeds in which you do not believe. Be free. You have perhaps formed some sensual habits of mind or body; abandon them. You still indulge in distrustful fears that things will go wrong, or that people will betray you, or mistreat you; get above all of them. You still act selfishly in many ways and on many occasions; cease to do so. Abandon all these, and in place of them put the best actions you can form a conception of in your mind. If you desire to advance, and you are not doing so, remember that it can be only because your thought is better than your practice. You must do as well as you think.

Let your thoughts be ruled by principle, and then live up to your thoughts.

Let your attitude in business, in politics, in neighborhood affairs, and in your own home be the expression of the best thoughts you can think. Let your manner toward all men and women, great and small, and especially to your own family circle, always be the most kindly, gracious, and courteous you can picture in your imagination. Remember your viewpoint; you are a god in the company of gods and must conduct yourself accordingly.

The steps to complete consecration are few and simple. You cannot be ruled from below if you are to be great; you must rule from above. Therefore you cannot be governed by physical impulses; you must bring your body into subjection to the mind; but your mind, without principle, may lead you into selfishness and immoral ways; you must put the mind into subjection to the soul, and your soul is limited by the boundaries of your knowledge; you must put it into subjection to that Our soul which needs no searching of the understanding but before whose eye all things are spread. That constitutes consecration. Say: "I surrender my body to be ruled by my mind; I surrender my mind to be governed by my soul, and I surrender my soul to the guidance of God." Make this consecration complete and thorough, and you have taken the second great step in the way of greatness and power.

Chapter IX

Identification

Having recognized God as the advancing presence in nature, society, and your fellow men, and harmonized yourself with all these, and having consecrated yourself to that within you which impels toward the greatest and the highest, the next step is to become aware of and recognize fully the fact that the Principle of Power within you is God Himself. You must consciously identify yourself with the Highest. This is not some false or untrue position to be assumed; it is a fact to be recognized. You are already one with God; you want to become consciously aware of it.

There is one substance, the source of all things, and this substance has within itself the power that creates all things; all power is inherent in it. This substance is conscious and thinks; it works with perfect understanding and intelligence. You know that this is so, because you know that substance exists and that consciousness exists; and that it must be substance that is conscious. Man is conscious and thinks; man is substance, he must be substance, else he is nothing and does not exist at all. If man is substance and thinks, and is conscious, then he is, Conscious Substance. It is not conceivable that there should be more than one Conscious Substance; so man is the original substance, the source of all life and power embodied in a physical form. Man cannot be something different from God. Intelligence is one and the same everywhere, and must be everywhere an attribute of the same substance. There cannot be one kind of intelligence in God and another kind of intelligence in man; intelligence can only be in intelligent substance, and Intelligent Substance is God. Man is of one and the same stuff with God, and so all the talents, powers, and possibilities that are in God are in man, not just in a few exceptional men but in everyone. "All power is given to man, in heaven and on earth." "Is it not written, ye are gods?" The Principle of Power in man is man himself, and man himself is God. But while man is original substance, and has within him all power and possibilities, his consciousness is limited. He does not know all there is to know, and so he is liable to error and mistake. To save himself from these he must unite his mind to that outside him which does know all; he must become consciously one with God. There is a Mind surrounding him on every side, closer than breathing, nearer than hands and feet, and in this mind is the memory of all that has ever happened, from the greatest convulsions of nature in prehistoric days to the fall of a sparrow in this present time; and all that is in existence now as well. Held in this Mind is the great purpose that is behind all nature, and so it knows what is going to be. Man is surrounded by a Mind that knows all there is to know, past, present, and to come. Everything that men have said or done or written is present there. Man is of the same one identical stuff with this Mind; he proceeded from it; and he can so identify himself with it that he may know what it knows. "My Father is greater than I," said Jesus, "I come from him." "I and my Father are one. He shows the son all things." "The spirit shall guide you into all truth."

Your identification of yourself with the Infinite must be accomplished by conscious recognition on your part. Recognizing it as a fact, that there is only God, and that all intelligence is in the one substance, you must affirm somewhat after this wise: "There is only one and that one is everywhere. I surrender myself to conscious unity with the highest. Not I, but the Father. I will to be one with the Supreme and to lead the divine life. I am one with infinite consciousness; there is but one mind, and I am that mind. I that speak unto you am he." If you have been thorough in the work as outlined in the preceding chapters; if you have attained to the true viewpoint, and if your consecration is complete, you will not find conscious identification hard to attain; and once it is attained, the power you seek is yours, for you have made yourself one with all the power there is.

Chapter X

Idealization

You are a thinking center in original substance, and the thoughts of original substance have creative power; whatever is formed in its thought and held as a thought-form must come into existence as a visible and so-called material form, and a thought-form held in thinking substance is a reality; it is a real thing, whether it has yet become visible to mortal eye or not. This is a fact that you should impress upon your understanding—that a thought held in thinking substance is a real thing; a form, and has actual existence, although it is not visible to you. You internally take the form in which you think of yourself; and you surround yourself with the invisible forms of those things with which you associate in your thoughts.

If you desire a thing, picture it clearly and hold the picture steadily in mind until it becomes a definite thought-form; and if your practices are not such as to separate you from God, the thing you want will come to you in material form. It must do so in obedience to the law by which the universe was created.

Make no thought-form of yourself in connection with disease or sickness, but form a conception of health. Make a thought-form of yourself as strong and hearty and perfectly well; impress this thought-form on creative intelligence, and if your practices are not in violation of the laws by which the physical body is built, your thought-form will become manifest in your flesh. This also is certain; it comes by obedience to law.

Make a thought-form of yourself, as you desire to be, and set your ideal as near to perfection as your imagination is capable of forming the conception. Let me illustrate: If a young law student wishes to become great, let him picture himself (while attending to the viewpoint, consecration, and identification, as previously directed) as a great lawyer, pleading his case with matchless eloquence and power before the judge and jury; as having an unlimited command of truth, of knowledge and of wisdom. Let him picture himself as the great lawyer in every possible situation and contingency; while he is still only the student in all circumstances let him never forget or fail to be the great lawyer in his thought-form of himself. As the thought-form grows more definite and habitual in his mind, the creative energies, both within and without, are set at work, he begins to manifest the form from within and all the essentials without, which go into the picture, begin to be impelled toward him. He makes himself into the image and God works with him; nothing can prevent him from becoming what he wishes to be.

In the same general way the musical student pictures himself as performing perfect harmonies, and as delighting vast audiences; the actor forms the highest conception he is capable of in regard to his art, and applies this conception to himself. The farmer and the mechanic do exactly the same thing. Fix upon your ideal of what you wish to make of yourself; consider well and be sure that you make the right choice; that is, the one that will be the most satisfactory to you in a general way. Do not pay too much attention to the advice or suggestions of those around you: do not believe that any one can know, better than yourself, what is right for you. Listen to what others have to say, but always form your own conclusions. DO NOT LET OTHER PEOPLE DECIDE WHAT YOU ARE TO BE. BE WHAT YOU FEEL THAT YOU WANT TO BE.

Do not be misled by a false notion of obligation or duty. You can owe no possible obligation or duty to others that should prevent you from making the most of yourself. Be true to yourself, and you cannot then be false to any man. When you have fully decided what thing you want to be, form the highest conception of that thing that you are capable of imagining, and make that conception a thought-form. Hold that thought-form as a fact, as the real truth about yourself, and believe in it.

Close your ears to all adverse suggestions. Never mind if people call you a fool and a dreamer. Dream on. Remember that Bonaparte, the half-starved lieutenant, always saw himself as the general of armies and the master of France, and he became in out-ward realization what he held himself to be in mind. So likewise will you. Attend carefully to all that has been said in the preceding chapters, and act as directed in the following ones, and you will become what you want to be.

Chapter XI

Realization

If you were to stop with the close of the last chapter, however, you would never become great; you would be indeed a mere dreamer of dreams, a castle-builder. Too many do stop there; they do not understand the necessity for present action in realizing the vision and bringing the thought-form into manifestation. Two things are necessary; firstly, the making of the thought-form and secondly, the actual appropriation to yourself of all that goes into, and around, the thought-form. We have discussed the first, now we will proceed to give directions for the second. When you have made your thought-form, you are already, in your interior, what you want to be; next you must become externally what you want to be. You are already great within, but you are not yet doing the great things without. You cannot begin, on the instant, to do the great things; you cannot be before the world the great actor, or lawyer, or musician, or personality you know yourself to be; no one will entrust great things to you as yet for you have not made yourself known. But you can always begin to do small things in a great way.

Here lies the whole secret. You can begin to be great today in your own home, in your store or office, on the street, everywhere; you can begin to make yourself known as great, and you can do this by doing everything you do in a great way. You must put the whole power of your great soul in to every act, however small and commonplace, and so reveal to your family, your friends, and neighbors what you really are. Do not brag or boast of yourself; do not go about telling people what a great personage you are, simply live in a great way. No one will believe you if you tell him you are a great man, but no one can doubt your greatness if you show it in your actions. In your domestic circle be so just, so generous, so courteous, and kindly that your family, your wife, husband, children, brothers, and sisters shall know that you are a great and noble soul. In all your relations with men be great, just, generous, courteous, and kindly. The great are never otherwise. This is your attitude.

Next, and most important, you must have absolute faith in your own perceptions of truth. Never act in haste or hurry; be deliberate in everything; wait until you feel that you know the true way. And when you do feel that you know the true way, be guided by your own faith though the entire world shall disagree with you. If you do not believe what God tells you in little things, you will never draw upon his wisdom and knowledge in larger things. When you feel deeply that a certain act is the right act, do it and have perfect faith that the consequences will be good. When you are deeply impressed that a certain thing is true, no matter what the appearances to the contrary may be, accept that thing as true and act accordingly. The one way to develop a perception of truth in large things is to trust absolutely to your present perception of Truth in small things. Remember that you are seeking to develop this very power or faculty—the perception of truth; you are learning to read the thoughts of God. Nothing is great and nothing is small in the sight of Omnipotence; he holds the sun in its place, but he also notes a sparrow's fall, and numbers the hairs of your head. God is as much interested in the little matters of everyday life as he is in the affairs of nations. You can perceive truth about family and neighborhood affairs as well as about matters of statecraft. And the way to begin is to have perfect faith in the truth in these small matters, as it is revealed to you from day to day. When you feel deeply impelled to take a course that seems contrary to all reason and worldly judgment, take that course. Listen to the suggestions and advice of others, but always do what you feel deeply in the within to be the true thing to do. Rely with absolute faith, at all times, on your own perception of truth; but be sure that you listen to God—that you do not act in haste, fear, or anxiety.

Rely upon your perception of truth in all the facts and circumstances of life. If you deeply feel that a certain man will be in a certain place on a certain day, go there with perfect faith to meet him; he will be there, no matter how unlikely it may seem. If you feel sure that certain people are making certain combinations, or doing certain things, act in the faith that they are doing those things. If you feel sure of the truth of any circumstance or happening, near or distant, past, present, or to come, trust in your perception. You may make occasional mistakes at first because of your imperfect understanding of the within; but you will soon be guided almost invariably right. Soon your family and friends will begin to defer, more and more, to your judgment and to be guided by you. Soon your neighbors and townsmen will be coming to you for counsel and advice; soon you will be recognized as one who is great in small things, and you will be called upon more and more to take charge of larger things. All that is necessary is to be guided absolutely, in all things, by your inner light, your perception of truth. Obey your soul, have perfect faith in yourself. Never think of yourself with doubt or distrust, or as one who makes mistakes. "If I judge, my judgment is just, for I seek not honor from men, but from the Father only."

Chapter XII

Hurry And Habit

No doubt you have many problems, domestic, social, physical, and financial, which seem to you to be pressing for instant solution. You have debts that must be paid, or other obligations that must be met; you are unhappily or inharmoniously placed, and feel that something must be done at once. Do not get into a hurry and act from superficial impulses. You can trust God for the solution of all your personal riddles. There is no hurry. There is only God, and all is well with the world.

There is an invincible power in you, and the same power is in the things you want. It is bringing them to you and bringing you to them. This is a thought that you must grasp, and hold continuously that the same intelligence that is in you is in the things you desire. They are impelled toward you as strongly and decidedly as your desire impels you toward them. The tendency, therefore, of a steadily held thought must be to bring the things you desire to you and to group them around you. So long as you hold your thought and your faith right all must go well. Nothing can be wrong but your own personal attitude, and that will not be wrong if you trust and are not afraid. Hurry is a manifestation of fear; he who fears not has plenty of time. If you act with perfect faith in your own perceptions of truth, you will never be too late or too early; and nothing will go wrong. If things appear to be going wrong, do not get disturbed in mind; it is only in appearance. *Nothing can go wrong in this world but yourself; and you can go wrong only by getting into the wrong mental attitude.* Whenever you find yourself getting excited, worried, or into the mental attitude of hurry, sit down and think it over, play a game of some kind, or take a vacation. Go on a trip, and all will be right when you return. So surely as you find yourself in the mental attitude of haste, just so surely may you know that you are out of the mental attitude of greatness. Hurry and fear will instantly cut your connection with the universal mind; you will get no power, no wisdom, and no information until you are calm. And to fall into the attitude of hurry will check the action of the Principle of Power within you. Fear turns strength to weakness.

Remember that poise and power are inseparably associated. The calm and balanced mind is the strong and great mind; the hurried and agitated mind is the weak one. Whenever you fall into the mental state of hurry you may know that you have lost the right viewpoint; you are beginning to look upon the world, or some part of it, as going wrong. At such times read Chapter Six of this book; consider the fact that this work is perfect, now, with all that it contains. Nothing is going wrong; nothing can be wrong; be poised, be calm, be cheerful; have faith in God.

Next as to habit, it is probable that your greatest difficulty will be to overcome your old habitual ways of thought, and to form new habits. The world is ruled by habit. Kings, tyrants, masters, and plutocrats hold their positions solely because the people have come to habitually accept them. Things are as they are only because people have formed the habit of accepting them as they are. When the people change their habitual thought about governmental, social, and industrial institutions, they will change the institutions. Habit rules us all.

You have formed, perhaps, the habit of thinking of yourself as a common person, as one of a limited ability, or as being more or less of a failure. Whatever you habitually think yourself to be, that you are. You must form, now, a greater and better habit; you must form a conception of yourself as a being of limitless power, and habitually think that you are that being. It is the habitual, not the periodical thought that decides your destiny. It will avail you nothing to sit apart for a few moments several times a day to affirm that you are great, if during all the balance of the day, while you are about your regular vocation, you think of yourself as not great. No amount of praying or affirmation will make you great if you still habitually regard yourself as being small. The use of prayer and affirmation is to change your habit of thought. Any act, mental or physical, often repeated, becomes a habit. The purpose of mental exercises is to repeat certain thoughts over and over until the thinking of those thoughts becomes constant and habitual. The thoughts we continually repeat become convictions. What you must do is to repeat the new thought of yourself until it is the only way in which you think of yourself. Habitual thought, and not environment or circumstance, has made you what you are. Every person has some central idea or thought- form of himself, and by this idea he classifies and arranges all his facts and external relationships. You are classifying your facts either according to the idea that you are a great and strong personality, or according to the idea that you are limited, common, or weak. If the latter is the case you must change your central idea. Get a new mental picture of yourself. Do not try to become great by repeating mere strings of words or superficial formulas; but repeat over and over the THOUGHT of your own power and ability until you classify external facts, and decide your place everywhere by this idea. In another chapter will be found an illustrative mental exercise and further directions on this point.

Chapter XIII

Thought

Greatness is only attained by the constant thinking of great thoughts. No man can become great in outward personality until he is great internally; and no man can be great internally until he THINKS. No amount of education, reading, or study can make you great without thought; but thought can make you great with very little study. There are altogether too many people who are trying to make something of themselves, by reading books without thinking; all such will fail. You are not mentally developed by what you read, but by what you think about what you read.

Thinking is the hardest and most exhausting of all labor; and hence many people shrink from it. God has so formed us that we are continuously impelled to thought; we must either think or engage in some activity to escape thought. The headlong, continuous chase for pleasure in which most people spend all their leisure time is only an effort to escape thought. If they are alone, or if they have nothing amusing to take their attention, as a novel to read or a show to see, they must think; and to escape from thinking they resort to novels, shows, and all the endless devices of the purveyors of amusement. Most people spend the greater part of their leisure time running away from thought, hence they are where they are. We never move forward until we begin to think.

Read less and think more. Read about great things and think about great questions and issues. We have at the present time few really great figures in the political life of our country; our politicians are a petty lot. There is no Lincoln, no Webster, no Clay, Calhoun, or Jackson. Why? Because our present statesmen deal only with sordid and petty issues—questions of dollars and cents, of expediency and party success, of material prosperity without regard to ethical right. Thinking along these lines does not call forth great souls. The statesmen of Lincoln's time and previous times dealt with questions of eternal truth, of human rights and justice. Men thought upon great themes; they thought great thoughts, and they became great men.

Thinking, not mere knowledge or information, makes personality. Thinking is growth; you cannot think without growing. Every thought engenders another thought. Write one idea and others will follow until you have written a page. You cannot fathom your own mind; it has neither bottom nor boundaries. Your first thoughts may be crude; but as you go on thinking you will use more and more of yourself; you will quicken new brain cells into activity and you will develop new faculties. Heredity, environment, circumstances—all things must give way before you if you practice sustained and continuous thought. But, on the other hand, if you neglect to think for yourself and only use other people's thought, you will never know what you are capable of; and you will end by being incapable of anything.

There can be no real greatness without original thought. All that a man does outwardly is the expression and completion of his inward thinking. No action is possible without thought, and no great action is possible until a great thought has preceded it. Action is the second form of thought, and personality is the materialization of thought. Environment is the result of thought; things group themselves or arrange themselves around you according to your thought. There is, as Emerson says, some central idea or conception of yourself by which all the facts of your life are arranged and classified. Change this central idea and you change the arrangement or classification of all the facts and circumstances of your life. You are what you are because you think as you do; you are where you are because you think as you do.

You see then the immense importance of thinking about the great essentials set forth in the preceding chapters. You must not accept them in any superficial way; you must think about them until they are a part of your central idea. Go back to the matter of the point of view and consider, in all its bearings, the tremendous thought that you live in a perfect world among perfect people, and that nothing can possibly be wrong with you but your own personal attitude. Think about all this until you fully realize all that it means to you. Consider that this is God's world and that it is the best of all possible worlds; that he has brought it thus far toward completion by the processes of organic, social, and industrial evolution, and that it is going on to greater completeness and harmony. Consider that there is one great, perfect, intelligent Principle of Life and Power, causing all the changing phenomena of the cosmos. Think about all this until you see that it is true, and until you comprehend how you should live and act as a citizen of such a perfect whole. Next, think of the wonderful truth that this great Intelligence is in you; it is your own intelligence. It is an Inner Light impelling you toward the right thing and the best thing, the greatest act, and the highest happiness. It is a Principle of Power in you, giving you all the ability and genius there is. It will infallibly guide you to the best if you will submit to it and walk in the light. Consider what is meant by your consecration of yourself when you say: "I will obey my soul." This is a sentence of tremendous meaning; it must revolutionize the attitude and behavior of the average person.

Then think of your identification with this Great Supreme; that all its knowledge is yours, and all its wisdom is yours, for the asking. You are a god if you think like a god. If you think like a god you cannot fail to act like a god. Divine thoughts will surely externalize themselves in a divine life. Thoughts of power will end in a life of power. Great thoughts will manifest in a great personality. Think well of all this, and then you are ready to act.

Chapter XIV

Action At Home

Do not merely think that you are going to become great; think *that you are great now*. Do not think that you will begin to act in a great way at some future time; begin now. Do not think that you will act in a great way when you reach a different environment; act in a great way where you are now. Do not think that you will begin to act in a great way when you begin to deal with great things; begin to deal in a great way with small things. Do not think that you will begin to be great when you get among more intelligent people, or among people who understand you better; begin now to deal in a great way with the people around you.

If you are not in an environment where there is scope for your best powers and talents you can move in due time; but meanwhile you can be great where you are. Lincoln was as great when he was a backwoods lawyer as when he was President; as a backwoods lawyer he did common things in a great way, and that made him President. Had he waited until he reached Washington to begin to be great, he would have remained unknown. You are not made great by the location in which you happen to be nor by the things with which you may surround yourself. You are not made great by what you receive from others, and you can never manifest greatness so long as you depend on others. You will manifest greatness only when you begin to stand alone. Dismiss all thought of reliance on externals, whether things, books, or people. As Emerson said, "Shakespeare will never be made by the study of Shakespeare." Shakespeare will be made by the thinking of Shakespearean thoughts.

Never mind how the people around you, including those of your own household, may treat you. That has nothing at all to do with your being great; that is, it cannot hinder you from being great. People may neglect you and be unthankful and unkind in their attitude toward you; does that prevent you from being great in your manner and attitude toward them? "Your Father," said Jesus, "is kind to the unthankful and the evil." Would God be great if he should go away and sulk because people were unthankful and did not appreciate him? Treat the unthankful and the evil in a great and perfectly kind way, just as God does.

Do not talk about your greatness; you are really, in essential nature, no greater than those around you. You may have entered upon a way of living and thinking which they have not yet found, but they are perfect on their own plane of thought and action. You are entitled to no special honor or consideration for your greatness. You are a god, but you are among gods. You will fall into the boastful attitude if you see other people's shortcomings and failures and compare them with your own virtues and successes; and if you fall into the boastful attitude of mind, you will cease to be great, and become small. Think of yourself as a perfect being among perfect beings, and meet every person as an equal, not as either superior or an inferior. Give yourself no airs; great people never do. Ask no honors and seek for no recognition, honors and recognition will come fast enough if you are entitled to them.

Begin at home. It is a great person who can always be poised, assured, calm, and perfectly kind and considerate at home. If your manner and attitude in your own family are always the best you can think, you will soon become the one on whom all the others will rely. You will be a tower of strength and a support in time of trouble. You will be loved and appreciated. At the same time do not make the mistake of throwing yourself away in the service of others. The great person respects himself; he serves and helps, but he is never slavishly servile. You cannot help your family by being a slave to them, or by doing for them those things that by right they should do for themselves. You do a person an injury when you wait on him too much. The selfish and exacting are a great deal better off if their exactions are denied. The ideal world is not one where there are a lot of people being waited on by other people; it is a world where everybody waits on himself. Meet all demands, selfish and otherwise, with perfect kindness and consideration; but do not allow yourself to be made a slave to the whims, caprices, exactions, or slavish desires of any member of your family. To do so is not great, and it works an injury to the other party.

Do not become uneasy over the failures or mistakes of any member of your family, and feel that you must interfere. Do not be disturbed if others seem to be going wrong, and feel that you must step in and set them right. Remember that every person is perfect on his own plane; you cannot improve on the work of God. Do not meddle with the personal habits and practices of others, though they are your nearest and dearest; these things are none of your business. Nothing can be wrong but your own personal attitude; make that right and you will know that all else is right. You are a truly great soul when you can live with those who do things that you do not do, and yet refrain from either criticism or interference. Do the things that are right for you to do, and believe that every member of your family is doing the things that are right for him. Nothing is wrong with anybody or anything, behold, it is all very good. Do not be enslaved by anyone else, but be just as careful that you do not enslave anyone else to your own notions of what is right.

Think, and think deeply and continuously; be perfect in your kindness and consideration; let your attitude be that of a god among gods, and not that of a god among inferior beings. This is the way to be great in your own home.

Chapter XV

Action Abroad

The rules that apply to your action at home must apply to your action everywhere. Never forget for an instant that this is a perfect world, and that you are a god among gods. You are as great as the greatest, but all are your equals.

Rely absolutely on your perception of truth. Trust to the inner light rather than to reason, but be sure that your perception comes from the inner light; act in poise and calmness; be still and attend on God. Your identification of yourself with the All-Mind will give you all the knowledge you need for guidance in any contingency that may arise in your own life or in the lives of others. It is only necessary that you should be supremely calm, and rely upon the eternal wisdom that is within you. If you act in poise and faith, your judgment will always be right, and you will always know exactly what to do. Do not hurry or worry; remember Lincoln in the dark days of the war. James Freeman Clarke relates that after the battle of Fredericksburg, Lincoln alone furnished a supply of faith and hope for the nation. Hundreds of leading men, from all parts of the country, went sadly into his room and came out cheerful and hopeful. They had stood face to face with the Highest, and had seen God in this lank, ungainly, patient man, although they knew it not.

Have perfect faith in yourself and in your own ability to cope with any combination of circumstances that may arise. Do not be disturbed if you are alone; if you need friends they will be brought to you at the right time. Do not be disturbed if you feel that you are ignorant, the information that you need will be furnished you when it is time for you to have it. That which is in you impelling you forward is in the things and people you need, impelling them toward you. If there is a particular man you need to know, he will be introduced to you; if there is a particular book you need to read it will be placed in your hands at the right time. All the knowledge you need is coming to you from both external and internal sources. Your information and your talents will always be equal to the requirements of the occasion. Remember that Jesus told his disciples not to worry as to what they should say when brought before the judges; he knew that the power in them would be sufficient for the needs of the hour. As soon as you awaken and begin to use your faculties in a great way you will apply power to the development of your brain; new cells will be created and dormant cells quickened into activity, and your brain will be qualified as a perfect instrument for your mind.

Do not try to do great things until you are ready to go about them in a great way. If you undertake to deal with great matters in a small way—that is, from a low viewpoint or with incomplete consecration and wavering faith and courage—you will fail. Do not be in a hurry to get to the great things. Doing great things will not make you great, but becoming great will certainly lead you to the doing of great things. Begin to be great where you are and in the things you do every day. Do not be in haste to be found out or recognized as a great personality. Do not be disappointed if men do not nominate you for office within a month after you begin to practice what you read in this book. Great people never seek for recognition or applause; they are not great because they want to be paid for being so. Greatness is reward enough for itself; the joy of being something and of knowing that you are advancing is the greatest of all joys possible to man.

If you begin in your own family, as described in the preceding chapter, and then assume the same mental attitude with your neighbors, friends, and those you meet in business, you will soon find that people are beginning to depend on you. Your advice will be sought, and a constantly increasing number of people will look to you for strength and inspiration, and rely upon your judgment. Here, as in the home, you must avoid meddling with other people's affairs. Help all who come to you, but do not go about officiously endeavoring to set other people right. Mind your own business. It is no part of your mission in life to correct people's morals, habits, or practices. Lead a great life, doing all things with a great spirit and in a great way; give to him that asks of you as freely as you have received, but do not force your help or your opinions upon any man. If your neighbor wishes to smoke or drink, it is his business; it is none of yours until he consults you about it. If you lead a great life and do no preaching, you will save a thousand times as many souls as one who leads a small life and preaches continuously.

If you hold the right viewpoint of the world, others will find it out and be impressed by it through your daily conversation and practice. Do not try to convert others to your point of view, except by holding it and living accordingly. If your consecration is perfect you do not need to tell anyone; it will speedily become apparent to all that you are guided by a higher principle than the average man or woman. If your identification with God is complete, you do not need to explain the fact to others; it will become self-evident. To become known as a great personality, you have nothing to do but to live. Do not imagine that you must go charging about the world like Don Quixote, tilting at windmills, and overturning things in general, in order to demonstrate that you are somebody. Do not go hunting for big things to do. Live a great life where you are, and in the daily work you have to do, and greater works will surely find you out. Big things will come to you, asking to be done.

Be so impressed with the value of a man that you treat even a beggar or the tramp with the most distinguished consideration. All is God. Every man and woman is perfect. Let your manner be that of a god addressing other gods. Do not save all your consideration for the poor; the millionaire is as good as the tramp. This is a perfectly good world, and there is not a person or thing in it but is exactly right; be sure that you keep this in mind in dealing with things and men.

Form your mental vision of yourself with care. Make the thought-form of yourself as you wish to be, and hold this with the faith that it is being realized, and with the purpose to realize it completely. Do every common act as a god should do it; speak every word as a god should speak it; meet men and women of both low and high estate as a god meets other divine beings. Begin thus and continue thus, and your unfolding in ability and power will be great and rapid.

Chapter XVI

Some Further Explanations

We go back here to the matter of the point of view, for, besides being vitally important, it is the one that is likely to give the student the most trouble. We have been trained, partly by mistaken religious teachers, to look upon the world as being like a wrecked ship, storm-driven upon a rocky coast; utter destruction is inevitable at the end, and the most that can be done is to rescue, perhaps, a few of the crew. This view teaches us to consider the world as essentially bad and growing worse; and to believe that existing discords and inharmoniousness must continue and intensify until the end. It robs us of hope for society, government, and humanity, and gives us a decreasing outlook and contracting mind.

This is all wrong. The world is not wrecked. It is like a magnificent steamer with the engines in place and the machinery in perfect order. The bunkers are full of coal, and the ship is amply provisioned for the cruise; there is no lack of any good thing. Every provision Omniscience could devise has been made for the safety, comfort, and happiness of the crew; the steamer is out on the high seas tacking hither and thither because no one has yet learned the right course to steer. We are learning to steer, and in due time will come grandly into the harbor of perfect harmony.

The world is good, and growing better. Existing discords and inharmoniousness are but the pitching of the ship incidental to our own imperfect steering; they will all be removed in due time. This view gives us an increasing outlook and an expanding mind; it enables us to think largely of society and of ourselves, and to do things in a great way.

Furthermore, we see that nothing can be wrong with such a world or with any part of it, including our own affairs. If it is all moving on toward completion, then it is not going wrong; and as our own personal affairs are a part of the whole, they are not going wrong. You and all that you are concerned with are moving on toward completeness. Nothing can check this forward movement but yourself; and you can only check it by assuming a mental attitude that is at cross-purposes with the mind of God. You have nothing to keep right but yourself; if you keep yourself right, nothing can possibly go wrong with you, and you can have nothing to fear. No business or other disaster can come upon you if your personal attitude is right, for you are a part of that which is increasing and advancing, and you must increase and advance with it.

Moreover your thought-form will be mostly shaped according to your viewpoint of the cosmos. If you see the world as a lost and ruined thing you will see yourself as a part of it, and as partaking of its sins and weaknesses. If your outlook for the world as a whole is hopeless, your outlook for yourself cannot be hopeful. If you see the world as declining toward its end, you cannot see yourself as advancing. Unless you think well of all the works of God you cannot really think well of yourself, and unless you think well of yourself you can never become great.

I repeat that your place in life, including your material environment, is determined by the thought-form you habitually hold of yourself. When you make a thought-form of yourself you can hardly fail to form in your mind a corresponding environment. If you think of yourself as an incapable, inefficient person, you will think of yourself with poor or cheap surroundings. Unless you think well of yourself you will be sure to picture yourself in a more or less poverty stricken environment. These thoughts, habitually held, become invisible forms in the surrounding mind-stuff, and are with you continually. In due time, by the regular action of the eternal creative energy, the invisible thought-forms are produced in material stuff, and you are surrounded by your own thoughts made into material things.

See nature as a great living and advancing presence, and see human society in exactly the same way. It is all one, coming from one source, and it is all good. You yourself are made of the same stuff as God. All the constituents of God are parts of you; every power that God has is a constituent of man. You can move forward as you see God doing. You have within yourself the source of every power.

Chapter XVII

More About Thought

Give place here to some further consideration of thought. You will never become great until your own thoughts make you great, and therefore it is of the first importance that you should THINK. You will never do great things in the external world until you think great things in the internal world; and you will never think great things until you think about *truth*; about the verities. To think great things you must be absolutely sincere; and to be sincere you must know that your intentions are right. Insincere or false thinking is never great, however logical and brilliant it may be.

The first and most important step is to seek the truth about human relations, to know what you ought to be to other men, and what they ought to be to you. This brings you back to the search for a right viewpoint. You should study organic and social evolution. Read Darwin and Walter Thomas Mills, and when you read, THINK; think the whole matter over until you see the world of things and men in the right way. THINK about what God is doing until you can SEE what he is doing.

Your next step is to think yourself into the right personal attitude. Your viewpoint tells you what the right attitude is, and obedience to the soul puts you into it. It is only by making a complete consecration of yourself to the highest that is within you that you can attain to sincere thinking. So long as you know you are selfish in your aims, or dishonest or crooked in any way in your intentions or practices, your thinking will be false and your thoughts will have no power. THINK about the way you are doing things; about all your intentions, purposes, and practices, until you know that they are right.

The fact of his own complete unity with God is one that no person can grasp without deep and sustained thinking. Anyone can accept the proposition in a superficial way, but to feel and realize a vital comprehension of it is another matter. It is easy to think of going outside of yourself to meet God, but it is not so easy to think of going inside yourself to meet God. But God is there, and in the holy of holies of your own soul you may meet him face to face. It is a tremendous thing; this fact that all you need is already within you; that you do not have to consider how to get the power to do what you want to do or to make yourself what you want to be. You have only to consider how to use the power you have in the right way. And there is nothing to do but to begin. Use your perception of truth; you can see some truth today; live fully up to that and you will see more truth tomorrow.

To rid yourself of the old false ideas you will have to think a great deal about the value of men—the greatness and worth of a human soul. You must cease from looking at human mistakes and look at successes; cease from seeing faults and see virtues. You can no longer look upon men and women as lost and ruined beings that are descending into hell; you must come to regard them as shining souls who are ascending toward heaven. It will require some exercise of will power to do this, but this is the legitimate use of the will—to decide what you will think about and how you will think. The function of the will is to direct thought. Think about the good side of men; the lovely, attractive part, and exert your will in refusing to think of anything else in connection with them.

I know of no one who has attained to so much on this one point as Eugene V. Debs, twice the Socialist candidate for president of the United States. Mr. Debs reverences humanity. No appeal for help is ever made to him in vain. No one receives from him an unkind or censorious word. You cannot come into his presence without being made sensible of his deep and kindly personal interest in you. Every person, be he millionaire, grimy workingman, or toil worn woman, receives the radiant warmth of a brotherly affection that is sincere and true. No ragged child speaks to him on the street without receiving instant and tender recognition. Debs loves men. This has made him the leading figure in a great movement, the beloved hero of a million hearts, and will give him a deathless name. It is a great thing to love men so and it is only achieved by thought. Nothing can make you great but thought.

We may divide thinkers into those who think for themselves and those who think through others. The latter are the rule and the for-

mer the exception. *The first are original thinkers in a double sense, and egotists in the noblest meaning of the word.* —Schopenhauer.

The key to every man is his thought. Sturdy and defiant though he look he has a helm which he obeys, which is the idea after which all his facts are classified. He can only be reformed by showing him a new idea which commands his own. —Emerson.

All truly wise thoughts have been thought already thousands of times; but to make them really ours we must think them over again honestly till they take root in our personal expression. —Goethe.

All that a man is outwardly is but the expression and completion of his inward thought. To work effectively he must think clearly. To act nobly he must think nobly. —Channing.

Great men are they who see that spirituality is stronger than any material force; that thoughts rule the world.
—Emerson.

Some people study all their lives, and at their death they have learned everything except to think.
—Domergue.

It is the habitual thought that frames itself into our life. It affects us even more than our intimate social relations do. Our confidential friends have not so much to do in shaping our lives as the thoughts have which we harbor?
—J. W. Teal.

When God lets loose a great thinker on this planet, then all things are at risk. There is not a piece of science but its flank may be turned tomorrow; nor any literary reputation or the so-called eternal names of fame that may not be refused and condemned. —Emerson.

Think! *Think!!* THINK!!!

Chapter XVIII

Jesus' Idea Of Greatness

In the twenty-third chapter of Matthew Jesus makes a very plain distinction between true and false greatness; and also points out the one great danger to all who wish to become great; the most insidious of temptations which all must avoid and fight unceasingly who desire to really climb in the world. Speaking to the multitude and to his disciples he bids them beware of adopting the principle of the Pharisees. He points out that while the Pharisees are just and righteous men, honorable judges, true lawgivers and upright in their dealings with men, they "love the uppermost seats at feasts and greetings in the market place, and to be called Master, Master"; and in comparison with this principle, he says: "He that will be great among you let him serve."

The average person's idea of a great man, rather than of one who serves, is of one who succeeds in getting himself served. He gets himself in a position to command men; to exercise power over them, making them obey his will. The exercise of dominion over other people, to most persons, is a great thing. Nothing seems to be sweeter to the selfish soul than this. You will always find every selfish and undeveloped person trying to domineer over others, to exercise control over other men. Savage men were no sooner placed upon the earth than they began to enslave one another. For ages the struggle in war, diplomacy, politics, and government has been aimed at the securing of control over other men. Kings and princes have drenched the soil of the earth in blood and tears in the effort to extend their dominions and their power to rule more people.

The struggle of the business world today is the same as that on the battlefields of Europe a century ago so far as the ruling principle is concerned. Robert O. Ingersoll could not understand why men like Rockefeller and Carnegie seek for more money and make themselves slaves to the business struggle when they already have more than they can possibly use. He thought it a kind of madness and illustrated it as follows: "Suppose a man had fifty thousand pairs of pants, seventy-five thousand vests, one hundred thousand coats, and one hundred and fifty thousand neckties, what would you think of him if he arose in the morning before light and worked until after it was dark every day, rain or shine, in all kinds of weather, merely to get another necktie?"

But it is not a good simile. The possession of neckties gives a man no power over other men, while the possession of dollars does. Rockefeller, Carnegie, and their kind are not after dollars but power. It is the principle of the Pharisee; it is the struggle for the high place. It develops able men, cunning men, resourceful men, but not great men.

I want you to contrast these two ideas of greatness sharply in your minds. "He that will be great among you let him serve." Let me stand before the average American audience and ask the name of the greatest American and the majority will think of Abraham Lincoln; and is this not because in Lincoln above all the other men who have served us in public life we recognize the spirit of service? Not servility, but service. Lincoln was a great man because he knew how to be a great servant. Napoleon, able, cold, selfish, seeking the high places, was a brilliant man. Lincoln was great; Napoleon was not.

The very moment you begin to advance and are recognized as one who is doing things in a great way you will find yourself in danger. The temptation to patronize, advise, or take upon yourself the direction of other people's affairs is sometimes almost irresistible. Avoid, however, the opposite danger of falling into servility, or of completely throwing yourself away in the service of others. To do this has been the ideal of a great many people. The completely self-sacrificing life has been thought to be the Christ-like life, because, as I think, of a complete misconception of the character and teachings of Jesus. I have explained this misconception in a little book that I hope you may all sometime read, "A New Christ."

Thousands of people imitating Jesus, as they suppose, have belittled themselves and given up all else to go about doing good; practicing an altruism that is really as morbid and as far from great as the rankest selfishness. The finer instincts which respond to the cry of trouble or distress are not by any means all of you; they are not necessarily the best part of you. There are other things you must do besides helping the unfortunate, although it is true that a large part of the life and activities of every great person must be given to helping other people. As you begin to advance they will come to you. Do not turn them away. But do not make the fatal error of supposing that the life of complete self-abnegation is the way of greatness.

To make another point here, let me refer to the fact that Swedenborg's classification of fundamental motives is exactly the same as that of Jesus. He divides all men into two groups: those who live in pure love, and those who live in what he calls the love of ruling for the love of self. It will be seen that this is exactly the same as the lust for place and power of the Pharisees. Swedenborg saw this selfish love of power as the cause of all sin. It was the only evil desire of the human heart, from which all other evil desires sprang. Over against this he places pure love. He does not say love of God or love of man, but merely love. Nearly all religionists make more of love and service to God than they do of love and service to man. But it is a fact that love to God is not sufficient to save a man from the lust for power, for some of the most ardent lovers of the Deity have been the worst of tyrants. Lovers of God are often tyrants, and lovers of men are often meddlesome and officious.

Chapter XIX

A View Of Evolution

But how shall we avoid throwing ourselves into altruistic work if we are surrounded by poverty, ignorance, suffering, and every appearance of misery as very many people are? Those who live where the withered hand of want is thrust upon them from every side appealingly for aid must find it hard to refrain from continuous giving. Again, there are social and other irregularities, injustices done to the weak, which fire generous souls with an almost irresistible desire to set things right. We want to start a crusade; we feel that the wrongs will never be righted until we give ourselves wholly to the task. In all this we must fall back upon the point of view. We must remember that this is not a bad world but a good world in the process of becoming.

Beyond all doubt there was a time when there was no life upon this earth. The testimony of geology to the fact that the globe was once a ball of burning gas and molten rock, clothed about with boiling vapors, is indisputable. And we do not know how life could have existed under such conditions; that seems impossible. Geology tells us that later on a crust formed, the globe cooled and hardened, the vapors condensed and became mist or fell in rain. The cooled surface crumbled into soil; moisture accumulated, ponds and seas were gathered together, and at last somewhere in the water or on the land appeared something that was alive.

It is reasonable to suppose that this first life was in single-celled organisms, but behind these cells was the insistent urge of Spirit, the Great One Life seeking expression. And soon organisms having too much life to express themselves with one cell had two cells and then many, and still more life was poured into them. Multiple-celled organisms were formed; plants, trees, vertebrates, and mammals, many of them with strange shapes, but all were perfect after their kind as everything is that God makes. No doubt there were crude and almost monstrous forms of both animal and plant life; but everything filled its purpose in its day and it was all very good. Then another day came, the great day of the evolutionary process, a day when the morning stars sang together and the sons of God shouted for joy to behold the beginning of the end, for man, the object aimed at from the beginning, had appeared upon the scene.

An ape-like being, little different from the beasts around him in appearance, but infinitely different capacity for growth and thought. Art and beauty, architecture and song, poetry and music, all these were unrealized possibilities in that ape man's soul. And for his time and kind he was very good.

"It is God that works in you to will and to do of his good pleasure," says St. Paul. From the day the first man appeared God began to work IN men, putting more and more of himself into each succeeding generation, urging them on to larger achievements and to better conditions, social, governmental, and domestic. Those who looking back into ancient history see the awful conditions which existed, the barbarities, idolatries, and sufferings, and reading about God in connection with these things are disposed to feel that he was cruel and unjust to man, should pause to think. From the ape-man to the coming Christ man the race has had to rise. And it could only be accomplished by the successive unfolding of the various powers and possibilities latent in the human brain. Naturally the cruder and more animal-like part of man came to its full development first; for ages men were brutal; their governments were brutal, their religions were brutal, and what appears to be an immense amount of suffering resulted from this brutality. But God never delighted in suffering, and in every age he has given men a message, telling them how to avoid it. And all the while the urge of life, insistent, powerful, compelling, made the race keep moving forward; a little less brutality in each age and a little more spirituality in each age. And God kept on working in man. In every age there have been some individuals who were in advance of the mass and who heard and understood God better than their fellows. Upon these the inspiring hands of Spirit was laid and they were compelled to become interpreters. These were the prophets and seers, sometimes the priests and kings, and oftener still they were martyrs driven to the stake, the block, or the cross. It is to these who have heard God, spoken his word, and demonstrated his truth in their lives that all progress is really due.

Again, considering for a moment the presence of what is called evil in the world, we see that that which appears to us to be evil is only undeveloped; and that the undeveloped is perfectly good in its own stage and place. Because all things are necessary to man's complete unfoldment, all things in human life are the work of God. The graft rings in our cities, the red-light districts and their unfortunate inmates, these he consciously and voluntarily produced. Their part in the plan of unfoldment must be played. And when their part has been played he will sweep them off the stage as he did the strange and poisonous monsters which filled the swamps of the past ages.

In concluding this vision of evolution we might ask why it was all done, what is it for? This question should be easy for the thoughtful mind to answer. God desired to express himself, to live in form, and not only that, but to live in a form through which he could express himself on the highest moral and spiritual plane. God wanted to evolve a form in which he could live as a god and manifest himself as a god. This was the aim of the evolutionary force. The ages of warfare, bloodshed, suffering, injustice, and cruelty were tempered in many ways with love and justice as time advanced. And this was developing the brain of man to a point where it should be capable of giving full expression to the love and justice of God. The end is not yet; God aims not at the perfection of a few choice specimens for exhibition, like the large berries at the top of the box, but at the glorification of the race. The time will come when the Kingdom of God shall be established on earth; the time foreseen by the dreamer of the Isle of Patmos, when there shall be no more crying, neither shall there be any more pain, for the former things are all passed away, and there shall be no night there.

Chapter XX

Serving God

I have brought you thus far through the two preceding chapters with a view to finally settling the question of duty. This is one that puzzles and perplexes very many people who are earnest and sincere, and gives them a great deal of difficulty in its solution. When they start out to make something of themselves and to practice the science of being great, they find themselves necessarily compelled to rearrange many of their relationships. There are friends who perhaps must be alienated, there are relatives who misunderstand and who feel that they are in some way being slighted; the really great man is often considered selfish by a large circle of people who are connected with him and who feel that he might bestow upon them more benefits than he does. The question at the outset is: Is it my duty to make the most of myself regardless of everything else? Or shall I wait until I can do so without any friction or without causing loss to any one? This is the question of duty to self vs. duty to others.

One's duty to the world has been thoroughly discussed in the preceding pages and I give some consideration now to the idea of duty to God. An immense number of people have a great deal of uncertainty, not to say anxiety, as to what they ought to do for God. The amount of work and service that is done for him in these United States in the way of church work and so on is enormous. An immense amount of human energy is expended in what is called serving God. I propose to consider briefly what serving God is and how a man may serve God best, and I think I shall be able to make plain that the conventional idea as to what constitutes service to God is all wrong.

When Moses went down into Egypt to bring out the Hebrews from bondage, his demand upon Pharaoh, in the name of the Deity, was, "Let the people go that they may serve me." He led them out into the wilderness and there instituted a new form of worship which has led many people to suppose that worship constitutes the service of God, although later God himself distinctly declared that he cared nothing for ceremonies, burned offerings, or oblation, and the teaching of Jesus if rightly understood, would do away with organized temple worship altogether. God does not lack anything that men may do for him with their hands or bodies or voices. Saint Paul points out that man can do nothing for God, for God does not need anything.

The view of evolution that we have taken shows God seeking expression through man. Through all the successive ages in which his spirit has urged man up the height, God has gone on seeking expression. Every generation of men is more Godlike than the preceding generation. Every generation of men demands more in the way of fine homes, pleasant surroundings, congenial work, rest, travel, and opportunity for study than the preceding generation.

I have heard some shortsighted economists argue that the working people of today ought surely to be fully contented because their condition is so much better than that of the workingman two hundred years ago who slept in a windowless hut on a floor covered with rushes in company with his pigs. If that man had all that he was able to use for the living of all the life he knew how to live, he was perfectly content, and if he had lack he was not contented. The man of today has a comfortable home and very many things, indeed, that were unknown a short period back in the past, and if he has all that he can use for the living of all the life he can imagine, he will be content. But he is not content. God has lifted the race so far that any common man can picture a better and more desirable life than he is able to live under existing conditions. And so long as this is true, so long as a man can think and clearly picture to himself a more desirable life, he will be discontented with the life he has to live, and rightly so. That discontent is the Spirit of God urging men on to more desirable conditions. It is God who seeks expression in the race. "He works in us to will and to do."

The only service you can render God is to give expression to what he is trying to give the world, through you. The only service you can render God is to make the very most of yourself in order that God may live in you to the utmost of your possibilities. In a former work of this series, *The Science of Getting Rich*, I refer to the little boy at the piano, the music in whose soul could not find expression through his untrained hands. This is a good illustration of the way the Spirit of God is over, about, around, and in all of us, seeking to do great things with us, so soon as we will train our hands and feet, our minds, brains, and bodies to do his service.

Your first duty to God, to yourself, and to the world is to make yourself as great a personality, in every way, as you possibly can. And that, it seems to me, disposes of the question of duty.

There are one or two other things that might be disposed of in closing this chapter. I have written of opportunity in a preceding chapter. I have said, in a general way, that it is within the power of every man to become great, just as in *The Science of Getting Rich* I declared that it is within the power of every man to become rich. But these sweeping generalizations need qualifying. There are men who have such materialistic minds that they are absolutely incapable of comprehending the philosophy set forth in these books. There is a great mass of men and women who have lived and worked until they are practically incapable of thought along these lines; and they cannot receive the message. Something may be done for them by demonstration, that is, by living the life before them. But that is the only way they can be aroused. The world needs demonstration more than it needs teaching. For this mass of people our duty is to become as great in personality as possible in order that they may see and desire to do likewise. It is our duty to make ourselves great for their sakes; so that we may help prepare the world that the next generation shall have better conditions for thought.

One other point; I am frequently written to by people who wish to make something of themselves and to move out into the world, but who are hampered by home ties, having others more or less dependent upon them, whom they fear would suffer if left alone. In general I advise such people to move out fearlessly, and to make the most of themselves. If there is a loss at home it will be only temporary and apparent, for in a little while, if you follow the leading of Spirit, you will be able to take better care of your dependents than you have ever done before.

Chapter XXI

A Mental Exercise

The purpose of mental exercises must not be misunderstood. There is no virtue in charms or formulated strings of words; there is no short cut to development by repeating prayers or incantations. A mental exercise is an exercise, not in repeating words, but in the thinking of certain thoughts. The phrases that we repeatedly hear become convictions, as Goethe says; and the thoughts that we repeatedly think become habitual, and make us what we are. The purpose in taking a mental exercise is that you may think certain thoughts repeatedly until you form a habit of thinking them; then they will be your thoughts all the time. Taken in the right way and with an understanding of their purpose, mental exercises are of great value; but taken as most people take them they are worse than useless.

The thoughts embodied in the following exercise are the ones you want to think. You should take the exercise once or twice daily, but you should think the thoughts continuously. That is, do not think them twice a day for a stated time and then forget them until it is time to take the exercise again. The exercise is to impress you with the material for continuous thought.

Take a time when you can have from twenty minutes to half an hour secure from interruption, and proceed first to make yourself physically comfortable. Lie at ease in a Morris chair, or on a couch, or in bed; it is best to lie flat on your back. If you have no other time, take the exercise on going to bed at night and before rising in the morning.

First let your attention travel over your body from the crown of your head to the soles of your feet, relaxing every muscle as you go. Relax completely. And next, get physical and other ills off your mind. Let the attention pass down the spinal cord and out over the nerves to the extremities, and as you do so think:

"My nerves are in perfect order all over my body. They obey my will, and I have great nerve force." Next bring your attention to the lungs and think:

"I am breathing deeply and quietly, and the air goes into every cell of my lungs, which are in perfect condition. My blood is purified and made clean." Next, to the heart:

"My heart is beating strongly and steadily, and my circulation is perfect, even to the extremities." Next, to the digestive system:

"My stomach and bowels perform their work perfectly. My food is digested and assimilated and my body rebuilt and nourished. My liver, kidneys, and bladder each perform their several functions without pain or strain; I am perfectly well. My body is resting, my mind is quiet, and my soul is at peace.

"I have no anxiety about financial or other matters. God, who is within me, is also in all things I want, impelling them toward me; all that I want is already given to me. I have no anxiety about my health, for I am perfectly well. I have no worry or fear whatever.

"I rise above all temptation to moral evil. I cast out all greed, selfishness, and narrow personal ambition; I do not hold envy, malice, or enmity toward any living soul. I will follow no course of action which is not in accord 'with my highest ideals. I am right and I will do right."

Viewpoint

All is right with the world. It is perfect and advancing to completion. I will contemplate the facts of social, political, and industrial life only from this high viewpoint. Behold, it is all very good. I will see all human beings, all my acquaintances, friends, neighbors, and the members of my own household in the same way. They are all good. Nothing is wrong with the universe; nothing can be wrong but my own personal attitude, and henceforth I keep that right. My whole trust is in God.

Consecration

I will obey my soul and be true to that within me that is highest. I will search within for the pure idea of right in all things, and when I find it I will express it in my outward life. I will abandon everything I have outgrown for the best I can think. I will have the highest thoughts concerning all my relationships, and my manner and action shall express these thoughts. I surrender my body to be ruled by my mind; I yield my mind to the dominion of my soul, and I give my soul to the guidance of God.

Identification

There is but one substance and source, and of that I am made and with it I am one. It is my Father; I proceeded forth and came from it. My Father and I are one, and my Father is greater than I, and I do His will. I surrender myself to conscious unity with Pure Spirit; there is but one and that one is everywhere. I am one with the Eternal Consciousness.

Idealization

Form a mental picture of yourself as you want to be, and at the greatest height your imagination can picture. Dwell upon this for some little time, holding the thought: "This is what I really am; it is a picture of my own perfect and advancing to completion. I will contemplate the facts of social, political, and industrial life only from this high viewpoint. Behold, it is all very good. I will see all human beings, all my acquaintances, friends, neighbors, and the members of my own household in the same way. They are all good.

Nothing is wrong with the universe, nothing can be wrong but my own personal attitude, and henceforth I keep that right. My whole trust is in God.

Realization

I appropriate to myself the power to become what I want to be, and to do what I want to do. I exercise creative energy; all the power there is, is mine. I will arise and go forth with power and perfect confidence; I will do mighty works in the strength of the Lord, my God. I will trust and not fear, for God is with me.

Chapter XXII

A Summary Of The Science Of Being Great

All men are made of the one intelligent substance, and therefore all contain the same essential powers and possibilities. Greatness is equally inherent in all, and may be manifested by all. Every person may become great. Every constituent of God is a constituent of man.

Man may overcome both heredity and circumstances by exercising the inherent creative power of the soul. If he is to become great, the soul must act, and must rule the mind and the body. Man's knowledge is limited, and he falls into error through ignorance; to avoid this he must connect his soul with Universal Spirit. Universal Spirit is the intelligent substance from which all things come; it is in and through all things. All things are known to this universal mind, and man can so unite himself with it as to enter into all knowledge.

To do this man must cast out of himself everything that separates him from God. He must will to live the divine life, and he must rise above all moral temptations; he must forsake every course of action that is not in accord with his highest ideals.

He must reach the right viewpoint, recognizing that God is all, in all, and that there is nothing wrong. He must see that nature, society, government, and industry are perfect in their present stage, and advancing toward completion; and that all men and women everywhere are good and perfect. He must know that all is right with the world, and unite with God for the completion of the perfect work. It is only as man sees God as the Great Advancing Presence in all, and good in all that he can rise to real greatness.

He must consecrate himself to the service of the highest that is within himself, obeying the voice of the soul. There is an Inner Light in every man that continuously impels him toward the highest, and he must be guided by this light if he would become great.

He must recognize the fact that he is one with the Father, and consciously affirm this unity for himself and for all others. He must know himself to be a god among gods, and act accordingly. He must have absolute faith in his own perceptions of truth, and begin at home to act upon these perceptions. As he sees the true and right course in small things, he must take that course. He must cease to act unthinkingly, and begin to think; and he must be sincere in his thought.

He must form a mental conception of himself at the highest, and hold this conception until it is his habitual thought-form of himself. This thought-form he must keep continuously in view. He must outwardly realize and express that thought-form in his actions. He must do everything that he does in a great way. In dealing with his family, his neighbors, acquaintances, and friends, he must make every act an expression of his ideal.

The man who reaches the right viewpoint and makes full consecration, and who fully idealizes himself as great, and who makes every act, however trivial, an expression of the ideal, has already attained to greatness. Everything he does will be done in a great way. He will make himself known, and will be recognized as a personality of power. He will receive knowledge by inspiration, and will know all that he needs to know. He will receive all the material wealth he forms in his thoughts, and will not lack for any good thing. He will be given ability to deal with any combination of circumstances that may arise, and his growth and progress will be continuous and rapid. Great works will seek him out, and all men will delight to do him honor.

Because of its peculiar value to the student of the Science of Being Great, I close this book by giving a portion of Emerson's essay on the "Oversoul." This great essay is fundamental, showing the foundation principles of monism and the science of greatness. I recommend the student to study it most carefully in connection with this book.

> What is the universal sense of want and ignorance, but the fine innuendo by which the great soul makes its enormous claim? Why do men feel that the natural history of man has never been written, but always he is leaving behind what you have said of him, and it becomes old, and books of metaphysics worthless? The philosophy of six thousand years has not searched the chambers and magazines of the soul. In its experiments there has always remained, in the last analysis, a residuum it could not resolve. Man is a stream whose

source is hidden. Always our being is descending into us from we know not whence. The most exact calculator has no prescience that somewhat incalculable may not balk the very next moment. I am constrained every moment to acknowledge a higher origin for events than the will I call mine.

As with events, so it is with thoughts. When I watch that flowing river, which, out of regions I see not, pours for a season its streams into me—I see that I am a pensioner—not a cause, but a surprised spectator of this ethereal water; that I desire and look up, and put myself in the attitude for reception, but from some alien energy the visions come.

The Supreme Critic on all the errors of the past and present, and the only prophet of that which must be, is that great nature in which we rest, as the earth lies in the soft arms of the atmosphere; that Unity, that Oversoul, with which every man's particular being is contained and made one with all other; that common heart, of which all sincere conversation is the worship, to which all right action is submission; that overpowering reality which confutes our tricks and talents, and constrains everyone to pass for what he is, and to speak from his character and not from his tongue; and which evermore tends and aims to pass into our thought and hand, and become wisdom, and virtue, and power, and beauty. We live in succession, in division, in parts, in particles. Meantime within man is the soul of the whole; the wise silence; the universal beauty, to which every part and particle is equally related, the eternal One. And this deep power in which we exist, and whose beatitude is all-accessible to us, is not only self-sufficing and perfect in every hour, but the act of seeing, and the thing seen, the seer and the spectacle, the subject and the object, are one. We see the world piece by piece, as the sun, the moon, the animal, the tree; but the whole, of which these are the shining parts, is the soul. It is only by the vision of that Wisdom, that the horoscope of the ages can be read, and it is only by falling back on our better thoughts, by yielding to the spirit of prophecy which is innate in every man, that we know what it saith. Every man s words, who speaks from that life, must sound vain to those who do not dwell in the same thought on their own part. I dare not speak for it. My words do not carry its august sense; they fall short and cold. Only itself can inspire whom it will, and behold! Their speech shall be lyrical and sweet, and universal as the rising of the wind. Yet I desire, even by profane words, if sacred I may not use, to indicate the heaven of this deity, and to report what hints I have collected of the transcendent simplicity and energy of the Highest Law. If we consider what happens in conversation, in reveries, in remorse, in times of passion, in surprises, in the instruction of dreams wherein often we see ourselves in masquerade—the droll disguises only magnifying and enhancing a real element, and forcing it on our distinct notice—we shall catch many hints that will broaden and lighten into knowledge of the secret of nature. All goes to show that the soul in man is not an organ, but animates and exercises all the organs; is not a function, like the power of memory, of calculation, of comparison—but uses these as hands and feet; is not a faculty, but a light; is not the intellect or the will, but the master of the intellect and the will—is the vast background of our being, in which they lie—an immensity not possessed and that cannot be possessed. From within or from behind, a light shines through us upon things, and makes us aware that we are nothing, but the light is all. A man is the facade of a temple wherein all wisdom and all good abide. What we commonly call man, the eating, drinking, planting, counting man, does not, as we know him, represent himself, but misrepresents himself. Him we do not respect, but the soul, whose organ he is, would he let it appear through his action, would make our knees bend. When it breathes through his intellect, it is genius; when it flows through his affection it is love.

After its own law and not by arithmetic is the rate of its progress to be computed. The soul's advances are not made by gradation, such as can be represented by motion in a straight line; but rather by ascension of state, such as can be represented by metamorphosis—from the *egg* to the worm, from the worm to the fly. The growths of genius are of a certain total character, that does not advance the elect individual first over John, then Adam, then Richard, and give to each the pain of discovered inferiority, but by every throe of growth the man expands there where he works, passing, at each pulsation, classes, populations of men. With each divine impulse the mind rends the thin rinds of the visible and finite, and comes out into eternity, and inspires and expires its air. It converses with truths that have always been spoken in the world, and becomes conscious of a closer sympathy with Zeno and Arrian, than with persons in the house.

This is the law of moral and of mental gain. The simple rise, as by specific levity, not into a particular virtue, but into the region of all the virtues. They are in the spirit that contains them all. The soul is superior to all the particulars of merit. The soul requires purity, but purity is not it; requires justice, but justice is not that; requires beneficence, but is somewhat better; so that there is a kind of descent and accommodation felt when we leave speaking of moral nature, to urge a virtue which it enjoins. For, to the soul in her pure action, all the virtues are natural, and not painfully acquired. Speak to his heart and the man becomes suddenly virtuous.

Within the same sentiment is the germ of intellectual growth, which obeys the same law. Those who are capable of humility, of justice, of love, of aspiration, are already on a platform that commands the sciences and arts, speech and poetry, action and grace. For whoso dwells in this mortal beatitude, does already anticipate those special powers which men prize so highly; just as love does justice to all the gifts of the object beloved. The lover has no talent, no skill, which passes for quite nothing with his enamored maiden, however little she may possess of related faculty. And the heart that abandons itself to the Supreme Mind finds itself related to all its works and will travel a royal road to particular knowledge and powers. For, in ascending to this primary and aboriginal sentiment, we have come from our remote station on the circumference instantaneously to the center of the world, where, as in the closet of God, we see causes, and anticipate the universe, which is but a slow effect.

THE POWER OF SEX TRANSMUTATION

Mitch Horowitz

Contents

Author's Note
— 289 —

Chapter 1
Why a Book on Sex Transmutation?
— 290 —

Chapter 2
What Is Sex Transmutation?
— 291 —

Chapter 3
Ways of Using Sex Transmutation
— 296 —

Chapter 4
Sex Energy in Ancient Cultures—
and Our Own
— 308 —

Author's Note

This book is based on a talk I delivered on sex transmutation in the spring of 2019. The response was so enthusiastic—and the questions that followed so spirited—that I decided to adapt the material into this concise book, *The Power of Sex Transmutation*. My hope is that it elucidates one of the most powerful and intriguing yet confounding points in Napoleon Hill's program of success.

Chapter 1

Why a Book on Sex Transmutation?

This book explores the taboo topic of Napoleon Hill. The use of sexual energy arrives as step ten of thirteen steps to riches in *Think and Grow Rich*. Hill calls it "the mystery of sex transmutation."

Sex transmutation is probably the most intriguing and, in some regards, the most powerful, but also least-understood step in Hill's philosophy of personal achievement. It is also the least discussed. This is because it engenders embarrassment and confusion. You can only imagine how much more so this topic seemed risqué, radical, and even fringe-like in the year 1937 when Napoleon Hill first wrote about it.

Before I get into the specifics of sex transmutation, I want to share a personal revelation that made me realize how taboo a topic this really is. In 1960, more than twenty years after Hill first published *Think and Grow Rich*, one of my heroes, the motivational writer and radio commentator Earl Nightingale recorded a condensed edition of the book. Earl's 1960 condensation omitted the chapter on sex transmutation almost entirely. He neutered it, so to speak, and changed it to "enthusiasm." Gone was any mention of sex transmutation, and in its place was the more benign and somewhat redundant section on the power of enthusiasm. If Earl Nightingale and his publisher were too embarrassed to discuss the topic of sex transmutation in 1960, admittedly a long time ago in a more conservative age, again how much more radical did this subject seem in 1937? And how brave was it of Napoleon Hill to tackle this topic at all?

Now, I was delivering an online seminar on *Think and Grow Rich* shortly before this writing, and I was hitting upon some of the key points of Hill's book. During the question-and-answer session, a participant asked, "Could you please talk about this topic of sex transmutation, because it's completely mysterious to me, it's lost on me, I don't understand it. Can you unpack it?"

I was struck by this question. For these many decades, readers have been reading and rereading *Think and Grow Rich*, as well as taking in audio editions, adaptations, commentaries, and online seminars—and still, after generations, the topic of sex transmutation remains mysterious, taboo, intriguing, and often confusing. Here we are in 2019, and a dedicated reader was asking, in effect, "what in the world did he mean by this?"

I was struck by the necessity to treat this topic more fully and openly; because I think it's on everyone's minds, and yet very few commentators on Napoleon Hill have ever really sought to expand on what he means by the "mystery of sex transmutation." That's what we're going to do.

Chapter 2

What Is Sex Transmutation?

Let me begin by explaining exactly what Napoleon Hill meant, because I do believe it can be described in simple terms, even though it is an esoteric subject and probably every explanation—including Hill's own—will bring with it a train of questions, which I will address. But it can be explained plainly, and here it is:

Hill believed, I think with great reason and with great antecedents in a variety of ancient traditions, that the force of life seeking to express itself within us, the force of creativity seeking to express itself in us, is experienced as the *sexual urge*. The sexual urge is what motivates our species to procreate. The sensate experience driving our species toward procreation is experienced as sexual desire. As such, it's extremely powerful, arguably it's overwhelmingly powerful, a topic that we will touch upon later.

It is an urge that brings great joy. It is an urge that brings great suffering. It is an urge that brings people into harmony with one another. It is an urge that brings people into profound conflict. But it is the essential creative urge. It is the life force, so to speak, seeking expression. The sensate experience of sexual satisfaction, of sexual pleasure is how we men and women experience life itself seeking procreation, not only on a biological level, *but on all levels.* We are by nature productive beings. We are generative beings. We build things. We solve problems. We create new ones. We create works of art. We maintain commerce. We foster households. We create and tear down buildings, bridges, highways, and structures of all kinds. We devise technologies and seek, with greater and lesser levels of success, to manage the problems and challenges that accompany them. We eradicate old things and put new things, sometimes but not always improved things, in their place.

All of these impulses within the individual, Hill taught, are *the force of life itself seeking expression.* And that force experienced on the most sensate level is the sexual urge. But it is more than simply physical desire or expression—it is the essence of life seeking propagation on all levels and in all ways. Every time you create something, whether financial, artistic, architectural, craft-based, or product-based, this same life force is replicating itself through you.

There is antecedent for Hill's observation in many different traditions: in Taoism, in Kabbalah, in Vedic teachings, and beyond. Sex transmutation is one the deepest aspects of Hill's philosophy. In fact, I think it is the aspect of Hill's philosophy that is most fully connected to other wisdom traditions, and it is the most esoteric.

Now, some seekers today regard Napoleon Hill's works as a kind of spirituality with training wheels. There are people on the path who consider themselves above Napoleon Hill's material, a point of view that I discourage. But among that group of critics there are also those who will concede that he had a very knowing, sophisticated, and practical grasp of the concept of sex energy as it's been expressed in religious traditions and esoteric traditions throughout the ages. They are correct. And here we arrive at the *actionable* part of his teaching.

As noted, Hill saw the sexual urge as the creative impulse seeking expression within men and women, not only biologic expression, but all forms of expression: creative, commercial, and so on. He took this keen observation a step further and said you can actually *harness* and *use* this energy in your life in ways that go beyond the familiar physical releases, and in a manner that adds power to the pursuit of your goals. You do it this way: When you feel a sexual urge, when you feel the wish to express sexual desire, *you as an individual are capable of redirecting that desire towards an expression other than the physical*, towards some other form of expression or creation, and you do this through the mental act of consciously redirecting the sexual urge from physical to creative expression. The creative expression takes the form of whatever your worldly wish is at a given period. This is the act of transmutation. It is, in effect, an act of mental alchemy. You can actually become consciously aware of redirecting or transmuting the urge for sexual expression away from the physical and towards something that you are seeking to create in the world, whether commercial, scholarly, artistic, something physically based, and so forth.

This transmutation adds unique energy, intellect, enthusiasm, resilience, and intuitive insight to whatever you are working on. This is because sexual transmutation consciously places the force of creation itself at the back of your personal efforts.

I must immediately note that Hill is not counseling you to sublimate or repress the sexual urge. Quite the opposite. In the same chapter, Hill also emphasizes that nothing is greater tonic for one's mood, spirit, and physical relaxation and wellness than healthfully expressed, consensual sexuality. He makes that point again and again.

This, too, is a very liberated attitude for the year 1937—that physical sexual expression is vital for a sense of wellbeing, and that it probably has greater therapeutic value than anything else we engage in.

So, he's not in any respect talking about sublimation, repression, or abstinence—not at all. But he is making the point that there exist other selective channels through which sexual energy can be expressed, which go beyond the physical. Physical expression is one vital, necessary, helpful means of expression. But there are other creative, commercial, artistic, intellectual, athletic channels through which the sexual impulse can be directed, at the time and place of your choosing.

In fact, Hill notes that greatly effective people in the world, in whatever walk of life—the entrepreneur, the person who excels at a certain art or craft or science, the writer, the actor, the salesman, people who tend to perform at a uniquely high level in their field, and people who tend to be magnetic and enthusiastic and demonstrate the capacity to persuade other people of the soundness of their plans and get other people to go along with them—all of them, often unconsciously, are using sexual energy, and channeling the sexual urge, at critical moments, into their presentation or works. This imbues their works or personalities with greater vigor, substance, and appeal.

Hill makes the observation that, in many cases, such people are of a very highly sexual nature. The sexual urge, he writes, is very heavily pronounced in them, and they are using it all the time, not always knowingly, not always consciously, but they are using it to forward their plans, to rally people to their side, to get things done. Hill specifically uses the example of a salesperson who is exceptionally persuasive—this person's magnetism, he notes, is sexual in nature. But it is a form of transmuted sexuality in which it is not directed toward physicality or intimacy, but rather it is expressed in the manner of charisma or sales appeal. This is why a customer sometimes feels, often mistakenly, that a sales agent is flirting. That may be occurring on some level, but what is more often occurring is the act of sex transmutation—although the practitioner and the subject are unaware of it.

Hill takes matters even further and maintains that people who are commonly regarded as geniuses, as icons, as impresarios are capable of rising to that level of excellence because sexual energy is at the back of their efforts. Again, this energy is the life force itself seeking expression and creation through us in myriad ways. Now, for the plural term geniuses, Hill uses the arcane plural *genii*. This is significant. Genii dates to Roman-Latin usage. It means not only great intellectual prowess but also suggests the Ancient Roman meaning that genius itself is a gift bestowed by higher spirits or daemons. The same term appears as *jinn* or genie in Arab folklore and culture, again referencing a spirit capable of possessing the individual or bestowing supernatural power. This suggests the connection Hill saw between higher forces of life and the individual's capacity for accomplishment.

A similar point was made by the great medical clairvoyant Edgar Cayce (1877–1945), who was roughly contemporaneous with Hill. I have no evidence that the two figures ever met or exchanged ideas. But they reached similar conclusions in this area. In my book, *Occult America*, I write about Cayce advising a young man from Kentucky, a distant cousin who writes to him in the 1930s to say that he is gay, and he doesn't know where to turn, he doesn't know what to do; he's been to different therapists and doctors, and he feels completely at a loss as to how to proceed with his life because all the people around him, given the time and era, pathologize his sexuality.

Cayce, remarkably enough, a man who was raised in the environs of a deeply conservative Bible belt region of the country, replies to this young man with extraordinary sensitivity and insight. Here is a portion of the seer's written response:

> *Sex, of course, is a great factor in everyone's life; it is the line between the great and the vagabond, the good and the bad; it is the*

expression of reactive forces in our very nature; allowed to run wild, to self-indulgence, becomes physical and mental derangement; turned into the real influence it should be in one's life, connects man closer with his God, and this is the use you should put it to. . . . That your experience has brought you manifestations that have at times, or often, expressed themselves in sex is not to be wondered at, when we realize that that is the expression of creative life on earth.

I wrote about this episode at the end of Occult America because I wanted to demonstrate what a remarkably sensitive, intuitive, and sympathetic figure Edgar Cayce was that he could write to a young man like that from Kentucky in the 1930s. Edgar's was probably one of the only voices that sounded that way at that time. And, looking back, I think he and Napoleon Hill were in comportment in their attitudes about sexuality. They viewed sexuality as a positive expression, a therapeutic expression, a healthful expression—and something more. Again, Edgar is expressing the view that while the biologic expression of sex is vital and necessary, the sexual urge, in its broadest terms, underscores everything creative that we do. And that's exactly what Hill was driving at.

Chapter 3

Ways of Using Sex Transmutation

I see two critical steps to employing the power of sex transmutation in your life.

The first is simply to become of aware of it—the concept of sexual energy and its potential transmutation adds a whole new dimension to how we understand human sexuality and creativity. It is certainly not something we're raised to observe. We must see and understand the sexual force in our lives as not only an urge towards physical release and procreation, but as something that is also at the back of our wishes, drives, desires, and efforts.

That awareness places you on more intimate terms with yourself and your nature, which is vitally important because the first step of all productive self-knowledge is knowing thyself. So, that is step one.

In knowing yourself sexually, it is also important to be aware of how this facet of your nature is used to manipulate you. Our consumer society repackages and resells everything, including heroism, rebelliousness, religion, and, of course, sexuality. Every human urge that has its own noble, primal basis in the life of the individual is ultimately repackaged and sold back to us, or potentially used to manipulate us.

Pornography has never been more prevalent in our society because of the digital revolution. I suppose our generation is the first generation that is dealing with the truly mass, 24/7 distribution of pornography. It's existed from time immemorial, of course, going back to Greek vases and Vedic tapestries. Our generation is not unique in this regard, but our generation is unique insofar as this material is being distributed worldwide on demand, and I suppose we have to ask ourselves how this going to affect us. And we don't fully know. I tend to have permissive attitudes towards all these things, but at the same time I do think that we as a species, at least here in the West, are getting somewhat reconditioned sexually because there's such a vast consumption of pornography today.

Now, again, I don't know whether that's a wholly good or bad thing, or, as is often the case, there are probably a wide range of consequences spread across a large field of possibilities. It is probable that adolescents, in particular, are getting conditioned along certain lines because of the nature of pornography. I also recognize that there are some people for whom pornography is a positive experience, for whom it alleviates loneliness and sexual urges, and I take that seriously. I also recognize that there are performers doing this for a living, who

I believe deserve respect and fair treatment financially. So, there's a complexity of things going on.

Probably the reason we're facing so many challenges in this area, and part of the reason why so much of the traffic that actually goes on within digital culture is sexual in nature, is because Napoleon Hill was correct: the sexual urge is at the back of so much in life. In *Think and Grow Rich*, Napoleon Hill notes that of all the things that seem to urge the individual in a certain direction, that play upon the individual's motivations and desires, and that stimulate the psyche, sexuality is the number-one stimulant. Here is Hill's list of "The Ten Mind Stimuli:"

1. The desire for sex expression
2. Love
3. A burning desire for fame, power, or financial gain, MONEY
4. Music
5. Friendship between either those of the same sex, or those of the opposite sex
6. A Master Mind alliance based upon the harmony of two or more people who ally themselves for spiritual or temporal advancement*
7. Mutual suffering, such as that experienced by people who are persecuted
8. Auto-suggestion
9. Fear
10. Narcotics and alcohol

Obviously, lots of things motivate us. We're motivated by the need for income. We're motivated by peer attitudes. We're motivated by the desire to be appreciated. We're motivated by our fears. As Hill notes, some motivations are substance-based. Our minds and emotions are

---

* I write about this in my book *The Power of the Master Mind* (G&D Media).

stimulated, sometimes heightened and sometimes dulled, by various drugs and by alcohol. The wish to know, the wish to attain higher knowledge, is also a form of motivation. Yet amid all of these diffuse motivations, Hill ranks at the top the sexual urge. So, it's natural that marketers and others around us are, in varying ways and either consciously or unconsciously, going to use sexuality to manipulate us. It's inevitable and it requires mindfulness and even wariness. Sometimes the people doing the manipulating are not aware themselves of what is going on.

The power of sex, even in our media-saturated society, is still something of a taboo topic. It still makes people uncomfortable. This is among the reasons why I want to reassure you that everything I am writing about, and the experiments I am about to posit here and in the next chapter, are your own personal, private inquiries. These things belong to the environs of your own psyche. You don't have to run out and share what you're doing. You don't have to seek anyone's approbation or approval. You don't have to identify yourself or adopt some label.

I think our greatest personal experiments are conducted in private, and I invite everyone to explore what I am about to describe knowing that you do not have to take a communal or congregational approach to any of this. These sexual explorations are yours alone, and I think that sense of privacy, that sense of silence, invites you to study, consider, experiment, to get to know yourself in a different way.

Now, the second step takes us further into the question of application. To review, Hill makes the contention, and I believe this is true from my own personal experience, that when you are possessed of the sexual urge, you can—by a shift in your attention—redirect that urge from physical satisfaction toward the accomplishment of another aim, whether commercial, artistic, educative, or creative. Remember: you're not repressing physical satisfaction. Rather, you are electing to make a choice in a self-selected situation. This act will place greater and deeper vigor, insight, and energy behind your efforts.

You may be writing a chapter in a book. You may be delivering a sales presentation. You may be building a home. You may be practicing a dance routine or a martial arts combination. Whatever you're dedicated to, you can do consciously what we're doing unconsciously all the time by harnessing sexual energy as a creative force, as a creative impetus. It's going on constantly whether we're directing it or not.

In life we're sitting in the passenger seat most of the time. But through a shift in our attention we can, at a choice moment, transmute these creative, sexual energies. Again, we already do it unconsciously; when people are filled with excitement and enthusiasm and a positive, fearless, can-do attitude; when they are passionately applying themselves in the direction of a natural and cherished task—there is sexual energy present.

People are always telling me things like, "You're so enthusiastic." "You seem never to sleep"—I do sleep, by the way. And, "you produce so much in terms of books and lectures and shows and narration. How do you do it?" I say, "It's love for the subject matter. I'm deeply impassioned towards my subjects. I'm very driven to do it." Napoleon Hill would say, in effect, "Yes, bravo to that—that's true; but there's sex energy at the back of all the terms you're using. You're using euphemisms."

He would probably make the point that passion itself is a euphemism. Magnetism is a euphemism. Even enthusiasm, that elixir that seems to make everything possible, is a euphemism. He would say behind all of that is the sexual urge which is the urge of life seeking creation, generativity, and productivity.

Now, we have to allow ourselves to relax about all of this. There are not always times where sexual redirection is possible. Sometimes sexual expression, of whatever form, requires engagement and release. That's just human nature. So, I don't want people to get hung up over this. I'm not trying to create another rule under which you feel driven to live. Sexuality doesn't obey rules, in any case. But there are select times where you will find, if you experiment, that you *can* redirect the sexual urge in a healthful, natural way along different lines, specifically creative lines.

There are also ways in which this occurs more subtly. One of the things that Napoleon Hill writes about—and here I'm a little hamstrung by some of the old-fashioned language and gender roles that Hill used back in 1937, but the point retains its substance—is that one of the greatest drives behind the creative process, in his language, is man's wish to please woman. Hill writes this in *Think and Grow Rich*, and here I use the original language:

> *Man's greatest motivating force is his desire to please woman! The hunter who excelled during prehistoric days, before the dawn of civilization, did so, because of his desire to appear great in the eyes of woman. Man's nature has not changed in this respect. The "hunter" of today brings home no skins of wild animals, but he indicates his desire for her favor by supplying fine clothes, motor cars, and wealth. Man has the same desire to please woman that he had before the dawn of civilization. The only thing that has changed, is his method of pleasing. Men who accumulate large fortunes, and attain to great heights of power and fame, do so, mainly, to satisfy their desire to please women.*

This same point is captured, albeit in a grim and haunting way, in the movie *The Social Network*, written by Aaron Sorkin. *The Social Network* is about the rise of Facebook as a new technology and media titan. In the movie, these young programmers are feverishly trying to assemble Facebook, particularly Mark Zuckerberg, who appears as a conflicted, socially awkward wizard. He and his generally male collaborators and competitors are in, in essence, trying to "hook up" by presenting themselves as successful, entrepreneurial, hard-driven models of achievement and money.

If you watch the film, which I highly recommend, you'll see the undercurrent of sexuality running through all two hours. It's a vexing and curious aspect of human nature, but what they were expressing in that film, in a somewhat critical way, was what Napoleon Hill was expressing in a more holistic way. He was saying that the nexus of sex and success is simply a fact of human nature. Great people throughout the ages, and in our own time, have often been driven to heights of success because of their desire to please or attract a mate.

In a more idealistic way, a friend of mine who is a champion bicyclist was told by a groomsman at his wedding: "Dude, you were nowhere without her." That, too, implies what Hill was driving at. Hill maintains that in a subtle but extremely powerful way the energy of the individual is very often directed and focused both by his or her mate and by the desire to please that mate.

Now, you'll notice I'm using gender-neutral language at this point, and for a reason. Hill's generation didn't use gender-neutral language; he wrote in the days where people would use expressions, like "behind every great man, there's a woman." It's no aspersion to say that he wrote in gender roles of an earlier generation. To address that, for any who are put off by it, I have also created a gender-neutral edition of *Think and Grow Rich*, and in that gender-neutral edition I preserve all of Hill's arguments faithfully but I break us out of some of the gender stereotypes a bit. If you like what I'm describing, you can go to the sexuality chapter of the gender-neutral edition of *Think and Grow Rich*, and you can take it in without feeling that you have to buy into the sexual roles that belong to an earlier generation.

My point is that whenever Hill talks about man's desire to please woman, we can talk about an individual's desire to please his or her mate or prospective mate. He says that there's a lot of people in our world and in history who have performed extraordinary services, demonstrated things never thought possible, produced enduring works of art, feats of entrepreneurship, acts of commerce that have changed the world, who were driven by this very intimate, sexualized wish to please a mate.

It's also important to note that Hill wanted people to express sexual energy in all of its facets, but never in ways there were destructive. That means expressing it in a manner that is obviously consensual, that is respectful, and that is, ultimately if not always, based in love or intimacy. It's interesting, I got into this discussion on an online seminar about *Think and Grow Rich* where somebody asked about the negative dimensions of sex energy. We live in a world today where we're seeing lots of lives that have been torn apart by the misuses of sexual energy. It strikes people as very curious sometimes.

Around the time of my seminar, I was at a dinner party where a very successful entrepreneur was sitting at the head of the table, and he was remarking that we live in a world today where some extreme high-achievers have gotten caught up in sexual scandals or acts of non-consensual behavior, and they seem to have put their whole lives and careers on the line, and hurt others, and it just seems to be a wild lapse of judgment. What's it all about? he wondered. I thought about some of what Napoleon Hill wrote. He talks about the dangers of sexual energy running amok; sexuality, he noted, is so powerful, and it's so irresistible a force when people aren't developed in some other way, that this force of ultimate creation becomes a force of ultimate destruction.

It's almost a part of natural law or human nature that what can nurture can also damage. Light concentrated can heat and heal, but can also cut like a laser. Water can sustain terrestrial life or in excess suffocate it. These are natural laws, and they're also psychological and physical laws. Hill warned that if misused, misdirected, or uncontrolled, the creative urge becomes a destructive urge, and I think that helps decipher some of what's gone on in our culture.

Now, for those of you who are interested in esoteric practices, it's entirely natural to ponder the connection between Hill's observation and the contemporary practice of what is called sex magick. He doesn't talk specifically about that connection, but I do think that what he's talking about relates to sex magick. Simply put, sex magick is setting an intention at the point of climax. I'm simplifying it, because there is often ceremony and ritual involved, but in various ways, sex magick is setting a personal intention or wish at the point of climax or orgasm.

A lot of what we call ceremonial magick, chaos magick, or spell work is actually New Thought along other ritual lines or channels. The basic premise behind modern magick is that the will can be externalized, and that the mental picture or wish can be concretized and actualized in the world around us, through rites, focus, and ceremony. Now, for those of us who are dedicated to New Thought, that practice generally involves externalizing thought through emotionalized focus, affirmations, visualizations, prayers, and mental imagery. But there are many people who I love, respect, and work with who are engaged in witchcraft, spell work, chaos magick, ceremonial magick, and other modalities, who are, to a very great extent, trying to accomplish the same thing—to render thoughts causative—through other means. They might be using herbs, ceremony, deity worship, rituals, symbols, sigils—but we're all attempting the same thing, which is to externalize the images and wishes of the psyche.

The method to which I've been referring has existed in magical tradition for many generations, but was popularized in the modern world by the artist and magician Aleister Crowley, among a handful of others, including the occultist Paschal Beverly Randolph. Their work occurred in the late nineteenth and early twentieth centuries and formed the basis for a lot of ceremonial magick today.

Sex magick as alluded, often involves focusing on a desire, focusing intentions, at the moment of climax. This practice is also used in a somewhat different way in chaos magick as part of the ceremony called sigil magick. In using sigil magick, you formulate a passionate desire—one that has some worldly means of realization—and, through a variety of methods, many of them very simple, render that desire into a symbol, an abstract symbol of the thing wished for. You then "charge" that symbol, so to speak, by working yourself up into a state of ecstasy or some kind of a meditative state that crosses over into a transcendental, surreal, or extra-rational state. Most often this is done through sexual climax.

The creation of the sigil is accomplished by writing down a simple statement of your desire, crossing out select letters, and then rearranging the remaining letters into an abstract symbol. There are myriad methods of doing this—you can create your own. And the key operation is then, during sexual climax, whether it's climax with a partner or whether it's solitary climax, focusing on your desire over the symbol or sigil and thus charging it. Although there are other methods, people generally use orgasm to charge the sigil with sexual-psychical energy. After this, you are effectively supposed to forget all about your desire, insofar as the ceremony itself has fulfilled it. Once charged, the abstract symbol, so the theory goes, becomes a subconscious router of your desire, and results in its fulfillment or outpicturing in the world. There is a gray area, or area of debate, as to how precisely this occurs. This is, after all, an occult practice—though some practitioners argue for its sheer rationality based on its success rate. If you want to learn about the practice, the finest book I personally know of is *Advanced Magick for Beginners* by Alan Chapman. Chapman's book is a marvel of clarity and wit.

Personally speaking, I have not had results with sigil magick—but lots of people I respect have. I think the hang up for me is the notion of "forgetting" one's desire. I am so impassioned toward my desires, and so driven toward them, that I cannot enter the proper psychical state of feeling fulfillment through alternate means, unless they are veritably equal to the thing sought. The ceremonial act in sigil magick is supposed to create a sense of satisfaction, but for me personally it has not. You may be different. Again, lots of people find success using the method. I encourage trying it. But what I've described in my experience is why I personally favor Hill's method of sexual transmutation, which channels sexual energy toward the actual production of the end being sought.

Hill doesn't specifically talk about any these operations I've been describing, such as sex magick or sigil magick. Their popularity came much later. I cannot say for sure what he knew or didn't know about this magical subculture or its methods. But the important thing, for me, is identifying those areas where earnest seekers reach parallel conclusions, even, or especially, if they are not directly in contact. Correspondences are, to me, a marker of truth. I think that what Hill explores affirms all of these operations. Because Hill is really saying that mental and sexual energy possess an extra-physical component, a non-local component. I am absolutely certain, from years of reading and studying and working with Hill's ideas, that he would have agreed that sexual energy, as with the emotions, as with the intellect, has an extra-physical component. He implies as much by identifying sexuality as the incipient life force in the individual.

In fact, in his chapter on sex transmutation he notes that the practice contributes to the development of a "sixth sense," or what we might call extra-sensitivity, ESP, telepathy, or heightened intuition. He did believe that channeled sexual energy could not only amp up your creative, physical, and intellectual abilities, but it would similarly amp up your intuitive abilities to the point where an individual could participate in a kind of "over-mind" or non-localized intelligence or Infinite Intelligence, as he called it. Indeed, Hill wrote that genius itself—again harkening to the Ancient Roman tradition—reaches us through the agencies of a sixth sense. This idea also appeared in the late-ancient Greek-Egyptian philosophy called Hermeticism, which is probably where the Romans received it.

For these reasons, I feel certain that Hill would have agreed that sex energy has an extra-physical component. It exists in the cosmos as an energetic reality and it is expressed through the individual. So, I think this is at the back of the operations performed by today's sex magicians or chaos magicians or people working with sigil magick. As I alluded earlier, the idea of sexually charging your sigil or symbol can seem very abstract. I'm using figurative language to describe operations whose workings we don't really understand. But there is empiricism present. And that empiricism is experienced in the congruency of the results. We certainly have reliable testimony, records of experiences, and successes, but, for all that, we don't really understand what's going on. Things that exist beyond the operation of the five senses can be very difficult to theorize over. In that sense, we don't yet possess a theory of delivery of sex magick. We don't know precisely what's happening. It's extra-physical. It's extrasensory. But I think Hill would affirm by observation, by testimony, by experience that's what's happening is actual, that it's real.

I think people who engage in those forms of magick would benefit from reading Hill's chapter, because it's a very simple and harmonious parallel path. It's interesting, to this day, you mention the name Aleister Crowley, and some people cringe and say, "Oh wow, the Great Beast." He has this outlaw image, which he cultivated. But you mention the name Napoleon Hill, and it seems very domestic. You think of guys sitting around a business roundtable, and it seems very familiar and tame by comparison. And yet, what Hill wrote about sex transmutation is every bit as radical, as daring, and experimental as what Crowley wrote on sex magick. And I personally find Hill's approach easer for the individual to enter into.

Now, I mentioned earlier that Hill's ideas also coalesce with ancient esoteric teachings on sexuality, including those found in Taoism and Tantra, where sexual energy is seen as an actual force that can be cultivated, stored, and used for purposes of transmutation or personal alchemy, by which I mean self-transformation. Now, remarkably enough, here's Napoleon Hill in 1937 in what, comparatively speaking, was a conformist, somewhat repressed society, dealing with some of this deeply esoteric material, sometimes echoing age-old esoteric traditions. It should bring us a new dimension of respect towards Napoleon Hill. When this man says he spent twenty years researching *Think and Grow Rich*, that should be taken very seriously because he looked in a lot of corners and byways and devised a truly remarkable, wide-ranging program, which I'm focusing on just one aspect of here.

But, for me, this focus feels like a kind of breakthrough because, for all the popularity of motivational and inspirational methods in our culture, this topic is rarely dealt with, and you and I have just broken that barrier.

Almost everyone would agree that the energy that we experience at the point of climax feels extraordinary. People cross oceans for it. Every sensitive reader of *Think and Grow Rich* for the past several decades has encountered this teaching on sex transmutation and has said to him or herself, "I know this is vital; I know this is powerful; I know this is important; but I don't know precisely what's going on here." There aren't a lot of places in our culture where you can have that exchange. So, I'm so glad we're having it. My hope is that this discussion becomes a true resource for people.

Chapter 4

Sex Energy in Ancient Cultures—and Our Own

A few months prior to this writing I traveled to Egypt with my friend Ronni Thomas, a brilliant filmmaker. Ronni and I are collaborating on a documentary about the occult book, *The Kybalion*. Although it's a modern book, written in 1908, *The Kybalion* does retain some ideas from the late-ancient Greek-Egyptian philosophy called Hermeticism, which I mentioned earlier. The author of that book was a thoughtful and dynamic New Thought writer named William Walker Atkinson (1862–1932), who wrote under the pseudonym Three Initiates. In *The Kybalion*, Atkinson writes about the principle of "mental gender," that is, about the male or conscious mind impregnating the female or subliminal mind with an idea, which the subliminal or subconscious mind allows to gestate and finally come to life in the world. In Egypt there are bas-reliefs and statues everywhere that are tributes to sexuality and fertility, both of the literal and metaphysical type. There are gods and goddesses specifically dedicated to beauty, to procreation, to fertility—and as the great Hermetic dictum goes, "as above, so below." In other worlds, all facets of the cosmos, nature, and our psyches reflect these energies of sexuality and impregnation, sometimes physically and sometimes metaphysically, not dissimilar from what Atkinson and Hill are writing about.

I was personally able to enter a chamber deep within the Valley of Kings in Luxor, which is normally closed off to the public. I was permitted to go deeply into this chamber and I was permitted to touch the bas-relief of a bull, which is associated in Ancient Egypt with both fertility and sexuality. I can only report back to you what I personally experienced: as I laid hands very gently on this bas-relief of a bull, this symbol of sexual energy and fertility, I felt a sense of absolute lightening go through my body. What was occurring? What was the actual process? I don't know, but I can testify that's what I experienced. The Egyptians clearly recognized the act of creation, the act of sexuality, as something that is as essential as life and death, or the passing to the other world; it was a foundational part of the existential psychology of Ancient Egypt, and it was enshrined within their pantheon.

There's an important point I want to make about personal appearance. You can heighten your magnetic power through your manner of dress, style, and personal comportment. Hill believed, and I've certainly seconded this in my writings, that there's a powerful and important psychology behind clothing and choice of appearance. He believed it necessary to dress in a personally comfortable and self-affirming way, or to adopt whatever kind of gait or composure you wish—and that the right decision in this area would make you feel magnetic, charismatic, confident. And you will actually *be* these things. We underestimate the interplay of the inner and the outer. Both are part of the same whole.

Hence, outer appearance can maximize sexual energy. When we're designing how we dress, wear our hair, the accouterments we wear, when we're designing our image—not just dressing up but designing our image, whatever our definition of that may be—we are seeking to exalt, build, and maximize our sexual energy, in the broadest sense. We're seeking to magnify that creative force, that force of attraction, within ourselves. I think that one should not underestimate or wave off as vanity the importance of dressing and comporting yourself the way that you wish.

I don't make a division between the inner and the outer. I think all of these divisions are artificial past a certain point. No one should feel embarrassed, or be made to feel like they're being shallow, if and when they wish to pay attention to the outer, to appearances, to what makes them look good, to what makes them feel good according to whatever one's internal lights may be, and in whichever way they're directed. It's a self-driven decision.

Of course, we all experience social pressure, peer pressure, consumer pressure; but bear in mind that every society in history—the Hebrews, the Greeks, the Maya, the ancient Vedic culture—every society in its works of art and communication has depicted beauty. We're not the first. And yes there's peer pressure, yes there's consumerism, there's pressure to conform, but every society has had its adornments and its symbols of beauty and its depictions of sexuality from the Song of Solomon to the headdresses of the Native Americans.

Every society has had a love for and appreciation of beauty, as they conceived it.

I just want the individual to feel as comfortable and at home in his or her own skin as possible, and I want the individual to feel the approbation to comport, dress, and conduct themselves in the world as comfortably as they personally wish. It's very powerful and its very relaxing. I believe that this is one of the reasons why a transgender person who is transitioning will often describe feeling a great and wonderful sense of relief because they finally feel like they're carrying themselves in the world as they wish, and that's vitally important.

I have two sons and I've been asked how, or whether, to teach kids about this material. I often tell people that when it comes to childrearing I'm reminded of something that was attributed to Napoleon. I don't know if he actually said it. So many things are attributed to Napoleon, apocryphally or not. But it's this: "Every plan immediately fails upon contact with the enemy." Forgive the metaphor, but that's been my experience with childrearing. Every well-laid plan that I seek to enact with my kids seems to completely fall apart in the to-and-fro of actual life; and yet at the same time, they do learn from me; they learn from example, both good and bad. They learn from what they witness in my behavior, strong and weak. And so I'll realize they are listening. They're just not listening at the times when I think they are.

So, it's a very personal question how everybody deals with this. It depends upon the nature of your household, the language you use, the necessity you feel in the matter, and, of course, their age. I've often thought that there should be a *Think and Grow Rich* for young people. I've often thought about writing such a book, and maybe these questions will reignite that in me. Perhaps I'll write such a book that can be handed to a sensitive 13-year-old and will include a chapter that's age-appropriate that deals with some of this material. That might be one response.

* * *

I want to reinforce that every being, every mature sexual being, is absolutely using his or her sexual energy in varied ways—the question is will we use it constructively, and how broad a definition are we willing to sustain of that? We understand something about what it means to encourage teens to be responsible from a sexual perspective, but if we broaden our perspective on sexuality, which is really what this book is about, then how much more so can we talk about the responsible and powerful uses of it for all of us? It's a daunting and promising prospect.

I don't want you to feel discouraged if some of this still seems far out or difficult to grasp. We are dealing with esoteric material, not only in the work of Napoleon Hill, but in many religious traditions across the ages. These were things that were matters of deep esotericism to Vedic masters to Taoist masters to Kabbalistic masters. I've tried to distill matters down in as clear a fashion as possible, but to a certain degree, there are places where you must go by yourself. And garnering experience is ultimately a solitary journey. You have to go into this journey yourself. Go into it privately. Glean your own insights. Arrive at your own testimony, at your own experiences.

I say that this material is esoteric because we're trying to find a way of channeling and directing some of the most mysterious forces in human life. The most important thing is that we *try* because that presents payoffs in your own life and encourages the work of other people. Your practice presents guideposts and testimony for others. If you read the book and you say, "I still don't know what he's talking about," you're not wrong—the completion comes with the effort. Try, try. This is mysterious material, and you shouldn't feel frustrated if it doesn't disclose itself all at once.

The Power of Sex Transmutation

* * *

I want to close with a guided meditation. Depending on what form you're experiencing this book, you can have someone read this passage to you, you can record it, or you can listen back to my narration at your own pace. Prepare by just relaxing and sitting or laying down comfortably. Close your eyes. Take a few deep breaths.

> *I'd like you to think of something that you deeply wish to achieve in life. Something that is profoundly and powerfully important to you. It can be a certain attainment, a personal achievement, an artistic or career goal. Something that is cherished by you as an aim, as a goal, as a wish.*
>
> *Once you have a clear picture of the desired or cherished thing, I want you to understand that there is, at the back of this desire, a great, eternal, universal force of self-expression seeking to actualize itself through you. There is a great force of creation seeking to express itself in your experience. This force goes under many names: enthusiasm, creativity, generativity.*
>
> *But it is ultimately the force of creation itself. It is sexual energy seeking expression and actualization. It is the sexual force that seeks to propagate our species, and this same all-powerful sexual force seeks expression not only as a biologic fact, but as a fact in all areas of creativity, productivity, generativity, and self-expression.*
>
> *I want you to feel heartened and enthused by the truth that this eternal, universal force exists at the back of your deepest desires and wishes. Because those same desires and wishes are life itself seeking expression through you.*
>
> *I want you to become aware of yourself as a conscious, creative being who, in your own person, is an individualized agent of this*

vast universal force of creation. This force is seeking an outlet right now through you and through the medium of your productive desires. Allow yourself to become aware of that.

Take a few more deep breaths in this awareness. Now, in a few moments, I invite you to open your eyes.

You are that.

YOUR INVISIBLE POWER

Genevieve Behrend

Contents

Introduction 317
Foreword 318

Chapter One *Order of Visualization* 321

Chapter Two *How to Attract to Yourself the Things You Desire* 324

Chapter Three *Relation Between Mental and Physical Form* 328

Chapter Four *Operation of Your Mental Picture* 330

Chapter Five *Expressions from Beginners* 337

Chapter Six *Suggestions for Making Your Mental Picture* 340

Chapter Seven *Things to Remember in Using Your Thought Power for the Production of New Conditions* 341

Chapter Eight *Why I Took Up the Study of Mental Science* 344

Chapter Nine *How I Attracted to Myself 20,000 Dollar* 347

Chapter Ten *How I Became the Only Personal Pupil of T. Troward, the Great Mental Scientist* 352

Chapter Eleven *How to Bring the Power in Your Word Into Action* 359

Chapter Twelve *How to Increase Your Faith* 360

Chapter Thirteen *The Reward of Increased Faith* 361

Chapter Fourteen *How to Make Nature Respond to You* 362

Chapter Fifteen *Faith With Works—What It Has Accomplished* 363

Chapter Sixteen *Suggestions As to How to Pray or Ask, Believing You Have Already Received* 366

Chapter Seventeen *Things to Remember* 371

Introduction

Genevieve Behrend was the only personal pupil that the great Thomas Troward ever had. She studied with him privately, at his home at Ruan Manor, Cornwall, England, for two years, 1912 to 1914, inclusive. She founded The School of the Builders in New York City and was the head of it until 1925. For five years thereafter she conducted the same school in Los Angeles and then toured the entire United States and Canada, presenting the Troward philosophy at its best, as only she was fully qualified to do, in almost every city of appreciable size.

She spent thirty-five years as one of America's greatest and best-known lecturers, teachers and practitioners. Millions heard and enjoyed her, not only on the public platform but over radio. Her students numbered tens of thousands all over the English-speaking world. Paris, France was her native city but she was half Scotch. This little book, *Your Invisible Power*, was her first. However it remains the most popular of all her books and has been, since its first edition, one of the world's best sellers on Mental Science. It has exhausted scores of editions.

Herein, Genevieve Behrend presents the Troward philosophy at its best, in her incomparable simple, direct and dynamic manner so well known to so many. Although she has written several other books this one remains her masterpiece.

—Worth Smith

Publisher's Note: Worth Smith, prominent author and authority on the Great Pyramid, has been the husband and closest collaborator of Genevieve Behrend for twenty-two years.

Foreword

These pages have been written for the purpose of furnishing you a key to the attainment of your desires, and to explain that Fear should be entirely banished from your consciousness in order for you to obtain possession of the things you want.

This pre-supposes, of course, that your desire for possession is based upon your aspiration for greater happiness. For example, you feel that the possession of more money, lands, or friends will make you happier, and your desire for possession of these things arises from a conviction that their possession will bring you freedom and contentment. In your effort to possess, you will discover that the thing you most need is to consistently "Be" your best self.

One morning after class a man came to me and asked if I would speak the word of supply for him, as he was sadly in the need of money. He offered me a $5 bill with the remark: "Dear Madam, that is half of every dollar I have in the world. I am in debt; my wife and child have not the proper clothing; in fact, I must have money." I explained to him that money was the symbol of differentiated substance, that this substance filled all space, that it was present for him at that very moment, and would manifest to him as the money he required. "But," he questioned, "it may come too late." I told him it could not come too late, as it was eternally present. He understood and got the uplift of my spoken word.

I did not see the man again, but six months later I had a letter from him stating he was in New Orleans. He said, "I am well established here in my regular profession of photography; I own my own home, have an automobile of my own, and am generally prospering. And dear Mrs. Behrend, I want to thank you for lifting me out of the depths that day in New York.

"Three days after I talked to you, a man whom I have not seen for years met me on the street. When I explained my situation to him, he loaned me the money to pay my bills and come down here. The enclosed check is to help you continue your wonderful work of teaching people how to mentally reach out and receive their never-failing supply. I would not take anything for my understanding as you have given it to me. God bless you."

A feeling that greater possessions, no matter of what kind they may be, will of *themselves* bring contentment or happiness, is a misunderstanding. No person, place, or thing can give you happiness. They may give you cause for happiness and a feeling of contentment, but the Joy of Living comes from within.

Therefore, it is here recommended that you should make the effort to obtain the things which you feel will bring you joy, provided that your desires are in accord with the Joy of Living.

It is also desired, in this volume, to suggest the possibilities in store for all who make persistent effort to understand the Law of Visualization, and who make practical application of this knowledge on whatever plane they may be. The word "effort," as here employed, is not intended to convey the idea of strain. All study and meditation should be without strain or tension.

It has been my endeavor to show that by starting at the beginning of the creative action, or mental picture, certain corresponding results are sure to follow. "While the laws of the Universe cannot be altered, they can be made to work under specific conditions, thereby producing results for individual advancement which cannot be obtained under the spontaneous workings of the law provided by Nature."

However far these suggestions I have given—of the possibilities in store for you, through visualizing, may carry you beyond your past experience, they nowhere break the continuity of the law of cause and effect.

If through the suggestions here given, any one is brought to realize that his mind is a center through and in which "all power there is" is in operation, simply waiting to be given direction in the one and only way through which it can take specific action—and this means reaction in concrete or physical form—then the mission to which this book is dedicated has been fulfilled.

Try to remember that the picture you think, feel, and see is reflected into the Universal Mind, and by the natural law of reciprocal action must return to you in either spiritual or physical form. Knowledge of this law of reciprocal action between the individual and the Universal Mind opens to you free access to all you may wish to *possess* or to *be*.

It must be steadfastly borne in mind that all this can be true only for the individual who recognizes that he derives his power to make an abiding mental picture from the All-Originating Universal Spirit of Life, and can be used constructively only so long as it is employed and retained in harmony with the nature of the Spirit which originated it. To insure this there must be no inversion of the thought of the individual regarding his relationship to this Universal Originating Spirit, which is that of a son, through which the parent mind acts and reacts.

Thus conditioned, whatever you think and feel yourself to be, the Creative Spirit of Life is bound to faithfully reproduce in a corresponding reaction. This is the great reason for picturing yourself and your affairs the way you wish them to be as existing facts—though invisible to the physical eye—and living in your picture. An honest endeavor to do this, always recognizing that your own mind is a projection of the Originating Spirit, will prove to you that the best there is, is yours in all your ways.

—G.B.

Los Angeles, California;
May, 1929.

Chapter One

Order of Visualization

The exercise of the visualizing faculty keeps your mind in order, and attracts to you the things you need to make life more enjoyable in an orderly way.

If you train yourself in the practice of deliberately picturing your desire and carefully examining your picture, you will soon find that your thoughts and desires proceed in a more orderly procession than ever before.

Having reached a state of ordered mentality, you are no longer in a constant state of mental hurry. Hurry is Fear, and consequently destructive.

In other words, when your understanding grasps the power to visualize your heart's desire and hold it with your will, it attracts to you all things requisite to the fulfillment of that picture by the harmonious vibrations of the law of attraction.

You realize that since Order is Heaven's first law, and visualization places things in their natural order, then it must be a heavenly thing to visualize.

Everyone visualizes, whether he knows it or not. Visualizing is the great secret of success.

The conscious use of this great power attracts to you multiplied resources, intensifies your wisdom, and enables you to make use of advantages which you formerly failed to recognize.

A lady once came to me for help in selling a piece of property. After I explained to her just how to make a mental picture of the sale, going through the details mentally, exactly as she would do if the property were sold, she came a week later and told me how one day she was walking along the street, when the thought suddenly occurred to her to go and see a certain real estate dealer, to whom she had not yet been.

She hesitated for a moment when she first got the idea, as it seemed to her that that man could not sell her property. However, upon the strength of what I had told her, she followed the lead and went to the real estate man, who sold the property for her in just three days after she had first approached him. This was simply following along with the natural law of demand and supply.

We now fly through the air, not because anyone has been able to change the laws of Nature, but because the inventor of the flying machine learned how to apply Nature's laws and, by making orderly use of them, produced the desired result. So far as the natural forces are concerned, nothing has changed since the beginning. There were no airplanes in "the Year One," because those of that generation could not conceive the idea as a practical, working possibility. "It has not yet been done," was the argument, "and it cannot be done." Yet the laws and materials for practical flying machines existed then as now.

Troward tells us that the great lesson he learned from the airplane and wireless telegraphy is the triumph of principle over precedent, the working out of an idea to its logical conclusion in spite of accumulated contrary testimony of all past experience.

With such an example before you, you must realize that there are still greater secrets to be disclosed. Also, "That you hold the key within yourself, with which to unlock the secret chamber that contains your heart's desire.

"All that is necessary in order that you may use this key and make your life exactly what you wish it to be, is a careful inquiry into the unseen causes which stand back of every external and visible condition. Then bring these unseen causes into harmony with your conception, and you will find that you can make practical working realities of possibilities which at present seem but fantastic dreams."

A woman came to me in New York City, asking for help, as she was out of work. I spoke the word of ever-present supply for her and intensified it by mentally seeing the woman in the position she dreamed of, but which she had been unable to make a practical reality.

That same afternoon she telephoned and said she could hardly believe her senses, as she had just taken exactly the kind of a position she wanted. The employer told her she had been wanting a woman like her for months.

We all knew that the balloon was the forefather of the airplane. In 1766 Henry Cavendish, an English nobleman, proved that hydrogen gas was seven times lighter than air. From that discovery the balloon came into existence, and from the ordinary balloon the dirigible, a cigar-shaped airship, was evolved.

Study of aeronautics and laws of the aerial locomotion of birds and projectiles led to the belief that mechanism could be evolved by which heavier-than-air machines could be made to travel from place to place and remain in the air by the maintenance of great speed, which would overcome by propulsive force the ordinary law of gravitation. Professor Langley of Washington, who developed much of the theory which others afterward improved upon, was subjected to much derision when he sent a model airplane up, only to have it bury its nose in the muddy waters of the Potomac. But the Wright Brothers, who experimented later, realized the possibility of traveling through the air in a machine that had no gas bag. They *saw* themselves enjoying this mode of transportation with great facility. It is said that one of the brothers would tell the other, when their varied experiences did not turn out as they expected: "It's all right, Brother, I can *see* myself riding in that machine, and it travels easily and steadily."

Those Wright Brothers knew what they wanted and kept their pictures constantly before them. Now transportation through the air is developing rapidly and we all feel sure it will in the near future become as ordinary a method of travel as the automobile.

In visualizing, or making a mental picture, you are not endeavoring to change the laws of Nature. You are fulfilling them.

Your object in visualizing is to bring things into regular order, both mentally and physically. When you realize that this method of employing the Creative Power brings your desires, one after another, into practical, material accomplishment, your confidence in the mysterious but unfailing law of attraction, which has its central power station in the very heart of your word-picture, becomes supreme. Nothing can shake it. You never feel that it is necessary to take anything from anybody else. You have learned that asking and seeking have, as their correlatives, receiving and finding. You know that all you have to do is to start the plastic substance of the Universe flowing into the thought-moulds your picture-desire provides.

Chapter Two

How to Attract to Yourself the Things You Desire

The power within you which enables you to form a thought-picture is the starting point of all there is. In its original state it is the undifferentiated formless substance of life. Your thought-picture makes the model, so to say, into which this formless substance takes shape.

Visualizing, or mentally seeing things and conditions as you wish them to be, is the condensing, the specializing power in you which might be illustrated by comparison with the lens of a magic lantern, which is one of the best symbols of the imaging faculty.

It illustrates the idea of the working of the Creative Spirit on the plane of initiative and selection—or in its concentrated, specializing form—in a remarkably clear manner.

The picture slide illustrates your own mental picture—invisible in the lantern of your mind until you turn on the light of your will.

That is to say, you light up your desire with absolute faith that the Creative Spirit of Life, in you, is doing the work. By the steady flow of the light of the Will on the Spirit, your desired picture is projected upon the screen of the physical world—an exact reproduction of the pictured slide in your mind.

A woman came to me for help to cause her husband to return to her. She said she was very unhappy and lonely without him and longed to be reunited. I told her she could not lose love and protection, because both belonged to her. She asked what she should do to get her husband back again. I told her to follow the great power of intuition and think of her husband as perfectly free, and the embodiment of all that a husband should be.

She went away quite happy, but returned in a few days to tell me that her husband desired a divorce in order to marry again. She was quite agitated and had evidently relaxed her will in following the instructions given at the former interview. Again I told her to hold constantly in her mind that the loving protection of the Spirit of Life would guide her in perfect happiness.

A month later she came again and said that her husband had married the other woman. This time she had completely lost her mental grip. I repeated the words for her as before, and she regained her poise. Two months later she came back to me, full of joy. Her husband had come to her, begging her forgiveness, and telling her what a terrible mistake he had made, as he could not be happy without her. They are now living happily together, and she, at least, learned the necessity of holding her pictured desire steadily in place by the use of her will.

Visualizing without a will sufficiently steady to inhibit every thought and feeling contrary to your pictured thought would be as useless as a magic lantern without the light.

On the other hand, if your will is sufficiently developed to hold your picture in thought and feeling, without any "ifs"; simply realizing that your thought is the great attracting power, then your mental picture is as certain to be projected upon your physical world as a picture slide put into a magic lantern shows on the screen.

Try projecting the picture in a magic lantern with a light that is constantly shifting from one side to the other, and you will produce the effect of an uncertain will. It is as necessary that you should always have back of your picture a strong, steady will, as it is to have a strong steady light back of a picture slide.

The joyous assurance with which you make your picture is the very powerful magnet of Faith, and nothing can obliterate it. You are happier than you ever were, because you have learned to know where your source of supply is, and you rely upon its never-failing response to the direction you give it.

All said and done, happiness is the one thing which every human being wants, and the study of visualization enables you to get more out of life than you ever enjoyed before. Increasing possibilities keep opening out, more and more, before you.

A businessman once told me that since practicing visualization, and forming the habit of devoting a few minutes each day to thinking about his work as he desired it to be, in a large, broad way, his orders had more than doubled in six months.

His method was to go into a room every morning before breakfast and take a mental inventory of his business as he had left it the evening before, and then enlarge upon it. He said he expanded and expanded in this way, until his affairs were in a remarkably successful condition. He would see himself in his office doing everything he wanted done. His occupation required him to meet many strangers every day.

In his mental picture he saw himself meeting these people, understanding their needs, and supplying them in just the way they wished.

This habit, he said, had strengthened and steadied his will in an almost inconceivable manner.

Furthermore, by thus mentally seeing things as he wished them to be, he had acquired the confident feeling that a certain Creative Power was exercising itself, for him and through him, for the purpose of improving his little world.

When you first begin to visualize seriously, you may feel, as many others do, that someone else may be forming the same picture you are, and that, naturally, would not suit your purpose. Do not give yourself any concern about this.

Simply try to realize that your picture is an orderly exercise of the Universal Creative Power specifically applied. Then you may be sure that no one can work in opposition to you. The universal law of harmony prevents that.

Endeavor to bear in mind that your mental picture is Universal Mind specifically exercising its inherent powers of initiative and selection. God, or Universal Mind, made man for the special purpose of differentiating Himself through him. Everything there is, came into existence in this same way, by this self-same law of self-differentiation, and for the same purpose. First came the idea, the mental picture, or the prototype of the thing, which is the thing itself in its incipiency.

The Great Architect of the Universe contemplated Himself as manifesting through his polar opposite—matter—and the idea expanded and projected itself until we have not only a world, but many worlds.

Many people ask, "But why should we have a physical world at all?" The answer is: "Because it is the nature of Originating Substance to solidify, under directivity rather than activity, just as it is the nature of wax to harden when it becomes cold, or plaster of Paris to become firm and solid when exposed to the air."

Your picture is this same Divine Substance in its original state, taking form through the individualized center of Divine operation, in your mind; and there is no power to prevent this combination of Spiritual Substance from becoming physical form. It is the nature of Spirit to complete its work, and an idea is not complete until it has made for itself a vehicle.

Nothing can prevent your picture from coming into concrete form except the same power which gave it birth—yourself.

Suppose you wish to have a more orderly room. You look about your room, and the idea of order suggests boxes, closets, shelves, hooks, and so forth. The box, the closet and the hooks, are all concrete ideas of order, because they are the vehicles through which order and harmony suggest themselves.

Chapter Three

Relation Between Mental and Physical Form

Some persons feel that it is not quite proper to visualize for *things*. "It's too material," they say. Why, material form is necessary for the self-recognition of Spirit from the individual standpoint, and this is the means through which the Creative Process is carried forward.

Therefore, far from matter being an illusion and something which ought not to be, matter is the necessary channel for the self-differentiation of Spirit.

However, it is not my desire to lead you into lengthy and tiresome scientific reasoning, in order to remove the mystery from visualization and to put it upon a logical foundation.

Naturally, each individual will do this in his own way. My only wish is to point out to you the easiest way I know, which is the road on which Troward guides me. I feel sure you will conclude, as I have, that the only mystery in connection with visualizing is the mystery of life taking form, governed by unchangeable and easily understood laws.

We all possess more power and greater possibilities than we realize, and visualizing is one of the greatest of these powers, it brings other Possibilities to our observation. When we pause to think for a moment, we realize that for a cosmos to exist at all, it must be the outcome of a Cosmic Mind, which binds "all individual minds to a certain generic unity of action, thereby producing all things as realities and nothing as illusions." If you will take this thought of Troward's and meditate upon it without prejudice, you will surely realize that concrete material form is an absolute necessity of the Creative Process; also "that matter is not an illusion but a necessary channel thru which life differentiates itself." If you consider matter in its right order, as the polar opposite to Spirit, you will not find any antagonism between them. On the contrary, together they constitute one harmonious whole. And when you realize this, you feel, in your practice of visualizing, that you are working from cause to effect, from beginning to end. In reality your mental picture is the specialized outworking of the Originating Spirit. One could talk for hours on purely scientific lines, showing, as Troward says, "that raw material for the formation of the solar systems is universally distributed throughout all space. Yet investigation shows that while the Heavens are studded with millions of suns, there are spaces which show no signs of cosmic activity. This being true, There must be something which started cosmic activity in certain places, while passing over others in which the raw material was equally available. At first thought, one might attribute development of cosmic energy to the etheric particles themselves. Upon investigation however, we find that this is mathematically impossible in a medium which is equally distributed throughout space, for all its particles are in equilibrium; therefore, no one particle possesses in itself a greater power of originating motion than the other. Thus we find that the initial movement, though working in and through the particles of primary substance, is not the particles themselves. It is this something we mean when we speak of Spirit."

This same power that brought universal substance into existence will bring your individual thought or mental picture into physical form. There is no difference in the power. The only difference is a difference of degree. The power and the substance themselves are the same. Only in working out your mental picture, it has transferred its creative energy from the Universal to the particular, and is working in the same unfailing manner from its specific center, your mind.

Chapter Four

Operation of Your Mental Picture

The operation of a large telephone system may be used as a simile. The main, or head central subdivides itself into many branch centrals, every branch being in direct connection with the main central, and each individual branch recognizing the source of its existence, reports all things to its central head. Therefore, when assistance of any nature is required: new supplies, difficult repairs to be done, or what not, the branch in need goes at once to its central head. It would not think of referring its difficulties (or its successes) to the main central of a telegraph system, though they might belong to the same organization. These different branch centrals know that the only remedy for any difficulty must come from the central out of which they were projected and to which they are always attached.

If we, as individual branches of the Universal Mind, would refer our difficulties in the same confident manner to the source from which we were projected, and use the remedies which it has provided, we would realize what Jesus meant when he said, "Ask and ye shall receive." Our every requirement would be met. Surely the Father must supply the child. The trunk of the tree cannot fail to provide for its branches.

A man came to me in great distress, saying he was about to lose his home in the South. In his own words, it was mortgaged to the hilt, and his creditors were going to foreclose. It was the house in which he had been born and had grown to young manhood, and the thought of losing it filled his heart and mind with sorrow, not only from a money standpoint, but from the standpoint of sentimental association. I explained to him that the Power that brought him into existence did so for the purpose of expressing its limitless supply through him; that there was no power on earth which could cut him off from his source except his own consciousness, and that in reality he would not be cut off then. I explained to him that he had it, but was unable to recognize that it was there, and said to him, "Infinite substance is manifesting in you right now." The next week, on Sunday, just before leaving my dressing room in the Selwyn Theatre to give my afternoon message, I received the following note: "Dear Mrs. Behrend: I want you to know that I am the happiest man in the whole city of New York. My home in the South is saved. The money came in the most miraculous way, and I have telegraphed enough to pay off the mortgage. Please tell the people this afternoon about this wonderful Power."

You may be sure I did, explaining to them that everything animate or inanimate is called into existence or outstandingness by a Power which itself does not stand out. The Power which creates the mental picture—the Originating Spirit Substance of your pictured desire—does not stand out. It projects the substance of itself, which is a solidified counterpart of itself, while it—the Power—remains invisible to the physical eye. Those will appreciate the value of visualizing who are able to realize Paul's meaning when he said, "The worlds were formed by the word of God. Things which are seen are not made of things which do appear."

There is nothing unusual or mysterious in the idea of your pictured desire coming into material evidence. It is the working of a universal, natural Law. The world was projected by the self-contemplation of the

Universal Mind, and this same action is taking place in its individualized branch which is the Mind of Man. Everything in the whole world, from the hat on your head to the boots on your feet, has its beginning in mind and comes into existence in exactly the same manner. All are projected thoughts, solidified. Your personal advance in evolution depends on your right use of the power of visualizing, and your use of it depends on whether you recognize that you, yourself, are a particular center through and in which the Originating Spirit is finding ever new expression for potentialities already existing within Itself. This is evolution.

Your mental picture is the force of attraction which evolves and combines the Originating Substance into specific shape. Your picture is the combining and evolving power house, in a generative sense, so to say, through which the Originating Creative Spirit expresses itself. Its creative action is limitless, without beginning and without end, and always progressive and orderly. "It proceeds stage by stage, each stage being a necessary preparation for the one to follow." Now let us see if we can get an idea of the different stages by which the things in the world have come to be. Troward says, "If we can get at the working principle which is producing these results, we can very quickly and easily give it personal application. First, we find that the thought of Originating Life, or Spirit, concerning Itself is its simple awareness of its own being, and this, demanding a relationship to something else, produces a primary ether, a universal substance out of which everything in the world must grow."

Troward also tells us that "though this awareness of being is a necessary foundation for any further possibilities, it is not much to talk about." It is the same with individualized Spirit, which is yourself. Before you can entertain the idea of making a mental picture of your desire as being at all practical, you must have some idea of your being; of your "I am"; and just as soon as you are conscious of your "I-amness," you begin to wish to enjoy the freedom which this consciousness suggests. You want to do more and be more, and as you fulfill this desire within yourself, localized spirit begins conscious activities in you. The thing you are more concerned with is the specific action of the Creative Spirit of Life, Universal Mind specialized. The localized God-germ in you is your personality, your individuality and since the joy of absolute freedom is the inherent nature of this God-germ, it is natural that it should endeavor to enjoy itself through its specific center. And as you grow in the comprehension that your being, your individuality, is God particularizing Himself, you naturally develop Divine tendencies. You want to enjoy life and liberty. You want freedom in your affairs as well as in your consciousness, and it is natural that you should. With this progressive wish there is always a faint thought-picture. As your wish and your recognition grow into an intense desire, this desire becomes a clear mental picture. For example, a young lady studying music wishes she had a piano in order to practice at home. She wants the piano so much that she can mentally see it in one of the rooms. She holds the picture of the piano and indulges in the mental reflection of the pleasure and advantage it will be to have the piano in the corner of the living room. One day she finds it there, just as she had pictured it.

As you grow in understanding as to who you are, where you came from, what the purpose of your being is, and how you are to fulfill the purpose for which you are intended, you will become a more and more perfect center through which the Creative Spirit of Life can enjoy itself. And you will realize that there can be but one creative process filling all space, which is the same in its potentiality whether universal or individual. Furthermore, all there is, whether on the plane of the visible or invisible, had its origin in the localized action of thought, or a mental picture, and this includes yourself, because you are Universal Spirit localized, and the same creative action is taking place through you.

Now you are no doubt asking yourself why there is so much sickness and misery in the world. If the same power and intelligence which brought the world into existence is in operation in the mind of man, why does it not manifest itself as strength joy, health and plenty? If one can have one's desires fulfilled by simply making a mental picture of that desire, holding on to it with the will, and without anxiety, doing on the outward plane whatever seems necessary to bring the desire into fulfillment, then there seems no reason for the existence of sickness and poverty. Surely no one desires either. The first reason is that few persons will take the trouble to inquire into the working principle of the Laws of Life. If they did, they would soon convince themselves that there is no necessity for the sickness and poverty which we see about us. They would realize that visualizing is a principle and not a fallacy. There are a few who have found it worth while to study this simple, though absolutely unfailing law, which will deliver them from bondage. However, the race as a whole is not willing to give the time required for the study. It is either too simple, or too difficult. They may make a picture of their desire with some little understanding of visualizing for a day or two, but more frequently it is for an hour or so.

If you will insist upon mentally seeing yourself surrounded by things and conditions as you wish them to be you will understand that the Creative Energy sends its substance in the direction indicated by the tendency of your thoughts. Herein lies the advantage of holding your thought in the form of a mental picture.

A man in the hardware business in New Jersey came to me in great distress. He would have to go into bankruptcy unless something happened in a fortnight. He said he had never heard of visualizing. I explained to him how to make a mental picture of his business increasing, instead of a picture of losing it. In about a month's time he returned very happy and told me how he had succeeded. He said, "I have my debts all paid, and my shop is full of new supplies." His business was then on a solid basis. It was beautiful to see his Faith.

The more enthusiasm and faith you are able to put into your picture, the more quickly it will come into visible form, and your enthusiasm is increased by keeping your desire secret. The moment you speak it to any living soul, that moment your power is weakened. Your power, your magnet of attraction is not that strong, and consequently cannot reach so far. The more perfectly a secret between your mind and your outer self is guarded, the more vitality you give your power of attraction. One tells one's troubles to weaken them, to get them off one's mind, and when a thought is given out, its power is dissipated. Talk it over with yourself, and even write it down, then destroy the paper.

However, this does not mean that you should strenuously endeavor to compel the Power to work out your picture on the special lines that you think it should. That method would soon exhaust you and hinder the fulfillment of your purpose. A wealthy relative need not necessarily die, or someone lose a fortune on the street, to materialize the $10,000 which you are mentally picturing. One of the doormen in the building in which I lived heard much of the mental picturing of desires from visitors passing out of my rooms. The average desire was for $500. He considered that five dollars was more in his line and began to visualize it, without the slightest idea of where or how he was to get it. My parrot flew out of the window, and I telephoned to the men in the courtyard to get it for me. One caught it, and it bit him on the finger. The doorman, who had gloves on, and did not fear a similar hurt, took hold of it and brought it up to me. I gave him five one dollar bills for his service. This sudden reward surprised him. He enthusiastically told me that he had been visualizing for just $5, merely from hearing that others visualized. He was delighted at the unexpected realization of his mental picture.

All you have to do is to make such a mental picture of your heart's desire, and hold it cheerfully in place with your will, always conscious that the same Infinite Power which brought the universe into existence, brought you into form for the purpose of enjoying Itself in and through you. And since it is all Life, Love, Light, Power, Peace, Beauty, and Joy, and is the only Creative Power there is, the form it takes in and through you depends upon the direction given it by your thought. In you it is undifferentiated, waiting to take any direction given it as it passes through the instrument which it has made for the purpose of self-distribution—you.

It is this Power which enables you to transfer your thoughts from one form to another. The power to change your mind is the individualized Universal Power taking the initiative, giving direction to the unformed substance contained in every thought.

It is the simplest thing in the world to give this highly sensitive Substance any form you will, through visualizing. Anyone can do it with a small expenditure of effort. Once you really believe that your mind is a center through which the unformed substance of all there is in your world, takes involuntary form, the only reason your picture does not always materialize is because you have introduced something antagonistic to the fundamental principle. Very often this destructive element is caused by the frequency with which you change your pictures. After many such changes, you decide that your original desire is what you want after all. Upon this conclusion, you begin to wonder why it (being your first picture) has not materialized. The Substance with which you are mentally dealing is more sensitive than the most sensitive photographer's film. If, while taking a picture, you suddenly remembered you had already taken a picture on that same plate, you would not expect a perfect result of either picture. On the other hand, you may have taken two pictures on the same plate unconsciously. When the plate has been developed, and the picture comes into physical view, you do not condemn the principle of photography, nor are you puzzled to understand why your picture has turned out so unsatisfactorily. You do not feel that it is impossible for you to obtain a good, clear picture of the subject in question. You know that you can do so, by simply starting at the beginning, putting in a new plate, and determining to be more careful while taking your picture next time. If these lines are followed out, you are sure of a satisfactory result. If you will proceed in the same manner with your mental picture, doing your part in a correspondingly confident frame of mind, the result will be just as perfect. The laws of visualizing are as infallible as the laws governing photography. In fact, photography is the outcome of visualizing.

Again, your results in visualizing the fulfillment of your desires may be imperfect, and your desires delayed, through the misuse of this power, owing to the thought that the fulfillment of your desire is contingent upon certain persons or conditions. The Originating Principle is not in any way dependent upon any person, place, or thing. It has no past and knows no future. The law is that the Originating Creative Principle of Life is "the universal here and everlasting now." It creates its own vehicles through which to operate. Therefore, past experience has no bearing upon your present picture. So do not try to obtain your desire through a channel which may not be natural for it, even though it may seem reasonable to you. Your feeling should be that the thing, or the consciousness, which you so much desire, is normal and natural, a part of yourself, a form of your evolution. If you can do this, there is no power to prevent your enjoying the fulfillment of the picture you have in mind, or any other you may create.

Chapter Five

Expressions from Beginners

Hundreds of persons have realized that "visualizing is an Aladdin's lamp to him with a mighty will." General Foch says that his feelings were so outraged during the Franco-Prussian war in 1870 that he visualized himself leading a French army against the Germans to victory. He said he made his picture, smoked his pipe, and waited. This is one result of visualizing with which we are all familiar.

A famous actress wrote a long article in one of the leading Sunday papers last winter, describing how she rid herself of excessive avoirdupois by seeing her figure constantly as she wished to be.

A very interesting letter came to me from a doctor's wife, while I was lecturing in New York. She began with the hope that I would never discontinue my lectures on visualization, which were helping humanity to realize the wonderful fact that they possessed the means of liberation within themselves. Relating her own experience, she said that she was born on the East Side of New York in the poorest quarter. From earliest girlhood she had cherished a dream of marrying a physician some day. This dream gradually formed a stationary mental picture. The first position she obtained was in the capacity of a maid in a physician's family. Leaving this place, she entered the family of another doctor. The wife of her employer died, and in the doctor married her—the result of long-pictured yearning. After that, both and her husband conceived the idea of owning a fruit farm in the South. They formed a mental picture of the idea and put their faith in its eventual fulfillment. The letter she sent me came from her fruit farm in the South. Her second mental picture had seen the light of materialization.

Many letters of a similar nature come to me every day. The following is a case that was printed in the New York Herald last May:

"Atlantic City, May 5—She was an old woman, and when she was arraigned before Judge Clarence Goldenberg in the police court today she was so weak and tired she could hardly stand. The Judge asked the court attendant what she was charged with. 'Stealing a bottle of milk, Your Honor,' repeated the officer. 'She took it from the doorstep of a downtown cottage before daybreak this morning.' 'Why did you do that?' Judge Goldenberg asked her. 'I was hungry,' the old woman said. 'I didn't have a cent in the world and no way to get anything to eat except to steal it. I didn't think anybody would mind if I took a bottle of milk.' 'What's your name?' asked the judge. 'Weinberg,' said the old woman, 'Elizabeth Weinberg.' Judge Goldenberg asked her a few questions about herself. Then he said: 'Well, you're not very wealthy now, but you're no longer poor. I've been searching for you for months. I've got $500 belonging to you from the estate of a relative. I am the executor of the estate.'

"Judge Goldenberg paid the woman's fine out of his own pocket, and then escorted her into his office, where he turned her legacy over to her and sent a policeman out to find her a lodging place."

I learned later that this little woman had been desiring and mentally picturing $500, while all the time ignorant of how it could possibly come to her. But she kept her vision and strengthened it with her faith.

In an issue of Good Housekeeping there was an article by Addington Bruce entitled "Stiffening Your Mental Backbone." It is very instructive, and would benefit anyone to read it. He says, in part: "Form the habit of devoting a few moments every day to thinking about your work in a large, broad, imaginative way, as a vital necessity to yourself and a useful service to society."

James J. Hill, the great railway magnate, before he started building his road from coast to coast, said that he took hundreds of trips all along the line before there was a rail laid. It is said that he would sit for hours with a map of the United States before him and mentally travel from coast to coast, just as we do now over his fulfilled mental picture. It would be possible to call your attention to hundreds of similar cases.

The method of picturing to yourself what you desire is both simple and enjoyable, if you once understand the principle back of it well enough to believe it. Over and above everything else, be sure of what it is you really want. Then specialize your desire along the lines given in the following chapter.

Chapter Six

Suggestions for Making Your Mental Picture

Perhaps you want to feel that you've lived to some purpose. You want to be contented and happy; you feel that good health and a successful business would give you contentment. After you have decided once and for all that this is what you want, you proceed to picture yourself healthy, and your business just as great a success as you can naturally conceive it growing into. The best times for making your definite picture are just before breakfast, and again, before retiring at night. As it is necessary to give yourself plenty of time, it may be necessary to rise earlier than you usually do. Go into a room where you will not be disturbed, meditate for a few moments upon the practical working of the law of visualizing, and ask yourself, "How did the things about me first come into existence? How can I get more quickly in touch with my invisible supply?"

Someone felt that comfort would be better expressed and experienced by sitting on a chair than on the floor. So the very beginning of a chair was the desire to be at ease. With this came the picture of some sort of a chair, The same principle applies to the hat and the clothes you wear. Go carefully into the thought of the principle back of the thing. Establish it as a personal experience; make it a fact to your consciousness. Then open a window, take about ten deep breaths, and during the time draw a large imaginary circle of light pound you. As you inhale—keeping yourself in the center of this circle of light—see great rays of light coming from the circle and entering your body at all points, centralizing itself at your solar plexus. Hold the breath a few moments at this central point of your body—the solar plexus—then slowly exhale. As you do this, mentally see imaginary rays, or sprays, of light going up through the body, and down and out through feet.

Mentally spray your entire body with this imaginary light. When you have finished the breathing exercise, sit in a comfortable upright chair and mentally know there is but one Life, one Substance, and this Life Substance of the Universe is finding pleasure in self-recognition in you. Repeat some affirmation of this kind, until you feel the truth and stimulating reality of the words which you are affirming. Then begin your picture. If you are thorough in this, you will find yourself in the deep consciousness beneath the surface of your own thought power.

Whether your desire is for a state of consciousness, or a possession, large or small, begin at the beginning. If you want a house, begin by seeing yourself in the kind of house you desire. Go all through it, taking careful note of the rooms, where the windows are situated, and such other details as help you to feel the reality of your picture. You might change some of the furniture about and look into some of the mirrors just to see how healthy, wealthy, and happy you look. Go over your picture again and again, until you feel the reality of it, then write it all down just as you have seen it, with the feeling that:

"The best there is, is mine. There is no limit to me, because my mind is a center of divine operation," and your picture is as certain to come true, in your physical world, as the sun is to shine.

Chapter Seven

Things to Remember in Using Your Thought Power for the Production of New Conditions

In Using Your Thought Power for the Production of New Conditions

1. Be sure to know exactly what conditions wish to produce. Then weigh carefully what further results the accomplishment of your desire will lead to.

2. By letting your thought dwell upon a mental picture, you are concentrating the Creative Action of Spirit in this center, where its forces are equally balanced.
3. Visualizing brings your objective mind into a state of equilibrium, which enables you to consciously direct the flow of Spirit to a definitely recognized purpose, and to carefully guard your thoughts from including a flow in the opposite direction.
4. You must always bear in mind that you are dealing with a wonderful potential energy, which is not yet differentiated into any particular form, and that by the action of your mind, you can differentiate it into any specific form that you will. Your picture assists you to keep your mind fixed on the fact that the inflow of this Creative Energy is taking place. Also, by your mental picture, you are determining the direction you wish the sensitive Creative Power to take, and by doing this, you make the externalization of your picture a certainty.
5. Remember when you are visualizing properly that there is no strenuous effort to hold your thought-forms in place. Strenuous effort defeats your purpose, and suggests the consciousness of an adverse force to be fought against, and this creates conditions adverse to your picture.
6. By holding your picture in a cheerful frame of mind, you shut out all thoughts that would disperse or dissipate the spiritual nucleus of your picture. Because the law is Creative in its action, your pictured desire is certain of accomplishment.
7. The seventh and great thing to remember in visualizing is that you are making a mental picture for the purpose of determining the quality you are giving to the previously undifferentiated substance and energy, rather than to arrange the specific circumstances for its manifestation. That is the work of Creative Power itself. It will build its own forms of expression quite naturally, if you will allow it, and save you a great deal of needless anxiety. What you

really want is expansion in a certain direction, whether of health, wealth, or what not, and so long as you get it—as you surely will, if you confidently hold to your picture—what does it matter whether it reaches by some channel which you thought you could count upon, or through some other of whose existence you had no idea. You are concentrating energy of a particular kind for a particular purpose. Keep this in mind and let specific details take care of themselves, and never mention what you are doing to anyone.

Remember always, that "Nature, from her clearly visible surface to her most arcane depths, is one vast storehouse of light and good entirely devoted to your individual use." Your conscious Oneness with the great Whole is the secret of success, and when once you have fathomed this, you can enjoy your possession of the whole, or a part of it, at will, because by your recognition you have made it, and can increasingly make it, yours.

Never forget that every physical thing, whether for you or against you, was a sustained thought before it was a thing. Thought, as thought, is neither good nor bad; it is Creative Action and always takes physical form. Therefore, the thoughts you dwell upon become the things you possess or do not possess.

A man came to me telling me how be longed to marry a certain young woman, but felt he could not afford to as his salary was small, and work uncertain. I spoke the word of ever-present Certain, Unlimited Supply and explained that Love knows no failure.

"It is yours to enjoy. See yourself in the kind of a home you both want. Do your part, keep on loving the girl, and believe absolutely in that which Lives and Loves in you."

A few months later they both came to my study looking radiantly happy. I knew they were married. The wife said to me: "Dear Mrs. Behrend, we are very happy because we now know how to use our thought power and hold our consciousness as one, with all we want."

So be yourself and enjoy Life in your own Divine way. Do not fear to be your true self, for everything you want, wants you.

Chapter Eight

Why I Took Up the Study of Mental Science

I have frequently been questioned about my reasons for taking up the study of Mental Science, and as to the results of my search, not only in the knowledge of principles, but also in the application of that knowledge for the development of my own life.

Such inquiries are justifiable, because one who essays the role of a messenger of psychological truths can only be convincing as he or she has tested them in the laboratory of personal mental experience. This is particularly true in my case, as the only personal pupil of Judge Troward, the great Master in Mental Science, whose teaching is based upon the relation borne by the Individual Mind toward the Universal Creative Mind, which is the Giver of Life, and the manner in which that relation may be invoked to secure expansion and fuller expression in the individual life.

My initial impulse toward the study of Mental Science was an overwhelming sense of loneliness. In every life there must come some such experience of spiritual isolation as pervaded my life at that period. Notwithstanding the fact that each day found me in the midst of friends, surrounded by mirth and gaiety, there was a persistent feeling that I was alone in the world. I had been a widow for about three years, wandering from country to country, seeking for peace of mind.

The circumstances and surroundings of my life were such that my friends looked upon me as an unusually fortunate young woman. Although they recognized that I had sustained a great loss when my husband died, they knew that he had left me well provided for, free to go anywhere my pleasure dictated.

Yet, if my friends could have penetrated my inmost emotions, they would have found a deep sense of emptiness and isolation. This feeling inspired a spirit of unrest, which drove me on and on in fruitless search upon the outside, for that which I later learned could only be found within.

I studied Christian Science, but it gave me no solace, though fully realizing the, great work the Scientists were doing, and even having the pleasure and privilege of meeting Mrs. Eddy personally. But it was impossible for me to accept the fundamental teachings of Christian Science and make practical application of it.

When about to abandon the search for contentment and resign myself to resume a life of apparent amusement, a friend invited me to visit the great Seer and Teacher, Abdul Baha. After my interview with this most wonderful of men, my search for contentment began to take a change. He had told me that I would travel the world over seeking the truth, and when I had found it, would speak it out. The fulfillment of the statement of this Great Seer then seemed to be impossible. But it carried a measure of encouragement, and at least indicated that my former seeking had been in the wrong direction. I began in a feeble groping way to find contentment within myself, for had he not intimated that I should find the truth? That was the big thing, and about the only thing I remember of our interview.

A few days later, upon visiting the office of a New Thought practitioner, my attention was attracted to a book on his table entitled "The Edinburgh Lectures on Mental Science," by T. Troward. It interested me to see that Troward was a retired Divisional Judge from the Punjab, India. I purchased the book, thinking I would read it through that evening. Many have endeavored to do the same thing, only to find, as I did, that the book must be studied in order to be understood, and hundreds have decided, just as I did, to give it their undivided attention.

After finding this treasure book, I went to the country for a few days, and while there, studied the volume as thoroughly as I could.

It seemed extremely difficult, and I decided to purchase another book of Troward's, in the hope that its study might not require so much of an effort. Upon inquiry I was told that a subsequent volume, "The Dore Lectures," was much the simpler and better of the two books. When I procured it, I found that it must also be studied. It took me weeks and months to get even a vague conception of the meaning of the first chapter of Dore, which is entitled "Entering Into the Spirit of It." I mean by this that it took me months to enter into the spirit of what I was reading.

But in the meantime a paragraph from page 26 arrested my attention, as seeming the greatest thing I had ever read. I memorized it and endeavored with all my soul to enter into the spirit of Troward's words. The paragraph reads:

"My mind is a center of Divine operation. The Divine operation is always for expansion and fuller expression, and this means the production of something beyond what has gone before, something entirely new, not included in the past experience, though proceeding out of it by an orderly sequence or growth. Therefore, since the Divine cannot change its inherent nature, it must operate in the same manner with me; consequently, in my own special world, of which I am the center, it will move forward to produce new conditions, always in advance of any that have gone before."

It took an effort on my part to memorize this paragraph, but in the endeavor toward this end, the words seemed to carry with them a certain stimulus Each repetition of the paragraph made it easier for me to enter into the spirit of it. The words expressed exactly what I had been seeking for. My one desire was for peace of mind. I found it comforting believe that the Divine operation in me could expand to fuller expression and produce more and more contentment—in fact, a peace mind and a degree of contentment greater than I had ever known. The paragraph further inspired me with deep interest to feel that the life-spark in me could bring into my life something entirely new. I did not wish to obliterate my past experience, but that was exactly what Troward said it would not do. The Divine operation would not exclude my past experience, but proceeding out of it would bring some new thing that would transcend anything that I had ever experienced before.

Meditation on these statements brought with it a certain joyous feeling. What a wonderful thing it would be if I could accept and sincerely believe, beyond all doubt, that this one statement of Troward's was true. Surely the Divine could not change its inherent nature, and since Divine life is operating in me, I must be Divinely inhabited, and the Divine in me must operate just as it operates upon the Universal plane. This meant that my whole world of circumstances, friends, and conditions would ultimately become a world of contentment and enjoyment of which "I am the center." This would all happen just as soon as I was able to control my mind and thereby provide a concrete center around which the Divine energies could play.

Surely it was worth trying for. If Troward had found this truth, why not I? The idea held me to my task. Later I determined to study with the man who had realized and given to the world so great a statement. It had lifted me from my state of despondency. The immediate difficulty was the need for increased finances.

Chapter Nine

How I Attracted to Myself 20,000 Dollars

In the laboratory of experience in which my newly revealed relation to the Divine operation was to be tested, the first problem was a financial one. My income was a stipulated one quite enough for my everyday needs, but it did not seem sufficient to enable me to go comfortably to England, where Troward lived and remain for an indefinite period to study with so great a teacher as he must be. So before inquiring whether Troward took pupils, or whether I would be eligible in case he did, I began to use the paragraph I had memorized. Daily, in fact, almost hourly, the words were in my mind: "My mind is a center of Divine operation, and Divine operation means expansion into something better than has gone before."

From the Edinburgh Lectures I had read something about the Law of Attraction, and from the Chapter on "Causes and Conditions" I had gleaned a vague idea of visualizing. So every night, before going to sleep, I made a mental picture of the desired $20,000 which seemed necessary to go and study with Troward.

Twenty imaginary $1,000 bills were counted over each night in my bedroom, and then, with the idea of more emphatically impressing my mind with the fact that this twenty thousand dollars was for the purpose of going to England and studying with Troward, I wrote out my picture, saw myself buying my steamer ticket, walking up and down the ship's deck from New York to London, and finally, saw myself accepted as Troward's pupil. This process was repeated every morning and every evening, always impressing more and more fully upon my mind Troward's memorized statement: "My mind is a center of Divine operations." I endeavored to keep this statement in the back part of my consciousness all the time, with no thought in mind of how the money might be obtained. Probably the reason why there was no thought of the avenues through which the money might reach me was because I could not possibly imagine where the $20,000 would come from. So I simply held my thought steady and let the power of attraction find its own ways and means.

One day while walking on the street, taking deep breathing exercises, the thought came:

"My mind is surely a center of Divine operation. If God fills all space, then God must be in my mind also; if I want this money to study with Troward that I may know the truth of Life, then both the money and the truth must be mine, though I am unable to feel or see the physical manifestations of either. Still," I declared, "it must be mine."

While these reflections were going on in my mind, there seemed to come up from within me the thought: "I Am all the substance there is," Then, from another channel in my brain the answer seemed to come, "Of course, that's it; everything must have its beginning in mind. The idea must contain within itself the only one and primary substance there is, and this means money as well as everything else." My mind accepted this idea, and immediately all the tension of mind and body was relaxed. There was a feeling of absolute certainty of being in touch with all the power Life has to give. All thought of money, teacher, or even my own personality, vanished in the great wave of joy which swept over my entire being. I walked on and on, with this feeling of joy steadily increasing and expanding until everything about me seemed aglow with resplendent light. Every person I passed appeared illuminated as I was. All consciousness of personality had disappeared, and in its place there came that great and almost overwhelming sense of joy and contentment.

That night when I made my picture of the twenty thousand dollars it was with an entirely changed aspect. On previous occasions, when making my mental picture, I had felt that I was waking up something within myself. This time there was no sensation of effort. I simply counted over the twenty thousand dollars. Then, in a most unexpected manner, from a source of which I had no consciousness at the time, there seemed to open a possible avenue through which the money might reach me.

At first it took great effort not to be excited. It all seemed so wonderful, so glorious, to be in touch with supply. But had not Troward cautioned his readers to keep all excitement out of their minds in the first flush of realization of union with Infinite supply, and to treat this fact as a perfectly natural result which had been reached through our demand? This was even more difficult for me than it was to hold the thought that "all the substance there is, I Am; I (idea) Am the beginning of all form, visible or invisible."

Just as soon as there appeared a circumstance which indicated the direction through which the twenty thousand dollars might come, I not only made a supreme effort to regard the indicated direction calmly as the first sprout of the seed I had sown in the absolute, but left no stone unturned to follow up that direction, thereby fulfilling my part. By so doing, one circumstance seemed naturally to lead to another, until, step by step, my desired twenty thousand dollars was secured. To keep my mind poised and free from excitement was my greatest effort.

This first concrete fruition of my study of Mental Science as expounded by Troward's book had come by a careful following of the methods he had outlined. In this connection, therefore I can offer to the reader no better gift than to quote Troward's book, "The Edinburgh Lectures," from which may be derived a complete idea of the line of action I was endeavoring to follow. In the chapter on Causes and Conditions he says:

"To get good results we must properly understand our relation to the great impersonal power we are using. It is intelligent, and we are intelligent, and the two intelligences must co-operate.) We must not fly in the face of the law expecting it to do for us what it can only do through us; and we must therefore use our intelligence with the knowledge that it is acting *as the instrument of a greater intelligence*; and because we have this knowledge we may and should cease from all anxiety as to the final result.

"In actual practice we must first form the ideal conception of our object with the definite intention of impressing it upon the Universal Mind—it is this thought that takes such thought out of the region of mere casual fancies and then affirm that our knowledge of the

Law is sufficient reason for a calm expectation of a corresponding result, and that therefore all necessary conditions will come to us in due order. We can then turn to the affairs of our daily life with the calm assurance that the initial conditions are either there already or will soon come into view. If we do not at once see them, let us rest content with the knowledge that the spiritual prototype is already in existence and wait till some circumstance pointing in the desired direction begins to shop itself. It may be a very small circumstance, but it is the direction and not the magnitude which is to be taken into consideration. As soon as we see it we should regard it as the first sprouting of the seed sown in the Absolute, and do calmly, and without excitement, whatever the circumstances seem to require, and then later on we shall see that this doing will in turn lead to a further circumstance in the same direction, until we find ourselves conducted, step by step, to the accomplishment of our object. In this way the understanding of the great principle of the Law of Supply will, by repeated experiences, deliver us more and more completely out of the region of anxious thought and toilsome labor and bring us into a new world where the useful employment of all our powers, whether mental or physical, will only be an unfolding of our individuality upon the lines of its own nature, and therefore a perpetual source of health and happiness; a sufficient inducement, surely, to the careful study of the laws governing the relation on between the individual and the Universal Mind."

To my mind, then as now, this quotation outlines the core and center of the method and manner of approach necessary for coming in touch with Infinite Supply. At least it, together with the previously quoted statement, "My mind is a center of Divine operation," etc., constituted the only apparent means of attracting to myself the twenty thousand dollars. My constant endeavor to get into the spirit of these statements, and to attract to myself this needed sum, took about six weeks, at the end of which time I had in my bank the required twenty thousand dollars. This could be made into a long story, giving all the details, but the facts, as already narrated, will give you a definite idea of the magnetic condition of my mind while the twenty thousand dollars was finding its way to me.

Chapter Ten

How I Became the Only Personal Pupil of T. Troward, the Great Mental Scientist

As soon as the idea of studying with Troward came to me, I asked a friend to write him for me, feeling that perhaps my friend could couch my desire in better or more persuasive terms than I could employ. To all the letters written by this friend, I received not one reply. This was so discouraging that I would have completely abandoned the idea of becoming Troward's pupil, except for the experience I had had that day on the street, when my whole world was illuminated, and I remembered the promise "All things whatsoever thou wilt, believe thou hast received, and thou shalt receive."

With this experience in my mind, my passage to England was arranged, notwithstanding the fact that apparently my letters were ignored. We wrote again, however, and finally received a reply, very courteous though very positive. Troward did not take pupils; he had no time to devote to a pupil. Notwithstanding this definite decision, I declined to be discouraged, because of the memory of my experience upon the day when the light and the thought had come to me, "I Am all the Substance there is." I seemed to be able to live that experience over at will, and with it there always came a flood of courage and renewed energy. We journeyed on to London, and from there telegraphed Troward, asking for an interview. The telegram was promptly answered, setting a date when he could see us.

At this time Troward was living in Ruan Manor, a little out-of-the-way place in the Southern part of England, about twenty miles from a railway station. We could not find it on the map, and with great difficulty Cook's Touring Agency, in London, located the place for us. There was very little speculation in my mind as to what Troward would say to me in this interview. There always remained the feeling that the truth was mine; also that it would grow and expand in my consciousness until peace and contentment were outward, as well as inward, manifestations of my individual life.

We arrived at Troward's house in a terrific rainstorm, and were cordially received by Troward himself, whom I found, much to my surprise, to be more the type of a Frenchman than an Englishman, (I afterward learned that be was a descendant of the Huguenot race), a man of medium stature, with a rather large head, big nose, and eyes that fairly danced with merriment. After we had been introduced to the other members of the family and given a cup of hot tea, we were invited into the living-room, where Troward talked very freely of everything except my proposed studies. It seemed quite impossible to bring him to that subject. Just before we were leaving, however, I asked quite boldly: "Will you not reconsider your decision to take a personal pupil? I wish so much to study with you," to which he replied, with a very indifferent manner, that he did not feel he could give the time it would require for personal instruction, but that he would be glad to give me the names of two or three books which he felt would not only be interesting but instructive to me. He said he felt much flattered and pleased that I had come all the way from America to study with him, and as we walked out through the lane from his house to our automobile, his manner became less indifferent, a feeling of sympathy seemed to touch his heart, and he turned to me with the remark: "You might write to me, if so inclined, after you get to Paris, and perhaps, if I have time in the autumn, we could arrange something, though it does not seem possible now."

I lost no time in following up his very kind invitation to write. My letters were all promptly and courteously answered, but there was never a word of encouragement as to my proposed studies, Finally, about two months later, there came a letter with this question in it: "What do you suppose is the meaning of this verse in the twenty-first Chapter of Revelation?"

"16. And the city lieth foursquare and the length is as large as the breadth; and he measured the city with the reed, twelve thousand furlongs. The length and the breadth and the height of it are equal."

Instinctively I knew that my chance to study with Troward hung upon my giving the correct answer to that question. The definition of the verse seemed utterly beyond my reach. Naturally, answers came to my mind, but I knew intuitively that they were incorrect. I began bombarding my scholarly friends and acquaintances with the same questions. Lawyers, doctors, priests, nuns, and clergymen, all over the world, received letters from me with this question in them. Answers began to return to me, but intuition told me not one was correct. All the while I was endeavoring to find the answer for myself, but no answer came. I memorized the verse in order that I might meditate upon it. I began a search of Paris for the books Troward had recommended to me, and after two or three days' search we crossed the River Seine to the Ile de Cite to go into some of the old bookstores there. The books were out of print, and these were the last places in which to find them. Finally we came upon a little shop which had them. The man had only one copy of each left, consequently the price was high. While remonstrating with the clerk, my eye rested upon the work of an astrologer, which I laughingly picked up and asked: "Do you think Prof.—— would read my horoscope?" The clerk looked aghast at the suggestion, and responded, "Why, no,

Madame, he is one of France's greatest astrologers. He does not read horoscopes."

In spite of this answer, there was a persistent impulse within me to go to the man. The friend who had accompanied me in my search for the books remonstrated with me, and tried in every way to dissuade me from going to the famous astrologer, but I insisted. When we arrived at his office, I found it somewhat embarrassing to ask him to read my horoscope. Nevertheless, there was nothing to do but put the question. Reluctantly, the Professor invited us into his paper-strewn study; reluctantly, and also impatiently he asked us to be seated. Very courteously and coldly he told me that he did not read horoscopes. His whole manner said, more clearly than words could, that he wished we would take our departure.

My friend stood up. I was at a great loss what to do next, because I felt that I was not quite ready to go. Intuition seemed to tell me there was something for me to gain there. Just what it was I was unable to define, so I paused a moment, much to my friend's displeasure and embarrassment, when one of the Professor's enormous Persian cats jumped into my lap. "Get down, Jack!" the Professor shouted. "What does it mean?" he seemed to ask himself. Then with a greater interest than he had hitherto shown in me, the Professor said with a smile:

"I have never known that cat to go to a stranger before, Madame; my cat pleads for you. I, also, now feel an interest in your horoscope, and if you will give me the data it will give me pleasure to write it out for you."

There was a great feeling of happiness in me when he made this statement, which he concluded by saying, "I do not feel that you really care for your horoscope." The truth of this statement shocked me, because I did not care about a horoscope, and could not give any reason why I was letting him do it. "However," he said, "may I call for your data next Sunday afternoon?"

On Sunday afternoon at the appointed time, the Professor arrived, and I was handing him the slip of paper with all the data of my birth, etc., when the idea came to ask the Professor the answer to the question Troward had given me from the 16th verse of the twenty-first Chapter of Revelation. The thought was instantly carried into effect, and I found myself asking this man what he thought this verse meant. Without pausing to think it over, he immediately replied, "It means: the city signifies the truth, and the truth is non-invertible; every side from which you approach it is exactly the same." Intuitively and undoubtingly I recognized this answer as the true one, and my joy knew no bounds, because I felt sure that with this correct answer in my possession, Troward would accept me as his pupil in the fall.

As the great astrologer was leaving, I explained to him all about my desire to study with Troward, how I had come from New York City for that express purpose, seemingly to no avail, until the answer to this test question had been given to me by him. He was greatly interested and asked many questions about Troward, and when asked if he would please send me his bill, he smilingly replied, "Let me know if the great Troward accepts you as his pupil," and bade me good afternoon. I hastened to my room to send a telegram to Troward, giving my answer to the question from the 16th verse of the 21st Chapter of Revelation.

There was an immediate response from Troward which said: "Your answer is correct. Am beginning a course of lectures on The Great Pyramid in London. If you wish to attend them, will be pleased to have you, and afterward, if you still wish to study with me, I think it can be arranged." On receipt of this reply preparations were at once made to leave Paris for London.

I attended all the lectures, receiving much instruction from them, after which arrangements were made for my studying with Troward. Two days before leaving for Cornwall, I received the following letter from Troward clearly indicating the line of study he gave me:

> 31 Stanwick Road,
> W. Kensington, England.

Dear Mrs. Behrend:

I think I had better write you a few lines with regard to your proposed studies with me, as I should be sorry for you to be under any misapprehension and so to suffer any disappointment.

I have studied the subject now for several years, and have a general acquaintance with the leading features of most of the systems which, unfortunately, occupy attention in many circles at the present time, such as Theosophy, The Tarot, The Kabala, and the like, and I have no hesitation in saying that, to the best of my judgment, all sorts and descriptions of *so-called* occult study are in direct opposition to the real life-giving Truth, and therefore, you must not expect any teaching on such lines as these.

We hear a great deal these days about initiation; but, believe me, the more you try to become a so-called "Initiate" the further you will put yourself from living life.

I speak after many years of careful study and consideration when I say that the Bible and its Revelation of Christ is the one thing really worth studying, and that is a subject large enough in all conscience, embracing, as it does, our outward life and of everyday concerns, and also the inner springs of our life and all that we can in general terms conceive of the life in the unseen after putting off the body at death.

You have expressed a very great degree of confidence in my teaching, and if your confidence is such that you wish, as you say, to put yourself entirely under my guidance, I can only accept it as a very serious responsibility, and should have to ask you to exhibit that confidence by refusing to look into such so-called "Mysteries" as I would forbid you to look into.

I am speaking from experience; but the result will be that much of my teaching will appear to be very simple, perhaps to some extent dogmatic, and you will say you have heard much of it before.

Faith in God, Prayer and Worship, approach to the Father through Christ—all this is in a certain sense familiar to you; and all I can hope to do is perhaps to throw a little more light on these subjects, that they may become to you, not merely traditional words, but *present living facts.*

I have been thus explicit as I do not want you to have any disappointment, and also I should say that our so-called course of study will be only friendly conversations at such times as we can fit them in, either you coming to our house, or I to yours, as may be most convenient at the time.

Also, I will lend you some books which will be helpful, but they are very few, and in no sense occult.

Now, if all this falls in with your ideas, we shall, I am sure, be very glad to see you at Ruan Manor, and you will find that the residents there, though few, are very friendly and the neighborhood very pretty.

But, on the other hand, if you feel that you want some other source of learning, do not mind saying so, only you will never find any substitute for Christ.

I trust you will not mind my writing you like this, but I do not want you to come all the way down to Cornwall, and then be disappointed.

With kindest regards,
Yours sincerely,
(Signed) T. Troward.

This copy of Troward's letter, to my mind, is the greatest thing I can give you.

Chapter Eleven

How to Bring the Power in Your Word Into Action

In every word you use, there is a power germ which expands and projects itself in the direction your word indicates, and ultimately develops into physical expression. For example, you wish the consciousness of joy. Repeat the word "joy" secretly, persistently and emphatically. The repetition of the word joy sets up a quality of vibration which causes the joy germ to begin to expand and project itself until your whole being is filled with joy. This is not a mere fancy, but a truth. Once you experience this power, you will daily prove to yourself that these facts have not been fabricated to fit a theory, but the theory has been built up by careful observation of facts; Everyone knows that joy comes from within. No one can give it to you. Another may give you cause for joy, but no one can be joyous for you. Joy is a state of consciousness, and consciousness is purely mental.

Troward says the "Mental faculties always work under something which stimulates them, and this stimulus may come either from without, through the external senses, or from within, by the consciousness of something not perceptible on the physical plane. The recognition of this interior source of stimulus enables you to bring into your consciousness any state you desire." Once a thing seems normal to you, it is as surely yours, through the Law of growth and attraction, as it is yours to know addition after you have learned the use of figures.

This method of repeating the word makes the word in all of its limitless meaning yours, because words are the embodiment of thoughts, and thought is creative; neither good nor bad, simply creative. This is the reason why Faith builds up and Fear destroys.

"Only believe, and all things are possible unto you."

It is Faith that gives you dominion over every adverse circumstance or condition. It is your word of Faith that sets you free not faith in any specific thing or act, but simple Faith in your best self in all ways. It is this ever-present Creative Power within the heart of the word that makes your health, your peace of mind, and your financial condition a reproduction of your most habitual thought. Try to believe and understand this, and you will find yourself Master of every adverse circumstance or condition, for you will become a Prince of Power.

Chapter Twelve

How to Increase Your Faith

But you ask, "How can I speak the word of Faith when I have little or no faith?"

Every living thing has faith in something or somebody. Faith is that quality of Power which gives the Creative Energy a corresponding vitality, and the vitality in the word of Faith you use causes it to take corresponding physical form. Even intense fear is alive with faith. You fear smallpox because you *believe* it possible for you to contract it. You fear poverty and loneliness because you *believe* them possible for you. It is the Faith which understands that every creation had its birth in the womb of thought-words, that gives you dominion over all things, your lesser self included, and this feeling of faith is increased and intensified through observing what it *does*.

Your constant observation should be of your state of consciousness when you did; not when you hoped you might, but feared it was too good to be true. How did you feel that time when you simply had to bring yourself into a better frame of mind and did, or you had to have a certain thing and got it? Live these experiences over again and again—mentally—until you really feel in touch with the self which knows and does, and then the best there is, is yours.

Chapter Thirteen

The Reward of Increased Faith

Your desire to be your best has expanded your faith into the faith of the Universe which knows no failure, and has brought you into conscious realization that you are not a victim of the universe, but a part of it. Consequently you are able to recognize that there is that within yourself which is able to make conscious contact with the Universal Law, and enables you to press all the particular laws of Nature, whether visible or invisible, into serving your particular demand or desire. Thereby you find yourself Master, not a slave, of any situation. Troward tells us that this Mastering is to be "accomplished by knowledge, and the only knowledge which will afford this purpose in all its measureless immensity is the knowledge of the personal element in universal spirit," and its reciprocity to our own personality. In other words, the words you think, the personality you feel yourself to be, are all reproductions in miniature of God, "or specialized universal spirit." All your word-thoughts were God word-forms before they were yours.

The words you use are the instruments—channels—through which the creative energy takes form. Naturally, this sensitive Creative Power can only reproduce in accordance with the instrument through which it passes. All disappointments and failures are the result of endeavoring to think one thing and produce another. This is just as impossible as it would be for an electric fan to be used for lighting purposes, or for water to flow through a crooked pipe in a straight line. The water must take the shape of the pipe through which it flows. Even more truly this sensitive, invisible Substance must reproduce outwardly the shape of the thought-word through which it passes.

This is the law of its Nature; therefore, it logically follows,

"As a man thinketh, so is he."

Hence, when your thought or word-form is in correspondence with the Eternal constructive and forward movement of the Universal Law, then your mind is the mirror in which the Infinite Power and Intelligence of the Universe sees itself reproduced, and your individual life becomes one of harmony.

Chapter Fourteen

How to Make Nature Respond to You

It should be steadily borne in mind that there is an Intelligence and Power in all Nature and all space, which is always creative, and infinitely sensitive and responsive. The responsiveness of its nature is two-fold: it is creative, and amenable to suggestion. Once the human understanding grasps this all-important fact, it realizes the simplicity with which the law of life supplies your every demand. All that is necessary is to realize that your mind is a center of Divine operation, and consequently contains that within itself which accepts suggestions, and expect all life to respond to your call. Then you will find suggestions which tend to the fulfillment of your desire coming to you, not only from your fellowmen, but also from the flowers, the grass, the trees, and the rocks, which will enable you to fulfill your heart's desire, if you act upon them in confidence on this physical plane. "Faith without works is dead," but Faith *with* Works sets you absolutely free.

Chapter Fifteen

Faith With Works—What It Has Accomplished

It is said of Tyson, the great Australian Millionaire, that the suggestion to "make the desert land of Australia blossom as the rose" came to him from a modest little Australian violet while he was working as a bushman for something like three shillings a day. He used to find these friendly little violets growing in certain places in the woods, and something in the flower touched something akin to itself in the mind of Tyson. He would sit on the side of his bunk at night and wonder how flowers and vegetable life could be given an opportunity to express themselves in the desert land of Australia. No doubt he realized that it would take a long time to save enough money to put irrigating ditches in the desert lands, but his thought and feeling assured him it could be accomplished, and if it could be done, he could do it. If there was a power within himself which was able to capture the idea, then there must be a responsive power within the idea itself which could bring itself into a practical physical manifestation. He resolutely put aside all questions as to the specific ways and means which would be employed in bringing his desire into physical manifestation, and simply kept his thought centered upon the idea of making fences and seeing flowers and grass where none existed at that time.

Since the responsiveness of Reproductive Creative Power is not limited to any local condition of mind, his habitual meditation and mental picture set his ideas free to roam in an infinitude, and attract to themselves other ideas of a kindred nature.

Therefore, it was not necessary for Tyson to wait until he had saved from his three shillings a day enough money to irrigate the land, to see his ideas and desires fulfilled, for his ideas found other ideas in the financial world which were attuned in sympathy with themselves, and doors of finance were quickly opened.

All charitable institutions are maintained upon the principle of the responsiveness of life. If this were not true, no one would care to give, simply because another needed.

The law of demand and supply, cause and effect, can never be broken. Ideas attract to themselves kindred ideas. Sometimes they come from a flower, a book, or out of the invisible.

You are intent upon an idea not quite complete as to the ways and means of fulfillment, and behold along comes another idea, from no one can tell where, and finds friendly lodging with your idea; one idea attracting another, and so on until your desires are physical facts. You may feel the necessity for improvement in your finances, and wonder how this increase is to be brought about, when there seems suddenly to come from within the idea itself, the realization that everything—even money—had its birth in thought, and your thoughts turn their course. You simply hold to the statement or affirmation that the best, and all there is, is yours. Since you are able to capture ideas from the Infinite through the instrument of your intuition, you let your mind rest upon that thought, knowing full well that this very thought will respond to itself. Your inhibition of all doubt and anxiety enables the reassuring ideas to establish themselves and attract to themselves "I can" and "I will" ideas, which gradually grow into the physical form of the desire in your mind.

In the conscious uses of the Universal Power to reproduce your desires in physical form, three facts should be borne in mind:

First—All space is filled with a Creative Power.

Second—This Creative Power is amenable to suggestion.

Third—It can only work by deductive methods.

As Troward tells us, this last is an exceedingly important point, for it implies that the action of the ever-present Creative Power is in no way limited by precedent. It works according to the essence of the spirit of the principle. In other words, this Universal Power takes its creative direction from the word you give it. Once man realizes this great truth, the character with which this sensitive, reproductive power is invested becomes the most important of all his considerations. It is the unvarying law of Creative Life Principle that "As a man thinketh in his heart, so is he." If you realize the truth that the Creative Power can be to you only what you feel and think it to be, it is willing and able to meet your demands.

Troward says, "If you think your thought is Powerful, your Thought is Powerful."

"As a man thinketh in his heart, so is he" is the law of life, and the Creative Power can no more change this law than an ordinary mirror can reflect back to you a different image than the object you hold before it. "As you think, so are you" does not mean "as you tell people you think," or "as you would wish the world to believe you think." It means your innermost thoughts; that place where no one but you knows. "None can know the Father save the son," and "No one can know the son but the Father." Only the reproductive Creative Spirit of Life knows what you think until your thoughts become physical facts and manifest themselves in your body, your brain, or your affairs. Then everyone with whom you come into contact may know, because the Father, the Intelligent Creative Energy which heareth in secret your most secret thoughts, rewards you openly reproduces your thoughts in physical form. "As you think, that is what you become" should be kept in the background of your mind constantly. This is watching and praying without ceasing, and when you are not feeling quite up to par physically, pray.

Chapter Sixteen

Suggestions As to How to Pray or Ask, Believing You Have Already Received

Scientific Thinking Positive Thought Suggestions for Practical Application

Try, through careful, positive, enthusiastic (though not strenuous) thought, to realize that the indescribable, Invisible Substance of Life fills all space; that its nature is Intelligent, Undifferentiated Substance.

Five o'clock in the morning is the best time to go into this sort of meditation.

If you will retire early every night for one month, and before falling asleep, impress firmly upon your subjective mind the affirmation: "My Father is the ruler of all the world, and is expressing His directing power through me," you will find that the substance of life takes form in your thought molds. Do not accept the above suggestion simply because it is given to you. Think it over carefully until the impression is made upon your own subconscious mind understandingly. Rise every morning, as was suggested before, at five o'clock, sit in a quiet room in a straight-back chair, and think out the affirmation of the previous evening, and you will realize and be able to put into practice your Princely Power with the realization to some extent, at least, that your mind really is a center through which all the Creative Energy and Power there is, is taking form.

Scientific Prayer The Principle Underlying Scientific Prayer

In prayer for a change in condition, physical, mental, or financial, for yourself or another, bear in mind that the fundamental necessity for the answer to prayer is the understanding of the scientific statement:

"Ask, believing you have already received, *And you shall receive*"

This is not as difficult as it appears on the surface, once you realize that:

Everything has, its origin in the mind, and that which you seek outwardly, you already possess.

No one can think a thought in the future.

Your thought of a thing constitutes its origin.

THEREFORE:

*The Thought Form of the Thing
is Already Yours As soon as you think it.*

Your steady recognition of this Thought Possession causes the thought to concentrate, to condense, to project itself, and to assume physical form.

To Get Rich Through Creation

The recognition or conception of new sources of wealth is the loftiest aspiration you can take into your heart, for it assumes and implies the furtherance of all noble aims.

Items to be remembered about Prayer for Yourself or Another

Remember that that which you call treatment or prayer is not, in any sense, hypnotism. It should never be your endeavor to take possession of the mind of another.

Remember that it should never be your intention to make yourself believe that which you know to be untrue. You are simply thinking into God or First Cause with the understanding that:

"If a thing is true at all, there is a way in which it is true throughout the universe."

Remember that the power of thought works by absolutely scientific principles. These principles are expressed in the language of the statement:

"As a man thinketh in his heart, so is he." This statement contains a world of wisdom, but man's steady recognition and careful application of the statement itself is required to bring it into practical use. Remember that the principles involved in being as we think in our heart are elucidated and revealed by the law: "As you sow, so shall you reap."

Remember that your freedom to choose just what you will think, just what thought possession you will affirm and claim, constitutes God's gift to you.

It shows how First Cause has endowed every man with the power and ability to bring into his personal environment whatever he chooses.

Cause and Effect in reference to Getting.

If you plant an ACORN, you get an OAK.

If you sow a GRAIN OF CORN, you reap a stalk and MANY kernels of corn.

You always get the manifestation of that which you consciously or unconsciously AFFIRM and CLAIM, habitually declare and expect, or, in other words, "AS YOU SOW."

Therefore, sow the seeds of—I AM . . . I OUGHT TO DO . . . I CAN DO . . . I WILL DO.

Realize
—that because you ARE you OUGHT to do;
—that because you OUGHT to, you CAN do;
—that because you CAN do, you DO do.

The manifestation of this truth, even in a small degree, gives you the undisputable understanding that DOMINION IS YOUR CHARTER RIGHT.

You are an heir of First Cause, endowed with all the power He has.

God has given you everything. ALL is yours, and you know that all you have to do is to reach out your mental hand and take it.

This Formula may serve as a pattern to shape your own Prayer or Affirmation into God for the benefit of another or yourself.

If for another, you speak the Christian name of the person you wish to help; then dismiss their personality entirely from your consciousness.

Intensify your thought by meditating upon the fact that there is that in you which finds the way, which is the Truth and is the Life.

You are affirming this fact, believing that since you are thinking this, it is already yours. Having lifted up your feeling to the central idea of this meditation, you examine your own consciousness and see if there is aught which is unlike God. If there is any feeling of fear, worry, malice, envy, hatred, or jealousy turn back in your meditation to cleanse your thought through the affirmation that God's love and purity fills all space, including your heart and soul. Reconcile your thought with the love of God, always remembering that:

You are made in the Image and Likeness of Love.

Keep this cleansing thought in mind until you feel that you have freed your consciousness entirely of all thoughts and feelings other than:

Love and Unity with all Humanity.

Then if denials do not disturb you, deny all that is unlike your desired manifestation. This accomplished, you almost overlay your denial with the affirmative thought that You are made in the Image and Likeness of God, and already have your desire fulfilled in its first, its original thought-form.

Closing of prayer

Prayer as a method of thought is a deliberate use of the Law which gives you the power of dominion over everything which tends in any way to hamper your perfect liberty.

> YOU HAVE BEEN GIVEN LIFE THAT YOU
> MAY ENJOY IT MORE AND MORE FULLY.

The steady recognition of this Truth makes you declare yourself a

> PRINCE OF POWER.

You recognize, accept, and use this power as

> THE CHILD OF A KING, AND HENCE
> DOMINION IS YOUR BIRTHRIGHT.

Then when you feel the light of this great truth flooding your consciousness—open the flood-gates of your soul in heartfelt praise because you have the understanding that
> THE CREATOR AND HIS CREATION ARE ONE;

also that the Creator is continually creating through his creation.

Close your treatment in the happy assurance that the prayer which is fulfilled is not a form of supplication, but a steady habitual affirming that: "The Creator of all creation is operating specifically through me," therefore—

> THE WORK MUST BE PERFECTLY DONE. YOUR MIND
> IS A CENTER OF DIVINE OPERATION

Hints for application and Practice

For every five minutes given to reading and study of the theories of Mental Science, spend fifteen minutes in the use and application of the knowledge acquired.

1. Spend one minute in every twenty-four hours to conscientiously thinking over the specification that must be observed in order to have your prayers answered.

2. Practice the steady recognition of desirable thought possession for two periods of fifteen minutes each every day. Not only time yourself each period to see how long you can keep a given conception before your mental vision, but also keep a written record of the vividness with which you experience your mental image. Remember that your mental senses are just as varied and trainable as your physical ones.

3. Spend five minutes every day between 12 noon and 1 o'clock with a mental research for new sources of wealth.

Chapter Seventeen

Things to Remember

That the greatest Mental Scientist the world has ever known (Jesus Christ, the Man) said all things are possible unto you. Also, "the things I do, you can do." Did he tell the truth?

Jesus did not claim to be more divine than you are. He declared the whole human race children of God. By birth he was no exception to this rule. The power be possessed was developed through His personal effort. He said you could do the same if you would only believe in yourself.

A great idea is valueless unless accompanied by physical action. God gives the idea; man works it out upon the physical plane.

All that is really worth while is contentment. Self-command alone can produce it.

The soul and body are one. Contentment of mind is contentment of soul, and contentment of soul means contentment of body.

If you wish health, watch your thoughts, not only of your physical being, but your thoughts about everything and everybody. With your will, keep them in line with your desire, and outwardly act in accordance with your thoughts, and you will soon realize that all power both over thoughts and conditions has been given to you.

You believe in God. Believe in yourself as the physical instrument through which God operates.

Absolute dominion is yours when you have sufficient self-mastery to conquer the negative tendency of thoughts and actions.

Ask yourself daily: "What is the purpose of the Power which put me here?"

"How can I work with the purpose for life and liberty in me?"

After having decided these questions, endeavor hourly to fulfill them. You are a law unto yourself.

If you have a tendency to overdo *anything*: eat, drink, or blame circumstances for your misfortunes, conquer that tendency with the inward conviction that *all power* is yours. Eat less, drink less, blame circumstances less, and the best there is will gradually grow in the place where the worst seemed to be.

Always remember that all is yours to use as you will. You can if you *will*; if you *will*, you do.

God the Father blesses you with all He has to give. Make good Godly use of it.

The reason for greater success when you first began your studies and demonstrations in Mental Science, was your joy and enthusiasm at the simple discovery of Power within, which was greater than you were able to put into your understanding later. With increased understanding comes increasing joy and enthusiasm, and the results will correspond.

AT YOUR COMMAND

Neville Goddard

Letter From Neville

This book contains the very essence of the Principle of Expression. Had I cared to, I could have expanded it into a book of several hundred pages but such expansion would have defeated the purpose of this book.

Commands, to be effective, must be short and to the point: the greatest command ever recored is found in the few simple words, "And God said, 'Let there be light.'"

In keeping with this principle I now give to you, the reader, in these few pages, the truth as it was revealed to me.

—**Neville**

Introduction

You do not command things to appear by your words or loud affirmations. Such vain repetition is more often than not confirmation of the opposite. Decreeing is ever done in consciousness. That is; every man is conscious of being that which he has decreed himself to be. The dumb man without using words is conscious of being dumb. Therefore he is decreeing himself to be dumb.

Instead of looking upon the Bible as the historical record of an ancient civilization or the biography of the unusual life of Jesus, see it as a great psychological drama taking place in the consciousness of man. Claim it as your own and you will suddenly transform your world from the barren deserts of Egypt to the promised land of Canaan. Every one will agree with the statement that all things were made by God, and without him there is nothing made that is made, but what man does not agree upon is the identity of God. All the churches and priesthoods of the world disagree as to the identity and true nature of God. The Bible proves beyond the shadow of a doubt that Moses and the prophets were in one hundred per cent accord as to the identity and nature of God. And Jesus' life and teachings are in agreement with the findings of the prophets of old. Moses discovered God to be man's awareness of being, when he declared these little understood words, "I AM hath sent me unto you." David sang in his psalms, "Be still and know that I AM God." Isaiah declared, "I AM the Lord and there is none else. There is no God beside me. I girded thee, though thou hast not known me. I form the light, and create darkness; I make peace, and create evil. I the Lord do all these things."

The *awareness of being* as God is stated hundreds of times in the New Testament. To name but a few: "I AM the shepherd, I AM the door; I AM the resurrection and the life; I AM the way; I AM the Alpha and Omega; I AM the beginning and the end"; and again, "Whom do you say that I AM?"

Every one will agree with the statement that all things were made by God, and without him there is nothing made that is made, but what man does not agree upon is the identity of God. All the churches and priesthoods of the world disagree as to the identity and true nature of God. The Bible proves beyond the shadow of a doubt that Moses and the prophets were in one hundred per cent accord as to the identity and nature of God. And Jesus' life and teachings are in agreement with the findings of the prophets of old. Moses discovered God to be man's awareness of being, when he declared these little understood words, "I AM hath sent me unto you." David sang in his psalms, "Be still and know that I AM God." Isaiah declared, "I AM the Lord and there is none else. There is no God beside me. I girded thee, though thou hast not known me. I form the light, and create darkness; I make peace, and create evil. I the Lord do all these things."

The *awareness of being* as God is stated hundreds of times in the New Testament. To name but a few: "I AM the shepherd, I AM the door; I AM the resurrection and the life; I AM the way; I AM the Alpha and Omega; I AM the beginning and the end"; and again, "Whom do you say that I AM?"

At Your Command

Can man decree a thing and have it come to pass? Most decidedly he can! Man has always decreed that which has appeared in his world and is today decreeing that which is appearing in his world and shall continue to do so as long as man is conscious of being man. Not one thing has ever appeared in man's world but what man decreed that it should. This you may deny, but try as you will you cannot disprove it, for this decreeing is based upon a changeless principle. You do not command things to appear by your words or loud affirmations. Such vain repetition is more often than not confirmation of the opposite. Decreeing is ever done in consciousness. That is; every man is conscious of being that which he has decreed himself to be. The dumb man without using words is conscious of being dumb. Therefore he is decreeing himself to be dumb. So he is dumb.

When the Bible is read in this light you will find it to be the greatest scientific book ever written. Instead of looking upon the Bible as the historical record of an ancient civilization or the biography of the unusual life of Jesus, see it as a great psychological drama taking place in the consciousness of man.

Claim it as your own and you will suddenly transform your world from the barren deserts of Egypt to the promised land of Canaan.

Every one will agree with the statement that all things were made by God, and without him there is nothing made that is made, but what man does not agree upon is the identity of God. All the churches and priesthoods of the world disagree as to the identity and true nature of God. The Bible proves beyond the shadow of a doubt that Moses and the prophets were in one hundred per cent accord as to the identity and nature of God. And Jesus' life and teachings are in agreement with the findings of the prophets of old. Moses discovered God to be man's awareness of being, when he declared these little understood words, "I AM hath sent me unto you." David sang in his psalms, "Be still and know that I AM God." Isaiah declared, "I AM the Lord and there is none else. There is no God beside me. I girded thee, though thou hast not known me. I form the light, and create darkness; I make peace, and create evil. I the Lord do all these things."

The *awareness of being* as God is stated hundreds of times in the New Testament. To name but a few: "I AM the shepherd, I AM the door; I AM the resurrection and the life; I AM the way; I AM the Alpha and Omega; I AM the beginning and the end"; and again, "Whom do you say that I AM?"

It is not stated, "I, Jesus, am the door. I, Jesus, am the way," nor is it said, "Whom do you say that I, Jesus, am?" It is clearly stated, "I AM the way." The awareness of being is the door through which the manifestations of life pass into the world of form.

Consciousness is the resurrecting **power**—resurrecting that which man is conscious of being. Man is ever out-picturing that which he is conscious of being. This is the truth that makes man free, for man is always self-imprisoned or self-freed.

If you, the reader, will give up all of your former beliefs in a God apart from yourself, and claim God as your awareness of being—as Jesus and the prophets did—you will transform your world with the realization that, "I and my father are one." This statement, "I and my father are one, but my father is greater than I," seems very confusing—but if interpreted in the light of what we have just said concerning the identity of God, you will find it very revealing. Consciousness, being God, is as "father." The thing that you are conscious of being is the "son" bearing witness of his "father." It is like the conceiver and its conceptions. The conceiver is ever greater than his conceptions yet ever remains one with his conception. For instance; before you are conscious of being man, you are first conscious of being. Then you become conscious of being man. Yet you remain as conceiver, greater than your conception—man.

Jesus discovered this glorious truth and declared himself to be one with God—not a God that man had fashioned. For he never recognized such a God. He said, "If any man should ever come, saying, 'Look here or look there,' believe them not, for the kingdom of God is within you." Heaven is within you. Therefore, when it is recorded that "He went unto his father," it is telling you that he rose in consciousness to the point where he was just conscious of being, thus transcending the limitations of his present conception of himself, called "Jesus."

In the awareness of being all things are possible, he said, "You shall decree a thing and it shall come to pass." This is his decreeing—rising in consciousness to the naturalness of being the thing desired. As he expressed it, "And I, if I be lifted up, I shall draw all men unto me." If I be lifted up in consciousness to the naturalness of the thing desired I will draw the manifestation of that desire unto me. For he states, "No man comes unto me save the father within me draws him, and I and my father are one." Therefore, consciousness is the father that is drawing the manifestations of life unto you.

You are, at this very moment, drawing into your world that which you are now conscious of being. Now you can see what is meant by, "You must be born again." If you are dissatisfied with your present expression in life the only way to change it, is to take your attention away from that which seems so real to you and rise in consciousness to that which you desire to be. You cannot serve two masters, therefore to take your attention from one state of consciousness and place it upon another is to die to one and live to the other.

The question, "Whom do you say that I AM?" is not addressed to a man called "Peter" by one called "Jesus." This is the eternal question addressed to one's self by one's true being. In other words, "Whom do you say that you are?" For your conviction of yourself—your opinion of yourself will determine your expression in life. He states, "You believe in God—believe also in me." In other words, it is the me within you that is this God.

Praying, then, is seen to be recognizing yourself to be that which you now desire, rather than its accepting form of petitioning a God that does not exist for that which you now desire.

So can't you see why the millions of prayers are unanswered? Men pray to a God that does not exist. For instance: To be conscious of being poor and to pray to a God for riches is to be rewarded with that which you are conscious of being—which is poverty. Prayers to be successful must be claiming rather than begging—so if you would pray for riches turn from your picture of poverty by denying the very evidence of your senses and assume the nature of being wealthy.

We are told, "When you pray go within in secret and shut the door. And that which your father sees in secret, with that will he reward you openly." We have identified the "father" to be the awareness of being. We have also identified the "door" to be the awareness of being. So "shutting the door" is shutting out that which "I" am now aware of being and claiming myself to be that which "I" desire to be. The very moment my claim is established to the point of conviction, that moment I begin to draw unto myself the evidence of my claim.

Do not question the how of these things appearing, for no man knows that way. That is, no manifestation knows how the things desired will appear.

Consciousness is the way or door through which things appear. He said, "I AM the way"—not "I," John Smith, am the way, but "I AM," the awareness of being, is the way through which the thing shall come. The signs always follow. They never precede. Things have no reality other than in consciousness. Therefore, get the consciousness first and the thing is compelled to appear.

You are told, "Seek ye first the kingdom of Heaven and all things shall be added unto you." Get first the consciousness of the things that you are seeking and leave the things alone. This is what is meant by "Ye shall decree a thing and it shall come to pass." Apply this principle and you will know what it is to "prove me and see." The story of Mary is the story of every man. Mary was not a woman—giving birth in some miraculous way to one called 'Jesus.' Mary is the awareness of being that ever remains virgin, no matter how many desires it gives birth to. Right now look upon yourself as this virgin Mary—being impregnated by yourself through the medium of desire—becoming one with your desire to the point of embodying or giving birth to your desire.

For instance: It is said of Mary (whom you now know to be yourself) that she know not a man. Yet she conceived. That is, you, John Smith, have no reason to believe that that which you now desire is possible, but having discovered your awareness of being to be God, you make this awareness your husband and conceive a man child (manifestation) of the Lord, "For thy maker is thine husband; the Lord of hosts is his name; the Lord God of the whole earth shall he be called." Your ideal or ambition is this conception—the first command to her, which is now to yourself, is "Go, tell no man." That is, do not discuss your ambitions or desires with another for the other will only echo your present fears. Secrecy is the first law to be observed in realizing your desire.

The second, as we are told in the story of Mary, is to "Magnify the Lord." We have identified the Lord as your awareness of being. Therefore, to "magnify the Lord" is to revalue or expand one's present conception of one's self to the point where this revaluation becomes natural. When this naturalness is attained you give birth by becoming that which you are one with in consciousness.

The story of creation is given us in digest form in the first chapter of John.

"In the beginning was the word." Now, this very second, is the "beginning" spoken of. It is the beginning of an urge—a desire. "The word" is the desire swimming around in your consciousness—seeking embodiment. The urge of itself has no reality, for "I AM" or the awareness of being is the only reality. Things live only as long as I AM aware of being them; so to realize one's desire, the second line of this first verse of John must be applied. That is, "And the word was with God." The word, or desire, must be fixed or united with consciousness to give it reality. The awareness becomes aware of being the thing desired, thereby nailing itself upon the form or conception—and giving life unto its conception—or resurrecting that which was heretofore a dead or unfulfilled desire. "Two shall agree as touching anything and it shall be established on earth."

This agreement is never made between two persons. It is between the awareness and the thing desired. You are now conscious of being, so you are actually saying to yourself, without using words, "I AM." Now, if it is a state of health that you are desirous of attaining, before you have any evidence of health in your world, you begin to FEEL yourself to be healthy. And the very second the feeling "I AM healthy" is attained the two have agreed. That is, I AM and health have agreed to be one and this agreement ever results in the birth of a child which is the thing agreed upon—in this case, health. And because I made the agreement I express the thing agreed. So you can see why Moses stated, "I AM hath sent me." For what being, other than I AM could send you into expression? None—for "I AM the way—Beside me there is no other." If you take the wings of the morning and fly into the uttermost parts of the world or if you make your bed in Hell, you will still be aware of being. You are ever sent into expression by your awareness and your expression is ever that which you are aware of being.

Again, Moses stated, "I AM that I AM." Now here is something to always bear in mind. You cannot put new wine in old bottles or new patches upon old garments. That is; you cannot take with you into the new consciousness any part of the old man. All of your present beliefs, fears and limitations are weights that bind you to your present level of consciousness. If you would transcend this level you must leave behind all that is now your present self, or conception of yourself. To do this you take your attention away from all that is now your problem or limitation and dwell upon just being. That is; you say silently but feeling to yourself, "I AM." Do not condition this "awareness" as yet. Just declare yourself to be, and continue to do so, until you are lost in the feeling of just being—faceless and formless. When this expansion of consciousness is attained, then, within this formless deep of yourself give form to the new conception by FEELING yourself to be THAT which you desire to be.

You will find within this deep of yourself all things to be divinely possible. Everything in the world which you can conceive of being, is to you, within this present formless awareness, a most natural attainment.

The invitation given us in the Scriptures is—"to be absent from the body and be present with the Lord." The "body" being your former conception of yourself and "the Lord"—your awareness of being. This is what is meant when Jesus said to Nicodemus, "Ye must be born again for except ye be born again ye cannot enter the kingdom of Heaven." That is; except you leave behind you your present conception of yourself and assume the nature of the new birth, you will continue to out-picture your present limitations.

The only way to change your expressions of life is to change your consciousness. For consciousness is the reality that eternally solidifies itself in the things round about you. Man's world in its every detail is his consciousness out-pictured. You can no more change your environment, or world, by destroying things than you can your reflection by destroying the mirror. Your environment, and all within it, reflects that which you are in consciousness. As long as you continue to be that in consciousness so long will you continue to out-picture it in your world.

Knowing this, begin to revalue yourself. Man has placed too little value upon himself. In the Book of Numbers you will read, "In that day there were giants in the land; and we were in our own sight as grasshoppers. And we were in their sight as grasshoppers." This does not mean a time in the dim past when man had the stature of giants. Today is the day—the eternal now—when conditions round about you have attained the appearance of giants (such as unemployed, the armies of your enemy, your problems and all things that seem to threaten you) those are the giants that make you feel yourself to be a grasshopper. But, you are told, you were first, in your own sight a grasshopper and because of this you were to the giants—a grasshopper. In other words, you can only be to others what you are first to yourself. Therefore, to revalue yourself and begin to feel yourself to be the giant, a center of power, is to dwarf these former giants and make of them grasshoppers. "All the inhabitants of the earth are as nothing, and he doeth according to his will in the armies of Heaven and among all the inhabitants of the earth; and none can stay his hand, nor say unto him, 'What doest thou'?" This being spoken of is not the orthodox God sitting in space but the one and only God—the everlasting father, your awareness of being. So awake to the power that you are, not as man, but as your true self, a faceless, formless awareness, and free yourself from your self-imposed prison.

"I am the good shepherd and know my sheep and am known of mine. My sheep hear my voice and I know them and they will follow me." Awareness is the good shepherd. What I am aware of being, is the "sheep" that follow me. So a good "shepherd" is your awareness that it has never lost one of the "sheep" that you are aware of being.

I am a voice calling in the wilderness of human confusion for such as I am aware of being, and never shall there come a time when that which I am convinced that I am shall fail to find me. "I AM" is an open door for all that I am to enter. Your awareness of being is lord and shepherd of your life. So, "The Lord is my shepherd; I shall not want" is seen in its true light now to be your consciousness. You could never be in want of proof or lack the evidence of that which you are aware of being.

This being true, why not become aware of being great; God-loving; wealthy; healthy; and all attributes that you admire?

It is just as easy to possess the consciousness of these qualities as it is to possess their opposites for you have not your present consciousness because of your world. On the contrary, your world is what it is because of your present consciousness. Simple, is it not? Too simple in fact for the wisdom of man that tries to complicate everything.

Paul said of this principle, "It is to the Greeks" (or wisdom of this world) "foolishness." "And to the Jews" (or those who look for signs) "a stumbling block"; with the result, that man continues to walk in darkness rather than awake to the being that he is. Man has so long worshipped the images of his own making that at first he finds this revelation blasphemous, since it spells death to all his previous beliefs in a God apart from himself. This revelation will bring the knowledge that "I and my father are one but my father is greater than I." You are one with your present conception of yourself. But you are greater than that which you are at present aware of being.

Before man can attempt to transform his world he must first lay the foundation—"I AM the Lord." That is, man's awareness, his consciousness of being is God. Until this is firmly established so that no suggestion or argument put forward by others can shake it, he will find himself returning to the slavery of his former beliefs. "If ye believe not that I AM he, ye shall die in your sins." That is, you shall continue to be confused and thwarted until you find the cause of your confusion. When you have lifted up the son of man then shall you know that I AM he, that is, that I, John Smith, do nothing of myself, but my father, or that state of consciousness which I am now one with does the works.

When this is realized every urge and desire that springs within you shall find expression in your world. "Behold I stand at the door and knock. If any man hear my voice and open the door I will come in to him and sup with him and he with me." The "I" knocking at the door is the urge.

The door is your consciousness. To open the door is to become one with that which is knocking by FEELING oneself to be the thing desired. To feel one's desire as impossible is to shut the door or deny this urge expression. To rise in consciousness to the naturalness of the thing felt is to swing wide the door and invite this one into embodiment.

That is why it is constantly recorded that Jesus left the world of manifestation and ascended unto his father. Jesus, as you and I, found all things impossible to Jesus, as man. But having discovered his father to be the state of consciousness of the thing desired, he but left behind him the "Jesus consciousness" and rose in consciousness to that state desired and stood upon it until he became one with it. As he made himself one with that, he became that in expression.

This is Jesus' simple message to man: Men are but garments that the impersonal being, I AM—the presence that men call God—dwells in. Each garment has certain limitations. In order to transcend these limitations and give expression to that which, as man—John Smith— you find yourself incapable of doing, you take your attention away from your present limitations, or John Smith conception of yourself, and merge yourself in the feeling of being that which you desire. Just how this desire or newly attained consciousness will embody itself, no man knows. For I, or the newly attained consciousness, has ways that ye know not of; its ways are past finding out. Do not speculate as to the HOW of this consciousness embodying itself, for no man is wise enough to know the how. Speculation is proof that you have not attained to the naturalness of being the thing desired and so are filled with doubts.

You are told, "He who lacks wisdom let him ask of God, that gives to all liberally, and upbraideth not; and it shall be given unto him.

But let him ask not doubting for he who doubts is as a wave of the sea that is tossed and battered by the winds. And let not such a one think that he shall receive anything from the Lord." You can see why this statement is made, for only upon the rock of faith can anything be established. If you have not the consciousness of the thing you have not the cause or foundation upon which the thing is erected.

A proof of this established consciousness is given you in the words, "Thank you, father." When you come into the joy of thanksgiving so that you actually feel grateful for having received that which is not yet apparent to the senses, you have definitely become one in consciousness with the thing for which you gave thanks. God (your awareness) is not mocked. You are ever receiving that which you are aware of being and no man gives thanks for something which he has not received. "Thank you father" is not, as it is used by many today, a sort of magical formula. You need never utter aloud the words, "Thank you, father." In applying this principle as you rise in consciousness to the point where you are really grateful and happy for having received the thing desired, you automatically rejoice and give thanks inwardly. You have already accepted the gift which was but a desire before you rose in consciousness, and your faith is now the substance that shall clothe your desire.

This rising in consciousness is the spiritual marriage where two shall agree upon being one and their likeness or image is established on earth.

"For whatsoever ye ask in my name the same give I unto you." "Whatsoever" is quite a large measure. It is the unconditional. It does not state if society deems it right or wrong that you should ask it, it rests with you. Do you really want it? Do you desire it? That is all that is necessary. Life will give it to you if you ask "in his name."

His name is not a name that you pronounce with the lips. You can ask forever in the name of God or Jehovah or Christ Jesus and you will ask in vain. "Name" means nature; so, when you ask in the nature of a thing, results ever follow. To ask in the name is to rise in consciousness and become one in nature with the thing desired, rise in consciousness to the nature of the thing, and you will become that thing in expression. Therefore, "what things so ever ye desire, when ye pray, believe that ye receive them and ye shall receive them."

Praying, as we have shown you before, is recognition—the injunction to believe that ye receive is first person, present tense. This means that you must be in the nature of the things asked for before you can receive them.

To get into the nature easily, general amnesty is necessary. We are told, "Forgive if ye have aught against any, that your father also, which is in Heaven, may forgive you. But if ye forgive not, neither will your father forgive you." This may seem to be some personal God who is pleased or displeased with your actions but this is not the case.

Consciousness, being God, if you hold in consciousness anything against man, you are binding that condition in your world. But to release man from all condemnation is to free yourself so that you may rise to any level necessary; there is, therefore, no condemnation to those in Christ Jesus.

Therefore, a very good practice before you enter into your meditation is first to free every man in the world from blame. For LAW is never violated and you can rest confidently in the knowledge that every man's conception of himself is going to be his reward. So you do not have to bother yourself about seeing whether or not man gets what you consider he should get. For life makes no mistakes and always gives man that which man first gives himself.

This brings us to that much abused statement of the Bible on tithing. Teachers of all kinds have enslaved man with this affair of tithing, for not themselves understanding the nature of tithing and being themselves fearful of lack, they have led their followers to believe that a tenth part of their income should be given to the Lord. Meaning, as they make very clear, that, when one gives a tenth part of his income to their particular organization he is giving his "tenth part" to the Lord—(or is tithing). But remember, "I AM the Lord." Your awareness of being is the God that you give to and you ever give in this manner.

Therefore when you claim yourself to be anything, you have given that claim or quality to God. And your awareness of being, which is no respecter of persons, will return to you pressed down, shaken together, and running over with that quality or attribute which you claim for yourself.

Awareness of being is nothing that you could ever name. To claim God to be rich; to be great; to be love; to be all wise; is to define that which cannot be defined. For God is nothing that could ever be named.

Tithing is necessary and you do tithe with God. But from now on give to the only God and see to it that you give him the quality that you desire as man to express by claiming yourself to be the great, the wealthy, the loving, the all wise.

Do not speculate as to how you shall express these qualities or claims, for life has a way that you, as man, know not of. Its ways are past finding out. But, I assure you, the day you claim these qualities to the point of conviction, your claims will be honored. There is nothing covered that shall not be uncovered. That which is spoken in secret shall be proclaimed from the housetops. That is, your secret convictions of yourself—these secret claims that no man knows of, when really believed, will be shouted from the housetops in your world. For your convictions of yourself are the words of the God within you, which words are spirit and cannot return unto you void but must accomplish whereunto they are sent.

You are at this moment calling out of the infinite that which you are now conscious of being. And not one word or conviction will fail to find you.

"I AM the vine and ye are the branches." Consciousness is the "vine," and those qualities which you are now conscious of being are as "branches" that you feed and keep alive. Just as a branch has no life except it be rooted in the vine, so likewise things have no life except you be conscious of them. Just as a branch withers and dies if the sap of the vine ceases to flow towards it, so do things in your world pass away if you take your attention from them, because your attention is as the sap of life that keeps alive and sustains the things of your world.

To dissolve a problem that now seems so real to you all that you do is remove your attention from it. In spite of its seeming reality, turn from it in consciousness. Become indifferent and begin to feel yourself to be that which would be the solution of the problem.

For instance; if you were imprisoned no man would have to tell you that you should desire freedom. Freedom, or rather the desire of freedom, would be automatic. So why look behind the four walls of your prison bars? Take your attention from being imprisoned and begin to feel yourself to be free. FEEL it to the point where it is natural—the very second you do so, those prison bars will dissolve. Apply this same principle to any problem.

I have seen people who were in debt up to their ears apply this principle and in the twinkling of an eye debts that were mountainous were removed. I have seen those whom doctors had given up as incurable take their attention away from their problem of disease and begin to feel themselves to be well in spite of the evidence of their sense to the contrary. In no time at all this so called "incurable disease" vanished and left no scar.

Your answer to, "Whom do you say that I AM"? ever determines your expression. As long as you are conscious of being imprisoned or diseased, or poor, so long will you continue to out-picture or express these conditions.

When man realized that he is now that which he is seeking and begins to claim that he is, he will have the proof of his claim. This cue is given you in words, "Whom seek ye?" And they answered, "Jesus." And the voice said, "I am he." "Jesus" here means salvation or savior. You are seeking to be salvaged from that which is not your problem.

"I am" is he that will save you. If you are hungry, your savior is food. If you are poor, your savior is riches. If you are imprisoned, your savior is freedom. If you are diseased, it will not be a man called Jesus who will save you, but health will become your savior. Therefore, claim "I am he," in other words, claim yourself to be the thing desired. Claim it in consciousness—not in words—and consciousness will reward you with your claim. You are told, "You shall find me when you FEEL after me." Well, FEEL after that quality in consciousness until you FEEL yourself to be it. When you lose yourself in the feeling of being it, the quality will embody itself in your world.

You are healed from your problem when you touch the solution of it. "Who has touched me? For I perceive virtue is gone out of me." Yes, the day you touch this being within you—FEELING yourself to be cured or healed, virtues will come out of your very self and solidify themselves in your world as healings.

It is said, "You believe in God. Believe also in me for I am he." Have the faith of God. "He made himself one with God and found it not robbery to do the works of God." Go you and do likewise. Yes, begin to believe your awareness, your consciousness of being to be God. Claim for yourself all the attributes that you have heretofore given an external God and you will begin to express these claims.

"For I am not a God afar off. I am nearer than your hands and feet—nearer than your very breathing." I am your awareness of being. I am that in which all that I shall ever be aware of being shall begin and end. "For before the world was I AM; and when the world shall cease to be, I AM; before Abraham was, I AM." This I AM is your awareness. "Except the Lord build the house they labor in vain that build it." "The Lord," being your consciousness, except that which you seek is first established in your consciousness, you will labor in vain to find it. All things must begin and end in consciousness.

So, blessed indeed is the man that trusteth in himself—for man's faith in God will ever be measured by his confidence in himself. You believe in a God, believe also in ME.

Put not your trust in men for men but reflect the being that you are, and can only bring to you or do unto you that which you have first done unto yourself.

"No man taketh away my life, I lay it down myself." I have the power to lay it down and the power to take it up again.

No matter what happens to man in this world it is never an accident. It occurs under the guidance of an exact and changeless Law.

"No man" (manifestation) "comes unto me except the father within me draw him," and "I and my father are one." Believe this truth and you will be free. Man has always blamed others for that which he is and will continue to do so until he find himself as cause of all. "I AM" comes not to destroy but to fulfill. "I AM," the awareness within you, destroys nothing but ever fills full the molds or conception one has of one's self.

It is impossible for the poor man to find wealth in this world no matter how he is surrounded with it until he first claims himself to be wealthy. For signs follow, they do not precede. To constantly kick and complain against the limitations of poverty while remaining poor in consciousness is to play the fool's game. Changes cannot take place from that level of consciousness for life is constantly out-picturing all levels.

Follow the example of the prodigal son. Realize that you, yourself, brought about this condition of waste and lack and make the decision within yourself to rise to a higher level where the fatted calf, the ring, and the robe await your claim.

There was no condemnation of the prodigal when he had the courage to claim this inheritance as his own. Others will condemn us only as long as we continue in that for which we condemn ourselves. So:

"Happy is the man that condemneth himself not in that which he alloweth." For to life nothing is condemned. All is expressed.

Life does not care whether you call yourself rich or poor; strong or weak. It will eternally reward you with that which you claim as true of yourself.

The measurements of right and wrong belong to man alone. To life there is nothing right or wrong. As Paul stated in his letters to the Romans: "I know and am persuaded by the Lord Jesus that there is nothing unclean of itself, but to him that esteemeth anything to be unclean, to him it is unclean." Stop asking yourself whether you are worthy or unworthy to receive that which you desire. You, as man, did not create the desire. Your desires are ever fashioned within you because of what you now claim yourself to be.

When a man is hungry, (without thinking) he automatically desires food. When imprisoned, he automatically desires freedom and so forth. Your desires contain within themselves the plan of self-expression.

So leave all judgments out of the picture and rise in consciousness to the level of your desire and make yourself one with it by claiming it to be so now. For: "My grace is sufficient for thee. My strength is made in weakness."

Have faith in this unseen claim until the conviction is born within you that it is so. Your confidence in this claim will pay great rewards. Just a little while and he, the thing desired, will come. But without faith it is impossible to realize anything. Through faith the worlds were framed because "faith is the substance of the thing hoped for—the evidence of the thing not yet seen."

Don't be anxious or concerned as to results. They will follow just as surely as day follows night.

Look upon your desires—all of them—as the spoken words of God, and every word or desire a promise. The reason most of us fail to realize our desires is because we are constantly conditioning them. Do not condition your desire. Just accept it as it comes to you. Give thanks for it to the point that you are grateful for having already received it—then go about your way in peace.

Such acceptance of your desire is like dropping seed—fertile seed—into prepared soil. For when you can drop the thing desired in consciousness, confident that it shall appear, you have done all that is expected of you. But, to be worried or concerned about the HOW of your desire maturing is to hold these fertile seeds in a mental grasp, and, therefore, never to have dropped them in the soil of confidence.

The reason men condition their desires is because they constantly judge after the appearance of being and see the things as real—forgetting that the only reality is the consciousness back of them.

To see things as real is to deny that all things are possible to God. The man who is imprisoned and sees his four walls as real is automatically denying the urge or promise of God within him of freedom.

A question often asked when this statement is made is; If one's desire is a gift of God how can you say that if one desires to kill a man that such a desire is good and therefore God sent? In answer to this let me say that no man desires to kill another. What he does desire is to be freed from such a one. But because he does not believe that the desire to be free from such a one contains within itself the powers of freedom, he conditions that desire and sees the only way to express such freedom is to destroy the man—forgetting that the life wrapped within the desire has ways that he, as man, knows not of. Its ways are past finding out. Thus man distorts the gifts of God through his lack of faith.

Problems are the mountains spoken of that can be removed if one has but the faith of a grain of a mustard seed. Men approach their problem as did the old lady who, on attending service and hearing the priest say, "If you had but the faith of a grain of a mustard seed you would say unto yonder mountain 'be thou removed' and it shall be removed and nothing is impossible to you." That night as she said her prayers, she quoted this part of the Scriptures and retired to bed in what she thought was faith. On arising in the morning she rushed to the window and exclaimed:

For this is how man approaches his problem. He knows that they are still going to confront him. And because life is no respecter of persons and destroys nothing, it continues to keep alive that which he is conscious of being.

Things will disappear only as man changes in consciousness. Deny it if you will, it still remains a fact that consciousness is the only reality and things but mirror that which you are in consciousness. So the heavenly state you are seeking will be found only in consciousness, for the kingdom of heaven is within you. As the will of heaven is ever done on earth you are today living in the heaven that you have established within you. For here on this very earth your heaven reveals itself. The kingdom of heaven really is at hand. NOW is the accepted time. So create a new heaven, enter into a new state of consciousness and a new earth will appear.

"The former things shall pass away. They shall not be remembered nor come into mind any more. For behold, I, come quickly and my reward is with me."

I am nameless but will take upon myself every name (nature) that you call me. Remember it is you, yourself, that I speak of as "me." So every conception that you have of yourself—that is every deep conviction—you have of yourself is that which you shall appear as being—for I AM not fooled; God is not mocked. Now let me instruct you in the art of fishing. It is recorded that the disciples fished all night and caught nothing. Then Jesus came upon the scene and told them to cast their nets in once more, into the same waters that only a moment before were barren—and this time their nets were bursting with the catch.

This story is taking place in the world today right within you, the reader. For you have within you all the elements necessary to go fishing. But until you find that Jesus Christ (your awareness) is Lord, you will fish, as did these disciples, in the night of human darkness. That is, you will fish for THINGS thinking things to be real and will fish with the human bait—which is a struggle and an effort—trying to make contact with this one and that one: trying to coerce this being or the other being; and all such effort will be in vain. But when you discover your awareness of being to be Christ Jesus you will let him direct your fishing. And you will fish in consciousness for the things that you desire. For your desire will be the fish that you will catch, because your consciousness is the only living reality you will fish in the deep waters of consciousness.

If you would catch that which is beyond your present capacity you must launch out into deeper waters, for, within your present consciousness such fish or desires cannot swim. To launch out into deeper waters, you leave behind you all that is now your present problem, or limitation, by taking your ATTENTION AWAY from it. Turn your back completely upon every problem and limitation that you now possess.

Dwell upon just being by saying, "I AM," "I AM," "I AM," to yourself. Continue to declare to yourself that you just are. Do not condition this declaration, just continue to FEEL yourself to be and without warning you will find yourself slipping the anchor that tied you to the shallow of your problems and moving out into the deep.

This is usually accompanied with the feeling of expansion. You will FEEL yourself expand as though you were actually growing. Don't be afraid, for courage is necessary. You are not going to die to anything by your former limitations, but they are going to die as you move away from them, for they live only in your consciousness. In this deep or expanded consciousness you will find yourself to be a power that you had never dreamt of before. The things desired before you shoved off from the shores of limitation are the fish you are going to catch in this deep. Because you have lost all consciousness of your problems and barriers, it is now the easiest thing in the world to FEEL yourself to be one with the things desired.

Because I AM (your consciousness) is the resurrection and the life, you must attach this resurrecting power that you are to the thing desired if you would make it appear and live in your world. Now you begin to assume the nature of the thing desired by feeling, "I AM wealthy"; "I AM free"; "I AM strong." When these "FEELS" are fixed within yourself, your formless being will take upon itself the forms of the things felt. You become 'crucified' upon the feelings of wealth, freedom, and strength. Remain buried in the stillness of these convictions. Then, as a thief in the night and when you least expect it, these qualities will be resurrected in your world as living realities.

The world shall touch you and see that you are flesh and blood for you shall begin to bear fruit of the nature of these qualities newly appropriated. This is the art of successful fishing for the manifestations of life.

Successful realization of the thing desired is also told us in the story of Daniel in the lion's den. Here, it is recorded that Daniel, while in the lion's den, turned his back upon the lions and looked towards the light coming from above; that the lions remained powerless and Daniel's faith in his God saved him.

This also is your story and you too must do as Daniel did. If you found yourself in a lion's den you would have no other concern but lions. You would not be thinking of one thing in the world but your problem—which problem would be lions.

Yet, you are told that Daniel turned his back upon them and looked towards the light that was his God. If we would follow the example of Daniel we would, while imprisoned within the den of poverty or sickness, take our attention away from our problems of debts or sickness and dwell upon the thing we seek.

If we do not look back in consciousness to our problems but continue in faith—believing ourselves to be that which we seek, we too will find our prison walls open and the thing sought—yes, "whatsoever things"—realized.

Another story is told us; of the widow and the three drops of oil. The prophet asked the widow, "What have ye in your house?" And she replied, "Three drops of oil." He then said to her, "Go borrow vessels. Close the door after ye have returned into your house and begin to pour." And she poured from three drops of oil into all the borrowed vessels, filling them to capacity with oil remaining.

You, the reader, are this widow. You have not a husband to impregnate you or make you fruitful, for a "widow" is a barren state. Your awareness is now the Lord—or the prophet that has become your husband.

Follow the example of the widow, who instead of recognizing an emptiness or nothingness, recognized the something—three drops of oil.

Then the command to her, "Go within and close the door," that is, shut the door of the senses that tell you of the empty measures, the debts, the problems.

When you have taken your attention away completely by shutting out the evidence of the senses, begin to FEEL the joy—(symbolized by oil)—of having received the things desired. When the agreement is established within you so that all doubts and fears have passed away, then, you too will fill all the empty measures of your life and will have an abundance running over. Recognition is the power that conjures in the world. Every state that you have ever recognized, you have embodied. That which you are recognizing as true of yourself today is that which you are experiencing. So be as the widow and recognize joy, no matter how little the beginnings of recognition, and you will be generously rewarded—for the world is a magnified mirror, magnifying everything that you are conscious of being.

"I AM the Lord the God, which has brought thee out of the land of Egypt, out of the house of bondage; thou shalt have no other gods before me." What a glorious revelation, your awareness now revealed as the Lord thy God! Come, awake from your dream of being imprisoned. Realize that the earth is yours, "and the fullness thereof; the world, and all that dwells therein."

You have become so enmeshed in the belief that you are man that you have forgotten the glorious being that you are. Now with your memory restored DECREE the unseen to appear and it SHALL appear, for all things are compelled to respond to the Voice of God, Your awareness of being—the world is AT YOUR COMMAND!

THE MAGIC STORY

Frederick van Rensselaer Dey

*"If you have skill, apply it;
the world must profit by it,
and, therefore, you."*

Preface

This wonderful little story, written by Frederick Van Rensselaer Dey, first appeared in the December, 1900, and January, 1901, issues of *Success Magazine*. It created an immediate sensation, and urgent requests were made for its reprint in book form. A small edition of a little silver-gray book was published to meet these requests, and this, the First Edition, has virtually disappeared from sight. The fact that the publishers of *Success Magazine* are in almost daily receipt of requests for additional copies is sufficient evidence of the value placed by the holders of the original edition upon the copies in their possession, and of their desire to bring it to the attention of their friends; and the demand has now become so insistent as to lead to the production of this, the Second Edition.

Mr. Dey has woven into this story, in a remarkably effective way, some of the fundamental principles of the "New Thought Movement" which is sweeping over this country, and it is safe to say that the application of these principles, as outlined in the "Magic Story," will accomplish almost, if not quite, all that is herein claimed for them towards the upbuilding and development of a manly, self-reliant, *success-compelling* spirit.

Part One

I WAS sitting alone in the *café*, and had just reached for the sugar preparatory to putting it into my coffee. Outside, the weather was hideous. Snow and sleet came swirling down, and the wind howled frightfully. Every time the outer door opened, a draft of unwelcome air penetrated the uttermost corners of the room. Still, I was comfortable. The snow and sleet and wind conveyed nothing to me except an abstract thanksgiving that I was where it could not affect me. While I dreamed and sipped my coffee, the door opened and closed, and admitted—Sturtevant.

Sturtevant was an undeniable failure, but, withal, an artist of more than ordinary talent. He had, however, fallen into the rut traveled by ne'er-do-wells, and was out at the elbows as well as insolvent.

As I raised my eyes to Sturtevant's, I was conscious of mild surprise at the change in his appearance. Yet he was not dressed differently. He wore the same threadbare coat in which he always appeared, and the old brown hat was the same. And yet there was something new and strange in his appearance. As he swished his hat around to relieve it of the burden of snow deposited by the howling nor'wester, there was something new in the gesticulation. I could not remember when I had invited Sturtevant to dine with me, but involuntarily I beckoned to him. He nodded, and presently seated himself opposite to me. I asked him what he would have, and he, after scanning the bill of fare carelessly, ordered from it leisurely, and invited me to join him in coffee for two. I watched him in stupid wonder, but, as I had invited the obligation, I was prepared to pay for it, although I knew I hadn't sufficient cash to settle the bill. Meanwhile, I noted the brightness of his usual lackluster eyes, and the healthful, hopeful glow upon his cheek, with increasing amazement.

"Have you lost a rich uncle?" I asked.

"No," he replied, calmly, "but I have found my mascot."

"Brindle bull, or terrier?" I inquired.

"Currier," said Sturtevant, at length, pausing with his coffee cup half way to his lips, "I see that I have surprised you. It is not strange, for I am a surprise to myself. I am a new man, a different man,—and the alteration has taken place in the last few hours. You have seen me come into this place broke' many a time, when you have turned away, so that I would think you did not see me. I knew why you did that. It was not because you did not want to pay for a dinner, but because you did not have the money to do it. Is that your check? Let me have it. Thank you. I haven't any money with me to-night, but I,—well, this is my treat."

He called the waiter to him, and, with an inimitable flourish, signed his name on the backs of the two checks, and waved him away. After that he was silent a moment while he looked into my eyes, smiling at the astonishment which I in vain strove to conceal.

"Do you know an artist who possesses more talent than I?" he asked, presently. "No. Do you happen to know anything in the line of my profession that I could not accomplish, if I applied myself to it? No. You have been a reporter on the dailies for—how many?—seven or eight years. Do you remember when I ever had any credit until to-night? No. Was I refused just now? You have seen for yourself. To-morrow my new career begins. Within a month I shall have a bank account. Why? Because I have discovered the secret of success."

"Yes," he continued, when I did not reply, "my fortune is made. I have been reading a strange story, and, since reading it, I feel that my fortune is assured. It will make your fortune, too. All you have to do is to read it. You have no idea what it will do for you. Nothing is impossible after you know that story. It makes everything as plain as A, B, C. The very instant you grasp its true meaning, success is certain. This morning I was a hopeless, aimless bit of garbage in the metropolitan ash can; to-night I wouldn't change places with a millionaire. That sounds foolish, but it is true. The millionaire has spent his enthusiasm; mine Is all at hand."

"You amaze me," I said, wondering if he had been drinking absinthe. "Won't you tell me the story? I should like to hear it."

"Certainly. I mean to tell it to the whole world. It is really remarkable that it should have been written and should remain in print so long, with never a soul to appreciate it until now. This morning I was starving. I hadn't any credit, nor a place to get a meal. I was seriously meditating suicide. I had gone to three of the papers for which I had done work, and had been handed back all that I had submitted. I had to choose quickly between death by suicide and death slowly by starvation.

Then I found the story and read it. You can hardly imagine the transformation. Why, my dear boy, everything changed at once—and there you are."

"But what is the story, Sturtevant?"

"Wait; let me finish. I took those same old drawings to other editors, and every one of them was accepted at once."

"Can the story do for others what it has done for you ? For example, would it be of assistance to me?" I asked.

"Help you? why not? Listen and I will tell it to you, although, really, you should read it. Still, I will tell it as best I can. It is like this: you see, "The waiter interrupted us at that moment. He informed Sturtevant that he was wanted at the telephone, and, with a word of apology, the artist left the table. Five minutes later I saw him rush out into the sleet and wind and disappear. Within the recollection of the frequenters of that *café*, Sturtevant had never before been called out by telephone. That, of itself, was substantial proof of a change in his circumstances.

One night, on the street, I encountered Avery, a former college chum, then a reporter on one of the evening papers. It was about a month after my memorable interview with Sturtevant, which, by that time, was almost forgotten.

"Hello, old chap," he said; "how's the world using you? Still on space?"

"Yes," I replied, bitterly, "with prospects of being on the town. shordy. But you look as if things were coming your way. Tell me all about it."

"Things have been coming my way, for a fact, and it is all remarkable, when all is said. You know Sturtevant, don't you? It's all due to him. I was plumb down on my luck—thinking of the morgue and all that—looking for you, in fact, with the idea that you would lend me enough to pay my room rent, when I met Sturtevant.

He told me a story, and, really, old man, it is the most remarkable story you ever heard; it made a new man of me. Within twenty-four hours I was on my feet, and I've hardly known a care or a trouble since."

Avery's statement, uttered calmly, and with the air of one who had merely pronounced an axiom, recalled to my mind the conversation with Sturtevant in the *café* that stormy night, nearly a month before.

"It must be a remarkable story," I said, incredulously. "Sturtevant mentioned it to me once. I have not seen him since. Where is he now?"

"He has been making war sketches in Cuba, at two hundred a week; he's just returned. It is a fact that everybody that has heard that story has done well since. There are Cosgrove and Phillips—friends of mine—you don't know them. One's a real estate agent; the other a broker's clerk. Sturtevant told them the story, and they have experienced the same result that I have; and they are not the only ones, either."

"Do you know the story?" I asked. "Will you try its effect on me?"

"Certainly; with the greatest pleasure in the world. I would like to have it printed in big black type, and posted on the elevated stations throughout New York. It certainly would do a lot of good, and it's as simple as A, B, C; like living on a farm. Excuse me a minute, will you? I see Danforth over there. Back in a minute, old chap."

He nodded and smiled,—and was gone. I saw him join the man whom he had designated as Danforth. My attention was distracted for a moment, and, when I looked again, both had disappeared.

If the truth be told, I was hungry. My pocket at that moment contained exactly five cents; just enough to pay my fare up-town, but insufficient also to stand the expense of filling my stomach. There was a "night owl" wagon in the neighborhood, where I had frequently "stood up" the purveyor of midnight dainties, and to him I applied. He was leaving the wagon as I was on the point of entering it, and I accosted him.

"I'm broke again," I said, with extreme cordiality. "You'll have to trust me once more. Some ham and eggs, I think, will do for the present."

He coughed, hesitated a moment, and then re-entered the wagon with me.

"Mr. Currier is good for anything he orders," he said to the man in charge; "one of my old customers. This is Mr. Bryan, Mr. Currier. He will take good care of you, and 'stand for' you, just the same as I would. The fact is, I have sold out. I've just turned over the outfit to Bryan. By the way, isn't Mr. Sturtevant a friend of yours?"

I nodded. I couldn't have spoken if I had tried.

"Well," continued the ex-night-owl man, "he came here one night, about a month ago, and told me the most wonderful story I ever heard. I've just bought a place in Eighth Avenue, where I am going to run a regular restaurant—near Twenty-third Street. Come and see me." He was out of the wagon, and the sliding door had been banged shut before I could stop him; so I ate my ham and eggs in silence, and resolved that I would hear that story before I slept. In fact, I began to regard it with superstition. If it had made so many fortunes, surely it should be capable of making mine.

The certainty that the wonderful story—I began to regard it as magic—was in the air, possessed me. As I started to walk homeward, fingering the solitary nickel in my pocket and contemplating the certainty of riding down town in the morning, I experienced the sensation of something stealthily pursuing me, as if Fate were treading along behind me, yet never overtaking, and I was conscious that I was possessed with or by the story. When I reached Union Square, I examined my address book for the home of Sturtevant. It was not recorded there. Then I remembered the *café* in University place, and, although the hour was late, it occurred to me that he might be there.

He was! In a far corner of the room, surrounded by a group of acquaintances, I saw him. He discovered me at the same instant, and motioned to me to join them at the table. There was no chance for the story, however. There were half a dozen around the table, and I was the farthest removed from Sturtevant. But I kept my eyes upon him, and bided my time, determined that, when he rose to depart, I would go with him. A silence, suggestive of respectful awe, had fallen upon the party when I took my seat. Every one seemed to be thinking, and the attention of all was fixed upon Sturtevant. The cause was apparent. He had been telling the story. I had entered the *café* just too late to hear it. On my right, when I took my seat, was a doctor; on my left a lawyer. Facing me on the other side was a novelist with whom I had some acquaintance. The others were artists and newspaper men.

"It's too bad, Mr. Currier," remarked the doctor; "you should have come a little sooner. Sturtevant has been telling us a story; it is quite wonderful, really. I say, Sturtevant, won't you tell that story again, for the benefit of Mr. Currier?"

"Why, yes. I believe that Currier has, somehow, failed to hear the magic story, although, as a matter of fact, I think he was the first one to whom I mentioned it at all. It was here, in this *café*, too,—at this very table. Do you remember what a wild night that was, Currier? Wasn't I called to the telephone, or something like that? To be sure I, I remember, now; interrupted just at the point when I was beginning the story. After that, I told it to three or four fellows, and it 'braced them up,' as it had me. It seems incredible that a mere story can have such a tonic effect upon the success of so many persons who are engaged in such widely different occupations, but that is what it has done. It is a kind of never failing remedy, like a cough mixture that is warranted to cure everything, from a cold in the head to galloping consumption. There was Parsons, for example. He is a broker, you know, and had been on the wrong side of the market for a month. He had utterly lost his grip, and was on the verge of failure. I happened to meet him at the time he was feeling the bluest, and, before we parted, something brought me around to the subject of the story, and I related it to him. It had the same effect upon him that it had on me, and has had upon everybody who has heard it, as far as I know. I think you will all agree with me, that it is not the story itself that performs the surgical operation on the minds of those who are familiar with it; it is the way it is told—in print, I mean. The author has, somehow, produced a psychological effect which is indescribable. The reader is hypnotized. He receives a mental and moral tonic. Perhaps, doctor, you can give some scientific explanation of the influence exerted by the story. It is a sort of elixir manufactured out of words, eh?"

From that the company entered upon a general discussion of theories. Now and then slight references were made to the story itself, and they were just sufficient to tantalize me—the only one present who had not heard it.

At length, I left my chair, and, passing around the table, seized Sturtevant by one arm, and succeeded in drawing him away from the party.

"If you have any consideration for an old friend who is rapidly being driven mad by the existence of that confounded story, which Fate seems determined that I shall never hear, you will relate it to me now," I said, savagely.

Sturtevant stared at me in mild surprise.

"All right," he said. "The others will excuse me for a few moments, I think. Sit down here, and you shall have it. I found it pasted in an old scrapbook I purchased in Ann Street, for three cents; and there isn't a thing about it by which one can get any idea in what publication it originally appeared, or who wrote it. When I discovered it, I began casually to read it, and in a moment I was interested. Before I left it, I had read it through many times, so that I could repeat it almost word for word. It affected me strangely—as if I had come in contact with some strong personality. There seems to be in the story a personal element that applies to every one who reads it. Well, after I had read it several times, I began to think it over. I couldn't stay in the house, so I seized my coat and hat and went out. I must have walked several miles, buoyantly, without realizing that I was the same man who, only a short time before, had been in the depths of despondency. That was the day I met you here—you remember."

We were interrupted at that instant by a uniformed messenger, who handed Sturtevant a telegram. It was from his chief, and demanded his instant attendance at the office. The messenger had already been delayed an hour, and there was no help for it; he must go at once.

"Too bad!" said Sturtevant, rising and extending his hand. "Tell you what I'll do, old chap. I'm not likely to be gone any more than an hour or two. You take my key and wait for me in my room. In the *escritoire* near the window you will find an old scrapbook, bound in rawhide. It was manufactured, I have no doubt, by the author of the magic story. Wait for me in my room until I return."

With that he went out, and I lost no time in taking advantage of the permission he had given me.

I found the book without difficulty. It was a quaint, home-made affair, covered, as Sturtevant had said, with rawhide, and bound with leather thongs. The pages formed an odd combination of yellow paper, vellum and home-made parchment. I found the story, curiously printed on the last-named material. It was quaint and strange. Evidently, the printer had "set" it under the supervision of the writer. The phraseology was an unusual combination of seventeenth and eighteenth century mannerisms, and the interpolation of italics and capitals could have originated in no other brain than that of its author.

In reproducing the following story, the peculiarities of type, spelling, etc., are eliminated, but in other respects it remains unchanged.

Nothing worth while is attainable without effort. By the same token, a thoughtful reading of "The Magic Story" and a correct interpretation of its "lessons" are essential to a full appreciation of its inspirational value.

The author has woven into this story in a remarkably effective way the basic principles of a successful life, and it is safe to say that persistent application of these principles will accomplish almost, if not quite, all that is claimed for them in the development of a self-reliant, success-compelling spirit.

Enthusiastic readers of this unusual book, appreciating its inspiriting force, give it generous publicity, and as a result its sphere of influence is being constantly enlarged.

Part Two
In the Old Scrap Book

INASMUCH as I have evolved from my experience the one great secret of success for all worldly undertakings, I deem it wise, now that the number of my days is nearly counted, to give to the generations that are to follow me the benefit of whatsoever knowledge I possess. I do not apologize for the manner of my expression, nor for lack of literary merit, the latter being, I wot, its own apology. Tools much heavier than the pen have been my portion, and, moreover, the weight of years has somewhat palsied hand and brain; nevertheless, the fact I can tell, and that I deem the meat within the nut. What mattereth it, in what manner the shell be broken, so that the meat be obtained and rendered useful? I doubt not that I shall use, in the telling, expressions that have clung to my memory since childhood; for, when men attain the number of my years, happenings of youth are like to be clearer to their perceptions than are events of recent date; nor doth it matter much how a thought is expressed, if it be wholesome and helpful, and findeth the understanding.

Much have I wearied my brain anent the question, how best to describe this recipe for success that I have discovered, and it seemeth advisable to give it as it came to me; that is, if I relate somewhat of the story of my life, the directions for agglomerating the substances, and supplying the seasoning for the accomplishment of the dish, will plainly be perceived. Happen they may; and that men may be born generations after I am dust, who will live to bless me for the words I write.

My father, then, was a seafaring man who, early in life, forsook his vocation, and settled on a plantation in the colony of Virginia, where, some years thereafter, I was born, which event took place in the year 1642; and that was over a hundred years ago. Better for my father had it been had he hearkened to the wise advice of my mother, that he remain in the calling of his education; but he would not have it so, and the good vessel he captained was bartered for the land I spoke of. Here beginneth the first lesson to be acquired:

Man should not be blinded to whatsoever merit exists in the opportunity which he hath in hand, remembering that a thousand promises for the future should weigh as naught against the possession of a single piece of silver.

When I had achieved ten years, my mother's soul took flight, and two years thereafter my worthy father followed her. I, being their only begotten, was left alone; howbeit, there were friends who, for a time, cared for me; that is to say, they offered me a home beneath their roof,—a thing which I took advantage of for the space of five months. From my father's estate there came to me naught; but, in the wisdom that came with increasing years, I convinced myself that his friend, under whose roof I lingered for some time, had defrauded him, and therefore me.

Of the time from the age of twelve and a half until I was three and twenty, I will make no recital here, since that time hath naught to do with this tale; but some time after, having in my possession the sum of sixteen guineas, ten, which I had saved from the fruits of my labor, I took ship to Boston town, where I began work first as a cooper, and thereafter as a ship's carpenter, although always after the craft was docked; for the sea was not amongst my desires.

Fortune will sometimes smile upon an intended victim because of pure perversity of temper. Such was one of my experiences. I prospered, and, at seven and twenty, owned the yard wherein, less than four years earlier, I had worked for hire. Fortune, howbeit, is a jade who must be coerced; she will not be coddled. Here beginneth the second lesson to be acquired:

Fortune is ever elusive, and can only be retained by force. Deal with her tenderly and she will forsake you for a stronger man. [In that, methinks, she is not unlike other women of my knowledge.]

About this time, Disaster (which is one of the heralds of broken spirits and lost resolve), paid me a visit. Fire ravaged my yards, leaving nothing in its blackened paths but debts, which I had not the coin wherewith to defray. I labored with my acquaintances, seeking assistance for a new start, but the fire that had burned my competence seemed also to have consumed their sympathies. So it happened, within a short time, that not only had I lost all, but I was hopelessly indebted to others; and for that they cast me into prison. It is possible that I might have rallied from my losses but for this last indignity, which broke down my spirits so that I became utterly despondent. Upward of a year was I detained within the gaol; and, when I did come forth, it was not the same hopeful, happy man, content with his lot, and with confidence in the world and its people, who had entered there.

Life has many pathways, and of them by far the greater number lead downward. Some are precipitous, others are less abrupt; but ultimately, no matter at what inclination the angle may be fixed, they arrive at the same destination—failure. And here beginneth the third lesson:

Failure exists only in the grave. Man, being alive, hath not yet failed; always he may turn about and ascend by the same path he descended by; and there may be one that is less abrupt (albeit longer of achievement), and more adaptable to his condition.

When I came forth from prison, I was penniless. In all the world I possessed naught beyond the poor garments which covered me, and a walking stick which the turnkey had permitted me to retain, since it was worthless. Being a skilled workman, howbeit, I speedily found employment at good wages; but, having eaten of the fruit of worldly advantage, dissatisfaction possessed me. I became morose and sullen; whereat, to cheer my spirits, and for the sake of forgetting the losses I had sustained, I passed my evenings at the tavern. Not that I drank overmuch of liquor, except on occasion (for I have ever been somewhat abstemious), but that I could laugh, and sing, and parry wit and badinage with my ne'er-do-well companions; and here might be included the fourth lesson:

Seek comrades among the industrious, for those who are idle will sap your energies from you.

It was my pleasure at that time to relate, upon slight provocation, the tale of my disasters, and to rail against the men whom I deemed to have wronged me, because they had seen fit not to come to my aid. Moreover, I found childish delight in filching from my employer, each day, a few moments of the time for which he paid me. Such a thing is less honest than downright theft.

This habit continued and grew upon me until the day dawned which found me not only without employment, but also without character, which meant that I could not hope to find work with any other employer in Boston town.

It was then that I regarded myself a failure. I can liken my condition at that time for naught more similar than that of a man who, descending the steep side of a mountain, loses his foothold. The farther he slides, the faster he goes. I have also heard this condition described by the word Ishma elite, which I understand to be a man whose hand is against everybody, and who thinks that the hands of every other man are against him; and here beginneth the fifth lesson:

> *The Ishmaelite and the leper are the same, since both are abominations in the sight of man—albeit they differ much, in that the former may be restored to perfect health. The former is entirely the result of imagination; the latter has poison in his blood.*

I will not discourse at length upon the gradual degeneration of my energies. It is not meet ever to dwell much upon misfortunes (which saying is also worthy of remembrance). It is enough if I add that the day came when I possessed naught wherewith to purchase food and raiment, and I found myself like unto a pauper, save at infrequent times when I could earn a few pence, or, mayhap, a shilling. Steady employment I could not secure, so I became emaciated in body, and naught but a skeleton in spirit.

My condition, then, was deplorable; not so much for the body, be it said, as for the mental part of me, which was sick unto death. In my imagination I deemed myself ostracised by the whole world, for I had sunk very low indeed; and here beginneth the sixth and final lesson to be acquired (which cannot be told in one sentence, nor in one paragraph, but must needs be adapted from the remainder of this tale).

Well do I remember my awakening, for it came in the night, when, in truth, I did awake from sleep. My bed was a pile of shavings in the rear of the cooper shop where once I had worked for hire; my roof was the pyramid of casks, underneath which I had established myself. The night was cold, and I was chilled, albeit, paradoxically, I had been dreaming of light and warmth and of the repletion of good things. You will say, when I relate the effect the vision had on me, that my mind was affected. So be it, for it is the hope that the minds of others might be likewise influenced which disposes me to undertake the labor of this writing. It was the dream which converted me to the belief—nay, to the knowledge—that I was possessed of two identities; and it was my own better self that afforded me the assistance for which I had pleaded in vain from my acquaintances. I have heard this condition described by the word "double." Nevertheless, that word does not comprehend my meaning. A double can be naught more than a double, neither half being possessed of individuality. But I will not philosophize, since philosophy is naught but a suit of garments for the decoration of a dummy figure.

Moreover, it was not the dream itself which affected me; it was the impression made by it, and the influence that it exerted over me, which accomplished my enfranchisement. In a word, then, I encouraged my other identity. After toiling through a tempest of snow and wind, I peered into a window and saw that other being. He was rosy with health; before him, on the hearth, blazed a fire of logs; there was conscious power and force in his demeanor; he was physically and mentally muscular. I rapped timidly upon the door, and he bade me enter. There was a not unkindly smile of derision in his eyes as he motioned me to a chair by the fire; but he uttered no word of welcome; and, when I had warmed myself, I went forth again into the tempest, burdened with the shame which the contrast between us had forced upon me. It was then that I awoke; and here cometh the strange part of my tale, for, when I did awake, I was not alone. There was a Presence with me; intangible to others, I discovered later, but real to me.

The Presence was in my likeness, yet was it strikingly unlike. The brow, not more lofty than my own, yet seemed more round and full; the eyes, clear, direct, and filled with purpose, glowed with enthusiasm and resolution; the lips, chin—ay, the whole contour of face and figure was dominant and determined.

He was calm, steadfast, and self-reliant; I was cowering, filled with nervous trembling, and fearsome of intangible shadows. When the Presence turned away, I followed, and throughout the day I never lost sight of it, save when it disappeared for a time beyond some doorway where I dared not enter; at such places, I awaited its return with trepidation and awe, for I could not help wondering at the temerity of the Presence (so like myself, and yet so unlike), in daring to enter where my own feet feared to tread.

It seemed also, as if purposely I was led to the place and to the men where and before whom I most dreaded to appear; to offices where once I had transacted business; to men with whom I had financial dealings. Throughout the day I pursued the Presence, and at evening saw it disappear beyond the portals of a hostelry famous for its cheer and good living. I sought the pyramid of casks and shavings.

Not again in my dreams that night did I encounter the Better Self (for that is what I have named it), albeit, when, perchance, I awakened from slumber, it was near to me, ever wearing that calm smile of kindly derision which could not* be mistaken for pity, nor for condolence in any form. The contempt of it stung me sorely.

The second day was not unlike the first, being a repetition of its forerunner, and I was again doomed to wait outside during the visits which the Presence paid to places where I fain would have gone had I possessed the requisite courage. It is fear which deporteth a man's soul from his body and rendereth it a thing to be despised. Many a time I essayed to address it, but enunciation rattled in my throat, unintelligible; and the day closed like its predecessor.

This happened many days, one following another, until I ceased to count them; albeit, I discovered that constant association with the Presence was producing an effect upon me; and one night, when I awoke among the casks and discerned that he was present, I made bold to speak, albeit with marked timidity.

"Who are you?" I ventured to ask; and I was startled into an upright posture by the sound of my own voice; and the question seemed to give pleasure to my companion, so that I fancied there was less of derision in his smile when he responded.

"I am that I am," was the reply. "I am he who you have been; I am he who you may be again; wherefore do you hesitate ? I am he who you were, and whom you have cast out for other company. I am the man made in the image of God, who once possessed your body. Once we dwelt within it together, not in harmony, for that can never be, nor yet in unity, for that is impossible, but as tenants in common who rarely fought for full possession. Then you were a puny thing, but you became selfish and exacting until I could no longer abide with you, wherefore I stepped out. There is a plus-entity and a minus-entity in every human body that is born into the world. Whichever one of these is favored by the flesh becomes dominant; then is the other inclined to abandon its habitation, temporarily or for all time. I am the plus-entity of yourself; you are the minus-entity. I own all things; you possess naught. That body which we both inhabited is mine, but it is unclean, and I will not dwell within it. Cleanse It, and I will take possession.

"Why do you pursue me?" I next asked the Presence.

"You have pursued me, not I you. You can exist without me for a time, but your path leads downward, and the end is death. Now that you approach the end, you debate if it be not politic that you should cleanse your house and invite me to enter. Step aside, then, from the brain and the will; cleanse them of your presence; only on that condition will I ever occupy them again."

"The brain hath lost its power," I faltered. "The will is a weak thing, now; can you repair them?"

"Listen!" said the Presence, and he towered over me while I cowered abjectly at his feet. "To the plus-entity of a man, all things are possible. The world belongs to him—is his estate. He fears naught, dreads naught, stops at naught; he asks no privileges, but demands them; he *dominates*, and cannot cringe; his requests are orders; opposition flees at his approach; he levels mountains, fills in vales, and travels on an even plane where stumbling is unknown."

Thereafter, I slept again, and, when I awoke, I seemed to be in a different world. The sun was shining and I was conscious that birds twittered above my head. My body, yesterday trembling and uncertain, had become vigorous and filled with energy. I gazed upon the pyramid of casks in amazement that I had so long made use of it for an abiding place, and I was wonderingly conscious that I had passed my last night beneath its shelter.

The events of the night recurred to me, and I looked about me for the Presence. It was not visible. But anon I discovered, cowering in a far corner of my resting place, a puny, abject, shuddering figure, distorted of visage, deformed of shape, disheveled and unkempt of appearance. It tottered as it walked, for it approached me piteously; but I laughed aloud, mercilessly. Perchance I knew then that it was the minus-entity, and that the plus-entity was within me; albeit I did not then realize it. Moreover, I was in haste to get away; I had no time for philosophy. There was much for me to do—much; strange it was that I had not thought of that yesterday. But yesterday was gone—to-day was with me—it had just begun.

As had once been my daily habit, I turned my steps in the direction of the tavern where formerly I had partaken of my meals. I nodded cheerily as I entered, and smiled in recognition of returned salutations. Men who had ignored me for months bowed graciously when I passed them on the thoroughfare. I went to the washroom, and from there to the breakfast table; afterwards, when I passed the taproom, I paused a moment and said to the landlord:

"I will occupy the same room that I formerly used, if, perchance, you have it at disposal. If not, another will do as well, until I can obtain it."

Then I went out and hurried with all haste to the cooperage. There was a huge wain in the yard, and men were loading it with casks for shipment. I asked no questions, but, seizing barrels, began hurling them to the men who worked atop of the load. When this was finished, I entered the shop. There was a vacant bench; I recognized its disuse by the litter on its top. It was the same at which I had once worked. Stripping off my coat, I soon cleared it of *impedimenta*. In a moment more I was seated, with my foot on the vice-lever, shaving staves.

It was an hour later when the master workman entered the room, and he paused in surprise at sight of me; already there was a goodly pile of neatly shaven staves beside me, for in those days I was an excellent workman; there was none better, but, alas I now, age hath deprived me of my skill. I replied to his unasked question with the brief but comprehensive sentence: "I have returned to work, sir." He nodded his head and passed on, viewing the work of other men, albeit anon he glanced askance in my direction.

Here endeth the sixth and last lesson to be acquired, although there is more to be said, since from that moment I was a successful man, and ere long possessed another shipyard, and had acquired a full competence of worldly goods.

I pray you who read, heed well the following admonitions, since upon them depend the word "success" and all that it implies:

Whatsoever you desire of good is yours. You have but to stretch forth your hand and take it.

Learn that the consciousness of dominant power within you is the possession of all things attainable.

Have no fear of any sort or shape, for fear is an adjunct of the minus-entity.

If you have skill, apply it; the world must profit by it, and, therefore, you.

Make a daily and nightly companion of your plus-entity; if you heed its advice, you cannot go wrong.

Remember, philosophy is an argument; the world, which is your property, is an accumulation of facts.

Go, therefore, and do that which is within you to do; take no heed of gestures which would beckon you aside; *ask of no man permission to perform.*

The minus-entity requests favors; the plus-entity grants them. Fortune waits upon every footstep you take; seize her, bind her, hold her, for she is yours; she belongs to you.

Start out now, with these admonitions in your mind. Stretch out your hand, and grasp the plus, which, maybe, you have never made use of, save in grave emergencies. Life is an emergency most grave.

Your plus-entity is beside you now; cleanse your brain, and strengthen your will. It will take possession. It waits upon you.

Start to-night; start now upon this new journey.

Be always on your guard. Whichever entity controls you, the other hovers at your side; beware lest the evil enter, even for a moment.

My task is done. I have written the recipe for "success." If followed, it cannot fail. Wherein I may not be entirely comprehended, the plus-entity of whosoever reads will supply the deficiency; and upon that Better Self of mine, I place the burden of imparting to generations that are to come, the secret of this all-pervading good—*the secret of being what you have it within you to be.*

THE PRINCE
by Niccolò Machiavelli

Translated by N.H. Thomson
Abridged by Mitch Horowitz

Contents

To the Reader 428

Chapter I On Acquiring a New Kingdom 429

Chapter II Against Occupation 431

Chapter III The Example of Alexander the Great 432

Chapter IV How to Control Formerly
Independent Territories 433

Chapter V When a Prince Conquers by Merit 434

Chapter VI When a Prince Conquers with
Help of Others or by Luck 437

Chapter VII When a Prince Conquers by Crime 438

Chapter VIII When a Prince Rules by Popular Consent 439

Chapter IX How the Strength of Princedoms
Should Be Measured 443

Chapter X Of Soldiers and Mercenaries 444

Chapter XI The Prince and Military Affairs 446

Chapter XII Better to Be Loved or Feared? 448

Chapter XIII Truth and Deception 450

Chapter XIV How to Avert Conspiracies 452

Chapter XV How a Prince Should Defend Himself 455

Chapter XVI How a Prince Should
    Preserve His Reputation 457

Chapter XVII A Prince's Court 458

Chapter XVIII Flatterers Should Be Shunned 459

Chapter XIX The Role of Fortune 461

Chapter XX Aphorisms from The Prince 463

To the Reader

I have found among my possessions none that I prize and esteem more than a knowledge of the actions of great men, acquired in the course of long experience in modern affairs and a continual study of antiquity. This knowledge has been most carefully and patiently pondered over and sifted by me, and now reduced into this little book. I can offer no better gift than the means of mastering, in a very brief time, all that in the course of so many years, and at the cost of so many hardships and dangers, I have learned, and know.

—Niccolò Machiavelli

Chapter I

On Acquiring a New Kingdom

The Prince cannot avoid giving offense to new subjects, either in respect of the troops he quarters on them, or of some other of the numberless vexations attendant on a new acquisition. And in this way you may find that you have enemies in all those whom you have injured in seizing the Princedom, yet cannot keep the friendship of those who helped you to gain it; since you can neither reward them as they expect, nor yet, being under obligations to them, use violent remedies against them. For however strong you may be in respect of your army, it is essential that in entering a new Province you should have the good will of its inhabitants.

Hence it happened that Louis XII of France speedily gained possession of Milan, and as speedily lost it. For the very people who had opened the gates to the French King, when they found themselves deceived in their expectations and hopes of future benefits, could not put up with the insolence of their new ruler.

True it is that when a State rebels and is again got under, it will not afterwards be lost so easily. For the Prince, using the rebellion as a pretext, will not hesitate to secure himself by punishing the guilty, bringing the suspected to trial, and otherwise strengthening his position in the points where it was weak.

I say, then, that those States which upon their acquisition are joined onto the ancient dominions of the Prince who acquires them are either of the same religion and language as the people of these dominions, or they are not. When they are, there is great ease in retaining them, especially when they have not been accustomed to live in freedom. To hold them securely it is enough to have rooted out the line of the reigning Prince; because if in other respects the old condition of things be continued, and there be no discordance in their customs, men live peaceably with one another. Even if there be some slight difference in their languages, provided that customs are similar, they can easily get on together. He, therefore, who acquires such a State, if he mean to keep it, must see to two things: first, that the blood of the ancient line of Princes be destroyed; second, that no change be made in respect of laws or taxes; for in this way the newly acquired State speedily becomes incorporated.

But when States are acquired in a country differing in language, usages, and laws, difficulties multiply, and great good fortune, as well as actions, are needed to overcome them. One of the best and most efficacious methods for dealing with such a State is for the Prince who acquires it to go and dwell there in person, since this will tend to make his tenure more secure and lasting. For when you are on the spot, disorders are detected in their beginnings and remedies can be readily applied; but when you are at a distance, they are not heard of until they have gathered strength and the case is past cure. Moreover, the Province in which you take up your abode is not pillaged by your officers; the people are pleased to have a ready recourse to their Prince; and have all the more reason if they are well disposed, to love, if disaffected, to fear him. A foreign enemy desiring to attack that State would be cautious how he did so. In short, where the Prince resides in person, it will be extremely difficult to oust him.

Another excellent expedient is to send colonies into one or two places, so that these may become, as it were, the keys of the Province; for you must either do this, or else keep up a numerous force of men-at-arms and foot soldiers. A Prince need not spend much on colonies. He can send them out and support them at little or no charge to himself, and the only persons to whom he gives offence are those whom he deprives of their fields and houses to bestow them on the new inhabitants. Those who are thus injured form but a small part of the community, and remaining scattered and poor can never become dangerous. All others being left unmolested, are in consequence easily quieted, and at the same time are afraid to make a false move, lest they share the fate of those who have been deprived of their possessions. In few words, these colonies cost less than soldiers, are more faithful, and give less offense, while those who are offended, being, as I have said, poor and dispersed, cannot hurt. And let it here be noted that men are either to be kindly treated, or utterly crushed, since they can revenge lighter injuries, but not graver. Wherefore the injury we do to a man should be of a sort to leave no fear of reprisals.

Chapter II

Against Occupation

If instead of colonies you send troops, the cost is vastly greater, and the whole revenues of the country are spent in guarding it; so that the gain becomes a loss, and much deeper offense is given; since in shifting the quarters of your soldiers from place to place the whole country suffers hardship, which as all feel, all are made enemies; and enemies who remaining, although vanquished, in their own homes, have power to hurt. In every way, therefore, this mode of defense is as disadvantageous as that by colonizing is useful.

In dealing with the countries of which they took possession the Romans diligently followed the methods I have described. They planted colonies, conciliated weaker powers without adding to their strength, humbled the great, and never suffered a formidable stranger to acquire influence.

Chapter III

The Example of Alexander the Great

Alexander the Great having achieved the conquest of Asia in a few years and, dying before he had well entered on possession, it might have been expected, given the difficulty of preserving newly acquired States, that on his death the whole country would rise in revolt.

Nevertheless, his successors were able to keep their hold, and found in doing so no other difficulty than arose from their own ambition and mutual jealousies.

If anyone think this strange and ask the cause, I answer that all the Princedoms of which we have record have been governed in one of two ways: 1) either by a sole Prince, all others being his servants permitted by his grace and favor to assist in governing the kingdom as his ministers; or 2) by a Prince with his Barons who hold their rank, not by the favor of a superior Lord, but by antiquity of bloodline, and who have States and subjects of their own who recognize them as their rulers and entertain for them a natural affection.

States governed by a sole Prince and by his servants—as with Alexander—vest in him a more complete authority; because throughout the land none but he is recognized as sovereign, and if obedience be yielded to any others, it is yielded as to his ministers and officers for whom personally no special love is felt.[1]

---

1 Machiavelli is saying that civic and military authority surpasses bloodline.—MH

Chapter IV

How to Control Formerly Independent Territories

When a newly acquired State has been accustomed to live under its own laws and in freedom, there are three methods whereby it may be held. The first is to destroy it; the second, to go and reside there in person; the third, to suffer it to live on under its own laws, subjecting it to a tribute and entrusting its government to a few of the inhabitants who will keep the rest your friends. Such a Government, since it is the creature of the new Prince, will see that it cannot stand without his protection and support, and must therefore do all it can to maintain him; and a city accustomed to live in freedom, if it is to be preserved at all, is more easily controlled through its own citizens than in any other way.

We have examples of all these methods in the histories of the Spartans and the Romans. The Spartans held Athens and Thebes by creating oligarchies in these cities, yet lost them in the end. The Romans, to retain Capua, Carthage, and Numantia, destroyed them and never lost them. On the other hand, when they thought to hold Greece as the Spartans had held it, leaving it its freedom and allowing it to be governed by its own laws, they failed, and had to destroy many cities of that Province before they could secure it. For, in truth, there is no sure way of holding other than by destroying, and whoever becomes master of a City accustomed to live in freedom and does not destroy it, may reckon on being destroyed by it. For if it should rebel, it can always screen itself under the name of liberty and its ancient laws, which no length of time, nor any benefits conferred will ever cause it to forget; and do what you will, and take what care you may, unless the inhabitants be scattered and dispersed, this name, and the old order of things, will never cease to be remembered, but will at once be turned against you whenever misfortune overtakes you.

If, however, the newly acquired City or Province has been accustomed to live under a Prince, and his line is extinguished, it will be impossible for the citizens, used, on the one hand, to obey, and deprived, on the other, of their old ruler, to agree to choose a leader from among themselves; and as they know not how to live as freemen, and are therefore slow to take up arms, a stranger may readily gain them over and attach them to his cause. But in Republics there is a stronger vitality, a fiercer hatred, a keener thirst for revenge. The memory of their former freedom will not let them rest; so that the safest course is either to destroy them, or to go and live in them.

Chapter V

When a Prince Conquers by Merit

Since men for the most part follow in the footsteps and imitate the actions of others, and yet are unable to adhere exactly to those paths which others have taken, or attain to the virtues of those whom they would resemble, the wise man should always follow the roads that have been trodden by the great, and imitate those who have most excelled, so that if he cannot reach their perfection, he may at least acquire something of its savor. Acting in this like the skillful archer, who seeing that the object he would hit is distant, and knowing the range of his bow, takes aim much above the destined mark; not designing that his arrow should strike so high, but that flying high it may strike the point intended.

I say, then, that in entirely new Princedoms where the Prince himself is new, the difficulty of maintaining possession varies with the greater or less ability of him who acquires possession. And, because the mere fact of a private person rising to be a Prince presupposes either merit or good fortune, it will be seen that the presence of one or other of these two conditions lessens, to some extent, many difficulties. And yet, he who is less beholden to Fortune has often in the end the better success; and it may be for the advantage of a Prince that, from his having no other territories, he is obliged to reside in person in the State which he has acquired.

Looking first to those who have become Princes by their merit and not by their good fortune, I say that the most excellent among them are Moses, Cyrus, Romulus, Theseus, and the like. And though perhaps I ought not to name Moses, he being merely an instrument for carrying out the Divine commands, he is still to be admired for those qualities which made him worthy to converse with God. But if we consider Cyrus and the others who have acquired or founded kingdoms, they will all be seen to be admirable. And if their actions and the particular institutions of which they were the authors be studied, they will be found not to differ from those of Moses, instructed though he was by so great a teacher. Moreover, on examining their lives and actions, we shall see that they were debtors to Fortune for nothing beyond the opportunity which enabled them to shape things as they pleased, without which the force of their spirit would have been spent in vain; as on the other hand, opportunity would have offered itself in vain had the capacity for turning it to account been wanting. It was necessary, therefore, that Moses should find the children of Israel in bondage in Egypt, and oppressed by the Egyptians, in order that they might be disposed to follow him, and so escape from their servitude. It was fortunate for Romulus that he found no home in Alba, but was exposed at the time of his birth, to the end that he might become king and founder of the City of Rome. It was necessary that Cyrus should find the Persians discontented with the rule of the Medes, and the Medes enervated and effeminate from a prolonged peace. Nor could Theseus have displayed his great qualities had he not found the Athenians disunited and dispersed. But while it was their opportunities that made these men fortunate, it was their own merit that enabled them to recognize these opportunities and turn them to account, to the glory and prosperity of their country.

They who come to the Princedom, as these did, by virtuous paths, acquire with difficulty, but keep with ease. The difficulties which they have in acquiring arise mainly from the new laws and institutions that they are forced to introduce in founding and securing their government. And let it be noted that there is no more delicate matter to take in hand, nor more dangerous to conduct, nor more doubtful in its success, than to set up as a leader in the introduction of changes. For he who innovates will have for his enemies all those who are well off under the existing order of things, and only lukewarm supporters in those who might be better off under the new. This lukewarm temper arises partly from the fear of adversaries who have the laws on their side, and partly from the incredulity of mankind, who will never admit the merit of anything new, until they have seen it proved by the event. The result, however, is that whenever the enemies of change make an attack, they do so with all the zeal of partisans, while the others defend themselves so feebly as to endanger both themselves and their cause.

It should be borne in mind that the temper of the multitude is fickle, and that while it is easy to persuade them of a thing, it is hard to fix them in that persuasion. Wherefore, matters should be so ordered that when men no longer believe of their own accord, they may be compelled to believe by force. Moses, Cyrus, Theseus, and Romulus could never have made their ordinances be observed for any length of time had they been unarmed, as was the case, in our own days, with the Friar Girolamo Savonarola, whose new institutions came to nothing so soon as the multitude began to waver in their faith; since he had not the means to keep those who had been believers steadfast in their belief, or to make unbelievers believe.

Such persons, therefore, have great difficulty in carrying out their designs; but all their difficulties are on the road, and may be overcome by courage. Having conquered these, and coming to be held in reverence, and having destroyed all who were jealous of their influence, they remain powerful, safe, honored, and prosperous.

Chapter VI

When a Prince Conquers with Help of Others or by Luck

They who from private life become Princes by mere good fortune, do so with little trouble, but have much trouble to maintain themselves. They meet with no hindrance on their way, being carried as it were on wings to their destination, but all their difficulties overtake them when they alight. Of this class are those on whom States are conferred either in return for money, or through the favor of him who confers them.

Such Princes are wholly dependent on the favor and fortunes of those who have made them great; of supports none could be less stable or secure; and they lack both the knowledge and the power that would enable them to maintain their position. They lack the knowledge because, unless they have great parts and force of character, it is not to be expected that having always lived in a private station they should have learned how to command. They lack the power since they cannot look for support from attached and faithful troops. Moreover, States suddenly acquired, like all else that is produced and grows up rapidly, can never have such root or hold as that the first storm which strikes them shall not overthrow them; unless, indeed that they who suddenly become Princes have a capacity for learning quickly how to defend what Fortune has placed in their lap, and can lay those foundations after they rise which by others are laid before.

He who does not lay his foundations at first, may, if he be of great ability, succeed in laying them afterwards, though with inconvenience to the builder and risk to the building.

A certain type of man will judge it necessary, on entering a new Princedom, to rid himself of enemies, to conciliate friends, to prevail by force or fraud, to make himself feared yet not hated by his subjects, respected and obeyed by his soldiers, to crush those who can or ought to injure him, to introduce changes in the old order of things, to be at once severe and affable, magnanimous and liberal, to do away with a mutinous army and create a new one, to maintain relations with Kings and Princes on such a footing that they must see it for their interest to aid him, and dangerous to offend.

Chapter VII

When a Prince Conquers by Crime

A man may also rise from privacy to be a Prince in one of two ways, neither of which can be ascribed wholly either to merit or to fortune. The ways I speak of are, first, when the ascent to power is made by paths of wickedness and crime; and, second, when a private person becomes ruler of his country by the favor of his fellow-citizens.

Whoever examines the first man's actions and achievements will discover little or nothing in them which can be ascribed to Fortune, seeing that it was not through the favor of any but by the regular steps of the military service, gained at the cost of a thousand hardships and hazards, he reached the princedom, which he afterwards maintained by so many daring and dangerous enterprises. Still, to slaughter fellow-citizens, to betray friends, to be devoid of honor, pity, and religion, cannot be counted as merits, for these are means which may lead to power, but which confer no glory.

On seizing a state, the usurper should make haste to inflict what injuries he must, at a stroke, that he may not have to renew them daily, but be enabled by their discontinuance to reassure men's minds and afterwards win them over by benefits. Whosoever, either through timidity or from following bad counsels adopts a contrary course must keep the sword always drawn, and can put no trust in his subjects, who suffering from continued and constantly renewed severities, will never yield him their confidence. Injuries, therefore, should be inflicted all at once that their ill savor being less lasting may the less offend; whereas, benefits should be conferred little by little that so they may be more fully relished.

But, above all things, a Prince should so live with his subjects that no vicissitude of good or evil fortune shall oblige him to alter his behavior; because, if a need to change should come through adversity, it is then too late to resort to severity; while any leniency that you may use will be thrown away, for it will be seen to be compulsory and gain you no thanks.

Chapter VIII

When a Prince Rules by Popular Consent

I come now to the second case, namely, of the leading citizen who, not by crimes or violence, but by the favor of his fellow-citizens is made Prince of his country. This may be called a Civil Princedom, and its attainment depends not wholly on merit, nor wholly on good fortune, but rather on what may be termed a fortunate astuteness. I say then that the road to this Princedom lies either through the favor of the people or of the nobles. For in every city are to be found these two opposed humors having their origin in this: that the people desire not to be domineered over or oppressed by the nobles, while the nobles desire to oppress and domineer over the people. And from these two contrary appetites there arises in cities one of three results: a Princedom, or Liberty, or License. A Princedom is created either by the people or by the nobles, according as one or other of these factions has occasion for it. For when the nobles perceive that they cannot withstand the people, they set to work to magnify the reputation of one of their number, and make him their Prince, to the end that under his shadow they may be enabled to indulge their desires. The people, on the other hand, when they see that they cannot make head against the nobles, invest a single citizen with all their influence and make him Prince, that they may have the shelter of his authority.

He who is made Prince by the favor of the nobles, has greater difficulty to maintain himself than he who comes to the Princedom by aid of the people, since he finds many about him who think themselves as good as he, and whom, on that account, he cannot guide or govern as he would. But he who reaches the Princedom by the popular support, finds himself alone, with none, or but a very few about him who are not ready to obey. Moreover, the demands of the nobles cannot be satisfied with credit to the Prince, nor without injury to others, while those of the people well may, the aim of the people being more honorable than that of the nobles, the latter seeking to oppress, the former not to be oppressed. Add to this, that a Prince can never secure himself against a disaffected people, their number being too great, while he may against a disaffected nobility, since their number is small. The worst that a Prince need fear from a disaffected people is that they may desert him, whereas when the nobles are his enemies he has to fear not only that they may desert him but also that they may turn against him; because, as they have greater craft and foresight, they always choose their time to suit their safety, and seek favor with the side they think will win. Again, a Prince must always live with the same people but need not always live with the same nobles, being able to make and unmake these from day to day, and give and take away their authority at his pleasure.

But to make this part of the matter clearer, I say that as regards the nobles there is this first distinction to be made. They either so govern their conduct as to bind themselves wholly to your fortunes, or they do not. Those who so bind themselves, and who are not grasping, should be loved and honored. As to those who do not so bind themselves, there is this further distinction. For the most part they are held back by pusillanimity and a natural defect of courage, in which case you should make use of them, and of those among them more especially who are prudent, for they will do you honor in prosperity, and in adversity give you no cause for fear. But where they abstain from attaching themselves to you of set purpose and for ambitious ends, it is a sign that they are thinking more of themselves than of you, and against such men a Prince should be on his guard, and treat them as though they were declared enemies, for in his adversity they will always help to ruin him.

He who becomes a Prince through the favor of the people should always keep on good terms with them; which it is easy for him to do, since all they ask is not to be oppressed. But he who against the will of the people is made a Prince by the favor of the nobles, must, above all things, seek to conciliate the people, which he readily may by taking them under his protection. For since men who are well treated by one whom they expected to treat them ill feel the more beholden to their benefactor, the people will at once become better disposed to such a Prince when he protects them than if he owed his Princedom to them.

There are many ways in which a Prince may gain the goodwill of the people, but, because these vary with circumstances, no certain rule can be laid down respecting them, and I shall, therefore, say no more about them. But this is the sum of the matter, that it is essential for a Prince to be on a friendly footing with his people since otherwise he will have no resource in adversity.

And what I affirm let no one controvert by citing the old saw that "he who builds on the people builds on mire," for that may be true of a private citizen who presumes on his favor with the people, and counts on being rescued by them when overpowered by his enemies or by the magistrates. In such cases a man may often find himself deceived. But when he who builds on the people is a Prince capable of command, of a spirit not to be cast down by ill-fortune, who, while he animates the whole community by his courage and bearing, neglects no prudent precaution, he will not find himself betrayed by the people, but will be seen to have laid his foundations well.

The most critical juncture for Princedoms of this kind, is at the moment when they are about to pass from the popular to the absolute form of government: and as these Princes exercise their authority either directly or through the agency of the magistrates, in the latter case their position is weaker and more hazardous, since they are wholly in the power of those citizens to whom the magistracies are entrusted, who can, and especially in difficult times with the greatest ease, deprive them of their authority, either by opposing or by not obeying them. And in times of peril it is too late for a Prince to assume to himself an absolute authority, for the citizens and subjects who are accustomed to take their orders from the magistrates will not when dangers threaten take them from the Prince, so that at such seasons there will always be very few in whom he can trust. Such Princes, therefore, must not build on what they see in tranquil times when the citizens feel the need of the State. For then everyone is ready to run, to promise, and, danger of death being remote, even to die for the State. But in troubled times, when the State has need of its citizens, few of them are to be found. And the risk of the experiment is the greater in that it can only be made once. Wherefore, a wise Prince should devise means whereby his subjects may at all times, whether favorable or adverse, feel the need of the State and of him, and then they will always be faithful to him.

Chapter IX

How the Strength of Princedoms Should Be Measured

In examining the character of these Princedoms, another circumstance has to be considered, namely, whether the Prince is strong enough, if occasion demands, to stand alone, or whether he needs continual help from others. To make the matter clearer, I pronounce those to be able to stand alone who, with the men and money at their disposal, can get together an army fit to take the field against any assailant; and, conversely, I judge those to be in constant need of help who cannot take the field against their enemies, but are obliged to retire behind their walls, and to defend themselves there. As to the latter there is nothing to be said, except to exhort such Princes to strengthen and fortify the towns in which they dwell, and take no heed of the country outside. For whoever has thoroughly fortified his town, and put himself on such a footing with his subjects as I have already indicated and shall further speak of, will always be attacked with much caution; for men are always averse to enterprises that are attended with difficulty, and it is impossible not to foresee difficulties in attacking a Prince whose town is strongly fortified and who is not hated by his subjects.

A Prince, therefore, who has a strong city, and who does not make himself hated, cannot be attacked, or should he be so, his assailant will come badly off, since human affairs are so variable that it is almost impossible for anyone to keep an army posted for a whole year without interruption of some sort. Should it be objected that if the citizens have possessions outside the town and see them burned they will lose patience, and that self-interest, together with the hardships of a protracted siege, will cause them to forget their loyalty, I answer that a capable and courageous Prince will always overcome these difficulties by holding out hopes to his subjects that the evil will not be of long continuance; by exciting their fears of the enemy's cruelty; and by dexterously silencing those who seem to him too forward in their complaints. Moreover, it is to be expected that the enemy will burn and lay waste the country immediately on their arrival, at a time when men's minds are still heated and resolute for defense. And for this very reason the Prince has less to fear because after a few days, when the first ardor has abated, the injury is already done and suffered and cannot be undone; and the people will now, all the more readily, make common cause with their Prince from his seeming to be under obligations to them, their houses having been burned and their lands wasted in his defense. For it is the nature of men to incur obligation as much by the benefits they render as by those they receive.

If the whole matter be well considered, it ought not to be difficult for a prudent Prince, both at the outset and afterwards, to maintain the spirits of his subjects during a siege; provided always that provisions and other means of defense do not run short.

Chapter X

Of Soldiers and Mercenaries

The arms with which a Prince defends his State are either his own subjects, or they are mercenaries, or they are auxiliaries, or they are partly one and partly another. Mercenaries and auxiliaries are at once useless and dangerous, and he who holds his State by means of mercenary troops can never be solidly or securely seated. For such troops are disunited, ambitious, insubordinate, treacherous, insolent among friends, cowardly before foes, and without fear of

God or faith with man. Whenever they are attacked defeat follows; so that in peace you are plundered by them, in war by your enemies. And this is because they have no tie or motive to keep them in the field beyond their paltry pay, in return for which it would be too much to expect them to give their lives. They are ready enough, therefore, to be your soldiers while you are at peace, but when war is declared they make off and disappear. I ought to have little difficulty in getting this believed, for the present ruin of Italy is due to no other cause than her having for many years trusted to mercenaries, who though heretofore they may have helped the fortunes of some one man, and made a show of strength when matched with one another, have always revealed themselves in their true colors so soon as foreign enemies appeared.

The second sort of unprofitable arms are auxiliaries, by whom I mean troops brought to help and protect you by a potentate whom you summon to your aid; as when in recent times, Pope Julius II, observing the pitiful behavior of his mercenaries at the enterprise of Ferrara, betook himself to auxiliaries, and arranged with Ferdinand of Spain to be supplied with horse and foot soldiers.[2]

Auxiliaries may be excellent and useful soldiers for themselves, but are always hurtful to him who calls them in; for if they are defeated, he is undone; if victorious, he becomes their prisoner. Ancient histories abound with instances of this.

Let him, therefore, who would deprive himself of every chance of success, have recourse to auxiliaries, these being far more dangerous than mercenary arms, bringing ruin with them ready made. For they are united, and wholly under the control of their own officers; whereas, before mercenaries, even after gaining a victory, can do you hurt, longer time and better opportunities are needed; because, as they are made up of separate companies, raised and paid by you, he

---

2 Julius was later forced to make territorial concessions to Ferdinand.—MH

whom you place in command cannot at once acquire such authority over them as will be injurious to you. In short, with mercenaries your greatest danger is from their inertness and cowardice, with auxiliaries from their valor. Wise Princes, therefore, have always eschewed these arms, and trusted rather to their own, and have preferred defeat with the latter to victory with the former, counting that as no true victory which is gained by foreign aid.

Chapter XI

The Prince and Military Affairs

A Prince, therefore, should have no care or thought other than for war, and for the regulations and training it requires, and should apply himself exclusively to this as his peculiar province; for war is the sole art looked for in one who rules, and is of such efficacy that it not merely maintains those who are born Princes, but often enables men to rise to that eminence from a private station; while, on the other hand, we often see that when Princes devote themselves rather to pleasure than to arms, they lose their dominions. And as neglect of this art is the prime cause of such calamities, to be proficient in it is the surest way to acquire power.

Between an armed and an unarmed man no proportion holds, and it is contrary to reason to expect that the armed man should voluntarily submit to him who is unarmed, or that the unarmed man should stand secure among armed retainers. For with contempt on one side and distrust on the other it is impossible that men should work well together. Wherefore, as has already been said, a Prince who is ignorant of military affairs, besides other disadvantages, can neither be respected by his soldiers, nor can he trust them. A Prince, therefore, ought never to allow his attention to be diverted from warlike pursuits, and should occupy himself with them even more in peace than in war. This he can do in two ways, by practice or by study.

As to the practice, he ought, besides keeping his soldiers well trained and disciplined, to be constantly engaged in the chase, that he may inure his body to hardships and fatigue, and gain at the same time a knowledge of places, by observing how the mountains slope, the valleys open, and the plains spread; acquainting himself with the characters of rivers and marshes, and giving the greatest attention to this subject. Such knowledge is useful to him in two ways; for first, he learns thereby to know his own country, and to understand better how it may be defended; and next, from his familiar acquaintance with its localities, he readily comprehends the character of other districts when obliged to observe them for the first time. For the hills, valleys, plains, rivers, and marshes of Tuscany, for example, have a certain resemblance to those elsewhere; so that from a knowledge of the natural features of that province, similar knowledge in respect of other provinces may readily be gained. The Prince who is wanting in this kind of knowledge, is wanting in the first qualification of a good captain for by it he is taught how to surprise an enemy, how to choose an encampment, how to lead his army on a march, how to array it for battle, and how to post it to the best advantage for a siege.

Among the commendations that Philopoemen, Prince of the Achaeans, has received from historians is this: that in times of peace he was always thinking of methods of warfare, so that when walking in the country with his friends he would often stop and talk with them on the subject. "If the enemy," he would say, "were posted on that hill, and we found ourselves here with our army, which of us would have the better position? How could we most safely and in the best order advance to meet them? If we had to retreat, what direction should we take? If they retired, how should we pursue?" In this way he put to his friends, as he went along, all the contingencies that can befall an army. He listened to their opinions, stated his own, and supported them with reasons; and from his being constantly occupied with such meditations, it resulted, that when in actual command no complication could ever present itself with which he was not prepared to deal.

As to the mental training of which we have spoken, a Prince should read histories, and in these should note the actions of great men, observe how they conducted themselves in their wars, and examine the causes of their victories and defeats. And above all, he should, as many great men of past ages have done, assume for his models those persons who before his time have been renowned and celebrated, whose deeds and achievements he should constantly keep in mind.

A wise Prince, therefore, should pursue such methods as these, never resting idle in times of peace but strenuously seeking to turn them to account, so that he may derive strength from them in the hour of danger, and find himself ready should Fortune turn against him.

Chapter XII

Better to Be Loved or Feared?

I say that every Prince should desire to be accounted merciful and not cruel. Nevertheless, he should be on his guard against the abuse of this quality of mercy.

A Prince should disregard the reproach of being thought cruel where it enables him to keep his subjects united and obedient. For he who quells disorder by a very few signal examples will in the end be more merciful than he who from too great leniency permits things to take their course and so to result in pillage and bloodshed; for these hurt the whole State, whereas the severities of the Prince injure individuals only. And for a new Prince, of all others, it is impossible to escape a name for cruelty, since new States are full of dangers.

Nevertheless, the new Prince should not be too ready of belief, nor too easily set in motion; nor should he himself be the first to raise alarms; but should so temper prudence with kindliness that too great confidence in others shall not throw him off his guard nor groundless distrust render him insupportable.

And here comes in the question whether it is better to be loved rather than feared, or feared rather than loved. It might perhaps be answered that we should wish to be both; but since love and fear can hardly exist together, if we must choose between them, it is far safer to be feared than loved. For of men it may generally be affirmed that they are thankless, fickle, false, studious to avoid danger, greedy of gain, devoted to you while you are able to confer benefits upon them, and ready, as I said before, while danger is distant, to shed their blood, and sacrifice their property, their lives, and their children for you; but in the hour of need they turn against you. The Prince, therefore, who without otherwise securing himself builds wholly on their professions is undone. For the friendships which we buy with a price, and do not gain by greatness and nobility of character, though they be fairly earned are not made good, but fail us when we have occasion to use them.

Moreover, men are less careful how they offend him who makes himself loved than him who makes himself feared. For love is held by the tie of obligation, which, because men are a sorry breed, is broken on every whisper of private interest; but fear is bound by the apprehension of punishment which never relaxes its grasp.

Nevertheless a Prince should inspire fear in such a fashion that if he do not win love he may escape hate. For a man may very well be feared and yet not hated, and this will be the case so long as he does not meddle with the property or with the women of his citizens and subjects. And if constrained to put any to death, he should do so only when there is manifest cause or reasonable justification. But, above all, he must abstain from seizing the property of others. For men will sooner forget the death of their father than the loss of their estate. Moreover, pretexts for confiscation are difficult to find, and he who has once begun to live by pillaging always finds reasons for taking what is not his; whereas reasons for shedding blood are fewer and sooner exhausted.

Among other things remarkable in Hannibal, this has been noted: that having a very great army, made up of men of many different nations and brought to fight in a foreign country, no dissension ever arose among the soldiers themselves, nor any mutiny against their leader, either in his good or in his evil fortunes. This we can only ascribe to the transcendent cruelty, which, joined with numberless great qualities, rendered him at once venerable and terrible in the eyes of his soldiers, for without this reputation for cruelty these other virtues would not have produced the like results.

Chapter XIII

Truth and Deception

Everyone understands how praiseworthy it is in a Prince to maintain trust, and to live uprightly and not craftily. Nevertheless, we see from what has taken place in our own days that Princes who have set little store by their word, but have known how to overreach men by their cunning, have accomplished great things, and in the end got the better of those who trusted to honest dealing.

Be it known, then, that there are two ways of contending, one in accordance with the laws, the other by force; the first of which is proper to men, the second to beasts. But since the first method is often ineffectual, it becomes necessary to resort to the second. A Prince should, therefore, understand how to use well both the man and the beast. And this lesson has been covertly taught by the ancient writers who relate how Achilles and many others of these old Princes were given over to be brought up and trained by Chiron the Centaur; the only meaning of their having for an instructor one who was half man and half beast is that it is necessary for a Prince to know how to use both natures, and that the one without the other has no stability.

But since a Prince should know how to use the beast's nature wisely, he ought of beasts to choose both the lion and the fox; for the lion cannot guard himself from the traps nor the fox from wolves. He must therefore be a fox to discern traps and a lion to drive off wolves.

To rely wholly on the lion is unwise; and for this reason a prudent Prince neither can nor ought to keep his word when to keep it is hurtful to him, and the causes which led him to pledge it are removed. If all men were good this would not be good advice, but since they are dishonest and do not keep faith with you, you in return need not keep faith with them; and no prince was ever at a loss for plausible reasons to cloak a breach of faith. Of this numberless recent instances could be given, and it might be shown how many solemn treaties and engagements have been rendered inoperative and idle through want of faith in Princes, and that he who was best known to play the fox has had the best success.

It is necessary, indeed, to put a good color on this nature, and to be skillful in simulating and dissembling. But men are so simple, and governed so absolutely by their present needs, that he who wishes to deceive will never fail in finding willing dupes.

And you are to understand that a Prince, and most of all a new Prince, cannot observe all those rules of conduct in respect whereof men are accounted good, being often forced, in order to preserve his Princedom, to act in opposition to good faith, charity, humanity, and religion. He must therefore keep his mind ready to shift as the winds and tides of Fortune turn, and, as I have already said, he ought not to quit good courses if he can help it, but should know how to follow evil courses if he must.

A Prince should therefore be very careful that nothing ever escapes his lips that does not make him seem the embodiment of mercy, good faith, integrity, humanity, and religion. And there is no virtue which it is more necessary for him to seem to possess than this last; because men in general judge rather by the eye than by the hand, for everyone can see but few can touch. Everyone sees what you seem, but few know what you are, and these few dare not oppose themselves to the opinion of the many who have the majesty of the State to back them up.

Moreover, in the actions of all men, and most of all of Princes, where there is no tribunal to which we can appeal we look to results. Wherefore if a Prince succeeds in establishing and maintaining his authority the means will always be judged honorable and be approved by everyone. For the vulgar are always taken by appearances and by results, and the world is made up of the vulgar, the few only finding room when the many have no longer ground to stand on.

A certain Prince of our own days, whose name it is as well not to mention, is always preaching peace and good faith, although the mortal enemy of both; and both, had he practiced them as he preaches them, would, oftener than once, have lost him his kingdom and authority.

Chapter XIV

How to Avert Conspiracies

A Prince should consider how he may avoid such courses as would make him hated or despised; and that whenever he succeeds in keeping clear of these, he has performed his part, and runs no risk though he incur other infamies.

A Prince, as I have said before, sooner becomes hated by being rapacious and by interfering with the property and with the women of his subjects than in any other way. From these, therefore, he should abstain. For so long as neither their property nor their honor are touched the mass of mankind live contentedly, and the Prince has only to cope with the ambition of a few, which can in many ways and easily be kept within bounds.

A Prince is despised when he is seen to be fickle, frivolous, effeminate, pusillanimous, or irresolute, against which defects he ought therefore most carefully to guard, striving so to bear himself that greatness, courage, wisdom, and strength may appear in all his actions. In his private dealings with his subjects his decisions should be irrevocable, and his reputation such that no one would dream of overreaching or cajoling him.

The Prince who inspires such an opinion of himself is greatly esteemed, and against one who is greatly esteemed conspiracy is difficult; nor, when he is known to be an excellent Prince and held in reverence by his subjects, will it be easy to attack him. For a Prince is exposed to two dangers: from within in respect of his subjects, and from without in respect of foreign powers. Against the latter he will defend himself with good arms and good allies, and if he have good arms he will always have good allies; and when things are settled abroad, they will always be settled at home, unless disturbed by conspiracies; and even should there be hostility from without, if he has taken those measures, and has lived in the way I have recommended, and if he never abandons hope, he will withstand every attack.

As regards his own subjects, when affairs are quiet abroad, he has to fear they may engage in secret plots; against which a Prince best secures himself when he escapes being hated or despised, and keeps on good terms with his people; and this, as I have already shown, is essential. Not to be hated or despised by the body of his subjects is one of the surest safeguards that a Prince can have against conspiracy. For he who conspires always reckons on pleasing the people by putting the Prince to death; but when he sees that instead of pleasing he will offend them, he cannot summon courage to carry out his design. For the difficulties that attend conspirators are infinite, and we know from experience that while there have been many conspiracies, few of them have succeeded.

He who conspires cannot do so alone, nor can he assume as his companions any save those whom he believes to be discontented; but so soon as you impart your design to a discontented man, you supply him with the means of removing his discontent, since by betraying you he can procure for himself every advantage; so that seeing on the one hand certain gain and on the other a doubtful and dangerous risk, he must either be a rare friend to you or the mortal enemy of his Prince, if he keep your secret.

To put the matter shortly, I say that on the side of the conspirator there are distrust, jealousy, and dread of punishment to deter him; while on the side of the Prince there are the laws, the majesty of the throne, the protection of friends and of the government to defend him, to which if the general goodwill of the people be added, it is hardly possible that any should be rash enough to conspire. For while in ordinary cases, the conspirator has ground for fear only before the execution of his villainy, in this case he has also cause to fear after the crime has been perpetrated since he has the people for his enemy and is thus cut off from every hope of shelter.

In brief, a Prince has little to fear from conspiracies when his subjects are well disposed towards him; but when they are hostile and hold him in detestation he has then reason to fear everything and everyone. And well ordered States and wise Princes have provided with extreme care that the nobility shall not be driven to desperation, and that the commons shall be kept satisfied and contented; for this is one of the most important matters that a Prince must look to.

Chapter XV

How a Prince Should Defend Himself

To govern more securely some Princes have disarmed their subjects, others have kept the towns subject to them divided by factions; some have fostered hostility against themselves, others have sought to gain over those who at the beginning of their reign were looked on with suspicion; some have built fortresses, others have dismantled and destroyed them; and though no definite judgment can be pronounced respecting any of these methods, without regard to the special circumstances of the State to which it is proposed to apply them, I shall nevertheless speak of them in as comprehensive a way as the subject will admit.

It has never chanced that any new Prince has disarmed his subjects. On the contrary, when he has found them unarmed he has always armed them. For the arms thus provided become yours, those whom you suspected grow faithful, while those who were faithful at the first continue so, and from your subjects become your partisans. And though all your subjects cannot be armed yet if those of them whom you arm be treated with marked favor you can deal more securely with the rest. For the difference which those whom you supply with arms perceive in their treatment will bind them to you, while the others will excuse you recognizing that those who incur greater risk and responsibility merit greater rewards. But by disarming, you at once give offense, since you show your subjects that you distrust them, either as doubting their courage or as doubting their fidelity, each of which imputations begets hatred against you. Moreover, as you cannot maintain yourself without arms you must have recourse to mercenary troops. What these are I have already shown, but even if they were good, they could never avail to defend you at once against powerful enemies abroad and against subjects whom you distrust. Wherefore, as I have said already, new Princes in new Princedoms have always provided for their being armed; and of instances of this History is full.

But when a Prince acquires a new State, which thus becomes joined on like a limb to his old possessions, he must disarm its inhabitants, except such of them as have taken part with him while he was acquiring it; and even these, as time and occasion serve, he should seek to render soft and effeminate; and he must so manage matters that all the arms of the new State shall be in the hands of his own soldiers who have served under him in his ancient dominions.

I do not believe that divisions purposely caused can ever lead to good; on the contrary, when an enemy approaches, divided cities are lost at once, for the weaker faction will always side with the invader, and the other will not be able to stand alone.

Moreover methods like these argue weakness in a Prince, for under a strong government divisions would never be permitted, since they are profitable only in time of peace as an expedient whereby subjects may be more easily managed; but when war breaks out their insufficiency is demonstrated.

It has been customary for Princes, with a view to hold their dominions more securely, to build fortresses which might serve as a curb and restraint on such as have designs against them, and as a safe refuge against a first onset. I approve this custom, because it has been followed from the earliest times.

Fortresses are useful or not according to circumstances, and if in one way they benefit, in another they injure you. We may state the case thus: the Prince who is more afraid of his subjects than of strangers ought to build fortresses, while he who is more afraid of strangers than of his subjects should leave them alone.

All considerations taken into account, I shall applaud him who builds fortresses and him who does not; but I shall blame him who, trusting in them, reckons it a light thing to be held in hatred by his people.

Chapter XVI

How a Prince Should Preserve His Reputation

Nothing makes a Prince so well thought of as to undertake great enterprises and give striking proofs of his capacity.

It greatly profits a Prince in conducting the internal government of his State to follow striking methods. The remarkable actions of anyone in civil life, whether for good or for evil, afford him notability; and to choose such ways of rewarding and punishing cannot fail to be much spoken of. But above all, he should strive by all his actions to inspire a sense of his greatness and goodness.

A Prince is likewise esteemed who is a stanch friend and a thorough foe, that is to say, who without reserve openly declares for one against another, this being always a more advantageous course than to stand neutral. For supposing two of your powerful neighbors come to blows, it must either be that you have, or have not, reason to fear the one who comes off victorious. In either case it will always be well for you to declare yourself, and join in frankly with one side or other. For should you fail to do so you are certain, in the former of the cases put, to become the prey of the victor to the satisfaction and delight of the vanquished, and no reason or circumstance that you may plead will avail to shield or shelter you; for the victor dislikes doubtful friends, and such as will not help him at a pinch; and the vanquished will have nothing to say to you, since you would not share his fortunes sword in hand.

A Prince should be careful never to join with one stronger than himself in attacking others, unless he is driven to it by necessity. For if he whom you join prevails, you are at his mercy; and Princes, so far as in them lies, should avoid placing themselves at the mercy of others.

A Prince should show himself a patron of merit, and should honor those who excel in every art. He ought accordingly to encourage his subjects by enabling them to pursue their callings, whether mercantile, agricultural, or any other, in security, so that this man shall not be deterred from beautifying his possessions from the apprehension that they may be taken from him, or that other refrain from opening a trade through fear of taxes; and he should provide rewards for those who desire so to employ themselves, and for all who are disposed in any way to add to the greatness of his City or State.

He ought, moreover, at suitable seasons of the year to entertain the people with festivals and shows. And because all cities are divided into guilds and companies, he should show attention to these societies, and sometimes take part in their meetings, offering an example of courtesy and munificence, but always maintaining the dignity of his station, which must under no circumstances be compromised.

Chapter XVII

A Prince's Court

The choice of Ministers is a matter of no small moment to a Prince. Whether they shall be good or not depends on his prudence, so that the readiest conjecture we can form of the character and sagacity of a Prince is from seeing what sort of men he has about him. When they are at once capable and faithful, we may always account him wise, since he has known to recognize their merit and to retain their fidelity. But if they be otherwise, we must pronounce unfavorably of him, since he has committed a first fault in making this selection.

There are three scales of intelligence, one which understands by itself, a second which understands what it is shown by others, and a third which understands neither by itself nor by the showing of others, the first of which is most excellent, the second good, but the third worthless.

As to how a Prince is to know his Minister, this unerring rule may be laid down. When you see a Minister thinking more of himself than of you, and in all his actions seeking his own ends, that man can never be a good Minister or one that you can trust. For he who has the charge of the State committed to him, ought not to think of himself, but only of his Prince, and should never bring to the notice of the latter what does not directly concern him. On the other hand, to keep his Minister good, the Prince should be considerate of him, dignifying him, enriching him, binding him to himself by benefits, and sharing with him the honors as well as the burdens of the State, so that the abundant honors and wealth bestowed upon him may divert him from seeking them at other hands; while the great responsibilities wherewith he is charged may lead him to dread change, knowing that he cannot stand alone without his master's support. When Prince and Minister are upon this footing they can mutually trust one another; but when the contrary is the case, it will always fare ill with one or other of them.

Chapter XVIII

Flatterers Should Be Shunned

One error into which Princes, unless very prudent or very fortunate in their choice of friends, are apt to fall, is of so great importance that I must not pass it over. I mean in respect of flatterers.

These abound in Courts, because men take such pleasure in their own concerns, and so deceive themselves with regard to them, that they can hardly escape this plague; while even in the effort to escape it there is risk of their incurring contempt.

For there is no way to guard against flattery but by letting it be seen that you take no offense in hearing the truth: but when everyone is free to tell you the truth respect falls short. Wherefore a prudent Prince should follow a middle course, by choosing certain discreet men from among his subjects, and allowing them alone free leave to speak their minds on any matter on which he asks their opinion, and on none other. But he ought to ask their opinion on everything, and after hearing what they have to say, should reflect and judge for himself. And with these counselors collectively, and with each of them separately, his bearing should be such, that each and all of them may know that the more freely they declare their thoughts the better they will be liked. Besides these, the Prince should hearken to no others, but should follow the course determined on, and afterwards adhere firmly to his resolves. Whoever acts otherwise is either undone by flatterers, or from continually vacillating as opinions vary, comes to be held in light esteem.

A Prince ought always to take counsel, but at such times and reasons only as he himself pleases, and not when it pleases others; nay, he should discourage every one from obtruding advice on matters on which it is not sought. But he should be free in asking advice, and afterwards as regards the matters on which he has asked it, a patient hearer of the truth, and even displeased should he perceive that any one, from whatever motive, keeps it back.

But those who think that every Prince who has a name for prudence owes it to the wise counselors he has around him, and not to any merit of his own, are certainly mistaken; since it is an unerring rule and of universal application that a Prince who is not wise himself cannot be well advised by others, unless by chance he surrender himself to be wholly governed by some one adviser who happens to be supremely prudent; in which case he may, indeed, be well advised; but not for long, since such an adviser will soon deprive him of his Government. If he listen to a multitude of advisers, the Prince who is not wise will never have consistent counsels, nor will he know of himself how to reconcile them. Each of his counselors will study his own advantage, and the Prince will be unable to detect or correct them. Nor could it well be otherwise, for men will always grow rogues on your hands unless they find themselves under a necessity to be honest.

Hence it follows that good counsels, whenever they come, have their origin in the prudence of the Prince, and not the prudence of the Prince in wise counsels.

Chapter XIX

The Role of Fortune

I am not ignorant that many have been and are of the opinion that human affairs are so governed by Fortune and by God that men cannot alter them by any prudence of theirs, and indeed have no remedy against them, and for this reason have come to think that it is not worthwhile to labour much about anything, but that they must leave everything to be determined by chance.

Often when I turn the matter over, I am in part inclined to agree with this opinion, which has had readier acceptance in our own times from the great changes in things which we have seen and everyday see happen contrary to all human expectation. Nevertheless, that our freewill be not wholly set aside, I think it may be the case that Fortune is the mistress of one half our actions, and yet leaves the control of the other half, or a little less, to ourselves. And I would liken her to one of those wild torrents which, when angry, overflow the plains, sweep away trees and houses, and carry off soil from one bank to throw it down upon the other. Everyone flees before them, and yields to their fury without the least power to resist. And yet, though this be their nature, it does not follow that in seasons of fair weather men cannot, by constructing dams and barriers, take such precautions as will cause them when again in flood to pass off by some artificial channel, or at least prevent their course from being so uncontrolled and destructive. And so it is with Fortune, who displays her might where there is no organized strength to resist her, and directs her onset where she knows that there is neither barrier nor embankment to confine her.

I note that one day we see a Prince prospering and the next day overthrown, without detecting any change in his nature or character. This, I believe, comes chiefly from a cause already dwelt upon, namely, that a Prince who rests wholly on Fortune is ruined when she changes. Moreover, I believe that he will prosper most whose mode of acting best adapts itself to the character of the times; and conversely that he will be unprosperous with whose mode of acting the times do not accord. For we see that men in these matters which lead to the end that each has before him, namely, glory and wealth, proceed by different ways, one with caution, another with impetuosity, one with violence, another with subtlety, one with patience, another with its contrary; and that by one or other of these different courses each may succeed.

Again, of two who act cautiously, you shall find that one attains his end, the other not, and that two of different temperament, the one cautious, the other impetuous, are equally successful. All which happens from no other cause than that the character of the times accords or does not accord with their methods of acting. And hence it comes, as I have already said, that two operating differently arrive at the same result, and two operating similarly, the one succeeds and the other not. On this likewise depend the vicissitudes of Fortune. For if to one who conducts himself with caution and patience, time and circumstances are propitious, so that his method of acting is good, he goes on prospering; but if these change he is ruined, because he does not change his method of acting.

For no man is found so prudent as to know how to adapt himself to these changes, both because he cannot deviate from the course to which nature inclines him, and because, having always prospered while adhering to one path, he cannot be persuaded that it would be well for him to forsake it. And so when occasion requires the cautious man to act impetuously, he cannot do so and is undone: whereas, had he changed his nature with time and circumstances, his fortune would have been unchanged.

To be brief, I say that since Fortune changes and men stand fixed in their old ways, they are prosperous so long as there is congruity between them, and the reverse when there is not. Of this, however, I am well persuaded, that it is better to be impetuous than cautious. For Fortune to be kept under must be beaten and roughly handled; and we see that she suffers herself to be more readily mastered by those who so treat her than by those who are more timid in their approaches. And always she favors the young, because they are less scrupulous and fiercer, and command her with greater audacity.

Chapter XX

Aphorisms from *The Prince*

"One change always leaves a dovetail into which another will fit."

"Men are either to be kindly treated or utterly crushed since they can revenge lighter injuries but not graver."

"The wise man should always follow the roads that have been trodden by the great, and imitate those who have most excelled."

"Take aim much above the destined mark."

"He who is less beholden to Fortune has often in the end the better success."

"Those who come to the Princedom by virtuous paths acquire with difficulty but keep with ease."

"It should be borne in mind that the temper of the multitude is fickle, and that while it is easy to persuade them of a thing, it is hard to fix them in that persuasion."

"He who does not lay his foundations at first, may, if he be of great ability, succeed in laying them afterwards, though with inconvenience to the builder and risk to the building."

"A Prince can never secure himself against a disaffected people, their number being too great, while he may against a disaffected nobility, since their number is small."

"Men are always averse to enterprises that are attended with difficulty."

"Mercenaries and auxiliaries are at once useless and dangerous, and he who holds his State by means of mercenary troops can never be solidly or securely seated."

"A Prince ought never to allow his attention to be diverted from war-like pursuits, and should occupy himself with them even more in peace than in war."

"Many Republics and Princedoms have been imagined that were never seen or known to exist in reality."

"If we must choose between them, it is far safer to be feared than loved."

"If a man have good arms he will always have good allies."

"I do not believe that divisions purposely caused can ever lead to good."

"A Prince should show himself a patron of merit."

"The readiest conjecture we can form of the character and sagacity of a Prince is from seeing what sort of men he has about him."

"A Prince who is not wise himself cannot be well advised by others."

"A Prince who rests wholly on Fortune is ruined when she changes."

"It is better to be impetuous than cautious. Fortune suffers herself to be more readily mastered by those who so treat her than by those who are timid in their approaches."

www.ingramcontent.com/pod-product-compliance
Lightning Source LLC
Chambersburg PA
CBHW052007070526
44584CB00016B/1646